Now retired, Frances P. Lothrop Hawkins continues to work with young children on a voluntary basis. She resides in Boulder, Colorado, with her husband, David.

Journey With Children

THE AUTOBIOGRAPHY OF A TEACHER

Journey With Children

THE AUTOBIOGRAPHY OF A TEACHER

Frances P. Lothrop Hawkins

Foreword by Nel Noddings

UNIVERSITY PRESS OF COLORADO

Published by the University Press of Colorado
P.O. Box 849
Niwot, Colorado 80544
(303) 530-5337

The University Press of Colorado is a cooperative publishing enterprise supported, in part, by Adams State College, Colorado State University, Fort Lewis College, Mesa State College, Metropolitan State College of Denver, University of Colorado, University of Northern Colorado, University of Southern Colorado, and Western State College of Colorado.

The paper used in this publication meets the minimum requirements of the American National Standard for Information Sciences—Permanence of Paper for Printed Library Materials. ANSI Z39.48-1984.

Library of Congress Cataloging-in-Publication Data

Hawkins, Frances Pockman, 1913-
     Journey with Children : the autobiography of a teacher / Frances
P. Lothrop Hawkins.
          p.   cm.
     Includes bibliographical references.
     ISBN 0-87081-399-4 (alk. paper). -- ISBN 0-87081-451-6 (pbk. :
alk. paper)
     1. Hawkins, France Pockman, 1913-   . 2. Teachers--United
States--Biography.   I. Title
LA2317. H48A3   1997
371. 1'0092--dc21
     [B]   96-54058
                                                  CIP

10   9   8   7   6   5   4   3   2   1

Contents

Foreword

Frances Pockman Hawkins reveals one of the loveliest of human traits—a lifelong faith and delight in children. While so many other citizens, middle-aged and older, deplore the incompetence and immorality of new generations, "Franny Hawkins" shows that children still want to learn, still suffer dreadful hurts at the hands of negligent (and sometimes well-intentioned) adults, and still respond energetically to teaching that is responsive to their needs. With her husband, David, she has been part of some of the finest educational movements of this century—Open Education, Head Start, and Elementary Science Study. Her beautiful *Journey With Children* takes the reader to great research universities, inner cities, Indian reservations, Great Britain, and ordinary backyards where conversations sparkle.

In this account that stretches across a lifetime, we find proof that children will learn to write, read, figure, tell stories, explore science, and negotiate with adults—all without coercion. Back-to-basics advocates enrage Hawkins. She advises them to "look at history carefully. Some of us were there." Children who are protected from public failure and guided conscientiously in stimulating and worthwhile activities will acquire these skills; they need not be deprived of arts, projects, and creative activities and confined to narrow instruction and drill. Hawkins clearly rejects coercion and all the strategies that destroy children's confidence and curiosity. But her way is not hands-off, "let 'em do as they please." Her way is harder and requires far greater skill than either coercion or permissiveness. It requires careful analysis, meticulous preparation, and continual reflection. Even now, looking back, she sees things that she might have done better.

I was touched by many of the stories told here. Teacher-readers will recognize many of the troubled youngsters who appear in these papers, and there is nothing romantic or dreamy about Hawkins's analyses. She clearly does *not* think that teachers can routinely produce miracles with needy children through simple dedication and hard work. *Conditions* have to change, Hawkins insists, and to that I say, Amen. Both teachers and children deserve better working conditions than we are providing for them today.

I was also amused by many of Hawkins's comments. She remarks early on that she has never been able to understand how teachers can follow a lesson plan. Of course, she had to produce such plans and give them some attention. But *follow* them? How can we follow a plan when children lead us on all sorts of paths, eager to explore, ask questions, observe, and teach us while we teach them? A lesson plan may point us in an initial direction, but it should not chain us to one narrow path. As I read her criticism of lesson plans, I was reminded of my own objection to them. I have always believed that it is the teacher and the field, more than the lesson, that need preparation. Teachers who prepare adequately are always overprepared. We read and think extensively on the topics we intend to present, and we have far more material at hand than we can possibly share. But it is there, at the ready, if the right question or opportunity arises. Even then, overprepared and eager, we may encounter questions that send us scurrying for more information. Teaching in this way is thoroughly interactive, and there are opportunities for both teachers and students to grow.

Besides the teacher, the field must be prepared; that is, the environment must be rich in things that will call forth the interests we want to cultivate. And these things—objects, living creatures, pictures, instruments, books—must be provided with thought. Good teachers think about the uses to which the objects may be put. Further, such teachers are ready to move outside and use the outdoors as a laboratory. Exploration outside, guided wisely, can instill a sense of place in children in addition to promoting the acquisition of skills and information. A carefully prepared field and a superbly prepared teacher will almost certainly guarantee that fine lessons will develop.

Notice that I said "almost guarantee." I think that I am writing in the spirit of Frances Hawkins when I remind readers that there are no sure-fire formulas or guarantees in education. I think Hawkins, like Dewey, Montessori, and Pestalozzi before her, has demonstrated that teaching can be considerate of students and still intellectually vital. But such teaching cannot be reduced to recipes; it requires imagination, industry, sensitivity, faith, and yes, love.

NEL NODDINGS
Stanford University

Journey With Children

THE AUTOBIOGRAPHY OF A TEACHER

Introduction

You cannot make Remembrance grow
When it has lost its Root—
The tightening the Soil around
And setting it upright
Deceives perhaps the Universe
But not retrieves the Plant—
Real Memory, like Cedar Feet
Is shod with Adamant—
Nor can you cut Remembrance down
When it shall once have grown—
Its Iron Buds will sprout anew
However overthrown.
                    — *Emily Dickinson*[1]

Beginnings

About one hundred miles northeast of San Francisco lies the town of Oroville, where in 1911 a man called Ishi "startled the modern world by accidentally wandering into it from the Stone Age." In her classic book *Ishi*, a tragic but magnificent biography, Theodora Kroeber includes an introductory statement for all Americans: "The history of Ishi and his people is, inexorably, part of our own history. We have absorbed their lands into our holdings. Just so must we be responsible custodians of their tragedy, absorbing it into our tradition and morality."[2]

Ishi lived and worked in the University of California Museum, on Parnassus Hill, perhaps two miles from our house in San Francisco. He had been brought there in 1911, just two years before I was born, and he died of tuberculosis when I was four. By the chance of time and place, my father was privileged to watch and admire this last remaining Native American of the Wahi tribe. At work in the museum, Ishi fashioned obsidian arrow points, scrapers, and knives; instructed anthropologists in his complete process of fire making; carved salmon harpoons of wood; made deer snares of hemp fiber. To a still-young San Francisco, Ishi

1

Leonard and Julie Pockman, my parents, near Chinipas, Chihuahua, Mexico, about 1908.

brought all the ancient but vanishing ways of life from the valleys, rivers, and foothills of Mount Lassen in northern California and finally took the anthropologists back to explore his native land.

My father's ever-growing knowledge about the Native Americans of California and Mexico and his affection and sympathy for these people were important to my three brothers and me while growing up. Almost any San Francisco boy, like my father, born in the 1880s of white parents or grandparents from the East Coast, grew up sharing their parents' prevailing ethnic prejudices toward the Native Americans the westward movement had overwhelmed and especially toward recent Chinese immigrants, brought to the United States to build mines and railroads. Just so my father. But somehow he escaped deep racial prejudice, and his children were enriched.

In 1905, at twenty-five, my father traveled to Mexico to work as an assayer and later as superintendent of a mine in the Sierra Madre, in Chihuahua. There he permanently lost his heart to Mexico and its people, both Hispanic and native. The Tarahumara Indian blankets we slept under as children were tangible evidence to support his laudatory tales of these shy, proud, magnificent humans—runners and weavers all. Some tales seemed to us exaggerated. How wrong we were.

In 1911, my parents and their fifteen-month-old baby were escorted by revolutionaries from Chinipas to the town of Alamos in Sonora, from whence the train brought them back to San Francisco. My mother's sympathies were with the revolutionaries, whereas my father, "Don Leonardo," was on the side of "Don Porfirio"—Diaz. For both my father and the Mexicans he had worked with, however, friendship was stronger than politics. Friendship ruled.

Our growing family spent the next ten years in San Francisco and Los Angeles, a city that in 1920 had kept some of its heritage as an ancient northern province of Mexico. My three brothers and I found shameful the prejudices against Mexicans. We knew we were fortunate.

We returned to San Francisco in 1932—to "the City," as San Franciscans called it, only slightly conscious of the regional snobbery this reflected—to the house my father had built and in which I had been born. My two older brothers were at Stanford, and my younger brother was in high school. I was attending San Francisco State College, where my formal apprenticeship in early childhood education began.

To my great good fortune, the influences of the University of Chicago, of Columbia Teachers College and Bank Street College were strongly present in this far-western college. Like Columbia, San Francisco

State College expressed the influence of progressive education at its best. We studied the seminal ideas of John Dewey, the early investigations of Jean Piaget, and, above all, child development as it related to the art of teaching young children. All of this gave me the necessary beginning tools and insight for a life of teaching and—above all—of continued learning. Progressive education was not seen as a system or dogma, it was simply a fruitful way of developing as young teachers.

It was a propitious time for me to enter the field. I spent my senior year at Stanford studying Russian literature, seventeenth-century drama, sociology, psychology, abnormal psychology, statistics, and then, most significantly philosophy—in the form of a graduate student, David Hawkins, my future husband. We met in a writing class taught by a marvelous professor, Marjorie Bailey.

Another part of my story needs some introduction. That part came many years later, with the commitment of a seasoned teacher to rediscover, from notes and memory, some of her happy journeys with children. For me, therefore, this book is a final major product of an active teaching life. By its very nature, containing scenes and many children over past years, it has become a patchwork quilt. There is pattern in it, not always discerned at first but growing from the inherently varied ways children learn and from the way I have learned. Those many journeys have become for me all parts of one journey.

I want to include here just one small patch, a story that is not part of the quilt but that shows how my neighbor Joe validated what I have tried to communicate.

An Aside From Joe

One morning in fall 1967, when I was polishing a final revision of *The Logic of Action*, I became uneasy.[3] I was doubting my understanding of the deaf children I had so recently worked with, especially the detailed notes made by my young assistant, Claire Ulam Weiner. What kept niggling me was one of Claire's good questions. "I wondered," she wrote, "whether we are perhaps reading too much into the children's reactions— Are they reacting less than we think they are?"

Now it was I—struggling with words—who wondered, and so I left the typewriter and went in search of the nearest child: my next-door neighbor, Joe. I saw him—this lively, immediate, four-year-old—sitting in a small rocking chair, rocking. Snug within the walls of his house hollowed carefully from a great pile of leaves, just big enough for one, he rocked back and forth, back and forth. I slowed my pace. With Joe one proceeded cautiously, and I wanted *him* to choose the greeting or to be silent. He was a child who valued his words and used them with care.

Joe remained silent until I was in front of his leaf house, settled on the cool grass with my back to him, facing toward the sun.

"When I came out first, Mrs. Hawkins," he finally announced, "it made me cold."

The topic had been chosen, and I could respond. I too had felt cold when I first came out. But now, from our warm dwellings in the sun, we compared the long, cool shadows of our two "real" houses. My voiced approval for Joe's impeccable choice of site, for his golden leaf house far out of the shadows, was less a compliment than a statement, and he took it as such.

In such a conversation, long pauses become appropriate. They slow the tempo and encourage thought. I turned to face Joe now, and with the cool grass under me I envied him his rocking chair. I waited.

"It's winter now, isn't it, Mrs. Hawkins?"

"It's almost winter now," I agreed, "almost winter." I knew Joe would hear the amendment, but he responded with another affirmation.

"Yes," he sighed comfortably, "it's winter now."

Not wanting to affect our ease with each other and with the morning, I again stayed silent, but after another pause Joe pursued the amendment. As children can do in propitious settings, he thus signaled his wish and his readiness to release himself from his previous statement.

"Yes, it is almost winter . . . almost."

Our musing continued and turned to the ripe apples on our trees, the grapes on his vines, the ripening of fruit in the fall, the already fallen apples, even wine making from his purple grapes. Then Joe moved on, having assessed, as children can, the moment's auspiciousness.

"Guess what, Mrs. Hawkins?"

"Tell me," I responded, "go ahead and tell me."

"Once Meg and me found a mouse all dead by her house. A cat had eated it, but not the legs and the body. An' guess what?"

"Tell me," I encouraged.

"Once me and Meg found a bird back by her barn, an' it was dead . . . with some feathers. An' which was badder, which was badder, do you fink?"

Now I had to pause. Getting no further clue from Joe, I answered that I didn't know which was badder, the dead bird or the dead mouse. So, gently but surely, Joe gave me his own reasoning.

"Well, I fink the mouse was badder, 'cause more blood was gone. It was badder 'cause it didn't have a head. I fink it was badder."

Now that I had been shown his logic, I could solemnly agree. Only later did my mind recall that awful thud of frail bird against window, the hopeful watch that this one might only be stunned and would rise, phoenixlike, to fly off. But all those birds had also had their heads. Jim's and Meg's mouse "didn't have a head."

Later, over peanut butter sandwiches in his kitchen, Joe explained to his mother what we had been up to "so long out there in the sun."

"Me and Mrs. Hawkins were telling stories—not jus' stories. An' after lunch we are going back."

But for me the morning had to end. With my soul restored about some of the truths young children seek to understand and communicate, about their ability to live in a hazardous but, in this case, a decent world, I returned to what was then, temporarily, the world for me—writing about them.

This philosophical aside of Joe's had restored my faith. We were not reading too much into our children's reactions. We were trying to interpret them.

Seeking the Good Company

My earlier writing, of short essays or for professional meetings, had always seemed fluent enough and cogent. But as soon as I made the decision to write this book—an autobiography—I was in trouble. Too many memories would crowd my mind. Thickets of them had to be untangled, and every chapter threatened to become a book. For a time I stopped writing. In no sense had I given up my great expectations for this book, but a barrier loomed in my way, one I did not understand.

Then happiness intervened. An invitation to "liven up a class for the deaf" came my way, and for a semester Claire Ulam Weiner and I had weekly visits, with materials for early science, to a small class of four-year-olds who were profoundly deaf. When David read our accumulated notes and saw Claire's pictures, he said, "I think we should share this story with the teachers; just take out some of the diatribes against the style of the public schools!" *The Logic of Action* resulted.[4] And between our weekly visits that term I spent many happy days pursuing my education in the art of writing: I studied under some of my favorite authors to find the secrets of their narrative art.

I found, first, that I was not alone. Virginia Woolf spoke to me on one such day.

> Anger had snatched my pencil while I dreamt. Interest, confusion, amusement, boredom—all these emotions I could trace and name as they succeeded each other throughout the morning. Had anger, the black snake, been lurking among them? . . .
>
> It is fatal for a woman to lay the least stress on any grievance; to plead even with justice any cause; in any way to speak consciously as a woman, and fatal is no figure of speech; for anything written with that conscious bias is doomed to death. It ceases to be fertilized. Brilliant and effective, powerful and masterly, as it may appear for a day or two, it must wither at nightfall; it cannot grow in the minds of others. [5]

Virginia Woolf's anger was directed against her demons; mine was focused on the deprecation and neglect of childhood.

In that altered state of searcher, I returned to the pages of favorite authors I had learned from, as from a teacher; perhaps they could also offer help with my writing. What inner audiences had they listened to that I seemed to lack? I tried not just to enjoy Henry James's *What Mazie Knew* or Dickens's *Little Dorritt* but somehow to ferret out some of the secrets of such different writers. I gloried in *Pride and Prejudice* and more of Jane Austin. Then I read again Maxim Gorky's *My Childhood* and took from our shelves a worn copy of the first volume of Sean O'Casey's autobiography, *I Knock at the Door*. These authors' autobiographies came from their own memories of childhood, mine from the adult notes and memories of the many children I had taught.

I began to understand something my favorite authors had found for guidance, and I came to a road I had not adequately explored. What was most significant along that road was expressed vividly by Henry James's great novels and short stories but also with his own self-reflection and the time he took to write about writing. From his essay "The Art of Fiction," I take a quotation that is endlessly enriching to my understanding and my efforts. James was examining the advice, often given to young writers, to "write from experience." "Of course that is true," he said, passing over a truism. But:

> Humanity is immense, and reality has a myriad of forms; the most one can affirm of it is that some of the flowers of fiction

have the odor of it, and others have not. . . . It is equally excellent and inconclusive to say that one must write from experience. . . . What kind of experience is intended and where does it begin and end? Experience is never limited, and it is never complete; it is an immense sensibility, a kind of high spider-web of the finest silken threads suspended in the chamber of consciousness, and catching every air-borne particle in its tissue. It is the very atmosphere of the mind; and when the mind is imaginative . . . it takes to itself the faintest hints of life, it converts the very pulses of the air into revelations. The young lady living in a village has only to be a damsel upon whom nothing is lost to make it quite unfair (as it seems to me) to declare to her that she shall have nothing to say about the military stationed in her village. Greater miracles have been seen than that, imagination assisting, she should speak the truth about some of these gentlemen. . . . Try to be one of the people on whom nothing is lost![6]

When I first read this part of James's essay, I was caught by its similarities to the ways I knew I must think about working with the young. If one does not try to be a teacher "on whom nothing is lost"—nothing that might happen within a group or with a child in focus—the very touchstone is missing.

What *kind* of experience did I intend to capture; where would it begin and end? The question led me back in time to the recovery of a classroom secret: given a long and thoughtful apprenticeship, a teacher's brain can learn to retrieve with speed the very suggestion or response that might be appropriate, freeing children to retrieve and invent, from their own fresh and expanding storehouse. The memories I needed for guidance in my writing were made up of these constant turning points and insights, just waiting to be recalled and disentangled.

It was thus that I came to realize how to bridge the gap that had concerned me so—the gap between my teaching and my writing. The bridge, most simply, is: in this chronicle, wherever I try to capture moments or days or weeks and make them again come to life, I must rely upon the *degree and quality of my initial immersion in those occasions*. What brought that action alive at the time was the interplay, inventiveness, and responsiveness of children. What brings it alive for me later, in writing, is my own part in creating and maintaining the ambiance with which and to which the children responded and changed themselves. So I must winnow recall and memory to bring life from the original events *as I originally partook of them* and only then verify them in writing.

Rome and San Francisco

One morning in Rome, where David and I were living for several months in 1976, I was reworking a story of my first class of second graders in 1936. I was struggling with how one exemplifies the atmosphere or climate of a classroom. The climate of Room 15 had needed a transformation from fear. Gradually, the students and I succeeded, but more from desperation than through much analysis on my part. As I was looking back, trying to work from notes, trying to define some critical conditions for joyful learning, my own childhood kept intruding. So I lingered there, although impatient with this personal intrusion.

Many have tried to understand the relationship between a child and an adult, in literature and in life. There was the relationship of Sean O'Casey and his mother in the 1880 slums of Dublin and that of Maxim Gorky and his grandmother amid the feudal rural poverty of Russia in the same decade.[7,8] I had written, thought, and known that such relationships contained secret within secret for the searcher.[9] But in Rome I saw with new clarity a related and second key to the kind of atmosphere I was seeking to define. It was not just my love for my dear grandmother but something else that came to live within me from her way of living. When I was grown she once said to me, "I have learned to live in the present." Her life had been extremely difficult, and that was her way of being, her philosophy of the present. So if I was to learn from this intrusion of my early memories, I would have to go beyond my affectional ties with her.

In the leisure and joy of our immediate life in Rome, I could slow my pace and search familiar memories with an altered mind-set. It was as if I had removed the magnet of sentiment and replaced it with another sort of memory probe, as if the same field that previously had yielded magnetic particles would now be scanned by some other means—a microscope—and yield pollen grains instead. And so with this new probe, I encouraged myself to step back and stay.

In the early part of the twentieth century it was common for any San Franciscan to "cross the Bay" on the elegant ferries, but for some it meant a special trip, a "happening." In my grandmother's house, there was always a sense of high adventure and planning that started before the day itself was anticipated, savored. We baked gingerbread or coffee cake to eat when we arrived, and we eyed the garden to assess what would be in bloom to bring. Clothes were chosen and laid out early the previous night, after which we bathed and went to bed.

With my young grandmother, about 1917.

Secondary to the preparation was the destination, although it was not unimportant. Great Uncle Will and Great Aunt Effie lived in the East Bay, in sleepy San Leandro. I remember few actual details about them or their house, but something significant about them does return to me, something stored in another place than that which contains the mere sequence of events. It was my awareness that my grandmother revered them and my mother did not. How this came to me I cannot say, but we know that children—especially, perhaps, those occasionally unsure of belonging in the family they have been born into—can thrive on bringing together evidence of their acceptance elsewhere and of nonjudgmental relationships.

This can be one of the happy bindings, can create a sense of security, among children in a classroom. It is a state of grace that cuts across and supersedes jealousies. It can be learned early, as early as walking and language. After the early trips to San Leandro and for years continuing into my teens, there were many ferry boat trips—to Mill Valley, in Marin

County, to Great Aunt Annie's "camp," to Maggie's cottage in San Rafael. We were usually a little late leaving the house on such expeditions but were strangely unanxious. There was so much to stow and carry; I hear Nana's voice urging finally "a brisk walk to await the streetcar" that would begin our journey in time to make the 10:20 ferry as planned.

The "A" car would come clanging down the hill and stop at Anza and Tenth. With our packages and, always, a large bouquet of flowers, we usually found our favorite sideways seat, facing north once the car turned into Geary Boulevard. This seat allowed us to check the time from the clock on the tower of the car barn and then calculate the time we could make the next ferry. How I loved that car-barn clock! We trusted it absolutely. I can't remember not being able to tell the time, accurately to the minute, an art I think I must have learned from that great impressive clock in its tower. Seldom didactic, my grandmother expected I would "pick it up."

I have many other memories of events with my grandmother, many simply of details of life within her house. What aspect was it of such mundane matters that so bewitched this young child? Was it some conspiracy we shared, a conspiracy to outwit? Was it that my opinions counted, that I was consulted? Was it the excitement of riding a streetcar, ferryboat, or train—something visits to her often involved? At home we always had an automobile, and I never knew my mother or father to ride a streetcar or a bus.

In time, we hoped, we were there at the Ferry Building, having admired its elegant shape looming ahead of us at the end of Market Street. Gathering packages to dismount, we would hurry to the ticket window. Near the embarkation was a big not-real clock, set for the next departure, and that would determine our speed. THE NEXT BOAT FOR SAU-SALITO WILL LEAVE AT 10:20 A.M. If we could still make it, our next race began. A smiling attendant might wait to put down the bar that meant the boat was being loosed from its moorings and yet allow *us* to run on. Oh happiness!

Practice and Theory

From all the close and refreshing scrutiny Rome allowed me, I was gaining a new sense of the factors affecting the atmosphere or climate that was propitious for learning—a child's own sense of learning to complement that of a teacher. When a particular child stood out and dominated a story, I would feel the need to tell one centered on a group. Once again I would need to explore the way a child in trouble could take strength or guidance from another or from a group or take some new step of development, yielding to the temptation posed by other children of attractive materials and occupations, thus casting off "the trappings and the suits of woe."

In reflecting on this pattern, I have come to understand how practice and theory have been interwoven all along, a weft and warp that belong in all my stories. Beyond such other debts as those to the good company among novelists and to my grandmother, therefore, I have accumulated another debt to those who have helped most in my understanding of some of the universals of children's learning and development. The first of these is Dr. Frederick Allen, director of the Philadelphia Child Guidance Clinic from 1925 to 1956. His major written work is *Psychotherapy With Children*.[10] In the vast array of literature on child development and therapy, I have found Allen's case histories and the ways of thinking that show through them to be the most profoundly relevant to the developmental situations a teacher encounters with young children and to ways of steering through those situations. He appears more than once in this book, always with insight important to the story.

This juxtaposition of fiction, personal reminiscence, psychotherapy, and teaching will seem surprising to many. A searching professional life can lead to surprising associations. In my case there are three: first, one of the greatest novelists, known too little for his understanding of children;[11] second, a distinguished but currently too little-known therapist; and third, the teaching of young children itself. What the novelists and the therapists share that I deeply value is the ability to observe children and adults and the psychic forces that exist between and within them, molding and influencing both adult and child.

The thought that teachers of children can and must join this august company is not strange. It is part of the very mandate they already hold from an awareness of each participant.[12]

Notes

[1]Poem 1,508, from *The Complete Poems of Emily Dickinson,* edited by Thomas H. Johnson (Boston: Little, Brown, 1960), p. 633. Reprinted with permission of the publisher.

[2]Theodora Kroeber, *Ishi in Two Worlds: A Biography of the Last Wild Indian in North America* (San Francisco: University of California Press, 1976). The quotations are from the flowsheet.

³Frances Pockman Hawkins, *The Logic of Action* (Boulder: Colorado Associated University Press, 1986). Revised edition of a work first published in 1969 by the Elementary Science Advisory Center, University of Colorado, Boulder.

⁴Ibid.

⁵Virginia Woolf, *A Room of One's Own* (New York: Harcourt Brace Jovanovich, 1989), pp. 32, 108.

⁶Henry James, *The Art of Fiction and Other Essays by Henry James,* with an introduction by Morris Roberts (New York: Oxford University Press, 1948), pp. 10–11.

⁷Sean O'Casey, *I Knock at the Door* (New York: Macmillan, 1960), pp. 57–75, esp. pp. 61–63.

⁸Maxim Gorky, *My Childhood,* trans. Margaret Wittlin (Moscow: Foreign Languages Printing House, n.d.).

⁹I had been full of it when writing (with David Hawkins) "The Life of Learning," *Urban Review* 7, no. 3 (July 1974).

¹⁰See Frederick H. Allen, *Psychotherapy With Children* (New York: W. W. Norton, 1942).

¹¹See Eli Siegel, *James and the Children: A Consideration of Henry James's The Turn of the Screw* (New York: Definition Press, 1968). And surely Henry James, *What Mazie Knew* (Penguin Books, 1985).

¹²For just two examples, see the sections "Ronald" in Chapter 2 and "Only Ben" in Chapter 4. A very few stories do not appear here because they need the safeguard of a more clinical publication.

1: Introduction to San Francisco Schools

My first semester of teaching, which was as a substitute in mid-Depression San Francisco, permanently altered my middle-class perception of the city of my birth. During the first month I was moved almost daily to a new school, thus getting a taste of the inner city. Whether the details were significant or insignificant, I amassed—almost as a novelist would—germs, as Henry James calls ideas for his stories, to be thought about and fitted into my twenty-two-year-old understanding as a person and as a teacher.

One learns little of a city by living in a middle-class neighborhood or by eating in its ethnic restaurants. To be sent hither and thither was more profoundly instructive. Each school became a newly discovered window to some phase of the city's life, and each contrasted with the others far more than I had anticipated.

In North Beach I found an abundance of life Italian style. Two days in a kindergarten there raised my voice by several decibels in an effort just to be heard in the lovely, shouting mass of five-year-olds not yet traumatized by school. In that school the admonition of one of my instructors at San Francisco State came back to me: "Never raise your voice," she had said, "just speak very softly, and the children will begin to listen." Ha! Miss Alcott had obviously never taught among these marvelous, exploding Latins! Long after the last children had left on those two days, echoes of voices rang loudly in my ears. I have no memory of what I did to teach, amuse, or hold my own; everything is lost in that long-ago din. I do remember the feeling of challenge the children left with me. I knew I would enjoy working with such lively children—if I could survive the initial chaos and noise. My affection for teaching in inner cities had begun.

After North Beach I was sent to a classroom in the Mission District, which at that time was predominantly German, Norwegian, and otherwise North European. The school was quiet, and propriety reigned. The children were dressed neatly; their blond hair was brushed and shining. "My daddy's union," said proudly, was a phrase that was new to me. In 1936, still in the depth of the Depression, these children's parents were

15

16 Journey With Children

working, something that set them apart from most students I taught over the next five years, whether inner city or middle class.

To extend my range, I began to hope for an assignment in China-town, but with no luck. Before I could sort out my impression of that first month, a magical letter arrived: I had been "assigned to Lafayette School, second grade . . . until end of term." In those Depression years I was incredulous at my good fortune, although it turned out to be bad fortune as well. But the letter and the promise it held were enough to make my weekend a joyous one—I was a long-term substitute with my own class!

I had done practice teaching at Lafayette School in 1933, some of it with a superb teacher, Agnes Gilchrist, who had been my teacher in her private kindergarten eighteen years earlier. She had warned me about Miss Hauzelt, although with less than full candor. My dear friend and mentor Miss Gilchrist was at risk in that school's atmosphere, as were all of the teachers and children.

Teacher and Children

But when the letter came I knew nothing about the situation to temper my joy. During the term of practice teaching I had spent at Lafayette School two years before, the principal had never appeared at the kindergarten. Therefore, my father drove a beaming daughter to Lafayette School to begin teaching. The vice-principal greeted me quietly and immediately led me down the hall to my new classroom. I had time as we walked to wonder whether any of the children I remembered from two years before when I student-taught kindergarten would happen to be in this particular second-grade class. I hoped so.

It did not strike me as odd at the time that no one really greeted or welcomed me. Principal Hauzelt had nodded from her office and told the vice-principal to show me to my room. San Francisco schools were not noted for warmth and friendliness to children or to teachers. The month in which I had substituted in many schools had not changed the impression I had formed during practice teaching: that the administrative bureaucracy was fierce and was never to be counted on to add much to any teacher's life or to any child's because that bureaucracy sought to do as little as possible to enhance the learning environment. In the years since 1936, I have found a scattering of public schools in the United States that are less damaged than Lafayette and even a few that are friendly. On the whole, however, across sixty years and thousands of miles, I feel our public schools—especially in the inner cities—are rarely designed so children and teachers can thrive and learn.

At the end of that first wonderful and exhausting day at Lafayette, I sat down at my desk when the children had left and tried to sort out my impressions. I was pleased and apprehensive, perplexed, and very excited. Two or three of the children had greeted me with shy remembrance. They were indeed from the kindergarten of two years before. I remembered them and was touched that they remembered me. For some of these lowest-testing second graders, kindergarten with my beloved Miss Gilchrist had been their only happy year at school. [1]

This first day was exhilarating for me, but the children were so routinized or scared or lost in daydreams or all of these that it almost seemed as though they could, zombielike, have carried on by themselves. They accepted and instructed me. Was such independence good? Perhaps, but I was frightened by their correct, fearful behavior, and that had to be analyzed. Four or five read well for second graders, but the other twenty-four essentially did not read at all. How could this be? I knew seven of the children were repeaters; this meant they had been in school for three years with little learning to show for that time. They feared reading or were bored and almost resisted the decoding they were expected to undertake.

The entire first day I was witness to the children's preoccupation with order and external form. There were fixed monitors for passing out materials, watering both of the pallid plants, erasing the blackboard, sharpening the pencils. Being in that room was like being among small robots rather than young children. I was appalled. Only occasionally had I managed to break through and get responses to my conversational efforts—some hints of spontaneity.

I stayed very late the first day, as I was to do every afternoon. I was going over records, assessing and remembering, trying to understand. Mrs. Burt from across the hall came by to welcome me. She remembered me from my student teaching. She was one of the few relaxed members of the staff—indeed, to my knowledge the only one. It was she who explained to me that there were three sections of the second grade and that they were grouped according to their reading scores; my section ranked the lowest. Hers was the highest, which may have been in part the result of the students having this gentle, competent teacher.

Within that first week, as I allowed many of the established routines to grind on, it was obvious how profoundly ignorance and fear were affecting the children who did not read. They were normal children who had spent much of their school lives being traumatized. I firmly believed that they would quickly prove eager and capable once their binding cloths had been removed and their native abilities released and encouraged. Novice that I was, with that faith I began to move forward. For my evaluation, I would have the children themselves and their learning. (City-wide testing would come at the end of my term and that, too, would count—although some of us knew that testing gave only a thin slice of what children were learning or failing to learn.)

When I began to alter what the reading groups did, a wave of apprehension—almost fear—rippled through the entire class. I asked the two reading-book monitors to return all the books to the cupboard. I announced, "We will not use books for a long time." Many students silently raised their hands. The questions were substantially the same: "If we don't have reading groups, then how can we get to hear each other at our seats?" This, I realized, was precious time—teacher-free!—with a friend to go through arithmetic flash cards or spelling words or to draw, with whispering permitted, while the teacher was engaged with another group in the painful process so wrongly called reading. I reassured the children that we would still come together in three groups but for many other things, not just for reading out of readers. Guidance from children!

Before I recount some of the changes we made, let me sketch the state of those existing reading groups. I have mentioned that few children were reading. They were the ones who had been allowed to take a library book to their seats when they were not pressed into group work. In their reading groups, these readers were understandably bored by the aggravatingly slow pace. For them, to abolish group reading would be no real loss. At first, they did miss their superior status of always being the word-givers, but soon, as activities became more appropriate and challenging, these good readers did not miss the past.

At the other extreme were the repeaters, who had constantly been traumatized and ultimately were unable to recognize a single word. Between these extremes were the gallant stumblers. Still trying, they guessed right occasionally and politely requested most words. It was a slow, painful twenty minutes for this middle group, who sat resignedly waiting a turn to fail while others, with much help and almost no comprehension, decoded a few lines.

Among those who could not read, I choose Gordon to describe first. He was the most frightened of the students. When he held a reader, his hands shook so much that I wondered how he could even focus on the print, let alone read it. A repeater, he was finishing his second year of daily public exposure as a failure. Aldo, another repeater, had a much less painful strategy. When it was his turn, he would openly and with no shame ask someone to give him each and every word! Aldo was a fine artist. He would learn to read when he felt the need.

Then there was Donald. Sitting in his reading group Donald day-dreamed and hummed happily until it was his turn. Scanning the short sentence for a familiar word, he would ask someone to give him the rest and would stumble along with no interest, understanding, or observable self-consciousness. In retrospect, I thought of Donald as our poet; writing two- or three-line compositions soon became his delight.

Most of the girls in this class had learned to fake rather well, to sit next to a friend and "read" haltingly at a much slower and less mature level than they were capable of. They made the greatest strides: fear receding, they could race ahead

Even now I remain astonished, as was my long-ago young self, at how such a group of eager and competent children could be so cheated so soon, so devastatingly. The word *brainwashing* did not yet exist, but that was what they had endured and do endure. They had learned well what was of primary importance to the school and to most of its teachers—to behave well and quietly, to raise a hand for any recognition, never to talk or whisper to one another except in those allotted times (no wonder they loved them) when a twosome could "hear each other." They had learned to cover up any failure, to always act as if they knew how to read, and to make a friend of one who knew a little more and who could, on occasion, stealthily supply a word or an answer or a single sound. Yes, we had phonics!

Such were the basics for Lafayette School in 1936, masquerading under the labels of reading, writing, and arithmetic. The phrase "back to basics" had not yet been invented, although San Francisco schools could not go back to something they had never left. Lafayette was steadfastly dedicated to the three Rs. Although many children were failing, it was actually the school that had failed. I am enraged when I hear the back-to-basics cry. Let the criers do their homework and look at history carefully. Some of us were there. Wherever one finds a teacher who likes to teach, who loves learning and is not burdened with impossible numbers, children learn—along with and as a part of much else—to read and write and understand arithmetic, not just to "do" it. It was the Lafayette children who secured my belief that children learn with the same differences in style and tempo that characterized them as they learned to walk, to speak, to play and eat, and to navigate in their often hazardous world.

Even for a novice it was easy to define what the more fearful and failure-ridden children had not been allowed to know but would joyfully embrace: a little self-directed success. They had already accepted their dependency, their inadequacy, their shame, and they were locked into a fearful status quo. Was this the least threatening way for them to survive at school? They were powerless.

Written small, small enough for one young teacher to grasp and remedy, it is a reminder to me of much that lies at the roots of some of our social concerns. It is not a theme to be put forth simplistically, but for me, at least, it is never to be set aside. I think of Erich Fromm's *Escape From Freedom;* but for the essence of it there is a verse from the poem "Germinal," by the poet "A. E." George Russell:

In ancient shadows and twilights
Where childhood had strayed,
The world's great sorrows were born
And its heroes were made.
In the lost boyhood of Judas
Christ was betrayed. [2]

What these children needed was a first try in new directions rather than, as had been their lot, repeated "remedial" and failure-reinforcing activities. I began to feel this in every recess of my mind and heart. It has traveled with me ever since. My education was enlightened.

About this time I heard of a report Stanford University had published a few years before. A fourteen-year-old at the local junior high school had committed suicide. Stanford studied his school records. All of his Lafayette teachers and Principal Hauzelt had been interviewed. Hauzelt instructed the teachers to say nothing about this child that would imply that he had experienced "troubles" during his six years at Lafayette. All complied, and the slate of Lafayette was wiped clean—of the truth. The child had been miserable throughout his school years, which I learned privately from a few of his teachers.

This conviction of the school's failure informed my evolving plans. At Stanford and San Francisco State there had, fortunately, been little emphasis on method, on "how to do it." There had instead been a strong emphasis on educating us as teachers who would pick and choose from our store of living and learning, who would use our own minds once we had assessed the strengths and needs of the children we were to teach. It was a glorious heritage.

It remains a mystery to me—given the diversity of children and the variety of ways in which they thrive, and given our ignorance—why it is still so fashionable to label ourselves, thus narrowing the sources of new insight. Still in my own future was the University of California graduate school summer of 1939 with Kurt Lewin and George Stoddard and 1943 when Frederick Allen was to become my mentor; they all encouraged my offbeat ways and taught me from their respective disciplines.

I make these points to underscore that I had not been cheated by my own education, the fruits of which set me well on course to observe children, to analyze their strengths and provide for them. During the sixty-odd years since that class, I have sought and found ways to continue a process begun by two good universities.

My plans for changing the school life of these second graders stemmed from a consideration of what could be done *at once,* of how we could begin to move *away from that atmosphere created by daily, hopeless, and public failure.* I could lift the burden of each child whose life at school had been heavy. For awhile there would be no reading aloud, no asking a child to do something he or she could not do alone. Opportunities for self-help must be abundant and constantly available.

We began in our new small groups, with much talk about what we saw, liked, would like to have, had noticed on the way to school, what a friend or aunt or grandparent had for a pet—all the kinds of talk teachers should expect and encourage to stretch bridges between home and school, between child and child, between friends. There was nothing here that good teachers today would find unusual. This sort of communication is one of the universals. But the ways in which teachers and children can transpose and extend this sort of communication are critical, transforming it from routine pleasantry into a bond of learning that becomes unique.

With encouragement and expectation, these second graders began suddenly to deluge the classroom with treasures from home and from their daily walks to and from school. It was one of their ways of showing trust, I believed, and of making the room their own, newly reclaimed. The wide, continuous top of a row of low cupboards invited displays and became our "science" shelf for rocks, carrot tops growing, a coconut, grasses, a stolen rose, an ant in a pill box, a brown cocoon—and much more.

With such modest riches we began, at small-group time, to produce a cooperative newspaper written on large, stiff paper that could be pegged on the wall. At first, no one was allowed to read it out loud; only I was permitted to do so. After a child had dictated his or her own news story under his or her own byline, because of the use of names and personal events, children quickly found their own contributions and asked to read them—what fraction from text and what from memory I cared not a whit. By the end of the second week, even children like Gordon began to breathe naturally at group newspaper time. Donald stopped his continual day-dreaming; it was he, as I remember, who brought the cocoon one morning.

The success of the wall newspaper required some skill in large-letter printing, and I, a poor penwoman who had chafed at the college require-ment, now blessed San Francisco State for requiring proficiency and some elegance in this printing art from all its kindergarten-primary students, in addition to proficiency in children's art, music, children's literature, and so on.

We planted seeds in pots by the eastern windows—enough to watch growth and even taste a radish or two. The old plants—all two of them—were pruned, and new ones came, some on loan from parents, to stay until the end of the term.

The cumulative effects of all these small changes of direction and tempo, each modest enough in itself, proved dramatic. Days were sud-denly too short. The children elected not to go out for recess—unless I insisted—and raced home for a bite of lunch and raced back for the after-noon session. Sweet reward, that!

Knowing that the children were now focusing on school and its offer-ings—not all of them at once, but in rapidly growing numbers—I deep-ened the challenge. The next step was to increase the need for *silent* reading within the room. I made and displayed the required charts of *Songs We Know, Spelling Bee Team Winners for the Week, Poems We Know,* and so on. Then I hit on the idea of a chart that linked and contrasted the new era with the old. It was large and showed the names of monitors, in shallow envelopes, for each day of the week. When I first arrived, remem-ber, the monitors had been fixed for so long that no one ever questioned who would do what job. Because names on this chart changed frequently and were posted, any child might find that his or her turn had come rather unexpectedly. Next to the phrase describing each job I put a silhou-ette, cut out and mounted, of a child engaged in that task. The chart became grubby after some weeks, evidence that it was used well and enjoyed. For some children it remained important throughout the semes-ter. The surprise element challenged their budding reading abilities, which pleased them.

During the group sessions we soon branched out from reading and writing the daily newspaper into other matters. We began to play silent-reading games. I made tagboard cards with written commands: "run," "jump," "skip," "hop." Beside each command verb was a sketch of a child doing that activity. I could soon cut off these sketches and paste them on the backs of the cards, unseen except to verify if needed. Single words were replaced with more complicated commands such as "run around the library table," "skip to the front door," "hide under the teacher's desk." Reading out loud was forbidden. By this time all things and places in the room were labeled, and the few verbs were becoming familiar, so this plan worked!

Many of the verbs represented activities once forbidden within that classroom, such as running and skipping; hence the speed of learning may have been even more enhanced. "Clap three times" (or even four or five or twenty times) was a favorite card command. The cards were not used at the children's seats because I did not want them to be read aloud; they were special to group sessions with me.

All the children enjoyed this escape from sitting and boredom and shame, so much so that even the few competent readers wanted to take part. This was a game that used the written language as a language and not just as a transcription of speech to be sounded out, word by awkward word.

Late one afternoon I found a mimeograph machine in a closet down the hall, and I began to use it after school. I spent hours making new, appropriate, and required "seat work," as it was called. Ours was based on the things going on in our classroom. The science shelves and windowsills were now loaded with good things well labeled. Children were encouraged to get up from their seats to seek an answer or the spelling of a word. This provision for self-help, I hoped, would further release children from having to be given every other word. It did help, and it was fun.

Initially, I invented three levels of difficulty in the seat work from which a child could choose. The easiest might say "draw a caterpillar." In the blank space the child would draw a caterpillar but only after close observation of one of the many caterpillar-visitors we had on the science table on twigs in jars. The most difficult words might be "Constance brought three carrot tops. Draw two growing tall, or draw one not yet growing tall." Within days, all of the children were using all of the work, and I was hard put to expand and invent.

Tension was easing around anything having to do with the science shelves, so we used those changing materials more and more often. Fortunately, the children were bringing enough material so the displays and labels were not fixed; our discussions and reading and writing about them never became stale. There were times of high excitement, as when a caged canary visited, brought for a day by a parent.

Composition time was scheduled for after lunch. To enliven it, we took time in the mornings to compose on the blackboard what might be called cooperative stories. These differed from the newspaper in that the entire class, rather than just one reading group, contributed at least once a week. The stories were less personal, and there were no individual bylines. Both news and stories resulted from the events that were pulling us together as a group. These stories repeated so much of the group's growing vocabulary that some of my former nonreaders and stumblers were suddenly anxious to read out loud; some of the slower ones, who were not ready to read, became the best story composers.

So it was that when composition time came, we had the science shelf and two written sources to consult, all of which was our own good copy. Some children simply copied with one or two words changed, as beginners will, but they were soon able to read what they had written, which greatly helped to build self-confidence! Within two weeks composition time had been changed from a time for groaning to a time the students valued. It became, in fact, the quietest time of the day. Everyone had something to write, and no one had to wait a turn or be called on. I was constantly amazed that none of the children ever had trouble choosing or inventing the two or three most important sentences to express what each had taken from the morning's abundance of concerns and written stories. I realized only later that it would have been helpful to have given each child a small, private notebook for writing or drawing; in those early days, I too had much to learn.

This interweaving of collecting and observing, talking and telling, reading and writing made sense to these second graders, and we all knew it for what it was—a sweet breath of success. Although I was spending nine or ten hours a day at school, I don't remember being tired in those early weeks. It was only later, when the principal tried to alter our ways, that fatigue became my constant companion.

Spelling bees marked a favorite hour once a week. How this activity had escaped the pall that had stifled reading and arithmetic and writing is still a mystery. Did its team and competitive spirit suggest a sport, an out-of-school activity? Perhaps former teachers had enjoyed the spelling bees? Whatever the reason, I was grateful and made the most of it. Hearing each other's spelling created competence in this absurd language of ours. It involved pure memory, an isolated skill initially of little help in writing but one widely valued, especially by me, a notoriously poor speller. I applaud phonetic spelling, especially for some beginners (although not all). It can remove a major obstacle to children's story writing, an art our schools neglect too much.

The children explained to me the format of their spelling bees, and our first match could proceed. I chose the two captains, and they, with much prompting from friends, chose the teams. They chose by friendship rather than spelling ability—poor spellers were not ignored or chosen last. Nice, that. I saw a chance during the first match to introduce numbers tangentially by keeping score on the board. The children found this a welcome addition to the game and helped me list the number of words missed by each team. Halfway through the first match one boy pointed to the columns on the blackboard. "Miss Pockman! Look! It's just like arithmetic!" His pleasure of discovery was shared, and from then on I introduced numbers as often as seemed appropriate.

This informal, natural use of arithmetic seemed a must, given these children's lack of understanding of the simple formal arithmetic they were supposed to be memorizing for their second-grade required curriculum. Number combinations—addition and subtraction—were printed on flash cards. Early on, these had provided another escape route from boredom; children could work in chosen pairs, hearing each other's rote responses to the cards they flashed at each other. In analyzing this performance or gently asking questions, it became clear that the number symbols on the blue flash cards had no meaning behind them. No one had ever been asked to think about whether the answers made sense in terms of their common-sense, out-of-school understanding of numbers, of greater and lesser. I gradually tried to phase out the flash cards and concentrate on using arithmetic throughout the day. I tried mainly to put arithmetic to use and in this way to untangle some of the mumbo-jumbo.

By the fourth week the transformation of the class was evident, not just in the children's demeanor and the receding of fear and caution but also in the return of spontaneity in tackling simple reading and writing. Their compositions especially reflected the change. Not everyone had yet made great strides forward, but a comfortable majority had done so. At the time, my understanding and experience allowed me only to rejoice about and with the children over the speed of the transformation. I did not yet analyze, but I accepted and was ready to build something new into my developing framework of theory: the speed of recovery that can occur when children *are freed to change themselves, when an atmosphere of fun replaces one of fear.*

Our days of anticipation and fulfillment together continued. Parents began to stop by—for just a moment—to smile with a word of appreciation when they helped a child bring something for the science shelves. Since no one who was part of the school ever came by—except Mrs. Burt, perhaps twice after school—it was especially good to have parents' appreciation and involvement.

The atmosphere of hostility and fear in the entire school should have put me on guard, but hard work and pleasure in the children's budding happiness protected me. I was confident, if vulnerable, since all the responses I had from children and parents were positive. But then, I ask, how can one be prepared, busy below, for sudden disaster from the sky? As practice teachers we had been protected from administrators, and San Francisco State in those years made a heroic effort to select the few classrooms in which its students would be in the presence of learning rather than of dictatorial administrations. In my own elementary school in Los Angeles in the twenties, there had been laughter and fun among teachers. One episode is etched into my mind: two teachers from the upper grades on "yard duty," laughing and then breaking into song—"La donna è mobile." The children gathered around for some moments listening, enchanted.

On the last day of my fourth week, Donald's butterfly produced its marvelous last instar, or transformation. Someone's checking eye had found the cocoon being abandoned, and we crowded around, all twenty-eight plus one, to watch the slow process of the butterfly pumping up its wings before taking off. When it did fly, it circled the room more than once, showing its colors of orange and brown, and then, finding an open window and more light, it was gone.

The day and the hour, climaxing our own month of liberation, were fine enough. What a story we wrote on the board that morning! By the time we had finished it, no one moved. We sat while at least ten children wanted to read it aloud. We spoke of compositions we would have to write that afternoon, and then the children went off to their work at seats or tables.

Just at the conclusion of that happy episode, the door opened to a visitor and to a new phase of my life at Lafayette. Amid the miseries that were to follow would come the opportunity for these children, after their month of change, to sustain me and our new ways throughout the remaining weeks of the term.

The door opened, and in came the elegant and beautiful Mrs. Harris, the assistant deputy superintendent of the one hundred elementary schools in San Francisco. I had just met her at a teachers' meeting and had been impressed by her talk. I still remember my first reaction to her presence in my class: Why couldn't she have come an hour earlier? But then I welcomed her and invited her to wander and observe. One of the children read her the story about our butterfly, and others joined in excitedly to tell about it. Mrs. Harris seemed less interested in the children or the butterfly than in such matters as our wall newspaper and our charts. She asked if she could borrow the chart of silhouettes and daily tasks for the next kindergarten-primary meeting. I was pleased, and Mrs. Harris went rather quickly on her way. The visit lasted less than ten minutes.

Mrs. Harris's visit had been a surprise. I had understood through the grapevine that no member of the central administration was welcome at Lafayette following an incident in which Principal Hauzelt had slapped a teacher. The administration had made her apologize, the barriers went up, and the enmity was permanent.

During lunch that fateful day, I was told Miss Hauzelt wished to see me in her office. I naively thought our visitor must have told her something pleasant about the charts or the children's stories. In my happy state, it never crossed my mind that Mrs. Harris would leave behind an untactful complaint. She had, in fact, done both. When I walked into the principal's office, such a tirade of abuse was unleashed against me that it left me speechless and physically ill. In the midst of a hideous frothing of words, I heard what Mrs. Harris had reported: "Frances Pockman is doing some interesting things in her room. Her discipline could be better." Certain phrases said to me that day in terrible anger remain etched in my memory: "So you, Miss Pockman, are letting children do just what they want to do? Now I understand why parents have been calling me and saying that their children are happy in school for the first time since kindergarten. You, Miss Pockman, are responsible for children ending up out there," pointing toward Alcatraz Island, the old federal prison in San Francisco Bay. "That's where children end up who are not disciplined." It went on and on. With genuine fury she screamed at me, "How dare you run a class without proper discipline in my school? Children like yours, in the lowest group, will always run wild." I tried to defend the children by telling the truth about their self-direction and progress. Miss Hauzelt didn't let me finish but scoffed at my expectations for these lowest-level children. "Why, they aren't capable of really reading . . . they will learn at most a little bit of reading, a little bit of arithmetic."

I was nearly unable to breathe at this onslaught against me and the children. I just stood until, in the midst of a final accusation against "your kind of teaching," she rose, looked at the clock, and said with gusto, "Now we will just go down to your class together and see what state it is in." It was ten past one; the children had been back in our room for ten minutes, alone. Had she calculated this?

I remember the terrible walk down that long, gloomy hall. I was terrified about what had just happened and wondered what would happen next, what we would find. I had never left the children alone. Doing so was illegal!

We neared the room. Absolute quiet. Every child was seated properly and quietly, working on the afternoon's composition about our butterfly. The children were so involved with the butterfly miracle and with their compositions that at first they hardly noticed the two arrivals. For a moment I naively dared to hope Miss Hauzelt would be mollified, if not pleased, and would change her totally false view of these children who were under my care. But her face was contorted with fury as she stalked along the side of the room to the front where she stood and searched the silent twenty-eight children.

Then there was a gentle hum, a short and pleased sound. Miss Hauzelt's relief at this "misdemeanor" was evident in the way she yelled, "Who did that?" All eyes turned to her. "Who made that noise?" We all knew—Donald, of course. I only trusted that no one would betray the culprit. These children had, after all, survived this school; part of their technique for survival was to protect each other. (Only later does contagious corruption take effect, when some children give up and become informers to authority.)

The sin of the hum hung over us. After failing to get either a confession or an informer, Miss Hauzelt turned to me and said in her loud voice, "I shall come everyday to this class, Miss Pockman, to see how your discipline progresses." No more hums!

She did just that. She came everyday, unpredictably, at different times, for three weeks. We were always pleased when she came in the morning, because then we didn't have to be on guard all day. She came, sat at my desk working at papers, listening for trouble all the while. There was never a voice or a movement she could pounce on. She never spoke to a child or to me. She never noticed any of our work.

The children and I became co-conspirators, pledging silently not to give her an inch. They never let me down, and I tried in every way to make it up to them when she wasn't there by keeping to our former happy ways. Mrs. Burt laughingly told me she had been asked to teach me how to march the children to the schoolyard, about twenty feet beyond our door. But even Mrs. Burt obeyed—I can't say respected—Miss Hauzelt and asked me to let her go along on one occasion as my instructress.

No one in the entire school, it seemed, had ever crossed Miss Hauzelt, except the one teacher who had been slapped and who had then reported her to some higher authority. Mrs. Harris, the deputy superintendent who agreed with my philosophy, had, in praising my work, made only the slight but sycophantic concession that my "discipline could be better."

Things weren't easy after that. I couldn't sustain my former joy in teaching during times of such apprehension. It never occurred to me that I was in error or should change my ways—except when the ogre was present. Miss Hauzelt was wrong about everything. I hated and feared her for what she could do to a child she saw as erring or to my own beginning confidence as a teacher. Thus can be the power of the sick among us.

I have trusted all young children in my classes since that time. I have never been let down. Those second graders were, and have been ever since, a beacon of possibility. Their early support, the way they continued to learn under adversity, their unvoiced understanding, have been with me throughout all the years that have followed.

Toward the end of term, we gained tangible evidence of the children's progress. When the city-wide test for reading was given in May, these formerly lowest-scoring children tested on a par with Miss Burt's highest group of second graders. I was delighted, if a little disappointed that they hadn't tested even higher. I knew that if we could have spent the entire year together instead of just two-and-a-half months, when tested these children would have been the stars of the school.

A month later on the final day of the term, when I had packed and was leaving, Miss Hauzelt stopped by. She referred to the tests and said, "Well, I guess you must have learned from Mrs. Burt how to discipline your children." I looked at her and said, "Goodbye, Miss Hauzelt," and turned away. The children and I had survived.

Retrospect

Almost thirty years later in Boston, such principals—and their intimidated teachers—were abundant. I visited many following the Boston

South End kindergarten summer of 1963 (see Chapter 7). Soon after that, Jonathan Kozol wrote *Death at an Early Age.* [3]

Notes

[1]In tracked schools, such as Lafayette, and as they are today, "lowest-testing" children are put in the lowest track—and everyone knows it.

[2]From the poem "Germinal," by George Russell, in *Modern British Poetry* (Harcourt Brace Jovanovich, 1942), p. 155. Reprinted by permission on approval.

[3]Jonathan Kozol, *Death at an Early Age: The Destruction of the Hearts and Minds of Negro Children in the Boston Public Schools* (New York: Houghton-Mifflin, 1967).

2: The Emerson Years

Emerson

For this third-generation San Franciscan, history began with grand-parents and their memoirs of early days. Since our family was blessed with four willing historians, plus parents and uncles and their friends, the habit of living in a present interwoven with the past of a burgeoning city was one we happily acquired.

My paternal grandmother, upon hearing I was to teach at Emerson School, supplied me with much of San Francisco history for the period 1850–1860. "Why, there has been a public school there at California and Divisadero as long as I can remember . . . decades before the fire . . . we used to sled on the Divisadero Hill past the school . . . on sand, of course." She—Eliza Bryson Brodie—had come with her mother and baby brother from New York to "the Isthmus" and then traveled "by native's back" across the fifty-mile Panamanian jungle. Another ship brought the young family up the Pacific Coast to ultimately join her father, my great-grand-father, in San Francisco.

Our other grandmother, Fannie McDowell Boyd, was properly born in San Francisco at the "foot of Telegraph Hill" in 1869. She grew up in "the Mission District." Only later did I realize what a provincial, insu-lated city of less than half a million San Francisco was. This grandmother had sent her son Rudy to Emerson School for a year or so, after the fire. During "the earthquake and fire, we were all terrified that the flames would cross Filmore Street." Further details of the earthquake followed—especially the difficulty of saving frightened horses in the stable next to the school by covering their eyes.

My three brothers and I relished all of this—especially since we had lived in Los Angeles during our own school years before college. We spent all of our vacations in San Francisco and camping near Lake Tahoe until we moved back to San Francisco—to the house where I was born—in 1932. During the twelve years in Los Angeles, I understood why my mother always mentioned in conversations with neighbors that we didn't know how soon we would be returning to "the City."

31

I must add here, in a lighter vein, more history of the San Francisco School Department because of family memories. My mother had been born in San Francisco and had attended Pacific Heights School, where I did my first practice teaching in 1933. My mother did not speak easily or often of her childhood, and I was surprised by one voluntary reminiscence about Pacific Heights that she shared with me. I retell my mother's story because it relates something important about the traditions of the San Francisco School Department, going back at least to the turn of the century. As an undergraduate practice teacher I had become fully aware of the dictatorial character of the administration, and this earlier history fits.

One morning we were looking at a box of pictures I had never seen before. They included a photograph of her with her classmates from the eighth-grade graduating class at Pacific Heights in 1903. They were not more than fourteen years old, all girls, but they looked eighteen in their ankle-length dark skirts, their elegant shirtwaists with ties, and their long hair done up in pompadours or braids. On the back of the mounted photograph each girl had signed her name (how did they teach such penmanship in those days!). We read the names, and my mother identified the girls. I remarked that most of the names were Jewish. Her response was proud and emphatic: "Of course, it was the best school in the city." My mother never understood anti-Semitism.

My mother spoke of the great excitement that surrounded each lunch hour at Pacific Heights. Just before the students went home for lunch, a servant would arrive with a large silver tray of food for the principal—white linen, covered silver dishes, and the marvelous smell of some hidden gourmet food. Whence these feasts? Each day the wealthiest families in the school would vie with each other to present the most elegant noon meal. "And of course," said my mother matter-of-factly, "their children were treated properly in return." There must have been many students, closer in means to my mother's immediate family—which was of very modest means—who simply accepted the blatant bribery as the sort of thing that went on and, childlike, had enjoyed the sight and fragrance as those daily offerings were carried past them, often by a Chinese servant. In the 1930s, when I began to teach there, these earlier gross displays of privilege no longer occurred.

A Permanent Substitute

Emerson School was built about 1910 and reflected the economies and compromises public schools, with few exceptions, still exhibit. After Lafayette School I was sent to Emerson as a "permanent substitute" in the kindergarten. I stayed for four years. After a year and a half at Emerson, I was made a probationary teacher and received a small salary instead of my previous five dollars a day.

It may have been an honor, as I was told, to become a probationer after such a "brief" period of subbing (two years!), but I had long been aware that such honors brought burdens. I became one of the administration's showpieces during those years at Emerson and joined the most exploited group of beginning teachers in the system. I put up with the extra work this honor entailed because I counted it as a trade-off for being allowed to teach subversively in a child-oriented manner. The administration liked the sound of what I did and was pleased with the results on tests but knew little of its substance. Since only a handful of principals and even fewer administrators had a clue about how children learned well or how teachers could help in this learning, my subversive approach was essential.

I had worked as a graduate-student practice teacher under a superb principal, Miss Bradley, in Berkeley-Oakland; I had enjoyed six magnificent weeks in Lois Hayden's kindergarten at Pacific Heights School in San Francisco doing my first practice teaching. With such a background, I knew I was not alone in my commitments; I was just lonely.

In 1910 when the school was built, there had been no public kindergartens, so the room at Emerson that was to be mine for the next four years had been designed for a first grade. All of the children sat at stationary desks. The room was small and had good windows, although they were too high to allow kindergarten or primary children to see more than the sky. There was no running water, no lavatory nearby. There were, however, a decent piano, good small chairs and tables, and a few supplies such as Peg-Boards and pegs, and some good storybooks.

Was there ever play equipment on the schoolyards? "No," the principal answered when I asked, "it has all been removed from our schools; too dangerous—parents sued. And," she continued, "the kindergarten children must never be in the yard when others are at recess. Too dangerous."

There was one large lavatory off each of the two playgrounds, which were separated outside by a long flight of metal-edged cement stairs that became a daily horror. "The kindergarten children must be taken to the lavatories twice a morning; that way no child will ever have to go alone. We have too many loitering men." For me, to take thirty-nine five-year-olds twice each morning up the inner stairs, then down a long hall to the outside girls' lavatory, on down the long outside dangerous flight remained a nightmare until I decided that the danger would be halved by going once a morning.

Silence must reign, of course. I alternated between being an ogre and inventing games that required silence and were appealing. Our favorite became a game of Indians in moccasins, stalking deer. The second year I rebelled, and we used the boys' lavatory on our level for everyone. No one ever knew!

The toilet seats were old-fashioned, not divided, and a notice came that we were to teach our girls—all twenty of mine—to get on and off the full-size toilets without touching the seat. In the meantime, I was supposed to "supervise" the nineteen boys sitting outside on the bench. "Gonorrhea has been detected in more than one of the children in the school, and divided seats have been ordered." The divided seats never arrived during my four years at Emerson, and I never succeeded in instructing five-year-old girls how to swing on or off those seats without "touching."

In addition to these daily annoyances were such shameful episodes as Emerson's refusal to accept free "excess commodities." With three-quarters of its families on relief or Works Progress Administration (WPA), Emerson was well qualified for the government's New Deal program of free fruit. In California especially, free oranges were plentiful. The government had decided to distribute excess fruit to hungry children. A school could refuse the gift: democracy at work! Emerson did refuse the offer. The rage felt by a few of us who had not been consulted was hardly assuaged when we heard the reasons most teachers gave for the refusal after a trial first week: "Enthusiasm." (To qualify, one's father or mother had to be on relief or WPA.) "Children raised their hands willingly, without shame, to admit their disgrace!" "Teaches them to expect something for nothing." Also, some orange peels had been found on the empty playground, which was the final straw.

In any class I taught during those years, there might be four children who could afford to buy milk for their snack, but we were issued a large box of graham crackers whenever we ran out. I stole happily from that box, at least four a day for each child. Water and grahams were better than nothing.[1]

Some children who were hungrier than most would ask for the milk of an absent child. I would give them the milk secretly or hide it or even dump it; I couldn't bear the pleas. There was no milk fund. I wanted to supply the milk myself, but at the pay I received of five dollars a day, I couldn't manage about nine dollars a week for milk for thirty-nine children.

Fellow Teachers

Some surprises awaited me among the teachers and administrators at Emerson. The vice-principal, Miss Nelson, walked into my classroom one day, and we discovered that she had been my Uncle Rudy's eighth-grade teacher in 1909. She beamed when she heard I was Rudy's niece: "Oh, he was such a mischievous boy. I used to put him in the front row and sit on his desk to keep him from getting in trouble. I couldn't scold him, he was so handsome and charming. So young to be killed in the war—I read all about his death." For a few moments I could imagine a young Miss Nelson, not the dour one who was now feared by the teachers at Emerson. After that chance discovery, Miss Nelson visited our room during class and seemed to enjoy our rather boisterous ways. She was always a welcome visitor, and it became hard to relate her relaxed ways with us to her reputation and her observed treatment of others.

Such happy accidents were minor compared with the one that allowed Kathleen McGowan to cross my path at Emerson. Our friendship and professional association began, unknown to me at the time, in the teacher's lunchroom during the first week of school. It was to sustain me through four years.

I was invited to join the teachers with sack lunches, and for a miserable, brief time I did. Without exception, the staff was friendly and kind toward me. Unless questioned, I was silent. Certainly, I said nothing about any child. I couldn't trust myself because what these women said about the students was so cruel and unprofessional. Snatches ring in my ears still:

"Oh, that nigger girl is just getting too uppity. She thinks she is too good for the sixth grade"—on and on about Ruth Cooley's too-proud ways. Ruth was indeed too good to be only a sixth-grade student. I depended on her able assistance in the kindergarten. She also maintained the attendance record for the entire school of six hundred students. She kept the exact figures for average daily attendance (ADA) and could do her schoolwork in minutes.

Another snatch of that lunchroom nightmare: "Is that blond, Billy, really a nigger? Send him down for me to see this afternoon." Then came a barrage of worn-out clichés: "shiftless," "wouldn't work if he stumbled over a job." A few teachers didn't join the conversation; others, I learned later, ate in their rooms. Beginning the second week, I ate in my room.

But one of the other silent teachers had noticed me and came to my room during lunch one day. She was an older woman with a hat and a lovely smile. She introduced herself as Miss McGowan. "Well, Miss Pockman, I see you have given up the lunchroom rather soon. I knew you would—if you care for children it's impossible. A few of us never eat there. I certainly don't, except to meet a new teacher. I watched you last week, and even though you never said anything to disagree, your face and neck grew red. I could tell how you felt." (Oh, that telltale high blood pressure!)

Miss McGowan taught the ungraded class of sixteen genetically or environmentally damaged children. She saw them as indeed they were—whole human beings—and found them a challenge and a delight. Her battle to protect them in the hostile school environment was heroic; we became fast allies and friends from the first day we met. David and I still have the wedding present she and the children made: a hand-carved solid mahogany tray. It is a beauty and has been a reminder, over fifty years, of a treasured friend and of her classroom.

Kathleen McGowan and I developed and maintained an association between her older children and my four- and five-year-olds. Her students made playhouse furniture and doll clothes and brought scrap wood for our carpentry projects—cooperation and friendship developed between the two classes. The kindergarten would entertain Miss Mac's class whenever a gift was to arrive. Watching those sixteen bigger children beam as they were admired and thanked and appreciated was all Miss McGowan and I ever needed for evaluation. All of her children thrived, as did mine, taking and giving.

Where did Kathleen McGowan come from? Why was she so different, so clear of vision and courageous in that bleak and murky atmosphere? What had gone right for my dear new friend? I asked her one afternoon after we had been secret conspirators for many months.

She was born into an Irish Catholic family, a religion she shared with half, I would guess, the teachers at Emerson. She lived with a sister who was a nurse. Two salaries and no major obligations meant that even during the Depression she and her sister were financially very comfortable.

Miss McGowan had grown up in Joliet, Illinois, where her father was a physician to families in the steel mills. He cautioned his family: "I have watched," she quoted him, "sturdy and fine Polish, Hungarian, and Irish people come into these steel mills, work for five years, and be thrown out, finished, physical wrecks; and then, as if they were less than human, another force brought in with similar futures. Never forget," he said, "never forget." These attitudes reflected a dedicated and fine man with a historical perspective. His loving daughter, now—fortunately for me— my friend, carried on his tradition and gave strength to me. Her father would likely have practiced medicine with the poor in nineteenth-century industrial Chicago, America's builders.

I knew less about the three teachers with whom I shared that floor at Emerson. There were two first-grade teachers and another, Miss Mansfield, who taught the "sight saving" class. I taught next door to Mrs. Strouse, a "capable" first-grade teacher. After kindergarten, half of my children would go on to her class and the other half to Miss Casamayou down the hall. Because of their joint power over the children I was to send on to them, I made every effort to remain friends and never to challenge or argue over methods with them. We stayed friends, although it was not because of agreement about teaching.

Miss Casamayou was inept and miserable from having taught too many children. She confessed to me early on that her favorite part of teaching was "doing the registers." She would send me an immature child occasionally who drove her mad, and I would give her my register to do at the end of the month. It was a good trade.

Miss Casamayou invited me into her room one afternoon to show me something that pleased her. It was May 31, Memorial Day, and all around the room were pictures of her dead family members, draped in black by the children; what a holiday that must have been for the first graders. I remember my embarrassment at her claim that the children had loved draping the black. In that strict, punitive atmosphere, she was probably right.

Mrs. Strouse was an entirely different kind of person and teacher. Her greatest strength was her assumption that all children could learn and would learn if they would only "straighten up and fly right." She saw her job as twofold: first, to "whip" them into proper line, with no infraction of the tight rules allowed, and second, to teach them to read. With some children it worked, although the toll in fear was heavy. With others her system was a disaster; for them, learning to sit silently in seats and obey commands never blossomed into reading.

I tried to comfort parents and children who came back to the kindergarten over the years. Mrs. Strouse was not a dull woman. I had a certain admiration for her mind, even for her absolute confidence that she knew all there was to know about teaching beginners. One problem was that she suffered from constant insomnia. She would report to me often about how many nights it had been since she had slept, and although I was compassionate for her, I grieved for the children. She might follow her miserable tale of insomnia with "that Sonia better not try anything today," or "just let James talk once today and he'll regret it." I was amazed at the level of tension that existed in her class and wondered how she or the children could stand the five hours a day they spent together.

We needed the quiet, competent ways of Miss Mansfield. Strict but not mean, Miss Mansfield ran a decent, if uninspired, program for ten or twelve children who were nearly blind. She kept entirely to herself, never spoke out about anything, never ate in the lunchroom, and then surprised me one day with a straightforward request. Would I take her youngest two children for an hour one day or even three days a week? I was swamped with my thirty-nine, but her request was so heartfelt. Miss Mansfield explained that she had no experience with such young children, but she knew they needed some of the activities we had going in the kindergarten. I was so pleased at her understanding something of the nature and needs of five-year-olds that I said yes. It was a happy association and one I never regretted.

I was rather alone until my fourth semester, when a second young kindergarten teacher was finally sent to share in the teaching of our ninety or so children. Evelyn Levinson and I became good friends. She was a gentle, competent person, and I was delighted to have her next door. She married soon after David and I did, and we four occasionally had pleasant meals together. When I was leaving, Evelyn spoke to me with gratitude, especially, she said, for what I had helped her learn about parents in our neighborhood, thus helping her to better understand and appreciate the children. No wonder I had come to love her. We were allies, with our children, in a hostile world.

The Families

Most of the six hundred children at Emerson came from families at high risk. It was mid-Depression, but many families had been among the poorest before that. President Franklin Roosevelt had called a third of our nation poorly housed, poorly clothed, and poorly fed. San Francisco's quota of hungry children was concentrated around Emerson and some sister schools. No free lunches, no free milk, and a pervasive atmosphere of harsh and thoughtless blame toward families on relief or WPA.

The condition of those families was difficult for me to separate from my own good fortune. I did the only thing within my power: to try to make every day one of success and fun and learning for the children. The trying kept me sane. But not all of my suffering was of the redemptive kind. With teaching jobs at such a premium, it was not enough for my classes to test high, as they did, on standardized city-wide tests. One also had to be liked and approved of by the hierarchy. Ingratiation was necessary, and fear was its companion. Perhaps one secret bond between the parents and me was our tacit understanding about the hostility of the world in which we navigated. Their support and affection were constant. I survived the San Francisco School Department because of them and their children.

Vignettes come to me all through these pages, still crystal clear in my mind regardless of whether I write them down or, in the need of brevity, leave some out. Was it because I had only known the poor and hungry in the fiction I read that these parents remain so vivid in my memory?

Emergencies of all kinds are common to the poor, and those parents came to me with some of theirs. Often a confidence was offered from the simple human need to share with a sympathetic friend. The only money I was asked for in the four years was requested by an unwed mother of two who needed an abortion. The amount was very small, but I questioned her at length. I learned that the doctor, bless him, was a respectable man in a famous hospital who could not bear to see the hacks perform illegal abortions on a poor woman. The amount he asked for I could just afford.

Confidences about such matters as food were shared, often with dark humor. I remember the glut of raisins when they were declared "excess commodities." This meant that if one were on relief and could get to the nearest food depot, pounds of raisins would be given free (never oranges). "I have used raisins in every possible way; in pies, bread, just plain, and in gravy; and finally the children just groan and refuse them." This was from my close and beloved friend, Dora Cooley, of whom I have more to say later.

I was lax about keeping children out for colds—endemic among the poorly nourished—because they loved school so. Kenneth's mother reported to me one Monday that she had brought Kenneth and his baby brother to school the previous Saturday to prove to him that there was no school that day. "He tried the locked door!"

Ted—a young refugee from the dust bowl—came back one Friday with his mother after three days of absence. One eye was still swollen almost closed. His mother explained that the two of them had sat waiting the previous three days at the Stanford Lane free clinic before they could be seen. I didn't have the heart to tell her what I thought, that Ted belonged at home. If he could endure sitting and waiting for so long, then surely he could manage with us. "He was so sad to miss all them days at school."

Then there were problems like Ronald's ringworm, his mother's desperation, and my introduction to more of the Stanford and University of California free clinics. Ronald (whose story is given in the next section) had worn a clean thin cotton stocking for weeks over his shaven and infected head when his mother came to me about the ringworm's persistence. The Stanford doctor had suggested that she take him to a certain specialist at the University of California (UC) clinic, but the Stanford clinic office had to release him to the other clinic for treatment. The office refused her request, and the situation was at a stalemate.

It was a stalemate for everyone except another of my allies. My mother was irate at the story and immediately went into action. I was game. Knowing the aplomb and power of my elegant mother, I feared for anyone who would receive the special barbs she reserved for fools. Ronald, now in his second year with me, was to relish it all.

She went to the Stanford Clinic and obtained the release, and she had no cause to display her anger. But at the California clinic, where no trouble had been anticipated, the admitting clerk made the mistake of being less than courteous before my mother could state her relationship to Ronald, treating her, my mother said coldly, in the manner she (the clerk) "no doubt reserved for the poorest and most in need."

With the new treatment, Ronald's ringworm improved at once and was gone in a short time. His appreciative mother was told by the new doctor that his hair had been saved just in time.

I have said that the bond I had with parents was one of a shared perception of the hostile world in which we moved together, but that is only the negative side. The other face of the coin was that I learned so much from parents—about poverty but also about gallantry, about friendship and loyalty. It was because of them and their children that I fought and grew and learned in that inner-city atmosphere.

Let me try, by choosing one family, to give a suggestion of the courage and grace I met and came to know. I have spoken about the bigotry I encountered in the teachers' lunchroom, including the racist denigration of my sixth-grade assistant, Ruth Cooley, who was competent and proud. All six members of the Cooley family were proud, although they were excruciatingly poor. Mr. Cooley had lost his chauffeur's job early in the Depression. Ruth's mother gave them pride and was clear about racism. Once when I was at her house, "Mousey," the nine-year-old, came in irate: "You know what that Mrs. Rawley called me? A nigger—she said, 'why, you are nothing but a little nigger girl.'" Mrs. Cooley responded matter-of-factly, something to the effect that Mrs. Rawley was a very ignorant and silly person, and we went on with our conversation. By such people as Dora Cooley I was properly educated. I learned later that Ruth had become one of the administrators at Stanford-Lane Hospital.

Ronald—The Escape Artist

Late on the first day of school, Ronald's mother handed me his brief enrollment information: "Here is Ronald. The RDCH (Russian Day Care Home) will pick him up at twelve." And then, with no hint of a smile, "If you have anything left in your kindergarten by the end of the morning, you will be fortunate."

Before I could laugh at such a preposterous statement, this tiny boy's mother had closed the door gently behind herself, and I was left looking at the cleanest, palest, saddest four-year-old ever to focus wary eyes on me. He turned suddenly and disappeared into the teaming crowd of children and mothers.

His mother's warning was not only accurate but also prophetic. After two weeks with Ronald in the classroom with thirty-eight others, I felt defeated and ready to agree with the RDCH and with his mother that he could not be contained within any ordinary classroom. It was not his daily silence that first concerned me, or even the chaos he stealthily and speedily made of our room. From the beginning those incredible Depression-born classmates managed to accept Ronald and his mischief and would assist in putting things back together in a way that showed me a side of four- and five-year-olds that I had not expected. Somehow we managed to work and play, with Ronald as our joint baby brother who was "wrecking everything, Miss Pockman" but who, I cautioned, did not know any better, at least not yet. Most troubling, however, was the fact that as the days passed, he would disappear from the classroom. This escape maneuver defeated me.

We survived Ronald's first disappearances, such as the time he made his way to the boys' lavatory, removed every stitch of clothing, and was found by the custodian trying to flush all his clothes down the toilet. Then he learned how to open the school's heavy, intricate doors and once halted cable cars in the middle of the street before he was rescued. "If that happens again, he must be excluded from school." The principal was right, and of course I knew it. This child did not respond to any of us, he lived silently in our midst—or out of it. I despaired. I scolded Ronald and tried always to keep two of our most stalwart children on Ronald-duty. It was not possible.

Somehow we managed. Ronald wrecked and others restored, all of us laughed (and I wept at home) at his impossible ways. I realized the power he bestowed on the other children. Because of Ronald, they became competent five-year-olds. The situation was helped greatly by the fact that we were left alone by the principal. We also had help from several fifth- and sixth-grade girls. They were a godsend. Ruth Cooley, of whom I have spoken, was one of these girls. She could prevent or control all sorts of trouble. Coming from her poor but wonderful black family of six children, she was a model for the older Emerson students; thus, helping in the kindergarten became fashionable at the school.

Once Ronald had perfected his inner map of the school, as he soon did, none of us could match his cunning ways of getting out unseen into the wider world. "The escape artist," we called him privately. Once, just after the cable car episode, in desperation I fastened a rope around Ronald's waist and tied the other end to myself. It was the only way I could devise to protect him and to demonstrate that his freedom with us had boundaries, that they would take him away if he could not learn to honor those boundaries. I did not know whether he understood these admonishments. After two weeks I fearfully removed the rope. Ronald stayed with us, still not speaking, laughing, smiling, or crying, but he stayed. I was jubilant, and so were the other children.

I was not sure how long I could keep this child. Yet my discouragement and weariness did not quite send me to the principal to ask to have Ronald removed. The reverse was true: I hung on. From the information I had gathered about him, and from his behavior early on, I thought (correctly, as it turned out) that he might have been treated like a caged animal rather than like a child. How, I asked myself, had he managed within his small self to keep alive his endless, if often unfocused, seemingly destructive curiosity?

I often took stock: Ronald had written off human beings or somehow never written them on, both children and adults, along his way. He treated us as if we were not there—except to get in his way and to be outwitted. But one day the lady who ran the RDCH arrived to escort him and several other children to the home. Something happened that made me seriously reconsider having Ronald removed from the class. I felt his eyes on me in an evaluative way as he observed and seemed to listen while the director of the RDCH, with real and understandable frustration, spilled out the long list of Ronald's iniquities: "runs away, turns on the gas . . . "

I could easily have added to the list, but both hers and Ronald's manner kept me silent and attentive. Something in Ronald's attention was different. Was he able to understand more than I thought? Was he beginning to observe me as a kind of being to be considered in a new way? I had been unable to impute any such intent to him before. My intuition told me this was significant, that he may be able to distinguish between adults. The director of the RDCH went on and on and finally, with too much satisfaction, summed up the RDCH's worn verdict on this four-year-old. The RDCH staff had just been waiting for the public school to agree: Ronald must be sent to Glen Ellen, the home for the feebleminded. Her understandable but improper glee, and the momentary intelligence I read—or hoped I read—in Ronald's eyes, cast the dice, his and mine together, for the next two years.

During those early weeks, Ronald did not respond in words, but he engaged in a dogged, messy, almost senseless exploration of everything in the room. The fishpond was never stocked at that time, for example, because Ronald had a need to handle, fondle, mouth, smell, and scatter the assorted pebbles and scraps of paper.

That early behavior was relentlessly uniform. Ronald used his mouth and his sense of smell with everything he touched. He gave little response to words and used none himself.

The following spring, when breakthroughs were occurring, I reported his progress to his mother and she to me. She confessed that all was not going as well out of school as in. Did I realize he was stealing? She opened her purse and took out a collection of junk she had taken from his pockets—snips of colored paper, a broken crayon or two, paper clips, pebbles, and other small expendables. Some of these "treasures" I had given him, others he had taken. We talked of this "sin" and what we would do about it. I begged that she trust me and Ronald. I gave him more trinkets, and he and I sorted through his pockets when he left for the day—this to go home as his, that to stay at school for him to use there.

As his life became more tenable, as heavy-handed judgment was suspended, the "stealing" ceased.

But the promising days were still ahead, and my discouragement with Ronald's lack of progress was great. Thanksgiving week arrived, and I decided to celebrate with a party. The children and I made favors, and a friend brought cookies. Although it was not planned to address Ronald's destructive ways, the event prompted him to give the signal I needed to assure me that he was on his way. With Ronald by the hand, dear friend Jane walked all of the children down the long hall.

I set up a centerpiece, the cookies with their sparkling decorations, pushed the chairs back against the wall, and lit candles (which were illegal). The simple transformation was shining in the eyes of all of the children as they entered the room and then sat back in awe in their chairs. Ronald walked alone to the glowing table with the slowest steps I had ever seen him take. I joined him and held his hand, afraid he might grab one of those forbidden candles.

Together, we stood by the table, the other children silently watching. Ronald began to tremble uncontrollably. I knelt to reassure him, my arm around him. He turned to look at me then back to the candles. The trembling stopped. He turned to me again and *smiled,* his very first smile. I later cried with joy. I thought I knew what promise that first smile held and what it foretold. I was right.

After that, I could continue the battle to keep Ronald with renewed confidence. He *was* learning. Sharing the Thanksgiving story with the principal was a pleasure. She wanted to believe I was doing the right thing. The battle by the RDCH to remove Ronald, however, did not stop. During that first year, Ronald's mother had difficulty adjusting to his change. The following year she played a central role. She and Ronald were changing themselves and their relationship.

Word came from the central office that Ronald had been tested and had an I.Q. of 45. He should, therefore, be removed from kindergarten. I had been tempted to comply, but only briefly. The fight to keep him always paralleled my effort to learn *how* to keep him and help him without cheating the other students. My family and friends were as indignant as I that an abused and neglected child who didn't speak would or could be given an intelligence test. And their delight matched mine when a year later Ronald's second test result revealed an I.Q. of 86. The report was qualified with a comment that confirmed what I already knew: "Not reliable, because he seems to be learning so fast."

As Ronald became less inaccessible, his behavior less that of a mindless automaton, I decided to have him with me on Saturdays. At first I took him where I could trust the atmosphere to be safe and not too startling. I took him often to my parents' house by streetcar, a conveyance he loved, and once to visit a close friend who had a toddler in a playpen. Ronald was fascinated by it all: the fish in my parents' garden pool, the streetcar driver with his controls, his forward position, his brake, and often his friendliness. Ronald learned to stay with me and to let his eyes and mind observe. With baby Sally, he was gentle. That was reassuring and hopeful.

As time went on I observed Ronald's growing ability to focus and thus to learn without always having to act first. The Saturdays became easier and more fun. In his positive or negative reactions, Ronald was never devious. He could now say simply and straightforwardly, "Let's go." Once he decided to talk, as is common with children in the normal range who talk late, speech came full-blown.

Early in the second year, Ronald's mother told me she was putting him into an orphanage for a few months; the RDCH would no longer keep him. I was shocked and begged her to let me see what I could do about keeping him at Emerson. The orphanage was housed in a large old mansion on Lake Street, not far from where my parents lived, so we worked out transportation. My father both suffered and enjoyed Ronald's passion for driving with him and was strict enough to manage the two miles without mishap. I would take him back at noon on the streetcar.

Slowly, Ronald began to transform his boundless, undefined curiosity into the desire to learn what lay beyond the world of smells, sounds, and sights. I remember my chagrin and delight one morning on the way to the lavatory as I quieted the children before going past the principal's office. I whispered in my teacher's voice, "Now, who is talking?" Ronald whispered back with a broad smile and his old fight—now irreverence—intact, "Only you."

At the end of two years it was time for him to move on to the first grade. By then he had become a great help to the kindergarten. He knew where absolutely everything was to be found and how to care for the animals. He tried valiantly to organize each new class. His I.Q. had risen into the normal range. But I knew he still had a long way to travel; I knew he would have trouble in most first-grade classes, including in my friend Mrs. Strauss's next door.

When Mrs. Strauss came to hear about the children she was to receive from me the next semester, she started with her usual request. "Now

Frances, remember: don't tell me about them, just tell me whether they are good or bad." When we came to Ronald, she simply put his name down and said, "Well, Frances, we'll just see whether it's been worth all the time and effort you and David have put into *him!*" I feared that in her class Ronald was doomed from the start.

I was right. During the first two weeks of the new year, he was constantly in tears, standing in the hall. But chance intervened. There were too many first graders, so a new first-grade class and teacher, Rose Kael, had become necessary. After some begging by me to the principal, Ronald was transferred to the class of my new friend and ally.

Ronald ultimately made it. There were setbacks, hard times, good times too. But he made it, and from his struggles I gained a confidence in children that goes with me into every classroom. It is not a small legacy to a beginning teacher from an abused mother and child.

Only a few times have I learned of my children's later lives, but I did learn of Ronald's. We were living in Colorado when he sought out my parents in San Francisco, to tell his story. He had come back to San Francisco from the Korean War, honorably discharged. He was a skilled craftsman, and president of his union. I did not learn anymore, but it was enough.

When such stories of success occur, a defensive protection of the conventional, almost sacred categories that transform symptoms into permanent syndromes invariably occurs. "Ah, yes, marvelous, but of course that child must have been misdiagnosed" as having an I.Q. of only 45, as psychopathic, as autistically inaccessible to human communication. This defensive maneuver often confirms the permanence of the syndrome or deepens it. It violates a canon of teaching, of medicine, and of scientific research.

In present times, a child like Ronald would almost certainly be put on a tranquilizing drug. Such a treatment would probably ameliorate "antisocial" behavior and, at the same time, would seriously curtail the child's ability to learn, to remake himself or herself, and to interact humanly with others.

Let me push the point a little further. Of a hundred five-year-olds whose developmental character matched that of Ronald when I first knew him, how many would remain essentially in that state, how many would fail to regain the pathways of normal development? In the 1930s? In the 1980s and 1990s? Of those who did regain such pathways and grow to normal adult competency (a small minority, I think), we could indeed say, as in the case of Ronald, "misdiagnosis." But now we are logically committed to ask, of those who do not achieve such normalcy but remain with very low I.Q.s, with autistic characteristics, and so on, in how many cases should we also be prepared to say "misdiagnosis"? We simply do not know. But strong evidence exists that consistent, humane, appropriate, and powerful educational intervention in the lives of such children can induce rather major changes.[2] Although I was inexperienced and untrained as a therapeutic teacher, my two years' work with Ronald and his mother was certainly a consistent and powerful intervention. A second-grade teacher was resentful: "Fine, what you have done for Ronald—but to have his mother in your house!"

Today I find the family therapy approach more adequate in scope than older practices that isolate such children, and the approach is richer in hope for us all.[3] In an odd and somewhat different sense of the term, Ronald's kindergarten "family" surrounded him and gave him early, immeasurable support for growth and change, support his mother was unable to provide at that time.

When I think of and meet afresh the abusing adults, abusing teachers and parents, of deeply troubled children, I find it necessary to sound a strong note of caution about the conditions in which we should bring a wider range of children together in our classrooms. Where rigid, understaffed schools and totally inadequate education and guidance are the rule, tensions only increase. What we are learning about child abuse—subtle or obvious—at home illuminates abuse at school. One must feel the class atmosphere to understand its effect—negative or positive. Intellectual and emotional wounds to the minds of children are initially less visible, but no less crippling, than those to their bodies.

Would I take on again what I did with Ronald and with a few others in my experience? Absolutely not, unless I were provided with professional assistance and a lower-than-usual class size. The toll was too great on me, on the other children, and on my family. That sort of toll is too great on deeply committed teachers I meet. I later had the good fortune to be able to leave behind the stifling working conditions provided by most public schools and by most private or public day-care centers before I too became an abusing teacher.

The setting that is not supportive, both morally and emotionally, is one in which children do not thrive and in which adults find themselves incapable of creating a situation in which the children can learn and thrive. Parents and teachers cannot abide such a setting, and children survive with only a fraction of their potential realized. Their misery seems stored away intact, stored until they in turn can wreak abuse on others. A few, with help, break the chain. It is a victory to be studied, analyzed, and sustained.

Betty—A U.S. Migrant

From the beginning, Betty was one of the silent ones: wary, watching. When the lively ones had settled in that term, I had time to notice her. I saw her pale, very thin face, long blond hair, and the faded, too-big dress—all so clean. As a teacher can in retrospect, I concentrated my concern on Betty's first weeks with us. I had not seen her play spontaneously, she had never initiated anything. She did not stay by herself, which would have drawn my attention sooner. No, she had simply blended into the activities and atmosphere of the class. At last I began to get her into focus, to observe closely, and to plan.

Betty's parents came back clearly to my mind, as they had stood in the outer hall the first day of the term. I had never seen them again. They had refused to come in that first day, but they did have something to say. The father spoke, and I had not known how to respond: "Jus' tell us, jus' tell us if she ain't good, Teacher." I looked at the tiny girl and took his words as a plea for the defenseless child. His words were not unkind or mean: "She won't give you no trouble, but jus' tell us if she do." The father stood behind his emaciated wife when he spoke. What seemed to me then as age in their appearance, I realized later, was simply the consequence of malnourishment and bad teeth rather than of a long life. Another pair of parents for my innocence to weep over. No longer innocent, I still weep.

Even in the beginning, I knew that it was only through their child that I could help them. During my years of teaching hungry children in San Francisco, my political involvement with the Left mitigated my agony for the ills that stalked those years for these Dust Bowl families.

Once I began to observe Betty closely, I saw her calculated ways of remaining unnoticed. On guard, she first noted what others were doing and then joined them. Betty always came with others for stories, music, and dancing, but she could hardly be said to participate. Betty filled her free work and the play hour by looking at books and watching others paint at the easels or model at the clay table, or she might disappear to play in the beloved five-room playhouse.

Having seen and clearly defined her pattern, I set about to entice her. No success. There would be a faint smile but no play, no dance, no painting or even talking. For a time I was defeated. But in such a situation one remains alert to some secret temptation that might bring such a child to forget to be on guard.

The secret was revealed, finally, in an unexpected way. Dramatizing favorite stories had become increasingly popular with this group. The choice on this particular morning was Maj Lindjman's *Snipp Snapp Snurr and the Buttered Bread*.[4] Children listened to me read the story, already well known, and were pleased with the large orange sun painted by Beverly for the springtime return of the sun in that far northland world so that the grass would grow again and butter would be forthcoming from the cows. Then came choosing characters to act out the story. The "cows" were selected to graze in the "field"; Snipp, Snapp, and Snurr were chosen; and then we needed a child to raise the sun, on cue, as the drama unfolded. Betty's hand went up! I concealed my surprise and quickly handed her the big cardboard sun. So "the play's the thing" once again.

As the play took shape, Betty hid behind her sun in back of a table that we saw as a grass-covered meadow in far-off Sweden. Then after the long winter, with the cows sad in their stalls, the sun returned—rising. On cue, the sun rose slowly in Betty's arms. There it was—meadows transformed, cows giving milk for Mother to churn and make butter for bread. Hands clapped at *finis*, and there were cries of "let's do it again" from both audience and actors. A different cast was chosen the next time except for Betty, who was still cast as the rising sun, suddenly belonging through our world of drama.

There were no great strides after this small breakthrough, but slowly this child thawed. She made a few friends and joined in some activities. Clay remained threatening, but she would sometimes paint. Tools and wood were never touched.

The next step was big and bold and solidified a new place for quiet Betty. One Monday morning Betty came with her new-to-me shining smile: "I have something to tell." We all found chairs and settled down to listen. She told about a wedding she had been to with her parents that had delighted her. The details of long dresses and flowers fell on eager young ears. Question followed question as Betty grew flushed with excitement—with her small triumph. I no longer had to bring Betty into focus. She had taken the big step herself and continued to expand.

So it was that quiet Betty taught me a new reason, beyond the more obvious ones, why our offerings must be so varied. A painted cardboard sun to hold and hide behind, yet just so to join a group—that was right for her. From variety come those opportunities a child can seize but that one could never fully anticipate or plan. In later years, when early science gave me wider access to the phenomena of the world, I could provide a repertoire even more diverse. Yet here the art of acting out a story proved wide enough for one and brought happiness to many.

Variety enlarges the net of opportunity with which to catch the strengths or curiosity almost all children bring with them. Initially, Betty exemplified some of the severe effects the migratory poverty of Dust Bowl families had on its youngest, as we knew them in the 1930s and as we still know them today. Her story offers the basic challenge: whether school can matter, whether it can mitigate in any way the misery such children inherit.

I first used Betty's story when I took postgraduate courses at the University of California with Kurt Lewin, who had only recently emigrated from Nazi Germany. His discussions of atmosphere in classrooms as crucial to whether and how and what children learn were a balm to my battered self after three years of struggling as a teacher at Emerson in the San Francisco Public Schools. With him and with his colleague George Stoddard I knew I was not alone. A quote from Kurt Levin may enable the story of Betty to support a conviction that in turn has supported some of us who count the early years of school as crucial: "I consider it one of the fundamental tasks of pedagogy so to constitute the situation of children in difficulties that the severe injuries usually occasioned by the circular causal relation may be avoided or undone. For here at least lie genuine pedagogical possibilities which do not require changing the child's 'abilities.' "[5]

Joy's Battle

If Ronald was the sharpest thorn in the flank of the RDCH, I suspect Joy was its model child. She reflected precisely what she had been taught there: from her racial views against "coloreds" to her consistently precise paintings. In fact, the theme of every RDCH child's pictures was initially identical: one sun, one house, a half-dozen flowers, and one path from the house on which stood a girl. The scorn and ridicule the RDCH children in my class heaped on all the neophytes was devastating. I felt powerless at first to protect the efforts of beginning painters against this "expertise."

It was my first encounter with such a consolidated band or gang in a classroom, and I soon realized that I was up against a powerful and self-reinforcing phenomenon. I knew I had to act.

I began by dictating who could paint and who could not, something I had previously avoided. I praised rich color and filling the entire paper with "abstractions." For the majority, this was a positive move. For the RDCH children it must have been negative, so I devoted as much time as I could to understanding how to release the talents of that closed band while simultaneously ignoring their stereotyped paintings and superior ways.

I began to watch the RDCH children at play, the only place I saw them off guard and hence more spontaneous. I paid attention and praised them in passing for innovation and for being helpful to each other.

Joy, a leader in the gang, refused even in play to be near a black child. This behavior was limiting to Joy and startling to me. It stood in contrast to the growing ease of other children, including, in this respect, Joy's day-care companions.

Overall, no single effort helped the RDCH children to become less dominated by their own small group, to be more independent, and to belong to a larger, less demanding kindergarten group. I could feel how much belonging was beginning to mean to us all.

Individual styles emerged among the RDCH children as they recognized and felt the climate—not the dictates—of a bigger group. We gained their trust, and they became kindergartners. We were all needed.

Within such a climate, Joy stood out more and more, and I was at a loss to help her. As others thrived, Joy became more brittle. I did not understand in those days just how great an effort it was for a child like Joy to keep from changing; to see her compatriots from RDCH "desert" and begin to swim on their own; to be constantly on guard against any touching, playing, or communicating with a black child (her final bastion, I think now). To be in a classroom where our music—song and dance and a rhythm band—encouraged the recognition of talents other than her own initially further isolated her. Joy's beautiful masklike face became more masklike and her body more rigid. I never saw her smile in the early weeks.

In my ignorance I read her behavior, as it solidified, as regression and did not yet know that such regression often precedes a giant leap forward in a child's development. This was to be true for Joy.

The stage was set early one morning by our smallest and youngest, Margaret, who had brought a charming doll to school. It was a black baby, the color of Margaret—rare dolls in those days—and most of us had a brief turn to hold it.

Later I walked into the room just in time to see Joy knock the doll from Margaret's arms. Both Margaret and I were shocked; Joy left the field. Margaret picked up her doll from the floor and disappeared inside the playhouse. I found Joy and took her by the hand. As usual, she was silent. I wanted to communicate the consequences of her daily behavior, such as her aggression with Margaret. Stooping to be face-to-face with Joy I said: "We all know, Joy, that there are children in this room whom you dislike and do not wish to play with. I am taking you next door to Mrs. Strouse's room for the rest of the morning. No one plays in there, no one will bother you, and no one is allowed to talk." I led Joy next door. This was the first and last time I ever did such a drastic thing. Mrs. Strouse gave Joy a chair from the reading circle while rows of children in fixed desks stared at us. I whispered to Joy that she could return when she felt ready.

I hadn't been back in the kindergarten for long when I noticed that Joy had returned. She was in the playhouse with Margaret and that baby doll, playing happily!

As Joy was leaving that day, she walked close enough to me (on purpose?) so I could give her a goodbye hug, but the reward for Joy came in the days that followed. It was as if a burden had been thrown away, and so it had. I am in awe of the process by which young children can participate in changing themselves—how their behavior signals to us that they need only a little help from us.

Joy's silence disappeared. She told her first long story one morning, a story that reflected troubles not of her making. To earn a living during the Depression, some single mothers inevitably entertained men, one after another, in tiny apartments. Joy told in detail of such episodes while the other children listened, some understanding and others just listening politely. Is the oldest profession on earth less horrifying to children who are surrounded by it?

Joy disappears from my notes and memory, which is evidence that she made her way more smoothly for the rest of the year. The Russian Day Care Home added my effect on Joy's neat paintings—no single, clean pattern any more—to the long list of my sins. I can still hear a young teacher's words to me as she picked up her RDCH group one morning: "In Moscow my father paid many rubles each month to send us to school where we were beaten if we misbehaved; here in the public schools they ought to try it."

Melvin

Down the hall from the kindergarten room was the Sight-Saving Class. Miss Mansfield, mentioned earlier as the kind and competent teacher of that class, asked if she could send her youngest ones to me: "I really don't know what to do with these fives and sixes, Mrs. H. Could you possibly take them for dancing and stories?" Of course I could, and the children and I enjoyed these fives and sixes whose handicap was not severe enough to put them in classes for the totally blind.

Melvin came to us in this way, a very small five-year-old. I quote from a paper I wrote for Dr. George Stoddard when I was in graduate school at the University of California in 1939.

> We had in our class one term a visitor three times a week, a boy who was almost blind. Melvin was a child of rare beauty of character and did more toward the growth . . . of other children than would seem possible in hourly visits for such a short time as one term. "To take Melvin to the lavatory. To take Melvin to the nurse. . . ." These were experiences in which one could see something happening to the helping child. Melvin was the center of attention, and yet a shy child developed self-confidence before my eyes if he or she could take care of Melvin for the hour. A domineering child would step behind Melvin and efface himself. Melvin was given privileges gladly and willingly. After the first time, I never had to remember to put Melvin beside me for story time so that he could "see" better. Some unnoticed one would have put Melvin's chair beside mine with a couple of books on it, to save it for him.

Melvin beamed his way among us, unruffled. I can see his broad smile, his tilted-back head (to get more light?), and I can feel that soft brown hand in mine. I never met his parents, but Melvin reflected their love and guidance in spite of poverty and prejudice. His poor sight and gentle ways endeared him to the kindergarten and enriched it.

A Last Year at Emerson

In my last year at Emerson, 1939–1940, I had trouble eating. Many children's constant hunger and pale, pasty appearance had never been easy for me to live with, and its effect on me must have been cumulative. Fatigue was cumulative also—too many children, and little or no professional support in meeting their needs and supporting their talents.

I left the San Francisco School Department, never to return except in memory. The most important of these memories—those of the children— are described in their stories. But there are others that help me define the circuit of my life in those years. One of these stories relates to the fact that all during the Great Depression the schools had vast and overflowing supplies of two commodities: paper and graham crackers! In these supplies hangs a small story.

San Francisco had suffered a general strike in mid-Depression 1934, and the memory of that strike was still fresh in 1936. Vigilantism was rife in the East Bay and the agricultural valleys, stalwarts protecting us from the Communist Revolution. In the rich valleys, Sacramento and San Joaquin, camps of agricultural workers were "protected" by sheriff's deputies from much-feared union organizers.

A friend and I spent some time in one of those miserable migratory-worker communities. It was a government camp, slightly less primitive than the private ones. We went to visit a friend who was teaching in a pre-school for the two- and three-year-olds whose mothers were working in the fields. Our suitcases were full of paper and crayons stolen from those overflowing supply closets at our school. We felt like revolutionaries.

It was in that camp that I first observed, over time and age, the full phenomenon of malnutrition: adults and children who were not starving but were always hungry and malnourished. The two- and three-year-olds looked almost normal; they were paler than healthy children but not strikingly so. In those older than five the hunger was less hidden, the malnutrition more obvious. But the adults—often younger than my friend and I—looked gaunt, old, and hollow-eyed, with most teeth gone.

The memory has often been revived and linked to others, over many years, whenever I am in the presence of a similar human condition: in 1970 among Lakota Sioux Indians in South Dakota, of inner-city poverty in Boston in 1963, in industrial farm areas of Mexico in 1937, or in the slums of Newcastle-Upon-Tyne in northern England in 1968.

I have spoken of the fear that pervaded our school. Were there exceptions? Among the one hundred public schools in the district, there were perhaps five or six schools to which teachers longed to be sent and a dozen others that were kind and friendly. I basked in the stories of a friend who taught in one of the kind schools, but I never experienced such happiness as long as I taught in San Francisco.

Under any such tyrannical hierarchy there are networks of disrespect, especially among brave neophytes. No defeat, slight or major, for
the administration went unreported or unappreciated. The news of the
defeat traveled quickly, told in whispers but with relish. We cherished
such moments. The gossip traveling through the schools was a magic
winged phenomenon; the names of informants were not part of it.

So, who told me about our deputy's comeuppance by a sixth-grader
at Commodore Sloat? I cannot remember. At any rate, I knew about it
within hours: Miss Roberts, the feared head deputy, was inspecting one
of San Francisco's affluent schools, Commodore Sloat. She had been
walking across the school playground in her regal manner during a
recess when the children were in the yard. She had slowed to observe two
boys tussling, then walked over to punish them. With a teacher in tow,
she stopped the fight and began to tongue-lash the two boys. One of them
turned to her, looked her up and down, and said, "Why you old gray son-
of-a-bitch, get your hands off of me." Some further exchange took place,
and Miss Roberts had the boy expelled from school until he apologized.
Details of the incident livened the grapevine for a time. The boy, who was
from a wealthy family, would not apologize, and his family accused Miss
Roberts of hitting him. We relished the courage of that perceptive eleven-
year-old, although unfortunately it was underlined by his naughty language.

In 1936 the San Francisco school administration flirted briefly with
something called progressive education. Our deputy superintendent,
who had seemingly been there forever and whose word was law, liked
me! I became a marked woman. For three years my room was on display.
I was invited to speak to a hundred kindergarten teachers whenever they
met at our school. I spoke on a variety of topics, including Ronald (see the
section on Ronald earlier in this chapter). Ronald and a handful of other
children sang for the meeting, and then they were taken back to our
room. I had fought a pitched battled for Ronald all year and won. Miss
Roberts had finally allowed me to keep him.

In Depression times, among overworked and undereducated teachers of the young, I had enjoyed many privileges. I had a good education;
my clothes, which were very important to Miss Roberts and the principal,
were appropriate; I spoke correct English and had proper manners. I
don't think my actual teaching was appreciated until much later, but I
supplied the correct patina of progressive ideas for those times. My room
reflected good work in progress, and my children tested higher than
expected for inner-city children.

None of this recognition or praise amounted to tangible help in the classroom. But it did encourage and sustain me in developing what I knew children deserved in school. When I took the examination to become a probationary teacher, Deputy Superintendent Roberts asked me to defend having had a chicken in school for a week by having me tell the entire story. I believed she was getting some tenuous grasp of what I was up to. Yet I never ceased to live in fear of her—none of us did—and stories of her wrath were constant and pervasive. This constituted the corruption. Because I was afraid of her, I tried too hard to placate her, at least until my last year at Emerson. Would it have been easier without the recognition I received? I think so.

My principal, Miss Ryder, enjoyed the recognition I received. She understood little of my commitment to teaching but approved of me for a reason that exemplified pure chance. She had known my father and had had a crush on him when they were in high school in the 1890s! It seldom occurred to Miss Ryder to help or to make life more pleasant for the children and me by relaxing some rules or reducing the number of children in my class or demanding a second kindergarten teacher. But in a crunch I could count on her. She left us alone most of the time—a state profoundly to be desired.

Having said that, I tell of one important time when Miss Ryder's support mattered to me because it was based on an understanding of my racial attitudes, which were shared by few in the school. Our class had won a citywide "school beautiful" contest, and a reporter from the *San Francisco Chronicle* came to interview me and to take a picture of the kindergarten. Miss Ryder—proudly, I judge—had sent for us and, with the young reporter present, congratulated us. As we waited, I realized there was a problem. Miss Ryder and the reporter whispered to each other, and she then whispered to me: "He can't take a picture of Negro and white children together, and I told him I didn't think you would agree to any picture at all." With appreciation toward her and fury toward him, I agreed. The reporter shrugged his shoulders ruefully and said, " *Chronicle* policy."

I called the children together and said in a loud voice that we were going to go downstairs and have a great big party. We did while I seethed at the idiocy of San Francisco and its "liberal" newspaper. What did we have for the party? Mainly, as I remember, games and fun. We may have bought individual cartons of ice cream with wooden spoons—a special treat I could seldom afford. It would have been nice if a small cash fund had been available to teachers for such occasions. Extras came from our meager salaries.

It was the mounds of good food dumped in those Depression years that made some of us irate while others went hungry. For example, I visited a friend one weekend in 1934 whose brother-in-law was plowing under fields of magnificent artichokes. We all gorged on artichokes, and the rest were destroyed.

What, one may ask, is the place of such asides in a professional memoir? To come of age in such a time made me a radical in what I know to be the correct sense of the word: "going to the root or source; fundamental; basic." Never mind my youthful political radicalism and the trouble it got me into in the 1950s. What it did professionally that was lasting was to mold and encourage me to seek among all children for fundamental strengths, for roots, and to help them grow from those strengths. A child's treasure sought is always there to be found.

I have separated the final year at Emerson from those preceding because of my new-found strength for rebellion, the administration's anger, and the children's and my great year together. Miss Roberts's condemnation early in my final year was brief and succinct: "Mrs. Hawkins, you are too concerned with the children and their parents and not enough with the administration." She was absolutely correct. The administration must have looked at the children's test scores, which soared in that last year, because I was given tenure for the coming year. I vowed when I resigned never again to work for the public schools for a salary. I never have, although I have managed to find ways to give support—moral and professional—to those who do.

Notes

[1]The school nurse, who came twice a week, in answer to my complaint about hungry children, replied that Stanford Convalescent Home could only take the worst two or three and only if they were positive for tuberculosis. Since there was no provision for testing for tuberculosis, how would we know?

[2]See S. K. Escalona, *The Roots of Individuality* (Chicago: Aldine Publishing, 1968); Harold M. Skeels, see bibliography.

[3]See Lynn Hoffman, *Foundations of Family Therapy: A Conceptual Framework for Systems Change* (New York: Basic Books, 1981).

[4]Maj Lindjman, *Snipp, Snapp, Snurr and the Buttered Bread*, translated from Swedish (Chicago: Albert Whitman, 1943). I have long been grateful to the Scandinavian writers of children's literature.

[5]Kurt Lewin, *A Dynamic Theory of Personality: Selected Papers*; trans. Donald K. Adams and Karl E. Zener (New York: McGraw Hill, 1935). The "circular causal relation" he spoke of was the way in which children's early difficulties in learning could, under the all-too-standard conditions of schooling, make it impossible for them to learn what was needed to overcome those difficulties.

3: The War Years

Los Alamos

In retrospect, I believe the underlying sadness I felt during three years spent in wartime Los Alamos—in spite of happy personal times—was a continuation of my loss of hope that began with the fall of the Spanish Republic to *los quatro generales*—the Franco dictatorship. We had watched Hitler and Mussolini prove their strength in Spain. I still hear a friend's question: "How long before Franco falls, before babies are no longer bayoneted across Europe? How many years?" We had worked and hoped until the International Brigade fell and the end was near. We wept and talked and raged.

By 1943, when we went to Los Alamos, all those fears of a world war had come true. None of our earlier efforts as "premature antifascists" seemed to matter.[1] Here, in this wartime weaponeering laboratory with its strange new commitments to mass destruction, my earlier pacifism was once again stirring. This feeling remains. The extent of the Holocaust we did not yet imagine.

When I left Emerson in 1940 and began to recover from my exhaustion, our lives were tranquil although busy. David had finished his degree at Berkeley and had been appointed to his first academic job, at Stanford where we had first met. In July 1941 our daughter, Julie, was born! We lived in Berkeley (where David next taught) and San Francisco until May 1943.

Our daughter's appearance deeply affected my understanding of young children. Teacher-become-mother deserves a separate chapter! She has brought David and me joy for over fifty years and remains one of life's glories. With wonderful grandsons Scott and Tom now grown, our cup runneth over.

When Julie was nearly two, she and I followed David to Los Alamos. Soon after the fall of the Spanish Republic, we had known what horrors the great bomb might bring, the bomb we were now to be involved with.

Our going to work at Los Alamos in 1943 was accompanied by a recognition of deep defeat. But our lives had been close to the world of physicist friends, and David wanted to share and learn from their troubled commitment. Einstein, a confirmed pacifist, had been persuaded by physicist colleagues to explain to President Roosevelt the possibility of the fission bomb and of its development by Hitler's Germany. Best we do it first! It was a lesser-evil commitment—persuasive but troubled.

It was not my sphere, but I followed into this strange new world—strange in the way it coped with ambiguity, to do the very thing most feared.

David was invited because he was a philosopher of science who understood the physicists and enough of the physics and was also a friend of Robert Oppenheimer and his students. He was at first an administrative assistant and later wrote the official chronicle, down to the time of Hiroshima and Nagasaki.[2] The young philosopher's position was special—it was in, but not of, the laboratory. In a pleasant way, we were protected.

What I couldn't understand at first was, with few exceptions, the generally apolitical social atmosphere. I realized finally that this was a closed society—closed as a military post by fences and gates and patrolling MPs, closed because it was preoccupied by the extraordinary weaponeering commitment at hand, closed because in U.S. history political action had been discouraged, and scientific research and technology were increasingly rewarded. The focus of those engrossed in this work had narrowed, not so much the focus of the people as individuals but of their social ambiance. A still further part of that closure came, I perceived, from our European cohorts. An old friend from the scientific staff recently answered my question about his fellow refugees from Europe and their lack—beyond the continuing discussion of news from the war—of any evident political curiosity. "They grew up without it," was his primary answer. But so did David and I. It is a puzzle to me still.

There were exceptions: some who, like us, had seen defeat in Spain, in the terror of Hitler's rule, in the evil "flowering" of anti-Semitism. The great Niels Bohr, professionally senior to all our physicists and revered by us all, was a profound exception. Having fled occupied Denmark with his son, Aage, he came from London and Washington for periodic visits to Los Alamos, bringing his deep wisdom about the bomb, as I was to learn. What I knew at the time, to my delight, were his warmth and his interest in learning more about U.S. society.[3] We stood in line with him to see *Tall in the Saddle*—Westerns were his favorite films. It was startling to be intently questioned by him about such matters as the Dust Bowl, the migratory workers, and my trip to one camp in California—unexpected because I had become accustomed to the purity of nonwar scientific chitchat that usually dominated evening gatherings. Others that particular evening, not sharing these concerns of his and of mine, sought to engage him in conversation. But Bohr persisted in his questions to me, lighting match after match to keep his pipe burning and building towers with the used matches.

During that first year I helped organize the much-needed nursery school in a surprisingly good building with a large play area, built to proper specifications by the Army Corps of Engineers. I stayed as head teacher until we found a replacement who was from the University of New Mexico. The children were those of the scientific staff and others. As assistants I found wives of young scientists, untrained but willing. A young, well-educated, trained kindergarten teacher, June Labowitz, later came from Minnesota. She became one of the first staff members of a new, small elementary school. For the small children coming to their first school, we had one expert part-time teacher. He was Eddie Rivera, misclassified as our janitor.

At nursery school we had a kitchen and a cook. Lunch was served at small tables, with an adult at each table. I was soon besieged with questions: "Yours is the only table where children eat! What can I do?" I don't remember what I said, but I released each staff member at lunch for a week to join and observe my table and report to me and the others how it seemed to be managed. After a time it worked.

Having known the children and their families at Los Alamos more intimately than is usual, I find it awkward to write about them, my recollections being heavy with privileged information—professionally privileged, not military kind. Some of the children at Los Alamos were troubled, a few deeply so. Wartime anxieties and dislocations added their toll. But most, of course, were on their way.

Washington and Boulder

We left Los Alamos about a year after the end of the war in the Pacific. David's chronicle of wartime Los Alamos was essentially finished, and he had a new position in Washington, D.C., teaching philosophy again. Julie had turned five, and I found a private kindergarten—for her, not for me as teacher. I did the school's bookkeeping in exchange for tuition fees. The local public school had no kindergarten.

The outside world had changed irreversibly, as it had already for those of us who had lived with the bomb. David was involved with others in the "reluctant lobby" of young scientists who were struggling to educate senators and members of Congress about the nature of atoms and powers of ten.

During that Washington year we met Robert L. Stearns, president of the University of Colorado, and Ward Darley, dean of its medical school. In 1947 we moved to Boulder, David for work in philosophy and university education. We have lived here ever since—a stone's throw, literally, from the beginning of the Far West, the Rocky Mountains. For some of these fifty years we have been away, one or both of us, teaching.

Our first six years in and away from Boulder were a time when I was only marginally involved with children—other than Julie. Toward the end of 1950 our calm life was interrupted by subpoenas from the Un-American Activities Committee and, in the first months of 1951, by David's academic trial to determine whether he was a fit member of the academic community. This all stemmed from those "premature antifascist" commitments I have mentioned, combined with our Los Alamos background.

Few today will remember the hysteria that swept the country in those times or the congressional committee that mounted that hysteria, looking for spies who might have betrayed "the secret" of the bomb to the Soviets, or the panic that was created in the universities as the committee looked for Communist conspiracies—enemies in our midst, subverting our students. Some faculty members lost their jobs; some colleges and universities lost their dignity. Our faculty was friendly to us, as were the majority of our regents, so David survived.

Much of it seems, in retrospect, a low comedy; at the time, it was frightening. In response to the committee's demands, we had refused to "name names," although we spoke willingly of our early membership in Communist Party groups. As a result we were threatened with a trial for contempt of the committee and possibly prison. This held inevitable consequences for us, for a nine-year-old child, and even for the university. Fortunately, it did not materialize.

David was invited to spend the year 1952–1953 at Harvard, to be involved in a new general science course for freshmen. It was a good year for the three of us, except for the nerve-racking comedy of the committee, which repeated itself in the form of a Senate Internal Security subcommittee. This time they only summoned David. Like an epidemic virus well along in its course, this plague was no longer burgeoning; it had destroyed many and conferred a kind of immunity on its survivors, us among them. In the later years we were left alone, sometimes even rather respectfully.[4]

When we returned to Boulder in summer 1953, my life as a teacher, fully and happily committed, began once again.

Notes

[1]This term was coined by our wartime investigative agencies to distinguish between those of us, of the Left, who had "prematurely" and "subversively" urged support for the Spanish Republic and opposition to Mussolini, Hitler, and Hirohito. At the time, the United States and Britain were still "neutral" toward these new-style buffers against communism, and the United States was selling scrap iron to Japan. A famous Hollywood writer was fired by his studio for such beliefs, only to be rehired the very next day—the day in 1941 when the Nazi armies rolled eastward and the Soviet Union suddenly became a U.S. ally.

[2]David Hawkins, *Project Y: The Los Alamos Story, vol. 2, part 1, Toward Trinity.* In a series on the history of modern physics (Los Angeles: Tomash Publishers, 1983).

[3]Ruth Moore, *Niels Bohr: The Man, His Science, and the World They Changed,* with drawings by Sue Richert Allen (New York: Alfred A. Knopf, 1966).

[4]The story is included in Ellen W. Schrecker, *No Ivory Tower: McCarthyism and the Universities* (New York: Oxford, 1986).

4: *Farm School*

Those long-ago days in Boulder when I returned to full-time teaching were a time of high hopes and their realization, made possible when Dorothy Brown and her husband, Bobb, urged me to teach the four-year-olds in the nursery school they were establishing on their farm. That was in 1953, after the second go-round with congressional "un-American" committees, discussed in Chapter 3. I was unsure of Boulder's response to the publicity these events received. Bobb and Dorothy, who had not been close friends, wrote me a letter. "You may be worried about the committee, we are not. . . . The children need you, and you need them. . . . See you in September." In the aftermath, we encountered very little local hostility. Except for the Browns' insistence, however, I might not have returned to teaching nor experienced the years of learning and joy ahead. Some debts are remembered with deep affection.

The Browns had a farm on which they grew alfalfa and raised a few farm animals. The school was part of their plan. Dorothy and I became the school staff, Bobb our sometime assistant—always our farmer-in-residence.

Most of our children at Farm School were middle class. The Browns assumed all administrative burdens. By action and spirit they gave me a chance to think and teach in ways neither public schools nor wartime nursery school had permitted.

Dorothy and I painted, restructured, and enjoyed every moment of getting ready. Bobb invented and made some versatile furniture for their small farmhouse, which would double as an indoor nursery and be used for cooking, music, and dancing. The small-animal house across the large central courtyard was ideal for a spacious, messy workshop. Suddenly, after much scrubbing, we were ready, eager to start.

One early autumn afternoon, we made a pledge to each other: we would forget everything about procedure we thought we knew and learn instead with these four- and five-year-olds. Thus it was: Farm School became for children and staff a place where we could work through our fascinating self-set puzzles and hurdles of living and learning well together.

The summer begins.

When I think back to those two years at Farm School, it is not surprising that the seasons define and set the stage, in notes and in memory. It seemed that returning to full-time teaching at a school on a small, working farm, surrounded by the seasons, was the happiest accident of my professional life. It still seems that way.

In some stories from those two wonderful years, individual children come into focus. Here, because a group of children is foremost, I need a lens of wider angle. Of course, a group is always part of the context vital to the story of any of its members, but in writing—as in teaching—emphasis must winnow, now one way and now another. At times a group seems banded together in a special, if intermittent, way, and here I bring forward such a gathering.

The story of even one child is a page torn from a past and future biography of which one's knowledge or memory can hold little for certain. Why do I not note in these records the occasional children whose difficulties were not merely developmental but already profound? They deserve a place in our thinking and planning and writing, but they must be dealt with somewhat out of the mainstream life of their group. To preserve anonymity, their stories must often be restricted to a more clinical

It looks so big!

literature. I have told one such story (see "Ronald" in Chapter 2) with enough anonymity. Here and hereafter, the history is closer at hand and professional confidentiality more in order. I mention this because readers are right to question stories that include no children with serious problems and no failures of the teacher to understand and help.

There is a link between the affluence of those particular families whose child is in deep trouble and my inability to help. The adults do not, perhaps cannot, allow themselves to ask for help. I agree with Frederick Allen that when people ask for help, they are already halfway there. Usually, the children have also learned to hide their troubles or to deny them. The bond of denial can be strong and destructive to the development of the child and to the child's relationship with his or her parents.

A Pecking Tooth

For four- and five-year-olds there have been few seasons, even fewer remembered—one, perhaps, or two. For the teacher of these four- and

Flag Day.

five-year-olds (Dorothy had the three-year-olds) there had been many springs but none like this, none on a farm.

Most of the long and golden fall that first year was lived outside, where three- and four-year-olds could intermingle. The enclosed workshop stood in the center of things—a modest farmhouse with trees and grass, a big working barn, nearby orchard, fields, and corrals. The buildings surrounded a spacious courtyard and driveway, creating a space that was closed to traffic by gates during school hours and was elected by most to be the gathering place. In the autumn warmth the workshop doors were seldom closed, either to the enormous sandbox just to the east or to the courtyard outside the western door.

Although it was well provisioned and occasionally used in the fall, little went on indoors. There were more compelling engagements outside, such as hauling clay for the workshop and, happy task, sieving it! In one meadow Bobb Brown had discovered a clay deposit laid down by a "recent" stream perhaps ten thousand years ago. We made many trips with the little red wagons, digging out the hard and lumpy clay. More than one load, light enough when not overfull, was pulled across the field. "Take some out. It's too heavy"—this from an expert who had developed an eye to judge.

The sieving! We slanted a large window screen against an outside wall, put an old sheet under it, and a wiggly line of volunteers immediately formed to rub the lumpy chunks against the screen. Like magic, tiny particles fell through to the white sheet, and we slowly accumulated enough clay for endless modeling.

Space, time to explore; the pony, Blaze, to ride when Bobb was free; apples to harvest and their knobby trees to climb; the shallow irrigation ditch flowing on alternate days—as if all this were not enough a happy accident occurred. Foreseeing a muddy courtyard once winter set in, Bobb had ordered a large load of crushed, porous sandstone, to be dumped in mounds around the courtyard. Having two small boys of his own, he wisely decided to let all the children help spread it. Within a day, cities were growing like mushrooms under the shade of the cottonwoods, spreading over the entire flat, clear courtyard. Mountains and rivers, with a network of roads from city to city to lake to. . . . Construction on such a scale brought new ground rules, new vocabulary while this relief mapping took over our days. Sieving, in consequence, was almost out. On warm days, in addition to the irrigation ditch in its shallow culvert, the hose might trickle forth slow-flowing rivers, and cooperation became the order of the morning. Lakes were more carefully dammed, spillways mended, and yesterday's mountain ranges moved. If engineers were in communication, flood disasters could be averted or quickly repaired.

Just as in the larger world, recent roads suggested and spawned roadside changes: a farmhouse here, a fruit stand there, and once even a miniature corral with pony rides. This corral required a twig fence, and the children discovered that sandstone gravel wouldn't secure the tiny fenceposts. Buckets of dry sand were brought from the sandbox, mixed with water, smoothed, mounded, and that did it. A first lesson in scaling from nature. Forests of twigs began to line the stretches of road, planted securely in deep gravel hills or in shallower sand hills. Such construction lasted long enough to create, in this world of the young, a new landscape—their own. One saw in this landscape the beginning of a new sense of proportion, of one thing to another—of scale.

Not all the children were engrossed each day by such global enterprises. The youngest three-year-olds might be found in the sunny corner where the sandbox sprawled. Here they dug and tunneled and explored away from the center of things, away from the older ones. Another of their favorite places was the big, three-room playhouse inside the workshop. They had three-year-old and individual needs and could pick and choose to satisfy them.

There were other offshoots, separate tangents to the work of the engineers and earth movers. I remember, with good reason, a splinter group, a crew of sailors made up of almost-fives who had just missed kindergarten entrance that fall, whose loyalty went to another, more difficult venture on seas deeper than their courtyard lakes provided. Behind the barns and beyond a fence that divided the school from the fields was a shallow (two feet deep) thirty-by-fifty-foot stock pond. For weeks in the fall this water was declared inbounds if an adult was present to open the gate.

The pond offered a permanent invitation for floating homemade craft, and all ages initially had a go. Starting with small sticks pulled by strings along the edge of the pond, a few older children became boatwrights in a more mature sense. The original sticks evolved from a motley pickup variety into carefully selected pieces of sawed wood and were soon nailed together. These last had to be well weighted before they would float properly. One measure of the older children's development was their increasing preoccupation with function rather than with style or beauty. (In the minds' eyes of some early builders had been the silhouette of a ship with superstructure well above deck, but here form and function had collided.) The achievement of stability required much trial and error. Vocabulary kept pace: keel, stability, density.

There came a gusty day, and hence the temptation to try sails was great. A final die was cast: we would make our ships sail to the wind. Once again this small group was off and away, plans soaring, and here I remember a quick but important argument with myself: if I don't interpose some reality, these so recently successful boatwrights will be back to square one, back to earlier disappointments. I listened to their grandiose planning talk of "how we could nail on a stick and then nail a sail to that" and almost lost my resolve to wait patiently. Before this Farm School experience I would have intervened, believing they needed to be guided, but I too was learning and decided to allow more trial and error. These children had already shown me, I realized, that they could come for help when necessary to their ideas, their work. Setbacks wouldn't throw them. They were making their own significant choices, and their satisfaction was obvious.

And so it happened. Again, days of capsized boats, top-heavy with masts and sails, but little discouragement. "It's too high. It won't work. Make the sail smaller. Put some more wood underneath. That stick's too heavy for a mast." But finally, "Hey look! It sails!" But only briefly. Back to the workbench to trim a sail or to consider the relationship of the triangle's height to its width. Yes, I could now be useful when needed in their scene, but as one contributing member with only a little more experience. A true sailor would have suffered more keeping hands off than this landlubber! I have thought long about this stage of seemingly bizarre planning that lucky children often work through. They don't have to reinvent the wheel, but they understand something of how the wheel was originally invented—not overnight, certainly.

Finally, after successes were more frequent, someone discovered a refinement: sails that bowed, sails not nailed on too straight and perpendicular, were more seaworthy. So rigged (accidentally at first?), boats stayed afloat longer for some reason we did not understand but, having observed, could imitate and cheer.

Only three or four of the older children were caught in this final prolonged enterprise. Such offshoots do not become the clear descant they can be unless most children are involved elsewhere. At Farm School some were still composing and improvising and committed to cities, streams, lakes, and sandbox. Among all these different levels I felt the verification of earlier hopes and glimpses, of surmises about what children can be released to learn, to teach themselves, and I watched daily the initial and necessary capriciousness of learning before it settles in for the long and happy involvement, to the achievement of rigor.

More new words were added: capsize, top-heavy, bowed, overflow. But more than words alone were being learned: a dam either held water or it leaked; a craft with a sail either sailed or capsized. Pondworthiness could not be faked.

One might improvise, invent, make do, use principles only partly grasped, pull a capsized boat to shore, but certain laws and habits of nature ruled and could not be ignored. Finally, we were able to watch scruffy sailboats sail from shore to opposite shore, knowing a well-earned satisfaction—"Feeling pleasure," as my husband, David, has put it, "in an accomplishment peculiar to our kind; to make, to seek, and learn the right and proper polite form of address, directed to inanimate nature, which will produce a response we desire."

When we were pushed inside by the cold weather, the ambiance of learning together held. Dorothy and I often separated the younger from the older children and alternated the use of house and workshop. Mornings included cooking, singing, dancing, drama, blocks, sawing, hammering, clay, finger painting, and all the usual nursery school activities children enjoy. But those winter months mostly unfold in my memory for what individual children made of them.

When the signs of spring appeared that year, the season took possession first of certain days and then of our very lives. With the winter pattern of alternating thaw and freeze—characteristic of our marginal region at the eastern edge of the Rockies—children and adults were often literally stuck in the mud. We might come to school to find the lawn and driveway still covered with last night's light snow. We could trace with sticks and boots the shadow of a tall, slender black elm or spreading cottonwood. The bare trees' shadows on clean snow made a network different from that of the children's roads in the fall. We walked carefully on these roads.

Suddenly, one morning, we looked up, not down, and the elms were green, a furry, brilliant, springtime-overnight green. Or at least, so we saw the speed of transformation as we tried again to trace the less sharp shadows. That last change was irreversible; not so other evidence of warmth returning.

All winter the stock pond had been so frozen that we could only shoe-skate on it, but it had been a long time now since that slippery, sliding, falling fun. Instead, the melting edge of the pond came and went. Clear, cold nights alternating with the warm chinook wind saved only a thin edge of ice or dark water. Sticks and rocks could break the thin ice or skate across it; then overnight the pond would freeze solid once more against our testing, the edges holding.

We were living in a world where weather indeed dictated, and one could sense a growing power the older children were developing from watching, caring, and learning to monitor the state of our familiar but ever-changing world. Finally, spring began in creature form one morning with a soft but insistent call from Bobb, who was standing outside the workshop. He was pointing, "Look over in that meadow." There in the distance, walking toward us, was a slow and stately procession of two— our brown-and-white Hereford cow in the lead and, close behind, a wobbly, still-wet, white-faced calf. We knew it for her own and stood silent in awe at this miracle. So new was this birth that hanging from the cow was fresh placental stuff. Was I the only observer of this evidence of how recent the birth? It appeared I was, as all other eyes stayed on the pristinely white-faced calf, the primary miracle sufficient unto itself.

On another morning's investigation we made our way as best we could across the mud, jumping from snow hummock to snow hummock, heading for the bare apple trees. Delays on such walks to extricate boots from mud, to clean them in puddles, were never disastrous and were often useful to calculate the season's progress or, just as important, the stickiness of a patch of mud. When we read *In My Mother's House* and talked about the need for testing the adobe to make houses, it all made sense.[1] We were becoming experts at mud testing, like Pueblo Indians!

Once under the knobby bare apple tree, climbing seemed absolutely necessary. As the children climbed, memories crowded in. How many apples had we pulled in the little wagon last fall? A hundred? A trillion? Certainly more than we could eat—enough for people, pigs, and horses. "Little red wagon full of apples, skip to my Lou my darling. Applesauce! Baked apples! I'm hungry!" We had made them both.

Since the morning when the calf had come walking in, speculation had begun in earnest about Blaze, the Shetland. No one minded last fall when Bobb explained that Blaze was getting too big, too lazy, to give rides around the corral. The children knew that Bobb's Arabian, Zarook, had sired the foal Blaze was carrying, but interest had waned over the winter while Blaze lived contentedly in stall or meadow. Now she looked rather round, and there was talk that maybe she would have twins, she was so big.

I brought factual books at their level from the library, but none of the didactic tomes spoke to these children. Again and again it was that delightfully bourgeois *Babar and His Children* who caught their fancy and tripped their need to discuss.[2] Were these my engineers, my boatwrights? No kingly cannon shots to announce births in our farmyard, but Blaze just might have triplets like Queen Celeste; "she might, you know!" Would they be colts or fillies? Would they be born in the day or at night? Back we would go to King Babar and his daydreams, his imaginings. We kept our own dreams about Blaze fresh and abundant, but when Crescent was found waiting beside Blaze on her birthday morning, with her silky coat of brown and the delicate white crescent moon on her forehead, she surpassed any triplets or twins, elephants or colts.

Vocabulary again had to keep pace: filly, colt, bull calf, heifer, stallion, mare. For these words, first approximations in meaning, understanding was less complete than for the words from last fall's sailing or dam building, which came with less of a spectator's sense of sport, more a participant's.

Somewhere during this time, Dorothy and I paused to assess. Was the children's interest in details, in process, too easily satisfied? Where were all the questions? We were both loath to fish, but wondered whether the abundant, first-hand reality might be overwhelming. It almost was for me, a forty-year-old city-raised girl. In mulling over these events, we finally relaxed. As we discussed and traded information, degrees and varieties of children's learning penetrated our doubts and began to dispel them. Perhaps, we reasoned, for four- and five-year-olds it was right that only the deep sense or essence of springtime would push into consciousness—outlines, promises, doors opening, memories stored, with a lifetime ahead to fill in the colors, to clarify.

Blaze, with Crescent now a lively and unattached glider, once again offered rides. I, at least, was in awe of Crescent's trusting and gentle greeting to her new world, especially to the children. Arabian Zarook and Shetland Blaze—a good cross, that.

The memory of my first introduction to the Arabian bloodline and its gentle temperament takes me forward to another morning that spring. Near Farm School was an Arabian broodmare farm, and we were invited to bring our children when its foal population was well established. My apprehension for around twenty small children too near so many horses was underlined when the farm friends opened a rather small enclosure, closed the gate behind us, then opened another gate so the mares and foals could join us in that small enclosure. By this time we trusted our children's respect for and ease around a large animal, but my apprehension faded only as the mares walked into the enclosure, each with her own foal, to inspect *us*. Slowly and proudly they came among us, nuzzling, looking, touching. Our human young touched and petted or not while a mood of wonder, respect, curiosity of species about species held and overwhelmed us. After a very long time—five or ten minutes, perhaps—a stallion father sent neighing greetings from a near enclosure, and our braver children went to pet him through the rails of the wooden fence. This again was done with the encouragement of our hosts, who knew the character of their stallion, as well as of his mares and foals.

Back in our own Farm School meadowlands, the grass had been greening at such a rate that one constantly lived with a time-lapse sense of growth. Fruit blossoms lagged that year, but finally, following this slow and meticulous sort of natural stage setting, the children themselves blossomed in their own independent, human way. This blossoming came not with a mammal but with a hen and ten eggs to hatch.

Once the hen and eggs we had all walked to buy from a chicken farm had been given a quiet nest in a corner of the dark barn, impatience took many forms, which set another tempo for living and learning. If you are young, three weeks is a long time to wait for hatching. There were trips to take a peek on the first day, there was a calendar for crossing off the days. And there were books! The children pored over these in possessive fashion now that our own hen was setting. Among the books brought from the public library was one that held the children's curiosity, although after their previous rejection of similar realistic books on horses I had not expected it to. It was *Wonderful Egg,* which contained photographs of a farm and its chickens and diagrams of the developing embryo. [3] This book was selected again and again and seemed to have been written about our very own eggs in the barn. Although we could never catch our mother hen in the act of turning the eggs with her beak, this now-favorite book assured us that she must, so faith was great that it happened when we were not looking. As the days were crossed off on the calendar, children would go back to *Wonderful Egg* to see what the real eggs must look like inside the shell on that very day.

The sustained attention and discussion continued over these embryological diagrams, and I watched carefully. It was always the diagrams the children now devoured. They skipped photographs of farms and children, as expert fingers easily found the diagrams; by their selection they showed me where the action was for them, as did their discussions: "What's he doing here? See where his claws are? What is that round thing on top of him? Is he dead? Silly, he's just sleeping. It's really dark in there, isn't it, Mrs. H.? I'm glad I'm not in there. Me too! Will he get out? How will he get out?"

Back and back again they came to that final question. Apprehension, seeking, trying out, and deep interest punctuated the days and led us repeatedly to examine the whole sequence from the first day to the twenty-first when, in the diagrams, we could finally see a whole, wet chick sleeping, waiting inside its shell. And then the pecking. Resting, pecking, rest—until the final hard push cracks the shell and frees the chick. That pecking tooth on top of the bill was particularly engrossing and delighted our growing knowledge of these matters. None of us had known about such a tooth. [4]

"He did it! He did get out! He used his pecking tooth." There indeed the chick stood, in that picture, still wet and tired, taking a rest before trying out its wobbly legs. I was no less excited, with an ignorance of many more years than the children's dispelled! "But he's got food inside him, doesn't he?" That too we had read. "He doesn't have to eat for a long time!" That last piece of intelligence was reiterated in the way four- and five-year-olds like to share a new and delightful bit of knowledge, with that fresh sense of being on the inside, with pride. I had often wondered how chicks could be shipped at birth, and now I knew; it was the yolk sac—his lunch, we called it.

I should speak of my role here. It was that of a teacher rather ignorant in zoological matters, a role in which we must all find ourselves in many areas even if we are educated. The children and I were learning together.

One morning in the farmhouse with a group around the piano I hazarded, "You could be chicks." Almost instantaneously, at my feet were curled-up children, chicks in eggs, arms hugging knees. Very quickly about twelve chicks were born—heads curled under, all in egglike silence. After a time for sleeping, with soft, sustaining music, there came a whisper: "I'm sleeping." Finally, one chick head lifted with eyes still shut: "It's dark in here. Now I'm pecking my shell. I'm pecking. I'm sleeping still." This last from Lucy—no copying pattern there. "I have to rest now. I'm tired of pecking with my pecking tooth." Eyes stayed closed, although peeks were taken as the mood was transmitted and sustained on that first, inventive day. Individual children set their own pace, pecking, pushing, standing, falling, resting—lost, in fact, in the enactment of their own interpretations and understanding. On and on, with that quality of self-forgetting and enchanted seriousness that marks inventiveness in child drama at its highest. At the piano I simply improvised softly to accompany the action, following their leads.

At home that night in wonder, making plans, I tried to reconstruct what had gone on so I could allow the dance to develop and not cause any premature rigidity. Without being able to classify or name the gains, I counted them as exciting and positive. I was not concerned with surface reality, with how and what these inventive children were selecting and making their own. They were showing me their own ways of transforming profound information for their four- and five-year-old minds.

On the mornings that followed a stylization began, almost balletlike: "let's be baby chicks." Repetition and consolidation were satisfying, fulfilling the need to make an overwhelming external affair totally one's own. One morning, however, I judged that innovation had ceased to occur; it had not been provided by the group itself, so I entered. One makes such a try, and there are at least two possibilities if feedback is working: the suggestion may be ignored, or it may be followed too slavishly. If the latter occurs, one hopes to be quicker and more observant the next time.

So I tried again. "Leslie, don't those eggs need to be turned? (We all knew mother hens turned their eggs.) Could you do it?" She could and did. And then there were two mother hens, one with wings outstretched to keep her eggs warm, and Leslie with two hands together to form a beak. "Too heavy, it's hard to turn you; you have to roll over, chick, when I *touch* your head."

Now other change could come from the children, and the ballet alternated and evolved. Sometimes players couldn't keep up with their own innovations or those of others.

Later, on spring mornings, we planted seeds outside, waiting patiently to see the green shoots. We expanded the morning dance to include parts of a related sequence. It was seldom the same play on successive days; innovation had become part of it, so stimulating had been the spring's own changes.

And the real eggs? Most of them did hatch on the twenty-first day precisely, although such an exact, predictable timescale is not so impressive to four- and five-year-olds who live and investigate daily in a world of unlocking wonders. Eggs hatched, and we had baby chicks, downy and yellow, to watch and admire as they found the food we provided.

How the children added the food for the chicks and the farm ducks provides a final glimpse of the year. Bobb carried out a bucket of hard seed corn one warm day and announced that the ducks couldn't eat it unless it was cracked into smaller pieces. Such a call for help fell on ready ears. Out came the old sheets, making white patches on the now lush grass. Rocks were gathered for cracking the corn. Many useless rocks were discarded; those with smooth, flat surfaces for grinding were kept. Once again, *In My Mother's House* informed and transformed us. There on the green lawn on white sheets, groups of Indian children gathered, each with *metate y mano,* turning out enough cracked corn to feed all of the barnyard fowl, chicks and ducks, for many weeks.

Only Ben

I stood in the doorway one morning and watched a group of children tumble out of Dorothy's station wagon. My own car pool of children was already hard at work, and now the new batch raced toward me, but only to stow treasures in lockers behind me with an occasional "Hi." As they disappeared into the humming, busy workshop, something of the morning's atmosphere—the children's eagerness and sureness—made it a milepost to me. One watches for these.

The earliest school life of any child can be particularly revealing and exciting—to the child, the parent, the teacher. That may be why those of us who teach and who have had the luxury of choosing where and how we teach often become so addicted to the observation of beginnings.

It was only a few weeks into their first school for these twenty-five three- and four-year-olds, yet most were well launched—self-directing and filled with anticipation for what they would make of the day. Most, but not all. Today, Ben lagged far behind, as if to remind me of that "not all." I moved away, and he stepped up slowly to lean against the door, his small back stiff, his two fists clenched. I knew the set of his jaw, did not need to see it.

Recently, Ben's eagerness to get to school had lasted well into the morning. Not today. Today he spurned any offer of solace or diversion. He held in abeyance his ingenuity and ability to play alone. His search for a friend would dominate his day.

As two teachers in harmony with their own "shorthand" can do, Dorothy and I hurriedly conferred and agreed to separate her ten three-year-olds from my fifteen four-year-olds during the early part of this crisp fall day. All but one of the three-year-olds (floaters, we came to call such children) separated themselves from the older ones and with Dorothy in tow headed for the farmhouse. Looking at Ben's back, Dorothy whispered to me in passing, "Look out for him." Her message was clear: keep children away, protect him—and them!

I was busy getting everyone settled, but I kept the silent Ben very much in my mind. If only he wouldn't try so hard to make a friend, if only he would play by himself, if only . . . It was easy to forget, when there was such an impasse, how much Ben and I had already learned. I saw him as a competent four-year-old with a sturdy ego who had a developmental problem: difficulty with peers.

Very briefly, by a developmental—as distinguished from a profound—problem, I mean a problem that is appropriate to a particular age and is often delicately linked to a strength (as Ben's self-sufficiency was linked to his trouble with peers). Such a problem is not yet deep and is within a child's ability to work through if circumstances are supportive—individually and intelligently so. Such children often ask for boundaries, but boundaries within which they can be their own architects. For Ben at home? A divorce, a step-father, a new baby!

Nothing new was needed here from me today. In this climate I could continue my preoccupation with Ben. He still leaned against the doorframe, and I knew he would move only when he was ready.

I understood Ben's refusal to accept direct help: it was part of his strength. Again I wondered what had triggered this morning's impasse—had trouble at home been underlined by something in the car on the way to school? Dorothy had indicated that he was waiting on his usual big rock when she picked him up. Perhaps this morning the cohesive gaiety of the car full of children he had joined—last—defined and underlined his loneliness. Who has not at some time known this human experience?

For a few minutes I was helping in a far corner of the room, and when I returned the doorway was empty. Progress. I caught a glimpse of the top of Ben's head in the central playhouse. (We had roughed in and furnished a kitchen, bedroom, and living room.) Luckily, and surprisingly, the playhouse had remained empty, and there was Ben, standing in front of the "sink," body less tense, but fists still at his sides.

I kept an eye on Ben. He began to move. Unaware of me, he picked up a pitcher of water and poured some into a large bowl of fresh, dry sawdust. Unclenched fists! Next, he grabbed a big spoon and began stirring. More water—pour, mix, pour, mix. It was slow motion, dreamlike, but it was motion. He found some muffin tins and spooned in just enough of the wet sawdust to fill the empty cups, patting each sawdust muffin level. Silently, I applauded his unlikely choice of therapy and was once again grateful to Dorothy, whose early morning provisioning was impeccable. Sawdust, muffin tins, water, and an empty kitchen: not unlikely at all, I corrected myself, content and thoughtful now, with Ben close and mending.

Ben's times of high tension, the tantrums, and his need to cool off were becoming less frequent. So what was going on in that little head? Perhaps the children's understandable unwillingness to be pummeled had kept him away from earlier fights and tears. In his need to unwind after a crisis, his ability to work alone served him well; he could turn to it and use that strength to think and to catch his breath. I had just been witness to that process. Progress? Resignation? Withdrawal? I did not yet know which.

It was with Ben and the other children during these years at Farm School that Frederick Allen's *Psychotherapy With Children* came newly and increasingly to my professional rescue. [5] Allen's philosophy of the Present guided me as a teacher. It helped me to continue my personal reconstruction of the Freudian and Piagetian viewpoints. My postgraduate summer at the University of California with George Stoddard and Kurt Lewin had informed my teaching, sharpened my wits, and showed me more explicitly how to observe so that salient questions could be posed: Where is this child in his or her present world? How is he or she moving? What can be offered to support the positive steps *that only this child can take?*

It was in these years that I came to understand that to assess, act, and analyze are parts of an entire cycle that can occur almost automatically when things go well in a classroom. It is what the "happy few" learn to do when they teach, challenged constantly in their work with small enough groups by a sense of the importance of their own professional growth. I learned from Frederick Allen that no dividing line exists between his kind of art and theory and the art and theory a teacher needs. My philosopher, friend, and husband, David, formulated it thus for me:

> The structure of Allen's theory (and his way of making it opera-
> tive affords the full, active role of a teacher; that of Piaget's theory
> puts it out of focus, legitimately so for some purposes; that of
> Freud's builds a dividing line, indeed a wall, between teaching
> and therapy, legitimately for some other purposes, but cutting
> their rich connections. There are proper distinctions here, but a
> theory which separates can blind one-half of a therapist's vision
> and the other half of a teacher's.

Allen makes the search and provision for each child's strengths and present opportunities always focal. Although my early teaching, when it was successful, had such a focus, I had found little theoretical support and almost no practical support for it. Suddenly, in my own field, I had found in Allen an older, successful ally from whom I could learn.

It was against such insight as Allen's that I began to realize new truths with Ben. Even at the peak of early tantrums, he did not resent my necessarily forceful intervention. That fact, not the tantrum or its psycho-genesis, was salient. I read it to mean strength: Ben understood part of the reality of his situation—namely, that my act was a rescue operation for *him*, not just for the child he might have attacked, and was certainly not a punishment. Ben, taking my action in some such spirit, thus freed himself from anger toward me, *from fear of himself,* and could work through the real troubles with his peers.

Thus, Ben was protected for a little longer, and I walked on, looking and listening, content and assessing. My hunch had indeed been right: not to introduce anything new today. The children all seemed happily moving in their own worlds, and I found it especially right this morning to have these four-year-olds by themselves rather than mingled with the three-year-olds.

On my way back to check on Ben, I stopped by a construction made from an assortment of large and small boxes. Back and forth I wandered, not risking interference, while a mountain cabin was being built "high on an invisible mountain." The solid and visible cement floor seemed to be its base camp. Construction in no way interfered with dwelling inside, and Jeff, Jenny, and Tom were simultaneously busy with both. It was that mysterious and magic juxtaposition the young achieve in their play when they manage to arrange things—properly separate in time and space—so that order and sequence cease to offer trouble. Picasso certainly remembered how this felt to him as a child, since he could capture the phenomenon so well on canvas.

The cabin door of these young magicians was closed—an orange crate does make a fine door—and our usually silent but sturdy Tom opened it, stepped through, and began to demonstrate its marvels. "Open it, Jenny, but only when I ring." "Silly," Jenny yelled from inside, "you can't have a bell in the mountains; you have to have a knocker." Jenny's disdainful and often queenly manner was seldom ignored. There was much substance to her additions. She gave glamour to every situation she graced, and we all knew and prized this dimension.

"Here I go," Jenny cried, "looking for a knocker . . . looking, looking, looking." Back she came from the wood box, a stick in hand, and as her two attendants waited and watched respectfully, Jenny managed to transform the stick into a knocker and "attach" it to the orange-crate door. Now the builder-dwellers were back in full swing and continued going in and out, around, and onto their creation, adding, revamping, oblivious of that other world the rest of us inhabited. As I moved away, I heard the queen: "Go back, Tom, you forgot to knock. Three times, you know."

While all this was happening, Ben was still at work in the kitchen, but he seemed much more at peace. I sent him a first silent "bravo." I knew he had won some battle, and so I dared a spoken greeting through his window. "Hi," he grinned back at me. On I walked, also at peace, still keeping him in my mind.

I knew Ben was one of the easy ones to help. His collisions were so open and fierce, his cry for help so demanding. It is fear of their own ineptness, their own resulting violence, that I believe such children must change, not fears more deeply seated.

And now observe with me this four-year-old, and the three he would choose to become his friends they would accomplish more surely what no therapist, no parent, no teacher could provide. I came near Ben's hideout again just as he was leaving it. He walked by me and into the room, leaving behind the protection that had been made possible by adults but that had been chosen and used well by him. The chip was gone from his shoulder, but wherever he paused to watch, no one saw him, no one spoke. Could he understand this rejection yet? It was difficult to watch, and I warned myself again to stay out of it. He had that successful battle already behind him, and although I was momentarily apprehensive, I was also hopeful as I watched him move on.

His meander around the preoccupied groups slowed and stopped, and he stood for a long time by the mountain cabin. My heart sank. No, I reasoned, not that closed group of mountaineers. Only my professional self, not my impulse, saved Ben from "helpful" intervention. As I silently watched, he moved into action. He took Jenny's knocker and knocked on the orange-crate door—three times, so he had heard Jenny's instruction from his hideout. Out of a window popped Jenny's head. "Ya can't come in—only us!" Ben moved away, but only to sit nearby, thinking, keeping cool. He picked up a cardboard carton and carried it to the door. Again he knocked, and this time he called out, "Wanna buy a chimney?"

Jenny's refusal was less emphatic than before. "Uh . . . no . . . no chimney." I blessed her. She could be gentle as well as fierce. Perhaps she could recognize ingenuity, having such an abundance of it herself.

I believe Ben had heard and taken heart from Jenny's altered tone, but I couldn't know for sure. With his next move—away from the cabin to an adjacent pile of blocks and large boxes—Ben was purposeful; still not angry, but quiet and thoughtful. He seemed in control not only of himself now but also of the situation. My observation became less apprehensive, more curious—and more professionally appropriate. What next move would he make?

With great sureness, Ben showed me. Through the speedy use of mind and hands, his pile of boxes was transformed, and up he climbed into what was suddenly but obviously the engineer's seat in a magnificent locomotive. For a moment he sat there, still thoughtful. He jumped down, ran to a far box where the musical instruments were stored, rummaged through them, and found what he needed. With the large, old-fashioned brass bell in hand, holding the clapper still, he climbed back onto the engineer's seat and rang the bell resoundingly. "All aboard!" he called. "All aboard! Here comes the Mountain Train!"

The bell sounded again, and the buzzing room fell silent. Three respectful and curious faces looked out from the cabin, then out came Jenny, Jeff, and Tom. From around the room came a few more passengers, and the engineer watched as too many stood, sat, or touched the train as it pulled out.

"All aboard! Up the mountain!" Ben kept calling. "All aboard!" All this in that projected voice every good conductor uses. "Everybody on?

Okay?" Everybody was on—including Jenny, Jeff, and Tom—and the train pulled slowly out of the station once again. The engineer sat splendidly confident about the new trip he was making.

"Here we are on the mountain. Everybody off!" And there indeed they were, on the heights, with Ben leading the way to his destination— the mountain cabin. The confirmation came from Jenny: "Ben first. Only Ben." Hunting for a friend, Ben had made three. Not bad.

A Winter's Tale

I had not noticed Philip until he found his way to us one cold morning after Christmas break. This three-year-old had left his group and come alone and now stood behind the table of finger painters in my four-year-old group. He was so engrossed that I could take a good look at him. Thin, neat, and tight, he had a strangely worn and sallow look about him. His eyes darted, with little expression in his face except for a ticlike grimace that would come and go. I felt his uniqueness at once and some diffidence toward it.

He was a new arrival to Dorothy's three-year-old group, and she had asked me to notice her "strange little fellow" the next time we had our groups together. No wonder. I realized that in spite of the worn and wary look, there was a fierceness about this child, a combination I had not met before. My professional self was at once engaged, all diffidence gone. Later, Dorothy and I agreed that it might be better if Philip chose to join the four-year-olds, hoping he would be challenged to participate in the older group's activities.

Enrolled late in the fall, Philip came only on Tuesday and Thursday mornings, as did many beginning three-year-olds. Although he was to turn four in the early spring, the two days each week were to prove particularly advantageous to him because of his strenuous and fatiguing use of them. The spacing allowed me to concentrate my curiosity on him when he was present without neglecting those who came five days a week or three.

Philip remained in sharp focus for me, and he remained there in the months ahead, but it was not until the following school year that he settled in—still unique, yet one among his classmates. By then he had changed himself, but his strengths and odd ways were intact. (See the discussion in Chapter 5, especially "Transitions.") Misery, the victory, and some real agony will define the winter months for Philip, his teacher, and one other child.

These months of growth reveal much of the situation that exists with the few young children who find themselves in deep trouble. Their stories must be told and understood, their pain appreciated, before we can arrive at an adult's understanding of how to help.

In moving back and forth between the two groups, Philip was not unlike others of his peers. Our easy ways and inclinations encouraged these floaters, as we came to call them. This gave us extra signals to interpret about children, especially since the reasons for floating were never the same for any two. Two teachers to observe, two different settings and a set of peers for each child.

For some weeks Philip moved between the two groups. In neither group did he speak often or join in any activities. His mother reported that he couldn't wait for school. It was a puzzle. In the beginning, he seemed so sure of his watchful style of navigating alone that after several failed attempts I was inhibited about engaging him in any kind of conversation. He simply ignored my efforts to assist him and, in turn, was totally ignored by the children in both groups. [6] His visage alone continued to keep me at a distance.

I use the term *visage* because unlike Hamlet, who wore his "suits of woe," Philip dressed in the popular cowboy regalia: boots, shirt, jeans, all worn with bravado. But like Hamlet, Philip could have said of himself that "he had that within which passeth show." He wore his clothes as if they were pasted on, could never be mussed. In the beginning they never were, and even after he began to participate they seldom were. The gap between jeans and shirt? Impossible to imagine. No fat tummy, belt always secured. Had he ever had any baby fat? Some few of the well-fed don't, of course, and he must have been one of the sparse ones. With the pale yellow cast to his skin, it took me some time to realize that he was healthy.

I did not meet Philip's mother until the following fall. Her words were few; she, too, seemed quiet. (I learned later that she had been seriously ill—she died when Philip was seven.) Pressures and troubles within families are harder on some children than on others, and Philip's reactions were unique to him. The reactions, however, rather than the troubles themselves, were the only area in which I could help.

Philip was no exception to my belief that when a child has grown accustomed to carrying his defense with him, any breaking away must come from the child. I watched for his signs. He came in one morning with a Dennis the Menace doll and a new swagger to his step. A smile seemed almost to come through his mask, and before long he broke his long silence with a pronouncement.

"This here is ma li'l old Dennis the Menace doll, and ah'm just lak him. Ah'm a li'l old menace maself, that what ma daddy call me . . . his li'l old menace." It was not the Oklahoma accent that threw me but the confidence that accompanied this first broadcast. For most of the morning Philip forgot to observe intently and wandered, rather happily for him, around the busy children with Dennis under his arm and would say to no one in particular, "This is ma Dennis." It was like a rehearsed speech that asked for no response, only an ear. It was a recorded announcement.

The Dennis doll was a benign enough protection for awhile and lived under Philip's arm as he returned to his inspections. (One could not help but wonder at the irony of Philip's calling himself a menace. The last thing Philip would have done would have been to use anything at school, never mind misuse it. At home? I doubted the aptness of the label there either. It was probably a nice joke between Philip and his father.)

Other sorts of pronouncements followed, similarly thrown forth, similarly ignored by the other children. For days these announcements seemed satisfying to Philip. Were they his way of stepping cautiously away from his former silent self? He would pull the string tie around his neck even tighter and might announce, "Ah lak this tie ta be tight, ah jus lak it that way." His clothes were very important to him; they too were his protection, his armor, and were not to be commented on by the teacher.

And then, slowly, these broadcasts seemed to have direction. They were directed toward me, if not *to* me. I grew hopeful that communication was consciously intended and expected to reach me. I was not wrong. Philip could soon look me in the eye, if only fleetingly. It was not unique, this sort of breakthrough dance. Even less troubled children, who cannot hazard initial direct address, will test and judge whether their slant signals, their covert messages, are received and properly interpreted. Only when they have that assurance, it seems, will further trust be given to the chosen first receiver. For Philip I was that first receiver. It kept me alert.

Although I had never known a child such as Philip, there was a persistent deja vu in his appearance. In a flash the reason became clear: he was from an early Renaissance canvas or mural! Giotto had painted such infants. In those fourteenth-century portrayals, I had always assumed the artists were seeking to depict the wise look, the little man. And so, in a sense, they were. Now, with this Renaissance baby before me in my class, I wondered if there had not been more of these old-before-their-time babies in those days—days when childhood was short and risky, when nourishment was scarce and survival always in doubt. Among our abused children there is a wariness, an en garde look. And on our TV screens, in news and documentaries, children appear who reflect more than their share of the world's misery and hunger.

Remembering Giotto, I recall an aspect of Philip's proportions. If his head was too small for his age and in relation to his body, his arms were properly short. At the time I missed this, but I remember how the cuffs of the plaid cowboy shirt were always folded back on the sleeve before being buttoned. Even manufacturers of such cloths, fitting small boys in other proportions, did not understand those short arms. (Not so ignorant, most Africans; from teachers there we learned that one of the tests of whether a child was ready to enter school is whether he can touch the opposite ear with one hand over the top of his head. Sometime between five and six the human young can do this.) Philip was appropriately short-armed at just four.

Soon after the new direction in Philip's behavior—his closeness to me when he made his declarations—his inner, fearful world began to break through his protective facade. At first I didn't know what was happening. He scrutinized every activity, from clay modeling to carpentry or paint-ing, with an eagle, judgmental eye and then left it alone. "Ah sure cain't climb up thar with those li'l ole kids, not me. . . . Dennis don't lak for me to put him down, not for one minute." After this sort of pronouncement he would stalk off to another observation point—almost, I felt, as if dis-tance or variety would strengthen his inner resolve to abstain from partic-ipation.

What could a teacher do to help? There were times when I felt totally dissatisfied with my role. I was protecting Philip from possible reactions of laughter and disdain from the other children. As professionals, we understand how subtly but absolutely such feelings are communicated to a classroom of children.[7] I felt Philip's growing acceptance and trust of me, but I wasn't sure my understanding was adequate for future urgent needs. As this progress, seen in his choice to remain with the four-year-olds and to come to school in the first place, became clear, I began to appreciate the seriousness of his approaching battles; my self-analysis proved correct. I hadn't fully understood at the beginning. I had underes-timated both the depth of his troubles with growth and his newly form-ing decision to meet those troubles head on when and where he had chosen.

Even when Philip began to go to pieces, I was unaware of how signif-icant and necessary the violent change was for his eventual growth. I saw it at first as mere regression rather than as a part of growth. Through my ignorance of the unevenness of development, I have come to believe, I slowed his progress. I needed professional help with this child, but in Boulder at that time, none was available.

Philip's pronouncements became more shrill, endlessly repeated. Philip would dissolve into anger and tears. "Whyn't they lissen to me . . . whyn't they wanna do it the way I tell 'em? Ah'll kill 'em, ah will, ah'll kill 'em all." Variations on this theme punctuated his mornings, and the only solace I could offer was to listen with compassion and agree that it was indeed not easy to tell another what to do with his or her work, and so on. It was as if Philip had to monitor and suffer over every independent piece of work done by sixteen busy four-year-olds.

Philip was exhausted these days by his self-set and impossible role: to see and evaluate and comment on it all. There were times when he reminded me of one of the four fencing judges placed at four close observation positions in an épée fencing match—their eyes and attention fixed and alert for the one and only point of the match. Except that unlike Philip, those judges were only briefly en garde.

Philip seemed driven to carry his futile behavior to an extreme. Was this his way of getting it out of his system or of breaking the pattern of how to live at school? From later insight, I realized that all of this was part of his thawing, and it hurt him like hell. I again sought help from Dr. Frederick Allen. His careful discussions of children working through their problems and of the adult's role in that struggle came to my rescue. I have never felt that Allen tells us what to do but rather helps us step back and think again in new and fresh ways about this particular child, whom he never knew. It works.

Thus, slowly one comes to understand, through theory and practice together, something of the almost universal strain experienced by deeply troubled young children who are trying to leave behind their stifling and too-dependent ways. It must be close to panic, to terror. Are they sustained by whiffs of their new freedom? Occasionally so, would be my best guess. But the paradox here is that the very freedom and new courage to move away from fear, to change, is itself fearful in the beginning.

By definition, it must be a lonely voyage when such children take over some of their own navigation. Heretofore they have depended on and built their ways around signals from others—in this case Philip's family, with its serious health problems. The outer bravado and independence, as with Philip, are deceptive. Courage exists within, and independence too; but it seems as if these traits are used up in survival and in

Sand masons.

keeping up a front rather than contributing to the life-enhancing and innovative learning they promise. (See especially "Transitions" and "Ginger" in Chapter 5 for promises fulfilled.)

I remember here a warm and welcome break in the weather. With the respite from winter, with the spring beginning, Dorothy and I could bring the two groups of children together more often. One of us would be in the workshop, one in the small, south-facing play yard. Inside-outside, with schedule set by the weather, Dorothy and I watched with interest how in the beginning children chose to be with their own group, with their own teacher. Philip, we realized, was no exception. He belonged! He was near me one morning when I believed his confidence in me as a new friend was secure. It was, but the way he chose to tell me was so unexpected.

I was wandering outside, from small group to small group, with Philip close by. Together we watched Tom and Ralph. Tom was high on the platform we had built in the old cattle chute, and Ralph was on the ground below. The two had their own form of communication, as well as a rope, a pulley, and a plastic bucket. Ralph would fill the bucket with dry leaves, rocks, sticks, and toy trucks or cars and then would pull it up

Climbing the old cattle chute.

so that Tom, in his platform house, could remove and arrange all of the new equipment from the bucket and send it down empty. As we watched, and with the quietest possible movement, Philip slipped his hand into mine. Although I knew this was only a symbol of his entry into his whole new world, amazement and delight flooded me. I didn't look down at him, and we continued our inspection of what was going on, hand in hand.

With Philip's hand in mine, I thought about this small miracle and was amused at a new discovery. Most young four-year-olds, not all, have much soft cartilage still in place, making such soft hands. So why did this particular hand of Philip's seem so unexpectedly soft and babylike? What struck me was the contrast of his hand with his worn look and his heroic struggles. I expected an older hand. I feel that surprising softness now as I write about it.

Hand in hand we paused to admire the "cementing" of a small collection of junk into place with wet earth and trowels. Philip said nothing. We moved on, and Philip then dropped my hand and went toward two girls who were pumping up inner tubes. With Dennis under his arm he squatted, watching intently for a long time—he didn't just stand above the action.

There was a tub of water, and by putting the end of a bicycle pump into it one could pump bubbles. Because of his close attention to the bubbling and pumping and because he had given me his hand, I presumed. I offered to roll up Philip's sleeves so he could make bubbles. He was startled off balance. "But ah gotta have ma sleeves buttoned! Ah don't lak em rolled up . . . ah *never* roll 'em up." Irate and righteous, he stalked off on his own and left me to regret such rushing of his timetable.

Among Philip's strengths that I valued and respected was this very self-pacing, a trait he retained when it was no longer needed to protect him from the need to grow but rather to protect the growth he had achieved. His inner fight to understand and to get out of his cocoon on his own terms never deserted him. Unless a troubled child has some of this fight, too much is only done to him or her. There were days now when Philip seemed at a kind of resting stage, days when his fight to grow away from troubles seemed to have exhausted him. The scowling and tears when his suggestions were ignored occurred less frequently. There was more wistful watching, and although he and I were now admitted friends and could even converse a little, that friendship didn't seem to help in moving him to play, to use materials. I looked with hope for any small signs of his entering the world of playing, making, or doing. When and how friendships with children would come I couldn't guess.

Knowing that Philip was changing himself in spite of his occasional fierce encounters, I was optimistic that a further breakthrough was coming. At some level of consciousness, even young children know they are trapped. But children differ greatly in their levels of self-consciousness, and it was only later that Philip gave evidence that he knew he was changed and was pleased with his emerging strengths.

In addition to the fight Philip exhibited throughout, he had another advantage. Except when he was too tired, he generally retained some spontaneity. "Spontaneous applies to what comes naturally to a person by reason of temperament or native tendency and not from constraint or external stimulus," says the *American Heritage Dictionary.* I believe Frederick Allen had this sense of the word in mind when he quoted from Adolph Mayer: "The spontaneity of the person, that which he can do and actually does on his own and in his own way, without external prompting or coercion, is what interests us above everything else." [8] Allen continues in his own words: "This places the patient in the center of an experience designed to help him use what he has in order to effect a livable relation with his everyday realities." [9]

And so we found ourselves—the children, Philip, and I—in the midst of a drama worthy of the Bard himself. On the days when Philip put aside his "suits of woe," he could move differently and could cease to observe obsessively. He still criticized, but, I realized, he generally came directly to me to voice his annoyance; it was no longer broadcast. After watching two children build a complicated block construction, he came to me with puzzlement, not anger. "Whyn't they wanna do it the way I tell 'em? Whyn't they lissen ta me?" In the face of such reasonableness, we could talk. I would explain something about the structure belonging to those who were making it and would resist my inclination to suggest he try his own.

Because the place where one could count on finding Philip was near the finger painters, we tried to have finger-painting materials ready on his days at school. Was it significant that he would slip back—only here—into his old ways? "Put some red on, more red." More yellow or black would be put on by the painter, and Philip would be furious. The old question came: "Whyn't he wanna do what ah say?" By allowing himself to expect a response, Philip again allowed himself to become vulnerable.

"Ah'll kill 'em, ah'll kill 'em . . . they won't lissen." Tears streamed down his cheeks. He never accompanied such threats with even a push or a light swat, and to my knowledge no child ever responded except by ignoring his commands, threats, and tears. (Although he was so different from Ben, discussed in the previous section, Philip shared Ben's courage to find and enter the arena of battle. It was always an arena of his own choosing.)

Before Philip could take the next big step, which was to begin using materials, I again needed to assess. He had built strong and loving bridges of communication with one adult in his school life. I stood ready and at times felt helpful. So far so good. With a child as fearful as Philip, I think of a bird and its tentative perchings between short circling flights, ever closer to a new source of food or living. Never mind the occasional retreat to a farther tree or branch; with time and patience, the prize is worth the daring, and the first taste rewards the courage.

For all children to thrive in a group, I have spoken repeatedly of a climate of learning and friendship and fun as enhancing such development. For children as fearful as Philip, such an atmosphere is crucial. They are en garde and apprehensive to a high degree, and the presence of other children, actively involved, may at first be a threat. But even then, potentially, it is also a blessing. For the change that occurred in Philip's guarded walk away from fear, it was crucial that he had an adult friend to tip the balance. He had not yet been able to use the materials that, time and again, he showed us tempted him, and he had no kind of association with any other child. But I am confident, though, that activity and learning are infectious from one child to another, and this proved to be the case with the other children and Philip.

In the therapy of young children beset by developmental troubles, it has been common for no "outsiders" to be present in the therapist's office; thus the therapist and child shared the full responsibility for any developments that occurred. Frederick Allen apparently used this isolation from immediate family or broader social influences as a powerful asset. Allen was fully aware that the developmental problems of young children are enmeshed in the patterns and tensions of family and societal life. Indeed, his child guidance clinic required substantial family input and participation.

Since Allen's time—and very much in agreement with his focus on the dynamics of family life—there has been a major development in therapeutic circles away from the notion that individuals' psychic disabilities can be well understood or treated in isolation. The general movement toward various forms of family therapy, therefore, has enjoyed a justifiable welcome.

In lively classroom situations, where teachers have in their own way had to become therapists, where human beings are invited to involve themselves in a larger circle—inquiring into the phenomena and the affairs of a larger world than that of their own or of their immediate family—the therapeutic potential has barely been understood. It is from such a perspective, as a teacher long involved with the young, that I can speak of Philip's next moves. One morning he kicked over the boundaries between himself and materials and thus joined a group. That morning had begun stormily for him, whether triggered by home or the car pool I didn't know. The other children in Philip's car pool enjoyed an easy camaraderie, an awareness of differences and likenesses. (I have spoken of this car-pool effect with Ben also. [10]) Philip was not yet a participating member of the group, but with his growing involvement he could begin to sense the intended or inadvertent exclusion. His very thawing made him, once again, more aware and more vulnerable.

On the morning I now speak of, Philip haunted the finger painters with his insistence on how to spread and what color should be next. His behavior seemed to represent full regression, but there were no tears at first. No one listened, no one cared, and he was finally thrown into a fury. I watched his face crumple and his tears fall. I knew he wanted to finger paint. I was fearful of a rebuff if I suggested he try—and yet?

In desperation, an idea came. I tore off a small corner of paper, put some white starch on it, and suggested that he could paint with one finger and add his own color. It worked! He shook on some brown, put a forefinger to use, spread the paint, looked at his finger, washed it in the water bucket, and asked for another piece of paper. I kept the paper small, but Philip now used all colors in succession, washing his finger after each try. The small size soon appealed to the experienced children; they began to ask for small pieces: "I want a piece like Philip's." Such a victory was sweet indeed. He couldn't keep from grinning, in a new way, all the rest of the morning.

By the next session Philip was ready to tackle large paper, *roll up his sleeves,* and take home many of his productions. His mother was amused because he had announced that he would never get his hands dirty in that stuff. After three weeks Philip was through with finger painting. He had set it, one imagines, as a necessary hurdle with a high first priority. After that plunge he moved more easily, if still very selectively, into the use of other materials.

Philip was now involved with materials but not with other children. For awhile, using his hands and mind in these new and formerly self-forbidden ways was sufficient. One could tell by his face whether a particular enterprise was a success; he developed a crinkly smile that he forgot to hide. Sometimes he looked ridiculously pleased with himself—as well he might. I celebrated this state of grace and ease on the sidelines.

And then, inevitably, his very victory, his stepping forward into wider participation, brought him into conflict with his peers. When he was on the periphery, the children had accepted his verbose ways, had expected him to live on the edge. They were unprepared for this new Philip who now expected to be included and understood. Life again became iffy for Philip. If he tried to enter he might be ignored or rebuffed. He could return to his clay or painting and ignore the other children. But Philip's assessment of what he must do next was sure and brave: he must move on.

How would it happen, I asked myself, and who would understand? I knew it had to come from Philip and the children. It was now spring. Philip's crying became more childlike, no longer silent tears running down the thin cheeks. I knew this was a positive sign, but I would forget and suffer with him, trying not to show it. Between his sobs the message was clear: "She won't even . . . whyn't he . . . they didn't let me . . . ah'll kill 'em . . . ah'll jes kill 'em all." Then would return a time for him to work with materials, or he would wander and watch, not trying to move mountains. His days were still challenging, but in energy spent the cost was again high.

His rescue came one morning from our sturdy and imaginative Jenny. The doors were wide open, and our two groups were together again, inside and outside, with Dorothy in the big yard and I inside. As I reconstruct this memorable morning, Philip stormed through the open door, grabbed Dennis the Menace from his locker, and walked to a corner of the workshop where some children and I were modeling with clay. He came near me, but not too close, and since I trusted him to ask for help, I waited. In just a few moments Jenny came stalking him, and I watched. Some new phase had already begun. She looked toward Philip's back thoughtfully, washed the wet sand from her hands in the water bucket next to the clay table, sat herself down with purpose, and began to mold a piece of clay.

"Philip," Jenny called emphatically to his back, not even turning her head, "What kind of ashtray shall I make for your father?" A sniff and another sniff were Philip's only response, but Jenny and I heard that first sniff as a small but significant response. Jenny answered with a loud, theatrical sigh of annoyance. She left her chair, walked over behind him, and with exasperated confidence rephrased her question. "If you don't tell me how to make the ashtray, how do I know whether to make it big or small?"

Jenny, at age five, had not read Kurt Lewin or Wolfgang Köhler on vectors and distance, but she had just verified them by closing the gap between Philip and herself and by giving him a choice. [11] She continued to stand behind him, and Philip gulped a big, noisy gulp. Jenny turned toward the table, Philip followed her, and she sat down and began to mold the clay. Philip wiped his nose on that buttoned-back sleeve and collapsed into a chair beside her. "Aw, a big one, ah guess."

The friendship between Philip and Jenny, which to my eyes began that day, continued. It was a stormy friendship, never dull, but for Philip it was a first. He had chosen well. In Jenny he had a peer who demanded much but who also gave generously.

Philip stopped being a great concern to us as the year came to a close. Only in the fall, however, when he became a member of my Field School the following year, did he stride forth and fulfill his unique early promise.

Notes

[1]Ann Nolan Clark, *In My Mother's House,* illustrations by Velino Herrera (New York: Viking, 1941).

[2]Jean de Brunhoff, *Babar and His Children* (New York: Random House, 1938).

[3]G. Warren Shloat, *Wonderful Egg* (New York: Charles Scribner's Sons, 1952).

[4]For technical information about this tooth, see Hermann Rahn, Amos Ar, and Chac V. Paganelli, "How Bird Eggs Breathe," *Scientific American,* 240, no. 2 (February 1979).

[5]Frederick H. Allen, *Psychotherapy With Children* (New York: W. W. Norton, 1942).

[6]Observe this child's integrity through the winter and spring and in the following year with some of his classmates. He exemplifies once again Frederick Allen's central theme, that all of us can be helped to help ourselves.

[7]Teachers have confided and described how children treat a child badly who is in deep trouble. I suspect at once that the teacher is revealing the children's reflection of her own reactions toward that child in trouble.

[8]Aldolph Mayer, "Spontaneity," in *Proceedings of the Illinois Conference of Public Welfare,* Mental Hygiene Division (1933), p. 25.

[9]Allen, *Psychotherapy,* pp. 51–52.

[10]Children's first reaction to school-bound carpooling can be an important semaphor. Today it tyically comes to those much younger, and reactions are ever more important for teachers to know and to fathom: "all clear" or "trouble ahead."

[11]Kurt Lewin, *Principles of Topological Psychology* (New York: McGraw Hill, 1936); Wolfgang Köhler, *Gestalt Psychology* (New York: Liveright, 1947).

5: Field School

Close to the end of our two years together at Farm School, the Browns sold their farm and were off to Oregon. It was a fresh start, and they were looking forward to the move. I was happy for them, sad for the end of our work together.

This sadness, however, was almost indecently replaced with excitement, a sense of freedom. Why? I had never experienced a two-year span of learning and living such as that at Farm School. Each day had carried me farther from the misery I had known in San Francisco with an ignorant administration and had restored and clarified my old delight in and knowledge of children.

I soon realized I was ready for a school of my own: one where children and I could work together with no other adult. My wise husband, David, was not surprised. He had expected such a step, my need to go it alone. He supported all of my efforts actively and with good humor.

The anticipation I felt during the summer before Field School lives with me as I write. But the new year it led to, which twelve children and I shared, still eludes my efforts to recapture on paper. To some extent this is true of the entire book, but here especially I feel it deeply. This chapter is an offering to those teachers who keep the dream of understanding children's potentialities: to work for a year with only a few children under ideal circumstances. My dream of doing so in the inner city was partially to be realized in summer 1963 in the South End of Boston. But it was Field School that gave me the courage to dare to return to my first loves: inner-city children.

I rented a partially remodeled three-car garage in the countryside nine miles from Boulder. David and I worked to get it ready, first putting in the plumbing for an old sink, low enough for children, with cold water (the first time I had ever had running water in my classroom). We warmed linoleum floor tile, piece by piece, to mold onto the rough concrete floor. David built cubbies that divided the big room into two unequal parts, defining an enclosed playhouse area and leaving a large work and play and dance area.

With furniture and easels and blocks from Farm School plus a piano, a phonograph, rhythm instruments, books, paper, and all the rest, we were finally ready. During the last week of preparations, the children and their parents came by to see their new school. I already knew most of them from Dorothy's three-year-old group at Farm School and from my own group of four-year-olds. Four children were newly recruited. Most of the veterans said "Hi!" and rushed in as if, I thought, to see old friends or a favorite piece of remembered equipment, like the small sawhorses or the hollow building blocks or. . .

But not everyone rushed in. Johnny and his mother came and stopped in the yard at a distance from me. She and I kept the distance and beamed at this four-year-old while he leaned lovingly against his mother's legs. Finally, he raised his eyes to look and then, with the speed of a small tornado, he was in my arms, nestling his head. I took this warm greeting to be for Farm School and for Dorothy. He had not been in my group, but I was identified nevertheless and became his link between good memories from his past and the immediate present. Is it across such bridges of experience and friendship that we can greet the future? I remembered, with Johnny's fierce hug for me, how long he had clung to his mother at the start of last year and how patiently and lovingly she had stayed with or near him in those first days away from home. Now he carried his trust with him. He would need it. In less than two years, his beautiful mother was dead.

On the Road Again

In 1955 "On the Road Again" had not been written. But we had other songs, and on our drives to school we sang them all. "Goodbye, Old Paint" was a favorite, as were "Buffalo Girl" and "Skip to My Lou." Or we might just talk, talk, talk. Viki, the last one in the car pool, was usually overflowing with details of her sister's life in second grade: "Stella can spell every word, Mrs. Hawkins, she even teaches me! Y-E-S spells yes and N-O spells no and . . . " Then there was quiet Clay, always at my left shoulder, kneeling on the mattress behind me, whose older sister's tutelage was reflected in his reading all the road signs. Thoughtful Philip (see "A Winter's Tale" in Chapter 4), as will be remembered from the last year at Farm School, was not much for ordinary chitchat. But as the year progressed, most of these avid learners would chorus, "S-T-O-P, Mrs. Hawkins!" and "G-O S-L-O-W." The invisible second grade cast a pleasant shadow over some early mornings unless I subverted it.

The two youngest had been in the group of three-year-olds at Farm School. They were the first to be picked up, and before the older ones took over I enjoyed listening to the dialogue as they sat alone in the back. One morning their conversation went like this:

Sue: "You know who lives up in those mountains up there?"
Lisa: "Indians."
Sue: "Jesus really does . . . he hides up there . . . and watches you."
Lisa: "And Santa Claus, 'cause my daddy told me so."
Sue: "Well, I don't want Jesus to get me . . . and the FBI lives up there too, ya know."
Lisa: "Jesus doesn't really live there, he lives in the sky."
Sue: "But I don't want them to get me, so guess what I do? I pull the covers up over my head. . . . Then they can't see me."
Lisa: "Well, Indians can get you too."

This last comment was said as an offhand aside, and the final statement seemed to establish a mutual agreement and some reassurance, through comradeship, against all those things that were out to get you. Sue giggled, was less apprehensive, and seemed to let go of her initial fear. What a strange world and ways of thought we can pass on to our young.

When all the riders were in, we would focus on seeing what we could see. More seed pods along the roadside and in the fields provided us with hundreds of birds to watch. Red- and yellow-winged blackbirds by the thousands could always be found among the cattails. With so much seed bounty, we often stopped the car and collected for ourselves, learning quickly not to pinch off any seed from cattails or to open the milkweed pods while in the car!

One morning a stunning pheasant cock walked across the road in front of our station wagon. We all saw it, or said we did, and stories tumbled out about a father who hunted, and so on. There were usually cows to count on one hillside and bare apple trees to compare with remembered ones with apples and leaves at Farm School.

The focus on numbers was clear when we neared the pond of ducks, on which there were always six white and black ducks. Early on we found it fun to speculate on how many would be swimming and how many on the bank. One tells this dispassionately, but when good grist comes for children's learning mills, the occasions are vibrant. "Three swimming, three out!" "Go slow, Mrs. Hawkins, one duck is getting out!"

When you unpack such seemingly everyday episodes, it is obvious why they matter. For us, the morning's catch of ducks was always six, divided: one and five, four and two, three and three, and sometimes six in and none out. Children feel a sense of power making contact with the reality (what logicians call the invariance) of numbers. From such early contacts, vividly enjoyed, the foundations are built for later and wider understanding. It needn't be ducks. For four- and five-year-olds the world brims with numbers.

Off The Road Again—Seeing Friends

In the early days the children picked up the previous year's friendships or made new friends. For me there was a deep and satisfying sense of continuity. We were walking new paths, but we relied on some of the past to steady and guide us. What delighted me initially about the children from Farm School was their intact self-direction—which we had worked so hard to help the children keep and broaden. With only four children new to the school, it was as if I had eight "old boys and girls"—co-teachers to inform and model the initial steps of a good life at this school.

Philip returned to school with his same questioning mind but with far happier ways of meeting the world. It was a joy to watch this four-and-a-half-year-old expand, yet keep his own style, in the months ahead.

So the early days were ones of recovering old ways and exploring new ones. One morning early in October came a shift, one that was to alter our course for that day—and for the autumn ahead. Someone walked on out the opposite door and kept walking, through the unfenced yard and into the fields. Why did all the rest of us drop everything on that sun-drenched morning and head toward the southern hills? I can recover no reasons. Soon, as we walked, sequence and detail were overlaid with a kind of joyous madness. I keep a vivid memory of running, leaping, and yelling, like a band of wild things. We circled each other, held hands, ran in pairs through the tall, uncut autumn grass—making channels by our passage. We were on the far side of a looking glass, tasting an almost primitive freedom.

I was of necessity both part and observer of this new phenomenon. A protective professionalism stayed with me as ballast. We ran in separate directions, at different speeds, coming together again for laughter and greeting, slowed to catch a breath or two for more racing, shouting, testing lungs and legs.

Another morning with some accord we headed for a far, lone cottonwood tree. Once there, we collapsed in the shade of its branches. Our school looked tiny, we had traveled so far.

From school this cottonwood had stood unnoticed; but in the shade of its spreading, drooping branches it enclosed us, and we felt sheltered. Even on that first morning, this became *our* tree, standing just for us beside a now-dry farmer's ditch.

Thus are some great enterprises launched—among the young, among the lucky older ones of our species. Those early days in the golden autumn we used our schoolhouse as a magic gate to the meadow. We explored, we laughed, we fell in love with the meadowlands and with each other.

In the beginning, so separately new was it that I kept seeing part of another scene of children in a vast meadow in an old Russian film *The Childhood of Maxim.* Unforgettably, those children were pulling a homemade wagon with one small crippled child—he sitting and laughing, they dancing and laughing ahead, behind, on the sides, vying to pull the wagon away from their slum hovels. So I remember the film, based on Maxim Gorky's book *My Childhood.*[1]

On a later morning the roots of the cottonwood became the roots of another tree we knew from a favorite rabbit called Peter, who lived with his mother and three sisters in a bank of sand under the roots of a big pine tree in England. We had our *own* rabbits in this meadow. Well, we saw footprints and *thought* we occasionally saw a rabbit. Anyway, we could always *be* rabbits, and sometimes we were.

There were always more in our family than Flopsey, Mopsey, Cottontail, and Peter. "Babies," we called the overflow, and some mornings when drama dominated under our cottonwood we would put together snatches of a scenario. For a brief time this intertwining of reality and drama set the tone for the mornings, as we came to know intimately the wide spaces and sky.

On such a morning the basket might be transformed into Mrs. Rabbit's market basket, carried with her to the baker's for "a loaf of brown bread and five currant buns." Our basket carried juice and crackers for thirteen; all the better. The way children weave together suggestive props with reality can enhance any morning's routine. The Peter Rabbit theme soon became a sometime thing, a memory left behind in the tracking and wondering—wondering about who really lived under this cottonwood or under the tall grass. The same basket, when it carried string, magnifiers, or rocks we gathered, became a science kit.

New respect grew for Robin and Chip, whose home territory this was. Four-year-old Chip, less shy than Robin, shared much of what he knew and understood. Listening alternated with action. To a rapt audience beside the ditch one morning, he and Robin, who was six, unfolded the cycle, through the year, of the now-dry ditch. Pointing to the Rockies again and again as the source, Chip had the manner of a ranger-guide. Robin encouraged him. He described the snowbanks up there that melted each spring and sent water down the hills in creeks and rivers to be used by farmers in their summer irrigation ditches. "It's dry now," he might end, "'cause it only runs in summer and not when there is snow." Quiet Chip and quieter Robin had spoken of these weighty matters, and under the cottonwood was awed silence. The children heard, not just politely listened.

During these diverse and heady mornings a palpable unity grew. As children will do when circumstances and enough time contrive, tangible contributions were brought from home and neighborhood. A bit of driftwood came from forested foothills and a pitch-pine knot—almost skeletal—or just a story of a picnic. Thus I knew parents were being included, our love of meadow expanded with our grasp of words to tell of it.

Footprints in the occasional bare sand were sought and identified by the older ones. Clay was our cunning detective. His sharp eyes could find tiny mouse prints or those of a local dog. In between such times of observing and self-instruction would again be tunneling in the tall grass or racing and yelling. Calling to share, no one to stop us, no timetable to follow, no sense of incongruity; only the smells and sights and hunts and finally tired legs to suggest a temporary halt. Drama under the cottonwood! Life in the field.

It lingered, this intertwining of sense and nonsense; then, without prediction as to how the emphasis would shift again, it did. I like to think that the two previous years at Farm School, healing and joyous, restored my confidence to expect and suggest, but not to "plan," the next moves.

One morning we were heading south toward our tree and the hills when a child turned back and called out, "Wait a minute!" Back to school she ran and returned carrying a tall cattail. Everyone went back, even I, to fetch a cattail. We were pleased with our innovative leader, and rather than run ahead we followed behind her in stately procession. We carried the stiff cattail standards carefully upright. Our lead marcher brought us to a high rise of meadow, where we slowed and gathered to look at the high, snow-capped mountains, with Boulder and foothills at their base.

After a time attention shifted back from the far view to the cattails. A small pinch of seeds was released and went with the wind! Pinch after pinch followed, with awe and ceremonial dignity, with space and time for admiration. When the breeze blew gently, we could see it carry the minuscule umbrella-like seeds in a self-contained cloud far beyond us. With a gust, the near sky was alive with seeds. Strange, I realized—it was only in the meadow that all twelve children were thus engaged together, in a common bond, to enjoy a phenomenon. Was it the vast empty space around, the sky so blue, and—overall—the awe we felt at such moments for the world?

We stayed on the rise, and there was another small change of focus. "Look, Mrs. Hawkins!" Johnny was holding tightly to a pinch of the close-packed seeds while it expanded, flowing almost like golden honey, to cover his thumb and forefinger. To observe was to appreciate: other fingers reproduced again and again this slow-motion flow—not of liquid but of minutely stemmed seeds, held in a pinch while flowing open and only slowly, slowly released to go forth over the meadow.

Suddenly a child called out with joy, "Now we can say millions and billions and trillions of seeds, just like in *Millions of Cats*!"[2] On such mornings I felt William Blake accompanying us, he who, having no use for formal education, painted and wrote for our delight:

To see a World in a Grain of Sand
And a Heaven in a Wild Flower
Hold Infinity in the palm of your hand
And Eternity in an hour. [3]

As if, perhaps, to verify, one morning the high back range of the Rockies—the Continental Divide—was covered with snow. Johnny came to me, asking, "How come I can't see those white ones from my house?" Houses near the foothills had no view of the "white ones." This was too much for words to describe, so we turned a big packing box with its longest side vertical. This became our foothills, and some of us moved in behind it. No high, white beauties were visible until one moved back and back, and there came the white-capped ones into view! When one moved closer, they disappeared. Most children took a turn, making the snow-capped high ones disappear and then return. On the trip back to Boulder that day, we stopped the car and focused on the place where we lost the white ones and felt ourselves well into another secret. And so we were . . . daily.

I was at peace with the way things were going. We were learning from the world itself; just what and when had become secondary to the fact that each of us could now be counted on, again and again, "to see a world." Not mystical, all this—although at times it felt so—but rather "earthy."

Transitions

Harvest, Categories, Birds, Pendulums, Music/Dance

By mid-November not even a warm Chinook wind could lure more than two or three outside. We were happily housebound. For most, the shift away from a life of wandering and wondering about our world had occurred. Now that we were inside, different explorations were taking over, individual searches were planned and carried out, and new wondering, observing, and speculating were taking place.

I had not fully recognized the momentum our meadow days would transfer to our indoor lives. Appreciation came gradually as the projects we tackled slowly evolved. I knew we had a tangible harvest to be savored and assimilated, but in addition a new spirit of enterprise was a legacy of the days in the meadow.

Some of the harvest was literally that. For the first cold days we spent inside, it seemed as if each bit of grain, each pod, pebble, and grain of sand had to be studied and discussed, the place we had found it recalled. We expressed gratitude to the blackbirds who had identified our field of cattails for us.

The harvest of the spirit was more diverse. The two youngest—Lisa and Sue of the back-seat dialogues—gave little notice to science director Philip's setups. They spent their time living in the big playhouse, with excursions to the worktable for scissors, tape, paper, and stapler. The playhouse became theirs, they made it so, with a sometimes devoted father Karl, often away from home. Only in retrospect did I recognize the behavior as a declaration of independence from the power of an older majority. Fortunately, our intuitions, if not our conscious understanding, can protect us. Without analyzing, I had encouraged these two girls to design their own days rather than to follow and copy in the wake of the older ones.

So it was; from outdoors to inside the spirit of the road and field came along to build bridges across the seasons and between our lives together.

I wondered occasionally why no one asked for a story or for music or for dancing. But first, how did these indoor days and our workshop evolve?

Four magnifiers, unless one or two were on loan around someone's neck, resided in our science corner. With the six-to-one magnification of the linen thread counter magnifiers, we were on a new path. [4] Philip announced he was "in charge," thus trying on a new and respected role. His cowboy regalia remained. Once a loner, as I described in Chapter Four, now his enthusiasm and self-directed pursuits carried him far and even rubbed off on others, not forced on them as were his last semester's ways of approaching other children and their affairs.

The need for classification arose one morning when some of us were sorting treasures from the early fall. After much discussion, two categories were declared sufficient: living and not living. [5] Later a fossil was examined with the magnifier, and another category was needed: once-living. Sometimes these discussions were with two or three children, occasionally with a bigger group. (See the next section for the growing classification of sugar, salt, cinnamon, and ginger.)

So it was that a magnifier, a human invention rather than something from outside nature, extended—for those few who were ready—much of the outside world we had gathered. This experience led into another realm—vocabulary. Somewhat self-consciously the children had already shown me their pleasure at collecting words. Long words were picked up with skill and delight. *Translucent* had long been a favorite; one child saw with excitement that many sand grains, when magnified, were translucent, whereas some were not. Some few were *transparent*, like glass. "Trans P, Trans L": a heady singsong developed. So I introduced *opaque* one morning—total failure, no one cared, (Page Piaget!).

Sue and Lisa, the two youngest, continued to divide their mornings between the playhouse and the worktable. With stapler, punch, and scissors, they polished and expanded new skills, using paper at a rapid rate. One morning I started to cut, using the small-print section of a newspaper. This allowed us to accentuate the height of animals by using two sheets opened for one creature. A strange zoo developed; my favorite was a giraffe-like fellow with two short legs, almost no body, and a neck long enough to overreach any tree we might make.

Karl remained a welcome father in the playhouse with the girls, but the two single mothers who lived there never seemed lonely. They basked in their domain of baby dolls to dress, undress, bathe, and dry. I overheard Susie one morning in a loud whisper: "Let's put the babies in the oven and close the door." Lisa helped, with delighted giggles from both, in this clandestine removal of babies. So much for those two baby sisters at home.[6]

I recall a significant beginning that was to dominate many mornings and, surprisingly, to enrich an activity still to come: the dance. Masking tape could be said to have started it all, although milkweed pods were equally responsible. In the mess of work in progress on the big table, the masking tape was always disappearing. After much hunting, it would be found buried under that work in progress. And so, in desperation I hung the tape from a rafter above the worktable. Voilà! We were all pleased, especially me: we had a pendulum!

Was it something about using the rafters or about the teacher standing on a table to secure the pendulum? Whatever the reason, bird bodies (as a child-poet had once dubbed our milkweed pods) were threaded, and it was as if we had released the pods to fly. Every one, even the youngest child, had a bird on a thread to swing from his or her hand. Each had a pendulum.

Becoming so brittle in the dry fall weather, these first birds were too fragile to last. The blunt needle for sewing on the thread caused large jagged holes. So one morning I wondered aloud about soaking the pods in water to remoisten and soften them. A chorus of "do it, Mrs. H., let's do it, try it" ensued, and with little confidence I agreed. A dishpan of water was placed in the center of the table, and a host of birds were soon floating, gently held down—held down because, of course, otherwise they floated. Water everywhere never dampens a child's spirit. After too short a time, I wrongly guessed, one tester took out her bird. It was pliable, it was soft enough!. "You were wrong, Mrs. H., weren't you? It worked." We had an orgy of shaping and stringing and just holding and molding those rejuvenated milkweed pods—"Mrs. H. thought it wouldn't work!"

The next session, of course, began with birds. We were still entranced with the flying creatures, and then a happy accident led to refinement. It was discovered that by cutting one pod from "tail" to "head," we had two wings to attach to a bird body. Their renewed pliability encouraged such discoveries and suggested further possibilities. Next we were stapling the wings onto the bodies. At first the angle of the wings didn't matter, just so there were two wings, but refinements crept in, and even I was caught up in being a creator (not just creative but a creator). For days, birds were "flying" everywhere, with their bodies molded closed or left open, wings askew or awry, all surprisingly birdlike. We discussed the magic of the effect of the water, on the pliability it had restored to the

pods. For the happy few, early on, the world is a series of magic phenomena not to be dwelt on but to be enjoyed and expected around any corner.
To be filed, perhaps?

In all this ease of making birds, essentially at first only *seeing* the pods
with subtly altered perception, a fresh challenge arose. The sequence was
similar to that of art or science. First, a long playful stage precedes or is
part of new insight. What had specifically offered challenge then grows.
Eventually: "I want mine to look like it is really flying" was announced,
and enough children understood and joined the request. For the youngest, a bird body on a thread was sufficient; refinement was sought or
came with experience and age.

We tried attaching the "flying" string through different parts of the
pod-back. Depending upon where the wings had been stapled, the center
of mass shifted, and we had nose dives, wing sags, or tail drags—and
much laughter. After innumerable attempts, our respect for birds *and* our
frustration at our own ineptness caused me to introduce the marvelous
stability of the triangle. It flew! Just how much the children understood of
this geometry is not of the essence. At the time I felt a need to inject it,
understood or not.[7] Three short threads were easy to sew on so that,
secured to the longer flying thread, the winged birds "flew." For fun we
tried it with two threads and laughed at the failure. Finally, "ya see,"
announced more than one child, "ya have to have three." That much was
now clear.

With such a large flock of birds on the wing, the children then settled
back to painting on paper and to clay and blocks, drama, and an occasional story. I now had an occasional lull, a luxury. We were in control of
our lives at school, and we all knew the power such autonomy brings.
Cooperation flourished.

I wondered more than once at the fact that we only sang in the car. I
missed music. One morning I went to the piano. Would one or two join
me? No one left his or her affairs; I was alone at the piano. This was a new
experience, and so I played folk songs we had sung in the car, old
marches, skips and jumps, enjoying the luxury of having a few minutes to
myself. After a couple of solo mornings, I added the "Night Herding
Song" from Beatrice Landeck's *Songs to Grow On*, still one of my favorites:
"I've circle herded and night-herded too. Bunch up little dogies, bunch
up, hi-ooo-hi-ooo." With this song the children's conversations quieted.
They were listening! I half expected a request, but none came.

Wondering, I walked around the busy room. Should I call the children to the piano? They would come, but I felt a reluctance to meddle

with this self-pacing band. I believed set plans might jar my confidence in what was developing. Send me back to "lesson plans"? Never!

The next time I began to play, there was an immediate general quieting, and a few voices joined in. Not turning to see who or to notice the change, I trusted that with these children I had discovered the way to go.

And so it proved to be. "Play 'Blow the Man Down,' Mrs. Hawkins. Play 'When the Farmer Comes to Town, with his wagon broken down, Oh the Farmer is the one who feeds us all.' 'Low Bridge, everybody down, low bridge, we're coming to a town.'" And then, in loud unison, "You will always know your neighbor, you will always know your pal, if you've ever navigated on the Erie Canal." From sea to canal to prairie we traveled that spring, but it was the prairie where we lingered again and again.

Beside me on the piano bench one morning, ever so quietly, sat Karl. I moved over to give him room and said to myself, "Karl? Shy Karl?" There he sat, unself-consciously playing softly with random notes, with perfect rhythm, a gentle descant. I knew at once this was not a first-time thing for him. He was bringing to school one of his delights from home. Hallelujah!

By now some form of music was becoming part of each morning. But before leaving Karl I want to follow another concern of his. He called me to the paint easel one morning and pointed to some letters he had written in the corner of his painting. "What does it say?" he asked with a frown. I read the capital letters: "P-O-T-S. You have written a word, Karl, 'pots'!" He still looked puzzled and then explained that he had wanted to write STOP, and he showed me where he had started. With the S at the far right he had to continue on the left, ending up with P. What fun. A backward word that made another word. Everyone came to inspect Karl's two-way word, and we touched on N-O and O-N and D-O-G and G-O-D. No one was reading yet, but some were close enough to appreciate this splendid chance joke of Karl's. Especially Karl.

Philip, in Karl's wake, brought another concern to music. He began standing near me at my left, while Karl or another child might be sitting on my right playing a sort of duet with me. Philip refused to sit and play, and so I offered him the Chinese drum, a hollow Chinese block, the triangle; nothing lasted past a try. Philip would return to stand by me at the piano, frowning and silent.

True to his own style, Philip finally showed me where his attention had been on all those mornings by the piano. With his old stance, one hand on his hip and tears of annoyance gathering, he spoke, "But I don't know how the piano MAKES the music, how does it make it?" So how did hitting those keys with fingers MAKE the sound, indeed?

I propped up the piano front, and there before us were the inner workings of that big brown mysterious box. Without having posed the question themselves, the other children could ride on Philip's question of "how does it make the music." They did just that, and the conversation and the exploration seemed only to fuel more questions. You touch the piano key—not very hard would do it too—then the key lifted the felt hammer and hit the thin wires, which made the high little sounds, while the big wrapped wires, when hit, sounded strong and loud. We could see it all, and we could question and try it with our fingers.

After some time I grew uneasy. I felt we were getting caught in something that was beyond our limits. Fingers, keys, hammers, strings vibrating, that mechanical sequence that makes the sounds but not the music! So knowing we were still together in our quest, I felt compelled to try something different. I first asked the children to come sit with me on the floor. With all of us down—even the fastidious Philip—something in the children's sharply focused attention goaded me, and I took the lead.

"Can you make your finger go tap, tap on the floor," I began, "and can you make these two fingers tap? Now make a scratching sound." We were all very quiet, listening to the scratching of many fingers. "How did you do that," I asked, "how did you make your finger first tap and then scratch?" Any response was properly slow in coming. "Remember," I said, "how one press on the piano key lifted the hammer and tapped it on the wire to make it hum? And we couldn't see that until we opened the piano?" Contributions came. "I told it to tap." "I say 'tap' and then I say 'scratch.'" We agreed that we really didn't understand, but maybe inside our brains were tiny things that worked when "we told them to"—or *thought* them to.

Anyone who has been with young children at such highly explorative moments, in such pathways, will know how astonishing is their readiness to touch on these mysteries—when curiosity stays in spite of minimal understanding. Some of us honor and appreciate this phenomenon; intent, children are so caught by it. Is it that occasionally they find themselves in touch with their own future ways of understanding? If this budding growth of the natural filing system is not hampered by being too soon tested or drilled, then some process functions well within the young to retrieve and refine—or modify—this early sketchy storehouse of the brain. And, I ask myself, if misery accompanies these early flashes, then is that misery also filed; will it surface later as a hindering valence to further seeking and learning? My own experience-based intuition assures me that some such mechanism is fully human.

After the piano and the trial analogy its mechanisms gave us, there were more obvious sounds to be explored, other thoughts to be followed. Tapped softly, we decided, window glass made music. Blocks, when tapped with Tinkertoy hammers, made differing sounds. And same-size blocks sometimes made different sounds when tapped. The small saw made clear tones when tapped. The triangle could be tapped and placed in some new file category in our brains.

However meager his early understanding, this all felt right to Philip, who by his wondering had initiated all of this exploration of sounds and ways of making them. He spurred the interest in instruments, and it held long enough to be extended. We visited Karl's house to hear his mother play her harp; to take turns was heady. Whistles were brought to school and wondered about. Our own percussion instruments were used, on occasion, with the piano.

Yet song and dance finally took precedence, and instruments were filed away: "Streets of Laredo," "Goodbye, Old Paint," and especially "Night Herding Song." The four small sawhorses were "saddled," string bridles adjusted—and we were on the prairie, taking off for Wyoming. Cowgirls and boys rode in fours; it worked well in tandem, and turns seemed easily shared. When "the sun went down at night," saddle blankets (unused resting mats) went down for sleeping next to the invisible herds of cattle. Voices sang softly "Bunch up, little dogies, bunch up; hi-ooo-hi-ooo." Cowboys and cowgirls rode while I might say a few soft words of a scenario to stay the mood. The mood returns even today with the words "I've circle herded and night-herded too. You know that Wyoming will be your last home."

And there, never caught in the singing but caught in that mood, rode Philip. Finally, his mood shifted. One morning he dismounted, called "Wait!" and rushed to his locker. Slowly he returned to us, carrying his cowboy hat in the crook of his left arm while with his right hand he "flew" his milkweed bird, ever so gently, from its thread: "I can nest him in my hat. Watch him come to his nest. Watch how he flies away." All watched while Philip's bird led its life of short pendulum arcs and settled in again and again to its nest. "I'm nesting him. See?" Oh Philip, what promise your last-year's misery was hiding (see Chapter 4, "A Winter's Tale")!

I asked myself that night and I wonder still: What triggers such delicate transformations, in this case using old materials in new ways? Had Philip thought at home of "nesting" his bird in his beloved cowboy hat? Or had riding his saddled sawhorse with friends' voices singing "Git along, little dogies" encouraged further imaginative juxtaposition? We cannot know, but we can remember and see, through the drawn memories of a Picasso, snatches from a childhood on the streets of Madrid: "this world of imaginative overlay or juxtaposition."

Where was Philip in his particular drama or canvas? I judge by his return after a brief solo ballet—flying and nesting his bird. Philip could rejoin his troupe, a troupe of children who had been caught up in a joint and sustaining enterprise: from meadow and roadside to classroom "prairie" with horses and birds. Who of us had not joined in the making and investing, to the birding and riding? To the singing or listening?

Mornings followed now when cowgirls and boys left their mounts briefly and danced, suspending their birds on strings. I came to believe the children were in some sort of joint glide with the pendulum swing. The simplest tempo would do, I just followed the rhythm they had taken from the suspended birds. Those who danced had the faraway look one sees again and again among children who are deep in their own dramatic play. It is still present among some great professional dancers and actors, creating for us their own realities.

I recognized, in this slow glide of accommodation to a "bird" on a string, an experimentation with another sort of motion. In my own early memories at age six or seven, I recall a pendulum in the form of a swing hung high in a giant redwood. What stayed permanently in my mind was its stately slow pace, which I did not understand at the time. In Golden Gate Park I knew all sorts of swings, but they went fast, and one had to pump hard and often to keep them going. With the swing at our cousins' place under the redwoods, an aunt might give one good push or a scary pull, back and high, and then it lasted and lasted and lasted. Not until middle age did I become curious enough about pendulums to understand something of the grand laws that govern their speed and period. What was filed by these children I do not know, but I trust it was some delight in observing, in experimenting, in participating in the laws of nature, improvising entire dances.

Ginger

After a prolonged Christmas vacation, we found ourselves in China. Mornings now included a time for reading and telling stories, and we read about Pun Kee in his Chinese village.

The title of the book was *Ginger*.[8] One morning I chose it. It could be that I thought we were all in need of a faraway setting to break from the smug contentment of our days. Some such rationale occasionally does tempt me. So we were transported to China—for a morning, I thought.

When I had finished the first paraphrasing of Pun Kee's quest for a gingerless house in his small village, there was an immediate request to "read it again." This time I read the book word for word. By the time I had finished, every child had joined us. It was a folk tale of Pun Kee's search, from grandmother's to aunt's and uncle's and cousin's, tasting and asking and not finding a gingerless cuisine. The listeners identified closely with the faraway Pun Kee: "I don't like ginger either. Not me. I hate ginger. Poor Pun Kee."

The subject had struck a sympathetic note because with this age group, conservative food habits are probably universal. In the midst of this gingerless feast of agreement, Philip's query came: "But I don't even know what ginger is!" A chorus of agreement joined him: "Not me either. But it's to eat." Philip tried not to smile at this success, but his pleasure showed.

With the time and inclination, some of us were launched. Others wandered off to previous occupations, some to listen from a distance. Most who stayed had something to contribute, from ignorance or to offer a list of personally preferred foods. My previously unexamined acquaintance with ginger was limited to Chinese food and to gingerbread or cookies, but I, too, offered statements from my own ignorance.

So, ginger came from a root, I pronounced (not yet knowing the difference between a rhizome and a root). "A root? The part that is in the dirt? I wouldn't eat it, not me. My mom doesn't let me eat dirty stuff. (Giggles) I wouldn't like it anyway. Poor Pun Kee." After a feast of sympathy for our ally in China, I posed some questions.

"Well, who likes potatoes? Carrots? Celery?"

"Potatoes grow in the dirt? And carrots?"

Incredulity, then belief, and more laughter. "Celery is a stem?" "I don't like spinach; it's a leaf?" "I don't eat leaves." Food preferences took over, with a host of agreement that peanut butter and jelly sandwiches were by far the favorite of all the children present.

And, of course, I couldn't resist. "Peanuts grow underground in the dirt, you know, and they are called groundnuts in some places."

"Awwww, Mrs. Hawkins!"

Going home in the car that day, ginger dominated the conversation. "You mean gingerbread has that ole root in it? But I love gingerbread." "I don't like gingerbread." "I do." And ginger snaps?

We had stumbled onto a favorite topic—shared preferences in food—which brought a new focus to our daily concerns. It was new because it came from words, from a book, from our tastes and our minds; because it was tripping new ideas and thus challenging my participation as an informant, as a questioner. Everyone agreed that we had to find out more about that spice, ginger. As Clay got out at his house, he turned to me: "And we could look at ginger under our microscope."

I mused that night at home at what the linen thread counter, our "microscope," had encouraged us to look at with magnified vision. Recently, Viki had come from the yard with an early dandelion in hand. Around her neck was a magnifier, and she wanted me to see "real" gold in the center. I looked and there it was, like real gold indeed. She looked away with embarrassment when I sang "dandelion growing there, is there sunshine in your hair?" Not for Viki any such sentimentality. However, amusement was there at my silliness. Clay would be his usual quiet, self-confident self with this new path we were walking. What else? Who else? We would see.

At home in the kitchen I shook a bit of ginger into my hand and spread it out. Surprise! With my naked eye I could see fibers! In all my years of cooking, I had never been curious enough to wonder. I took cinnamon and ginger to school and a whole nutmeg with its own small grater and some information from books.

I drove slowly and thoughtfully to Lisa's house that morning, putting the class into some new focus. Those who were turning five were showing me, I felt, that they were ready to concentrate and to delve into a deeper level of understanding, one that led perhaps from a known object to its origins, its history (those fibers of ginger were still fresh for me). We had already been surprised by sand under the magnifier—sand freshly seen as little crystal fragments, broken smaller and smaller from big rocks over millions of years. Because of the beauty and surprise of sand magnified, and after the children had known and loved sand for digging and tunneling, they had never asked about its history until they saw it magnified. Would the fibers take them a step farther? After the freewheeling glorious fall, it seemed just right that a new form of concentration was budding.

I had learned not to predict the particular paths that were to open. After some discussion, a few of us headed for the sunny science corner.

There was the viewing tray, neat and ready, kindness of our two curators Clay and Philip. "Ginger first, me first." "No, me." "It's full of sticks! Look, Mrs. Hawkins." "Let me see." "My turn." "You're in my

light." "I didn't have a very long turn." "Philip *always* takes too long."
After the initial chaos some appropriate order evolved, and "visitors" left
the "pros" to further examine and discuss. So one could call those sticks
fibers? Yes.

"And these fibers in the ginger," I said, "came from the underground
stem or the 'rhizome.'" I added that I had been wrong in saying that ginger came from the root. How they grinned at that! How they love it when
we confess! It is one way I know of keeping children honest—and ourselves as well.

A child then put the magnifier on the bits of cinnamon. More fibers!
More viewers, more talk and speculation—and smelling. And appreciation that these fibers came from the bark of a tree. Sugar, salt, and sand
were observed, and we realized that even though sugar comes from
sugar cane or beets (Boulder is on the edge of sugar-beet farms) we could
find no fibers, only the lovely crystal shapes—shinier than salt, we
thought.

I heard Karl, coming over from the adjacent playhouse: "Let me see
those fibers." He came, I realized, unable to resist a new word. He took a
long and careful look at the ginger fibers before he returned to his "family," Susie and Lisa. "They're looking at fibers over there," was his report.
Karl observed more carefully than his few words indicated. I knew from
the past that he would use *fiber* with accuracy and appreciation, as if he
had been waiting for just such a word to add to his collection. I remembered the ease and delight with which these same children had acquired
other favorite words: transparent, translucent, crystal, magnifier.

Discussions abounded. One morning, with my help, it went like this:
"Some things had once been living; some were living, like bugs and
leaves; some, like sand, had never lived." Fossils came up in the form of a
fossil shell, and we had enough to wonder about, I decided. "Why no
fibers in sugar?" we kept on wondering. We mixed a bit of sugar with
ginger and cinnamon. Not bad to taste, some thought. One or two brave
ones tasted ginger without sugar and pronounced it yucky. "Poor Pun
Kee, how could anyone like that icky poopy stuff?"

The swing from sense to nonsense being so wide, I was often
reminded of my days as a beginning teacher when laughter and silly
behavior became a threat. With too big a class it *can* be a threat, but the
failure to analyze the role of laughter and nonsense in this early world of
learning is the prime culprit. No class in psychology taught me what children have exemplified: that laughter, playing with new ideas, trying out
silly combinations, humor itself can help us all to sort, file, and recover; to

recombine and stumble into fresh thinking. Good physicists and mathematicians continue this sort of playfulness.

During this year I put into place crucial understandings. Old fears fell away, never to return—never, that is, without my appreciation of how fear comes and of why and what I could do to allay it. To have fun with the world around us, to explore it, to make pieces of it one's own, not like any other's—these concerns were becoming my sturdier guidelines.

Crystals stayed in a focus for a time—they were beautiful. I brought a large single crystal of amethyst to school from my collection. It dwarfed the sugar and salt; it did not, as they did, dissolve in water overnight. I explained to the children how I had found it when walking in the mountains on an old railroad bed. But I had been told (incorrectly, as I now know) that amethyst did not occur naturally in our nearby mountains. So where did this crystal come from? Had someone lost it? Maybe it had fallen from an old train? It was a small mystery the children enjoyed. We didn't know and we would never know. When we put the amethyst beside a sugar crystal it was like a giant beside an ant, and that made us all laugh.

Fresh ginger from a Japanese grocery store showed us the fibers in place. When we broke off a bud, we could see fibers exposed from each side of the break. No wonder we could see them in the dried ginger! Back to the magnifiers, back to the ginger "powder." There we found broken fibers! It was hard to slice the fresh ginger because the fibers were so tough. Ginger seemed to be carrying the message of transformation. (Only later did I learn that we could have planted that ginger and grown our own ginger plant.)

So it went that spring with the children and their teacher. Although ginger was a sturdy thread in the tapestry of our days, it was only one among many. One day near the end of the school year, I brought to school a small tin box of candied ginger. When we held it to the sun, there were the fibers! Long cooking in sugar water had not dissolved them. The sugar crystals on the candied pieces were bigger than any we had seen. A few brave tasters tried them. One of our "scientists" noticed the translucency. A reminiscent chant from last fall began again: "Trans-L, not Trans-P." The candied ginger was translucent, and everyone gathered to have a look at that attribute—light coming through. "Not like glass," one would explain to another. "I know that," the response.

We made gingerbread, which was its own kind of pleasure, for our final party. Everyone agreed that the mixing bowl should not be washed with so much dough in it, so twelve spooners licked it clean. As the smell of baking gingerbread filled the room, it was hard to wait, and every crumb was gathered and eaten.

Abraham Lincoln came to the party, kindness of the D'Aulaires in their story of young Abe.[9] The perhaps apocryphal incident tells of Abe sharing his rare gingerbread men and wondering why the good things of life are so scarce.

The ginger spree, with all its tangents, became a chapter in our shared memories. Echoes reverberated. From easel or clay table one might hear: "Do you like ginger?"

"No!" "Yes!"

"Raw ginger?"

A chorus of "no!"

"With sugar?"

"Yes!"

"Ginger ale?"

"Yes!" "No!"

The teasing and joking lasted and spread, especially around the newly acquired and shared understanding, not analyzed, that one question might not give enough information for an answer. A favorite question was, "Who likes candied ginger?" My reply, "I do," was greeted with giggles and laughter. "Not me!" "Only Mrs. Hawkins!"

We felt so competent and humorous and responsible for structuring each day.[10] In the words of Stendhal, we had become "We Happy Few."

Notes

[1]Maxim Gorky, *My Childhood*, translated from the Russian by Margaret Wettlin (Moscow: Foreign Languages Printing House, n.d.).

[2]Wanda Gag, *Millions of Cats* (New York: Coward-McCann, 1928).

[3]William Blake, "Auguries of Innocence" in *Great English Poets: William Blake* (New York: Clarkson N. Potter, 1986).

[4]Linen thread counters, available through Edmunds Scientific Company, Barrington, N.J. Much more pricey than they were! Eight-power loupes from camera shops will do.

[5]See my references to the young Charles Darwin in Chapter 6, "Trappers."

[6]See "Ginger" later in this chapter for more about word collecting.

[7]In this book there are several discussions of intervention and nonintervention; no simple rules!

[8]Ian MacNair and Ruth MacNair, *Ginger* (Poughkeepsie, N.Y.: Artist and Writers Guild, 1935). The story was written in England.

[9] Ingri and Edgar D'Aulaire, **Abraham Lincoln** (Doubleday & Co., Garden City, 1957).

[10]For further thoughts on "belonging" and its effects on learning, see Kurt Lewin, *Resolving Social Conflicts* (New York: Harper and Row, 1948).

6:   The Co-op School

A year had raced by since those twelve children and I had led our gypsy lives on the road and at the Field School. In that time our family had spent a beautiful half year defined by two fifteen-year-olds, a half-written book of David's, and a hilltop in Michoacán, Mexico.

In February 1957—with our godson Philip, daughter Julie, and a dachshund named Waldli—David and I headed south. Driving through the Four Corners region and a snowstorm, we traveled to Guaymas on the Sea of Cortez. There we were away from the university, the two high schools, and my own teaching.

At least one clear memory of Guaymas remains with me from that visit: two intent teenagers bent over drip sand castles, with dashes into the cool water of the sea, back and forth, busy shedding their teenage sophistication from the North. "One more day," they begged, "just one more day!" These were the two who had pushed us, on the first night in Guaymas, to "leave the next morning."

Mazatlán, Guadalajara, Morelia, Zinapequaro, Tsin-Tsun-Tsan, Lago de Zirahuen, Uruapan: for our yanqui souls, they are names of remembered magic. We stayed long in Morelia, where the younger two happily fraternized and learned to speak Spanish far better than the adults (who had come with some knowledge of the language). We closed our Mexican adventure in Mexico City. Living there was intensely social and heady for the younger ones—with an older teenage group of Mexicans and ex-Northerners, which was called *la flota,* the fleet. There our two quickly transformed their rustic Morelian Spanish into the rapid, clipped accent of the great city.

I refer to the Mexican trip because it intervenes between two years that were important teaching years for me. I have one last and vivid professional record of that trip. As we crossed the border for home, our two in the back seat continued their rapid Spanish to each other and groaned at the first gas station in the United States where only English was spoken. The two youngsters were now permanently at home in a wider world.

While in Mexico I had made no plans to teach, had been too happily engaged with my family and with Mexico itself even to think about what

117

I would do on returning. But then came a call from the Co-op School in
Boulder: Would I reconsider my past refusal to work as their head teacher
for the four-year-olds? I would certainly talk to them about it! I biked to
the school where two parents from the board were to meet me. By the
time I arrived, I was considering accepting.

I was early, and as I waited outside of the old carriage house, memories of the building flooded me. In this small nineteenth-century carriage
house the Unitarian Fellowship still met and rented the building to the
nursery school.

It was to become two happy years of association in which we all
learned and lived together in harmony. The parents ran their part of the
association, and I was the arbiter of how the school itself was to function.
We had only one impasse: this involved the safety of driving and of getting the children in and out of the school building. Two mothers had
appealed to me because others had been lax and even dangerous in caring for children in their cars. No child was allowed to sit in the front seat
(pre-seatbelts), but some drivers disregarded this rule. The same was true
for the role that children were not to be let out or picked up from across a
street. I finally threatened to resign because I simply could not teach professionally in a school where driving regulations were flouted. I shall
never understand why some parents refuse to accept rules that protect
their own children.

When I joined this group, the cooperative nursery school movement
was new, and the first two years for these parents had been exciting, if a
bit daunting. What had occurred, I quickly gathered from the parents,
was an outgrowth of their initial good sense in wanting to break with
authoritarian rules and regulations for their young children. What they
had not yet understood, and hence had failed to provide, had to do with
the positive provisioning—specifically, the necessary *boundaries*—that
would free their children once they came together in groups of twelve or
fifteen. Brief to state, this basic and immediate impasse was marvelously
complicated to untangle and implement. Parents were asking for help,
which gave me a welcome that would delight any teacher.

Tim and his mother, Joan, will give us a taste of the days of preparation. Tim, his mother, and his friend came to the "open house" a week
before school started. Before his mother, Joan, and I could do more than
nod, the two boys had raced up the stairs and did not come down until an
hour later when Joan called them. In spite of his haste, Tim and I
exchanged glances. What he made of me I do not know. What I saw was a
pale, wiry four-year-old with a mischievous gleam in his eyes. It was
enough. I knew we would become good friends.

The carriage house made a splendid nursery school. It was a bit run-down, but everything worked. It gave us two floors with two enormous rooms and two smaller ones, a toilet and washstand, a hall with a hot plate and an old electric oven I brought from home. I spent a luxurious settling-in week before school started: painting furniture, bringing much from my own store, rearranging, and generally transforming things. Parents came with children for a look: when Tim and his mother came, everything was almost ready.

Tim's mother was amazed at the spruced-up appearance and said that they hadn't painted the furniture because the children were too hard on it! We laughed together at this. She noticed all the supplies out on low shelves and warned me that this would never work, the children would use too much, and so on. I asked her to trust me, just to wait and see. She seemed reassured; she soon became a staunch supporter of all we did.

All through that first year I sensed the advantage to all of us of my being older, confident in my past experience. It encouraged the mother-teachers to lean on me a bit, much as grandmothers are meant to be leaned on. I was the ripe old age of forty-six, and recent experiences were fresh in my memory!

Occasionally that day, as Tim and his friend played upstairs, his mother spoke of the wildness of these children and finally about Tim's allergies. She seemed pleased to stay and unburden herself, although not at all unpleasantly. Suddenly, over our heads there was a deafening noise. Tim's mother held her ears. "There is that sitter thing. They love it, I hate it." Earlier I had found that "sitter thing" in a closet and wondered about it. It was a primitive skateboard, made from metal skates with a large board attached. When someone sat on it expertly, it could move across a hardwood floor at high speed. I decided it could not be used because of the potential danger, and no child ever even asked about it.

As Tim, his friend, and his mother were leaving, she turned to me beseechingly and said, "I don't know what you will make of him, he *is* a handful." I liked the way she said it, not unkindly but with compassion for Tim and for me. This chapter is filled with what Tim and I made of each other. It was to be a splendid partnership. I have given some detail about Tim's mother because she represents most of the parents from the Co-op who made my two years with them such a joy.

Tim and Friends

Pinned to the wall of the Co-op School I found a note: "Parents will be permissive at all times." This was the lead sentence of a brief guide to the nursery school's ground rules. Amused at the misuse of "will" to mean "shall"—customary only in the military—I tore up the injunction. No wonder these mothers were eager to have such a laissez-faire routine altered—whether they knew it or not.

With two parent helpers each school morning, including an occasional substitute father, I soon had refreshing new impressions to sort out. It was my first experience as a teacher in a cooperative school, and although parents were present, from day one most of the children gave evidence that their teacher was Mrs. Hawkins. A few changed their behavior when one of the parents was hers or his. Some ignored these parent-teachers, and some showed annoyance at having a mother around (none ignored a father). In the beginning, some of the younger children stayed close to mom. One parent stayed quietly each day for a month.

One mother told me: "Lorie always clings to me and doesn't want to stay without me." But in this new setting, Lorie seemed to have forgotten that part of herself or to have outgrown it. This upset her mother, so Lorie's father became the cooperating parent. This mother was the only parent, to my knowledge, who did not like the school's new ways. She complained that the children were too involved in what we had to offer and were too removed from the fights and squabbles she regarded as necessary, as obligatory for this age. But since the father came to replace her, her intention to remove Lorie must have been overruled.

Father participants were a joy. One once brought a bag of baby bull snakes—to the delight of most, the initial fears of a few. It was a pleasure to watch fears recede as we all got to know these six-inch charmers. Lorie expanded as she held and talked about the snakes. Whenever fathers participated, I observed, there was excitement and a higher noise level. It was a treat, and we all loved it.

The recent years at Field School and at Farm School had not prepared me for the primary impression I gained of these children. They seemed in the beginning to be shallowly engaged, never staying long with any self-chosen activity. We would see how much of this was the result of first-week syndrome, a new teacher, being back with old friends, and making new friends. They had every right, emotional as well as material, to knock at new doors. Watch them become deeply involved.

During those early days, Tim of that first day pointedly ignored me. He would find a friend, and the two might build with the large, hollow blocks near me. If I moved near the playhouse, there the two would appear. I soon realized that Tim was "accidentally" near me much of the morning. Observing and listening more carefully, I realized that his stage whispers to a friend were often intended for me as well: "Let's build a house. Let's go upstairs. Let's go chase birds." Although he seemed to ignore me, I was somehow often being informed of his whereabouts and activities. Was I being honored as the new one, although yet to earn my way?

In this manner Tim continued to structure our relationship. Early on we never spoke directly to each other, but we were aware of each other. If I was working at a table with some children, Tim might be on the edge but not actively participating. I took due note of his independence. I had been told he would only use blocks and race around on a tricycle. I had the feeling that he had thus typed himself as one who "never does" certain things. This is not unusual among conservative four-year-olds. Or the opposite: "I always do that" or "I like to do it that way."

A primary ground rule in the old carriage house was to use the very steep cement stairway only for going up or coming down. The children, I thought, knew and respected the fact that there was to be no stair play. Most did.

One morning early in the term when a few of us were around the piano, we heard two voices above our heads, Joel's and Tim's: "We're playing on the stairs," giggle, giggle, "we're on the stairs!" I looked up at them, sitting there together with mischief in both faces. I knew the gauntlet had been thrown. It was my move. I marked time, not relishing a first confrontation, and said to them in a seldom-used serious tone, "That's enough, get down from there at once and no fooling around!" In accord, the two moved up just one step and again called down their chant "we're playing on the stairs!"

Beside me now the voices were silent, time seemed to stop. Before the two stair sitters could gather their considerable wits for another move, I was up the flight and had two small culprits by two smaller arms, making our way down with no resistance. Through the big hushed playroom and into the back playhouse we marched. When I stooped down to scold them, they both looked already chastened, but I went on: "You may never come back to this school if you are not big enough to know what is dangerous. Your mothers will not allow it, and I will not allow it. Now, you play in here until you feel you can return to all of us. I don't want your little heads to be hurt on that cement."

I walked away feeling like an ogre. But I knew their challenge implied some readiness to ask for secure boundaries. After this episode such dangerous testing ended, and the two also showed a new ease with me and a blossoming of their own abilities. We had all gone through a testing. In such situations what frees most children, I believe, is the acceptance of necessary ground rules, their relieved sense that someone older is in charge of some parts of their exciting lives. Then *they* can begin to take over what is appropriately theirs. Watch these two throughout the year; watch them invent, take responsibility within a framework and context that adults could support.

As long as Tim's challenge to me remained in the realm of "I dare you to interest me," and as long as he maintained enough spontaneity of activity, I bided my time and focused on other children. I was watchful, concerned that he should move on but not concerned enough or invited to try to do anything overt. With the stair episode, they pulled me in. This was a new direction, Tim and Joel had chosen it; hence I could take a risk based on my judgment of what the two boys were telling me through their joint action. They were ready for, asking for intervention, for help—directly and clearly. Such four-year-olds must have great clarity of vision to lead them to such careful choosing of the arena—here the stairs—picking a moment out of time when the significant adult is within earshot and near enough to respond. Judging just how far to carry the defiance seemed deliberate. I had read the situation—correctly this time—as a request for guidance, for clarification of roles. Frederick Allen says it just right: when help is asked for, the first half of the battle for self-help is won.[1]

Often we err on both sides of the spectrum of response. Who among us, teacher or parent, has not known this? We fail to understand or take seriously the deep meaning of such behavior, such challenges on the part of a child, challenges that show us some of her or his capabilities. We then ignore or punish or placate, beg or plead—self-defeatingly. The atmosphere within which such challenges are made is, of course, of the essence. Unless there is mutual trust or the expectation of it, until great expectations are the order of the days outside the use of such challenges, we as the adults in this equation will move without guidance. The risk of response I took with Tim and Joel was informed by other children's actions and, peripherally, by these two in my immediate care. Otherwise the risk would be too great and could lead to transforming children's testing and seeking guidance into covert alienation or overt manipulative behavior.

At the beginning of this chapter I wrote jokingly about the rule the cooperating mothers had written: "You will be permissive at all times." Was this only a reaction against heavy-handed authority? It represented a beginning of wisdom, surely, but a meager one. In a lecture I once attended, Anna Freud herself confessed with great honesty that children brought up in ultrapermissive households seemed to acquire many of the same developmental troubles and later neuroses as children from traditionally authoritarian backgrounds. [2] Her father's theories had seemed to imply that the lessening of brittle adult authority would lead to healthier and happier child development, and she now felt this was too simplistic.

She did not, however, take the further step, to ask whether either of these two stereotypic categories—"authoritarian" or "permissive"—has much scientific or human value. Such patterns of parental behavior, when dominant, can be equally damaging—through coercion in one case and neglect in the other. Boundaries are essential; but those we define can be accepted, internalized as self-discipline, *if they are understood as boundaries within which children can still choose, explore, and thus flourish.* If no such boundaries are provided, then "permissiveness" can be read—by children as well as by observers and teachers—as indifference and neglect. And if children can so read our behavior toward them, the consequences may indeed be little different from those of the undiscriminating use of the heavy hand—which forces children to withdraw the kind of "misbehavior" that should be read as a plea for attention, a cry for help. In both cases, then, children are deprived of the very kind of adult support their young lives require.

Even when we have confidence that one has acted with good sense for the particular child, it is still reassuring and necessary to watch for confirmation in the form of that child's subsequent action. For both boys in my story, this episode was even more of a release than I had anticipated. I say release because of the speed with which they moved both toward and away from me. These two were freed from being preoccupied with my sheer adult presence and hence could seek me out for assistance or to share some happening or phenomenon. It is as if certain children become fascinated with and fixated on their power over consenting or otherwise helpless adults. The web woven by the addition of Tim's allergies to a complicated family structure produced some such inevitable distortion. Parents are often caught in these tangles, as too often are teachers and therapists.

Tim was ready for a new kind of relationship, and he achieved it in a new school and with a new teacher on terms that were mutually satisfying.

This is a kinship related to but separate from that of child and parent. It was to become one in which Tim thrived. Unless a co-op has an experienced teacher who is unrelated to any of the children, such new bonds may be harder to achieve.[3] Tim ended his transition period and entered a wider world with a sure step. I shall try to show what he made of it, with his imagination and energy (watch Tim throughout).

Tim could suddenly take or leave school offerings, he could try anything he wished, unrelated to adult offerings—within accepted boundaries. That was new and sweet, to him and to me. The hollow blocks had always interested him, and for awhile he became the architect-in -residence for buildings big and complicated, which one hated to dismantle at morning's end. He and friends could construct a fire engine so real that one watched it "arrive just in time to rescue people" and property and then slowly cruise back to the station. We had plenty of props: fireman's hats, ladders, rubber hoses, sirens; we had child firemen and excitement. Sometimes one wondered whether that structure didn't really move. Was there no smoke, were there no flames? For the children, there were no such questions. They were writers and actors and audience of a chosen scenario, concurrently.

And then Tim discovered paper and scissors and the stapler. From the very first he could transform a small beginning suggestion. I had shown a group of children how to make a "whirler" by cutting a spiral out of a circle of construction paper. With a thread knotted and run through the center, it made a sort of spinning kite on the end of a string when one ran with it or swirled it around one's head. Tim had made one or, rather, in quick succession he had made about seven of them.

Next, he took a large rectangular piece of paper and started to cut it into a square spiral. But instead of turning his scissors, he cut off his strip. Protecting his first strip, he quickly cut another and another and so on until he had cut the entire paper into a bundle of rather thin strips. Then one by one he stapled all the strips together. We were delighted and amazed at how far it would stretch across the room. "I can make it longer!" he asserted, and he did just that by cutting another piece of paper that was the same size into even thinner strips. With many staplings end to end, this one stretched on up the stairs. A nice piece of geometry, that. With young children one does not ask what things change and what stays the same through such a transformation; a sort of answer is there, however, for later harvesting. But one such innovation can spread and trigger more; soon other children were making all sorts of whirls, measures, and shapes. I learned that a popular request among these children for Christmas was a stapler.

A dear young friend, Karen Weisskopf Worth, a teacher of teachers of young children, said long ago, "Frances, you must tell about what you did and why, not just about the children!" I try to do so, especially in cases where children's performance has seemed to me in need of diagnosis and decisions on my part. This was the case in the earlier challenge from Tim and Joel.

My part in the story of scissors and staplers is of a different kind and may deserve some amplification. How does a teacher lead up to those doorways of invention and discovery that children may then open? One absolute is the provision of good materials, tried and tested or invented along the way. In my training I had been introduced to the uses of such materials. Scissors, paper, and paste—then and now—were part of the traditional kindergarten stock. We learned how to teach children to make things; nice little prescriptions but ones that were rather set. Along the way I had come to realize that the most important early learning developed when a child's work deviated from the pattern, often by accident. Such deviations can become starting points for fresh invention. The old tradition was the fruit of much past experience, still good for starters, but it was also limiting. The whirlers were that kind of starter, although I think they were my own invention, something to run with.

Most four-year-olds need help in learning to staple, and I spent some time giving it. After his invention Tim took over. I beamed to hear him explaining the stapler to a beginner: "When you push down, there are two bumps." I learned from that. Many would stop pushing after the first "bump," and the staple wouldn't go through. Tim could teach.

Investiture

There came a morning when I was witness to a process I had not specifically seen in school. One of the Babar books was the take-off, and it happened like this.[4]

Zephir will be remembered by King Babar's fans as the loyal friend of that rascal Arthur—Babar's cousin. A strange Horatio figure perhaps, but not so strange in the early world where friendship is being tried out, sending down roots: already familiar to boys like Tim and his cronies.

Because the Babar series had become a favorite, I brought a stuffed-stocking monkey one morning and introduced him as "Zephir" who wanted to listen to a story about himself. The long-legged fellow sat on the piano ledge while we read about "Arthur and Zephir."

I closed the book, and for a few seconds we sat in the still content-ment that can follow a good story. No one spoke, no one moved. Then quietly Tim walked to the piano and removed Zephir from his perch: "He's thirsty." No one showed surprise, and when Tim carried Zephir to the playhouse we all followed and arrived in time to watch Tim fit Zephir's long floppy legs into the doll's highchair. He opened the cup-board and found the teapot and a small cup. After putting the cup on the highchair tray in front of Zephir, he poured imaginary water into the cup and held it gently to Zephir's embroidered mouth—no spills. Tim turned toward the attentive audience with a look that seemed to say, "There we are, he *was* thirsty." Surrounding the ten or so children there was—if I interpreted correctly—silent awe and admiration.

Tim had breathed life into Zephir, and we had been witnesses to that investiture. For some time Zephir traveled with Tim. The highchair often came along to allow Zephir to sit upright by himself; Tim would explain, "He wants to sing with us."

But Zephir developed more needs, and not until the episode of the three-poster bed did other children feel Zephir might be shared. One of the mothers reported that Tim had arrived in the carpentry room and announced: "Zephir needs a bed." This was by no means the first request of our carpenters, Joel and John, who were often in the workshop. They would tackle anything and with hard work could manage to produce a respectable product. (See the next section, where Joel makes a loom, and "Nancy," later in the chapter, where Joel makes a stage for Nancy's pup-pets.)

With dispatch, Joel selected wood from the supply box: one flat rect-angular piece for the bed and three tall pieces for legs. He attached a leg at the middle of one end and two on the other end, near each corner. The bed legs were long and stood above the bed, as Joel left them, which made it a three-poster bed. Zephir could lie in it with his long legs hang-ing and resting on the floor: "Ya see, Mrs. Hawkins, if ya don't saw off the posts it's better, he can't slip off." Joel was an expert at explaining why his ideas or projects were the way they were. He was usually logical and right. Tim beamed, and the carpenters admired their three-poster bed—steady as only three legs can be. No covers, no pillow, no mattress, but in the land of make-believe a good primary prop suffices. Joel reminded me of a child in an article by Hans Otto Storm: "Children, when they con-struct things in play, normally play after the eolithic fashion: a painted board suggests the making of a boat, and the toy, in the process of con-struction, begins to look less and less like a boat, it can be conveniently turned into an airplane."[5]

At first Zephir was content in his school bed overnight, but Tim decided he would be happier if he went home with him each night: "With only a guinea pig at school, Zephir gets lonesome." The guinea pig only needed to go home with a child on the weekends, but Zephir was different. He now went home every night with Tim.

As Zephir's status became established and his needs were expanded and met, his popularity grew. There were accompanying pleasures and problems to be shared, discussed, agreed upon. A list went up for taking Zephir home for the night. The children had accepted, without a single question or gesture, that Tim was Zephir's natural parent in some way, and so Tim in return could show generosity. I have come to believe this stemmed from his being at peace with his creation and all it had added to our already rich communal life.

One sees this kind of generosity more and more as one learns how to help children expand the concomitant pleasures of competence and of contributing toward sharing. It stems from the climate and from the variety afforded by the environment. Almost no child lacks this potential for generosity. It is inevitably intertwined with his or her necessary - to-growth selfishness. When the child has enough, she or he can give— not as a sacrifice but as a further extension of what it means to have. Abuse breeds abuse, nourishment encourages nourishing. We know this, but it is nice to have our children exemplify it in class. To see it is another of the sure forms of evaluation, not superimposed by the teacher.

With the list growing for taking Zephir home, Tim had fewer turns. His thoughtful and imaginative mother solved the mathematics of one monkey for fifteen children. She made a duplicate, and Tim arrived one morning with two Zephirs and a wide grin: "We have two Zephirs now, my mom made him." The *we* is significant. *We* did have two everyday at school that were shared and played with by all. Tim took his Zephir home with him at night but never forgot to bring him back for others to enjoy. The twinning was a happy solution, and Tim's mother—whom I had met that week before school opened—had provided the imagination and skill to bring it to pass.

I Made a Loom

There was a good reason for building a loom, even if one were to forget in the excitement of watching our own "cloth" grow on the apple-box loom. With a linen thread counter on a string around her neck, Alexia had put the magnifier on the arm of her shirt and seen the crisscrossing individual threads. "It looks like rope!" All had to see, and the four magnifiers were kept busy so each child could see his or her shirtsleeve or sweater or a leaf.

The children had used and seen wonders of enlargement before, but this morning carried a special attribute, which I understood as no mere enlargement but as a transformation. Somehow threads, string, and rope were different when woven or knit. For most of the children the concept of *emergence* was new, and it was unexpected, judging from the reactions I saw. At story time we read *Pelle's New Suit.*[6] What else? I expected that this already favorite book would take on a fresh life, and it did.

We skipped nothing: we reread, we soared, we could do it all. "And," said Joel, "we could build a really big, big fire out back in our yard to dye it," in his eye the special gleam of roguish anticipation of that forbidden fire.

Appropriately absent from all this was any mention of what we would weave, or was it taken for granted that it would be a suit? These four- and five-year-olds were true to a universal for their ages: they did not worry about a finished product. Plans just spilled out. "An' a sheep, ya hafta have a sheep for the wool." "Where would he live?" was my spoilsport voice. "With the guinea pig." "But the cage is too little." "We could build a bigger one, couldn't we?" Finally came the voice of experience, of James, who had seen a sheep: "A sheep is pretty big, Mrs. H., I saw one on a farm an he was bigger than me."

I joined in all of this with no thought that much would come of it. Back we went to the book, staying now with the picture of the skeins of blue wool, already dyed and hanging on lines. For almost an hour we stepped back in time, across the ocean to Sweden, and breathed the damp forest air around Pelle's farm. We followed him as he searched for help and information to get himself a new suit. It was an hour of travel, a morning of ephemeral plans. There is indeed "no frigate like a book."[7] I was prepared to call *fini* to that lovely time, so satisfying and complete it had seemed in and of itself.

What did evolve from such a start was more exciting than anything I might have planned in advance. Perhaps my reluctance to get into weaving was useful. I had a seasoned disrespect for putting the young to weave. Too many dusty unloved ruglets had crossed my path.

Because the children pushed, we made a trip to a nearby farm where we knew they had half a dozen sheep. Some of the children wandered and watched ducks, chickens, and a tethered cow, but Steve and Joel spotted a ram and went toward his fence. I was as impressed as the boys with this monster. Because the ram stayed near the fence, the two "inspectors" could stand safely next to the animal. The farmer encouraged them to pet him. I reached through to the heavy gray coat—but not the boys.

Reality came with the enormous ram, but only to rethink and revamp plans. Size and scale could not be overlooked. Guinea pig looked awfully small in his large cage. Listening to their talk, I realized that the ringleaders of this weaving affair could and would accommodate. Others were about their own pursuits.

By this time, with my growing understanding, I knew enough to realize that we would happily stay for awhile in that fanciful time of plans when anything is possible. It is a phenomenon among the young to be cherished. We could trim our sail when necessary, when the pace of our work demanded it. First, I have come to believe, children thrive on having enough time to let their imaginations run wild and free, to play with ideas. A happy few adults in art and science know this sort of playfulness that precedes great breakthroughs.

Yes, somewhere in all the high-flung plans the decision had been reached that a rug was needed for the playhouse. We retraced some possibilities. Pelle's mother's loom was a large four-harness floor loom, rather like the one my husband and I were just learning to use at home. We went to my house to see the real loom. Like the ram, it overpowered. Floor pedals were pressed, the wool handled; but our back garden, with stepping stones and a juice-and-cracker picnic under the one pine tree, pushed the inappropriate loom out.

Two books about Navajo children and their lives showed us a much simpler loom than Pelle's mother's or than mine at home. Ann Nolan Clark's book for older children, *Little Navajo Bluebird,* contained clear pictures, and I could easily paraphrase the text. What pleased us was the picture of a loom "Uncle" had built for Doli next to her mother's loom. Here in Navajo land, other children were learning to weave. From then on Sweden receded for awhile, and our own American Indians became our guides. (Swedish ways were less foreign culturally than Navajo ways, but the loom was the thing.)

With some trepidation on my part and none on the children's, we began a loom. On a wooden apple box, with its sturdy ends, we hammered in fence-post staples, twelve on each end and not very close together. What surprised me was the kind of possessive delight some children quickly developed in their loom. From the first staple, the old box became our loom. For some time it led a life of its own: it was carried from place to place—the yard, upstairs, to the piano if we had music.

Just as surely as the investment in Zephir, the stocking monkey, had taken place (see the previous section), this bit of string, some nails, and an old box held magic for those who had heard about, imagined, hunted for, and now put together a real loom. It did for me, too. Margaret brought a large cotton-boll with seeds in situ for the seed collection, and we were hard put to imagine that the strong warp of the loom was spun from such fluffy white cotton. (I remember that collection of seeds in plastic bags with amusement. All hands contributed from time to time, and one or two like Margaret felt a proprietary interest. Charles Darwin reminisced with amusement about his own early collections: "I just wanted to have another kind of beetle in those early days. . . . I had no other interests early on."[8]) How the young, who are going around the clock for the first time, rely on their age and developing individual styles to examine the world!

The morning of color—of dyeing the white yarn—surpassed any plans or expectations of delight. We used dye from small packages, hot water, and smooth sticks for slow stirring. Everyone had a long turn. No one refused to help dissolve the powder before we put in the white skeins.

We suspended lines from walls and furniture. We had no leaves, only newspaper to soak up drips, but when the wet skeins were festooned and most hands were blue or red, there was high excitement. Only in retrospect did I analyze that it was not only the color dripping but also the curves-crossing-curves of yarn on lines that transformed the downstairs of the old carriage house. I have learned to call them "catenaries" since that time and have gathered some knowledge to bolster my early appreciation of their habits. I hope the festooned nursery school is filed in the memories of some of those now-past-thirty-year-olds.

We all felt something of what dyeing has given people since ancient times: a sense of power and wonder. Even the children who were not engaged in the weaving itself were captured by the transformation of snow-white and fluffy yarn into fierce red and brilliant blue.

Color itself intervened in the form of food colors in water, poster paint, "real" paint (which had been used to repaint the old tricycles), and the color we used to mix the dye. Remembering the joke on Pelle when he asked the house painter for paint to dye his yarn, we tried it ourselves. Try it yourself on a small bit of yarn. Water-color paints made shadowy shapes on old pieces of sheet or on paper towels, where they led lives of their own if used generously.

The drops of food colors in water were what then captured our fancy. Tall glass milk bottles, still used in the 1950s, displayed the color action well. (Clear plastic is safer and is available now.) The blue drops fell faster than the red, and we were amazed at how long it took for drops to mix into the water if the water was initially very still. I can see four bottles on top of the piano left to mix themselves. "Not yet," someone would announce, "not yet." Of all our "experiments," the action of red color dropped carefully into swirling water was the favorite: it was like "upside-down fire." Again and again we watched the liquid "flames" pulsate up, down, up, down. Many times we made our own show of color in water, mixing or just watching.

We returned to weaving. The dyed skeins of yarn dried quickly at our altitude. Since the loom was ready and waiting, we could start. Almost. First the warp had to be tightened, then a long wooden shuttle brought from my supplies, and finally we needed a wide-toothed new comb for a reed to beat each new line of weft. The younger children especially loved beating the weft. The comb pushed the latest weft strand into the rug so one felt like a weaver. In addition, those who couldn't weave could beat.

In the beginning, most of the children had "tries." But four children became the daily weavers, the faithful ones. Others might come for a lesson, some to "make like weaving." Joel became an expert, as did Alexia, Nancy, and a couple of others. Some few never picked up the shuttle. Steve was one such refuser, Tim was another. Only the men weave in Hopi land in Arizona on top of the mesas, but in our school weavers were of both sexes.

The small rug was growing in spite of early mistakes, and my expectations were met by the alternate blue and red stripes of different widths that seemed well along to being finished. Not to Joel. He came to me one morning: "Ya know, we haf ta put the pattern in *now*." We had never discussed such a thing. I had no idea how to put one in and told him so. In fact, at first I simply said I didn't have any idea how to help him. With a certain disdain, Joel met my statement: "Well," he countered, "we could find out, couldn't we? We could get a book, we could read how to do it."

Together we did put in a pattern, Joel and I. We got a book and learned how to set in two triangles point-to-point in Navajo interlaced style. The triangles were red in a blue stripe and were off center, but Joel and I thought they were rather elegant. When we had finished the background stripe, Joel announced it better than I could: "It's a pattern! It's a pattern!" he yelled, jumping up and down.

And suddenly it was time to cut off the rug. Many hands were ready to help—to tie the fringe close to the weaving at each end and finally to stand on the finished product, which barely held two small feet. Not Joel's. I had shared his wince when the first feet stepped on the rug. Joel quickly grabbed the rug in his hands: "I know, we could hang this one on the wall in our house and weave another for the floor, a bigger one." Who could resist such an enthusiastic presentation?

There never was another rug for the school, but about three weeks later Joel came to me from the carpentry room with his hands behind his back and a serious face. "I made a loom"—and with his words brought from behind him a flat piece of wood, perhaps eight inches square, with brads on two ends. As I tested the nails for steadiness, he continued: "Ten on each end, I counted 'em. It's to take home." And home it went, a simplified variation, ready for the warp.

One admires a five-year-old mind that selects from its growing storehouse of ideas—in this instance, foreign, primitive, grandiose, and simple. Selects and makes, as humans are meant to do. When young children so thrive, sometimes one and then another, we as teachers have our feedback. Such evaluation has the ring of truth.

Nancy

Nancy entered a month after school had started. Although there was a rule that children had to be accompanied by a parent on their initial morning, I was not about to follow it with this small, wary four-year-old. Send her home? Not welcome her? Hardly. She walked cautiously into the big room but did accept my offered hand. I took her with me on my rounds among the children.

In Nancy's first hour we wandered together, being helpful or just stopping to observe. If my hands were needed, Nancy stood beside me and watched and waited for my hand to be offered again. I had little feedback from this silent one and assumed, incorrectly, that she knew no English but felt at ease because she accepted my hand. I took Nancy's staying with me and our hand-in-hand communication as a giving of trust to me, as she meant it to be.

Juice was ready on a table, and we sat side by side with other children around us. Watching it all carefully, Nancy ate two crackers and drank the juice. I was impressed with this child's reserve, her acceptance of help offered, and her observation of what this school offered. Quite a bit of integrity there. What else, I wondered?

It was a warm morning, and most of the children went outside to play. Some stayed in. We watched one boy finish a painting at the easel, stow his painting, and then leave for outside. Nancy dropped my hand, walked to the easel, pointed to the brilliant array of paints, and, looking directly at me, asked, "I?" With a delighted grin, I answered something like, "Yes, you paint now, Nancy, it is your turn." I realized that we had just looked at each other for the first time.

Turning her back to me with slow-motion deliberateness, Nancy took a brush and carefully painted a large red circle, within which she slowly painted a line mouth. Dipping her brush for each eye, she painted them blue. Standing back to look at her creation, Nancy saw the blue begin to drip slowly from the eyes. With awe and delight in her voice, Nancy turned to me saying, "It cries!" We both watched and shared this small miracle.

I showed Nancy how to remove and stow her painting and thus to uncover a clean sheet, and then I left her. Her mother came early; she was pleasant but offhand, and yet I thought she seemed pleased that Nancy had enjoyed school. "No," she answered my question, "Nancy had never painted, only used crayons." I went with Mrs. A to where Nancy was still painting. Before her mother could speak, Nancy turned and looked at her, "I come back?" Mrs. A reassured her. Hand in hand the two started for the door. As she clutched her paintings, I heard Nancy repeat, "It my school. I come back."

To our delight, Nancy did come back to "her school," bringing intact her individual ways. She concentrated on the artistic aspect of school and thereby enhanced it for all the children. She transposed daily affairs into forms of dancing, painting, drama—on her own terms. In the beginning she shunned large groups. She might briefly join one for a story but would quietly withdraw if too many children came together or if the situation went on too long. Dancing in tutus pleased her if the group stayed small, but if too many wanted to take part Nancy would withdraw. I felt she was able to judge just what she should be about and was able to find it in "her school."

The informal puppet shows became Nancy's métier for a long spell. Two of the boys had constructed a sort of stage, and the supply of hand puppets with props engaged a happy few, including Nancy. One morning I sat in the audience as a lion puppet tried to sit in a chair that was much too small. Again and again the lion might knock over or fall off or push away the offending chair. The audience followed every move with laughter and appreciation. The audience and the puppeteers changed

constantly. On that morning Nancy became, or rather held, a kitten puppet and introduced a scaled-down sneeze. It was catching. Audience
sneezed, puppets sneezed, I sneezed . . . everyone careful to relate the size
of the sneeze to the size of the puppet, with giggles in between tiny
sneezes.

Nancy's early integrity held in other ways too. No child could make
her do anything she did not want to do. But she respected other children's good ideas, so Nancy was soon courted by others. Valerie, who
tended to be bossy, would try to advise or trick Nancy to join her and
take orders as other children did, but Nancy was quietly agile in refusing.
As her time at the school continued, I noticed that Nancy no longer
avoided large groups.

Perhaps the puppets Nancy loved encouraged her to bring and share
a treasure from home. It was a small replica of the three monkeys: see no
evil, hear no evil, speak no evil. She introduced the monkeys with a formal description, "You see, this is seenoivel, this hearnoivel, and this is
speaknoivel." Regardless of whether the children understood, they listened with respect. Only later did I learn that Nancy's pronunciation of
evil was Old English.

Trains and Planes

What struck me first one particular morning was a sense that a shift
had come: away from the early days of "where is it, he pushed me, I can't
find my other shoe." Nancy's hand took mine: "You play?" she asked
with her enchanting Norwegian accent. We walked to the piano. "I sit?"
she asked climbing into my lap, and we were off. "Lou, Lou, skip to my
Lou, skip to my Lou my darling." "Got me a cat, cat pleased me, fed my
cat under yonder tree." A small group gathered, and other favorites were
requested. From John: "Play the train music, and make it go far away,
Mrs. Hawkins." "Early in the morning, down by the station, see the cars
are standing all in a row. . . . Do you see the engineer pull the great big
throttle? . . . choo choo choo choo, off we go."

As the train went further away, hardly heard behind the mountains,
Steve registered his pleasure: "Ye-e-aa!" Others joined, Nancy climbed
down from my lap, song and tempo changed: "This train, this train is
bound for Glory, this train." We didn't know any more words, but we
could sing it near or far. By controlling the accompaniment and adding
a running dialogue, I kept the growing-audience train from chaos as we

listened for the train to come out of a tunnel, down into the valley, and slowly pull itself into the station. The steam—pshush, pshush—was deafening.

Suddenly the train's two engineers took over and called out: "ALL ABOARD, ALL ABOARD, this train is bound for Glory." To avoid having wrecks occur in the limited space, I suggested chairs and slowed the tempo to allow one more chair-car and still another. The lovely four-year-old intertwining of building, riding, accommodating, singing, and traveling was underway. Legs straddled the forward "car," but no one minded in the delight of such a long and curving train, "jus' like a real train."

"ALL ABOARD" but not quite. "Wait, stop the train, we got to have tickets." Most sat comfortably in their seats while the two conductors (how had they emerged?) dashed away for supplies to make tickets. Strips of colored paper were cut ticket-size into rectangles and "sold" to the passengers. The conductor punched out holes. "Punch, conductor, punch with care, punch in the presence of the passenger." Did I remember that from Mark Twain? "A red strip ticket is a five-cent fare, a blue strip ticket is a three-cent fare, a yellow strip ticket is a one-cent fare; punch, conductor, punch with care."

"This train is bound for Glory" but not quite yet. "Wait . . . wait . . . a caboose, it comes last, and it's red—always." A red chair was dragged from the playhouse and hitched on, but before we could take off into the mountains Valerie shouted, "Stop the train." After a pause she added "and don't start till I get back." All on board waited expectantly, watching to see what this sparkler was up to. Dragging the small yellow table with her and carrying a basket of dishes, Valerie returned: "You have to EAT on the train." Many hands moved chairs and helped set up the dining car while the music played a holding tempo until I finally called out, "All aboard who are going aboard."

But not yet—a softer voice than mine took precedence. Already out of her seat, Nancy turned on her way to the playhouse: "I get the food?" That Norwegian accent and politeness stymied even Valerie, who only called: "No, Nancy, remember I'm the one to get the food, remember?" Nancy disappeared and reappeared with a small suitcase, a baby, and a blanket. All watched as she made a bed in a chair next to hers, tucked the baby in, and nodded to me that now the train could start. Valerie's face reflected a connoisseur's pleasure, with a touch of envy. This was a new experience for Valerie, one no adult teacher could teach, only a shy Nancy.

Before we steamed off, two other "mothers" rushed to retrieve forgotten babies, but finally we waved goodbye to the nonexistent children on a phantom "platform" and slowly climbed the mountain. After curves and tunnels and long calm stretches with piano and songs in the background, we returned to the station where teacher-mothers waited to greet us. The children showed a reluctance to leave this trip behind and moved almost in slow motion, held by a sort of wonder at our trip together. [9]

To be part of such a day, of such play, is to be a participating bystander, an appreciative one. The far gaze on these children's faces I read as engagement—engagement of imagination, of the artist's eye to block, out or in, some essence from reality. At such moments, children seem to enhance their immediate world with the use of transformation, of juxtaposition, of new ideas put to instant use. Such play is a litmus test of appropriateness for children in their early world, when time and place and those minimal stage props come together in some liberating unity— the unity of drama. Mothers have consulted me because they have felt uneasy when a child of theirs had so little ability to play in this way. At the other extreme are children so constantly caught in this fantasy world that one is also concerned. But so it is with young humans who are already whole, already potentially able to lead rich and appropriate lives.

At home that night I was reliving the morning with relish, analyzing my own appreciation of its significance as I now do here, retelling the story. In my mind's eye I saw the young Pablo Picasso building, riding, playing in a train such as ours on the streets of Madrid. He never forgot it. Some of his drawings and paintings reflect that kind of juxtaposition, superimposition, and movement mapped I had been witness to: a child's delight and use of imagination to overlay a lesser reality. This morning I had seen minds inventing, total engagement, suggestions from one child leading to transformations and contributions of others. No wonder children's eyes glaze over with that faraway look. It is a look of wonderment, of appreciation for some human abilities . . . perhaps their own?

Renoir, with his artist's memory and eye, created children's portraits that carry some distilled essence of childhood. But then my thoughts jump to an earlier Spanish favorite, Francisco José de Goya.

The Goya child who lived in my memory is in the painting *La Familia de Carlos IV*. He is the smallest in that royal family portrait, with a wary look on his three- or four-year-old face. His hand is within his mother's; hers is almost flaccid, his is holding on. The later history of this child, Carlos Maria Isidro de Bourbon, who lived during a time of wars and violently oppressive orthodoxy, was indeed that of a life of fear. Goya caught it all, early on. It is consoling to find artists who can notice, who see and leave us evidence that we are not alone—we who work with children in classrooms and become privy to their fears and early inventions.

I come closer to home, where we lucky ones remember our own childhood. My grown brother Leonard, a physics graduate student, came occasionally from Stanford to visit my San Francisco kindergarten. After one such visit, we were reminiscing about our childhoods. Something about seeing these children triggered a twenty-year-old memory for him that he had never told. "Remember," he began, "how we would watch for a plane to take off from the Presidio?" "And then," I continued, "we would yell 'planes! planes!' and race up our hill to keep up with those low-flying, open-cockpit planes of pre-1920 vintage. Our day was made if we raced one plane."

The Presidio was at the end of our street, Twenty-First Avenue, and after takeoff the planes flew low over us. "Remember? Did they wave to us, Leonard?" "We thought they did!" he laughed, and then he told me of his connected fantasy. "I found a plank in the basement of just the right size to use as wings on my coaster, to transform it to a plane. I was very excited. I remember, when Mom would ask me to go around the corner to the market, I would decide whether to travel by slow car or fast airplane. For the plane trip I had to hold the plank on to the coaster, and that slowed me. I knew that; but still, I usually opted 'to fly' because airplanes were faster!"

Leonard became an experimental physicist. But built into his adult self was a playful approach to invention. Long before the august National Safety Council acknowledged such matters, he dramatized the importance of the automobile seat belt in scale-model, quantitative terms. When he was physically incapacitated by multiple sclerosis, a younger physicist, Keith Harworth, and my husband, David, had helped him with the experiments and the written reports.

Leonard did all this using an elegant but simple experiment-to-scale. This elementary experiment, or series of experiments, involved a scale-model study of automobile crashes and of what happens to the human occupants of the cars. A small wooden "car," big enough to hold an egg, was hung by two strings several feet long, as a pendulum. Hanging still, it would almost touch a brick wall. Pulled back through various distances and then released, it would crash into the wall, each time with a calculated velocity. Eggs with "seat belts" would break at much higher velocities than the unbelted ones, and these results could be translated to the impacts of cars with human occupants. Eggshells are roughly equivalent, at their size and these velocities, to human bones at realistic car-crash speeds.

This translation generally agreed with known accident statistics and pinpointed their cause with a simple demonstration of Newton's laws. Physicists already knew these causes, of course, but official and popular imaginations had been unwilling or unable to grasp the reality of high-speed impacts. And as often happens in matters of health and safety, many years elapsed before car seat belts appeared. Leonard's report was turned down for publication by the official journal of the National Safety Council, with no criticism or explanation. But years later his eggs did finally appear; some editorial conscience had, perhaps, revived. The early national seat-belt campaign, when it finally did get underway, used dramatic pictures of Leonard's eggs, unacknowledged, in their little pendulum-cars, the playful quality intact—a quality that is sometimes vital when we try to reach beyond our imagination's everyday grasp.

Trappers

Quiet Margaret's soft voice called us: "Come quick, they're here." Children tiptoed to the low window in time to see the flock of sparrows still feeding at the new station. "They sure do like it!" This was proud Joel, and all of us knew that by *it* he meant the feeding station. Joel's interest in birds was secondary to his affection for the station. He and John had been the master carpenters, transforming a large, three-foot square of plywood into this ungainly but serviceable feeder.

From the first hand-drilled hole, Joel had seen the feeder through to the finished product. "We drill in each corner, John; that way you get two to drill and I get two; me first." But once around led to twice around and, hence, four holes for each driller, eight holes finished at last: "This way ya go down a hole with the string and up a hole." It worked well, as he had foretold. At times like this I understood Joel's mother's remarks about him, not always made with pleasure: "He is always one jump ahead of us." Both boys used the arithmetic easily, as well as the drills.

To hang the feeder in the small elm tree outside the low window, more than two climbers had been needed. The tree was the right size for the children to climb and to secure, with help, the cords to branches. Leveling became a challenge. We worked as best we could by eye, but the first time the feeder was securely in place, the round seed rolled off. I brought a carpenter's level to school, with its captured bubble to tell us when all was level. The level remained at school in the carpentry room with other real tools and gave me a chance to share Robert Louis Stevenson's poem, "My Treasures," with the children:

> But of all of my treasures the last is the king,
> For there's very few children possess such a thing;
> And that is a chisel, both handle and blade,
> Which a man who was really a carpenter made. [10]

The bird watching surprised me. To watch birds go about their winged affairs requires such patience and stillness that it almost excludes the young. I asked myself what was so propitious about the timing and setting during that particular fall.

Some bird feeding must long have been associated with our building—an old carriage house with a loft. From the first days, flocks of sparrows seemed constantly, expectantly near. How long since the loft had stored and spilled from an abundance of hay and grain? We dwelt on that small history together.

As is common, some children only chased the birds at first, Tim leading. He would conspire aloud with deep satisfaction: "Come on, let's scare the birds." Three or four would join him in running toward the flock until all of the birds took flight. To vary this response, we began to throw out seed. Teasing the bird scarers evolved: "Only my baby scares the birds." After such taunts, more might join with Tim, responding "we are babies, come on, let's be babies." In these early years it is so important to be big that it was refreshing to have a ringleader like Tim who preserved the high spirits from those innocent earlier years when action was everything. The birds were undaunted in their perpetual search for grain; they were quite used, as city birds are, to being chased.

Fall came early that year, with winter soon to descend, and, we decided, it was as if the squirrels and birds had been getting ready, collecting and gorging themselves on the bursting seed pods and grasses. The population of busy harvesters in the form of squirrels inevitably caught the children's and my attention.

What kinds of seeds, we wondered at first, were those noisy squirrels stuffing into their cheeks and carrying off to hide? We began to answer such questions for ourselves. We watched, and because it took such patience for a squirrel to glean every seed from the long pod of the locust tree, we knew one kind of seed.

With such an original spur to our curiosity, a seed collection was begun. Small plastic bags were hung on a big bulletin board, and the display sharpened some children's awareness of the abundance around us. Two or three children found this collecting of seeds for its own sake just the thing. Quiet Margaret was one of these: she brought back a prize from a trip to California—a two-foot sugar pinecone that hung like a prehistoric monster beside the local varieties, which were much smaller although so similar in structure.

One morning Margaret's mother laughingly reported that Margaret was making their family aware of seeds—apple, orange, and others—that had been coming to school for display. The seed collection never went anywhere; we just collected. Much later I read *The Life and Letters of Charles Darwin*, written by his son Francis, and was delighted to find this quote in the grand old man's memories of his early days: "With respect to science, I continued collecting materials with much zeal, but quite unscientifically—all that I cared about was a new-named mineral, and I hardly attempted to classify them."[11] I remembered those many small bags of seeds with their names below, occasionally with a picture of the parent tree. We had, without knowing it, a distinguished precedent for just such unscientific collecting.

In observing and being a part of these children's ways with seeds, squirrels, birds, and old trees, I was often struck by the contrast with the children at Field School the year before last who had a totally different delight in the world of seeds and animals. Welcome evidence of the variety of responses from class to class, from child to child, remains one of the major and sustaining joys of knowing such a continuum of young children, as a long-time teacher does. How can the burying and masking of these differences continue under the aegis of narrow lesson plans and stiff models? No wonder there is so much teacher burnout, so many children lost, dropping out early because of boredom. And no one ever noticing each person's uniqueness.

Before that collection of seeds could gather dust, some of each package went onto the feeder to add to the commercial provisioning called Wild Bird Seed. We bought the latter in rather small packages because it was so much fun to make a trip to the feed store, where birds and small animals were also sold. In addition to our wildlife, we had other stock to provide for: the resident guinea pig. Commercial green alfalfa pellets were Guinea's (as we called him) staple, but faithful providers always supplemented this dried stuff by bringing fresh lettuce, carrots, or apples. Every weekend Guinea went home with one of the children, and although he was handled by the children in school—covered and pushed in a buggy—he seemed to thrive. When the weather allowed and we could be outside, Guinea went out too, into his makeshift corral—large hollow blocks around the choicest patch of green grass. It wasn't such a bad life, we decided.

During the year the understanding grew that all of us were responsible for this one small animal. I remember the abundance of fresh food brought after we had used hand lenses to look at a crushed alfalfa pellet. It was dry, pale, and certainly not fresh, like growing grass. So we took Guinea out at once to graze. We eventually began to see ourselves in the lives of our livestock, tame and wild, as providers—thoughtful providers. It was a heady new role for some of these children.

So it is with any group of children.

One day another happy accident flew into this arena. Lynn called out rather calmly, "There's a bluebird eating on the station." Most of the children were busy elsewhere, so this announcement brought only me running, but just in time to see brown sparrows leaving . . . with a flash of blue? I wasn't sure. "You scared 'em, Mrs. H." I certainly had.

Two or three others joined Lynn and me to watch, and I had time to wonder whether a mountain bluebird had been separated from the flock they always travel in. I was telling the children about these mountain birds when the sparrows returned—and a blue bird. No mountain creature, this blue beauty; it was a brilliant blue parakeet, minus tail feathers, who seemed very much at home with his adopted family of sparrows. I think I was the most excited of anyone—the world of the young is so rich with the unexpected or the previously unseen.

The parakeet separated itself on the feeding board of necessity. With his curved claws he gripped the edge to have access to enough seeds. Then, in a flash of feathers, they were gone, and Joel whispered: "Ya know what? We could catch that bird and . . . we could sell him." I turned to look at Joel, jolted from my reverie and trying not to laugh at his proposed business venture. How could we sell such a bird? It had escaped from someone's cage, it was a pet, and so on. How could we think of selling it? What had I said? We didn't have it.

For some days it was enough to watch this brilliant fellow return to the feeder with his modest brown companions. But inevitably we began to plot. There he would be on the edge of the station while the sparrows walked around and ate from an abundance and variety. The feeder was close enough to the window to allow us to see how the parakeet's claws curled under and thus prevented him from walking like a sparrow. That knowledge was exciting. And then, at a group time, Alex, who was already such a careful observer, gave us an "illustrated lecture" on her grandmother's parakeet's claws. She had looked very carefully: "There are claws that curl under like this." In her curled fingers we saw a claw like a parakeet's, and then, with palm and fingers almost flat, "and some go like this"—sparrows, of course.

In all of this observing and learning, the parakeet ceased being someone's lost bird and became ours. Such ownership of the wild, unobtainable but beloved phenomena may be a preface to delight in museums and their treasures. On a ferryboat from Victoria, British Columbia, to Seattle, I once met a young David, just two-and-a-half. We shared certain of the marvels of that four-hour trip, such as the three black-and-white dolphins or killer whales who jumped, high above our wake, for a good half hour. With small David's parents near and my David watching, we threw bread to the faithful seagulls that followed us for the entire trip. But it was the faithful, more distant moon rising and rising in the eastern sky that young David recognized as an older friend. He announced seriously to me toward the journey's end, with the proper caution in his voice, that I should respect his prior ownership: "It's my moon . . . my moon." With my ready agreement, David was satisfied as he turned toward, pointed to, and watched *his* moon rising in a darkened sky. My nearness was allowed.

Once the parakeet became ours, he became ours to catch. One mother laughingly said, "Why Frances, the children think they are going to catch that silly bird." As a member of the conspiracy, I could only answer that they just might be right and let her remain the doubting Thomas.

The first attempts to catch the parakeet were guileless. A child would simply sneak up and try to grab him. Even a tame bird is more wily than to allow that mode of capture, but somehow I felt these enchanted neophytes deserved a time when their initial plans could remain independent of my sage advice. (Besides, I didn't know how to capture that bird either.) No harm stemmed from the futile attempts, no one was discouraged. The parakeet, we observed, was much tamer than the sparrows, a fact that engendered hope among friends. Glued to the window, we would watch the quiet approach of a tiptoeing child, hold our breath, and console the empty-handed returnee. The difference in behavior between wild sparrows and a recently gone-wild parakeet gave us much to think about and discuss.

One morning Alex proudly brought an old green cage. Expectations soared. We baited the cage with seed, carried it to rest on the station, and rushed back inside to watch and wait. The plan was to wait until our bird went inside to eat, and then a child would tiptoe to the cage and close the door. Voilà! No one doubted that he would enter; after all, he was used to a cage and would like the wooden perches for eating from the seed cups.

To the delight of the children, he did just that. At first, it was enough to relish the fact that the prediction had come true. No one dashed out to capture him. Instead, we admired his ability to navigate within the confines of the small cage. As we had also predicted, no sparrow entered the cage. Finally, Joel could wait no longer. Quietly, he let himself out and edged toward the cage. Throughout his approach the bird stayed seemingly unaware but not, it developed, so incautious as to be caught: off went the bird. Someone remained on guard most of that morning. The parakeet returned, entered, and ate, but not one of us was fast enough to trick him. Even I tried, but with no success.

If this enterprise had been the best or the only path, my inclination to step in with more realistic plans would have been irresistible, but I was in tune with these beginning plotters—these four- and five-year-old trappers—and they indicated no need for any closure to their often unrealistic but engrossing scenario. After the cage fiasco, I saw no discouragement but rather an appreciation of the parakeet's artfulness and the challenge for us to invent another scheme to match it. Was the bird too clever? So far he had been.

There was a clumsy, halfhearted attempt to fix the cage door so it would close by itself. We realized that was the secret—a trapdoor. This insight or conviction was followed by the making of traps. These efforts resembled no trap I had ever seen, but to the designers and builders they were somehow traplike. They hardly left the workbench. They required tens of nails to hold trapdoors or drop doors together. Carpenter Joel got happily sidetracked and made a door for a "real house" with enough of a frame so it could open and close. He and Joe followed this with a sort of window that could open in a sort of frame, and Joel took both home. It's nice to have such carpenters in residence: they invest tools.

The object imagined or built to accomplish some real but difficult goal was itself to be honored. Even with this well-defined goal—here, of trapping a bird—caution not to push for early closure remained my responsibility as a teacher. This episode clarified my growing understanding of the need to protect early buds of imagination. Adults' imaginative ways of posing and solving problems, of painting, making music, or living well have, I am certain, significant origins in just such playful explorations of possibilities and fancies during childhood.

The cold was nearing, and I felt I needed to talk to a bird expert. I called Mr. Hough in the Classics Department, the only bird watcher I knew about in Boulder, to discuss our happy predicament and the urgency I suspected the impending cold weather presented. He assured me that if the parakeet were outside in the first frost he would die, and he offered his own live-bird trapping cage.

I brought the trapping cage to school the next session, and as had happened before, interest in the bird receded. For almost the entire morning the cage usurped our attention. Everyone wanted to examine and try out the elegant but simple mechanism.

I felt the power the children's failure now exerted. To invent such a mechanism had been beyond them, but they had tried, they had a vision. Hence the admiration and excitement—some had wrestled so gallantly with trap mechanisms. As the young do, they loved the sense of honesty that belonged to this new group: trap makers.

The trap was a marvel. Seed was placed in the seed holder, fingers were placed gently on the perch "like a bird," and that light pressure released and closed the door. It had two entrances, two doors, two perches, two seed cups, and wire between the two compartments. "What if we catch two birds? Aw, sparrows don't like cages. Where can ya buy such a cage, Mrs. H.?" We decided that Mr. Hough had not bought it but had made it, all of wire. Something about that discovery was sweet to these beginning trap makers. They were connoisseurs, inspecting, reminiscing, dreaming.

Finally we could part with this workable trapping cage long enough to try to rescue the parakeet from the future cold frost. Two children carried the trap to the station, two baited it, and two set the doors open and ready. At least two children remained glued to the window for the rest of the morning. At about eleven o'clock a watcher called softly. The birds were on the station. A crowd gathered and watched the blue parakeet go into the cage and then onto the perch by the seed cup. He ate his fill and left. The door stayed open. There was wild discussion of why this had happened: he didn't weigh enough, try again. With the bird gone, we checked the cage, and all seemed in working order.

It was time to leave for the weekend, so we called on our neighbor, whom we knew because she had given crumbs to the birds, and asked her to ring me when we had caught a bird. Only an hour later the telephone rang. "Mrs. Hawkins? You have caught yourselves a bird." I appreciated that plural usage. She had the cage inside her house and reported that the parakeet was pretty frightened. As I drove to retrieve our catch, I regretted the timing. Why had the cage not worked when the children were at school?

The frantic bird in the cage went home with me. He must have been free for many months, because escape seemed to be its only concern. I telephoned a few of our key birders, who spread the news.

Monday was a celebration day and one for admiring the parakeet. By then the bird was "tame," quiet. To our amazement, a happy accident occurred. "He" laid a small egg. Quiet pandemonium reigned as we rejoiced in her abilities. The children knew we could not keep the bird but would take it to the pet shop. Joel, however, did not give up. "We could sell the egg!"

We all took the bird in its cage to Mr. Korfaze's pet store, where he added to our mood of elation with a contribution of his own. He knew an old lady, he told the children, who wanted a parakeet very much but who didn't have enough money to buy one. He would give her this beauty free of charge! "The egg?" asked Joel. Mr. Korfaze assured us that very few parakeet eggs hatched. We left the small egg with him and returned to school, more confident now of future happy accidents.

John's School

Among all of the memories of the first year of the Co-op School, that of John Wilson (as I shall call him) has a secure and heroic place. The other fourteen children were experiencing ordinary growth, development, and learning with individual gusto; they are part of the fabric of this story. But John brought with him society's crushing effect on a family that happened to be black, one that was joining the graduate student academic world of the 1950s.

John was the second of four children under age six in his family. He was the recipient of the Co-op's scholarship, awarded each year to a minority family. His older brother, Ralph, had received the scholarship in 1957 and was in public kindergarten during the year I write of, 1958–1959.

I met John and his father on the first Monday morning of school. Mr. Wilson and I shook hands. Seeing the shy, immaculate child standing so still beside him, I invited Mr. Wilson to stay with John. "Oh, he'll be all right," was the response, and off went John's father—no nod, goodbye, or touch between the two. John stood still, eyes on the room, and did not move from where his father had left him. With such an introduction and brief leave-taking, I felt John had a right to stand still and not be bothered for awhile. I touched his shoulder with affection as I went to another part of the room I tried to keep him in sight, and he was certainly in my thoughts.

John did not move for a long time. When I took him a small red truck, he reached for it in slow motion, held on to that truck until his mother came for him almost two hours later. During the morning I noticed that he occasionally mouthed the truck but did not suck it. Not since Ronald, in my 1936 kindergarten, had I seen that gesture in place of sucking.

John made no contact with the other two teachers or with me apart from taking the red truck when I offered it to him. A small group went upstairs with me for records and stories, but John stayed downstairs— loyal to his original spot. During juice time I offered John a cup, which he took in his free hand but didn't drink. My notes tell me that I thought he was aware of much but was unable to move. I don't know how he disposed of his cup of juice. Perhaps one of the other teachers, in pity, took it away.

When John's mother came to pick him up, John saw her, turned toward the door, and walked slowly to the car. As John approached the car, he simply released his hold on the red truck and dropped it on the sidewalk. He had barely moved in well over an hour.

That first morning set John's basic pattern for the next couple of weeks. There were minor changes. He would move to stand near me and whatever group was working with me, clutching any object that was given to him. Sometimes I greeted him with a hug; he looked so forlorn, standing alone, so still and so constrained. At first I expected some resistance—stiffness, perhaps? In stepping out of my usual role of teacher, I hoped to get some clue about this silent and statuelike four-year-old.

I continued to give John a special and warm greeting because I believed he showed a subliminal response of pleasure. How, I now ask myself, did he show what I took for pleasure? Was it something in his eyes? He certainly did not smile. Was it finding him near me more often during a morning? The evidence was minimal, but the thawing was self-initiated. He *had* moved, and my confidence in his eventual breakthrough remained strong.

To appreciate the steady, resistant role this child maintained, one must be reminded of the other children's actions and explorations. The wild ones from last year had, from the first day, been heady with new worlds to structure. The fire engine of hollow blocks, with ladders and hoses and fire hats, had to grow to accommodate many more firefighters, boys and girls. It finally took up so much space that we had to move the tables we used for drawing and cutting and stapling.

Dancing took over in a new way because of Terry. Her love of dance brought her a coterie. We had tutus that could be tied over ordinary clothes. It was a joy to see unself-conscious Greg with a red tulle tutu over his jeans and cowboy shirt, dancing!

So in these first weeks, many activities were tried out in our old remodeled carriage house. From the slight evidence he gave I felt John liked to come to school, although he remained almost immobile. At first I tried to stay with a group that was involved with an activity near where John stood. Working with such a small group one morning, I handed John a big piece of colored paper, and he held it in his free hand. He stayed near, he observed, he looked at the paper. Progress!

Another morning I took John by the hand when a small group and I were going upstairs. He came along, but he needed much help from me on the stairs. Whether this was because of muscular weakness or unfamiliarity with climbing I could not determine. The other children and I sat in a small group on a blanket for a story, and John stayed near with his truck, also sitting but banging the truck on the floor. Before I could signal a concerned teacher to let him bang, she tried to entice him to go with her downstairs. At first he ignored her; then as she persisted, he came near me and, looking at me, said in a loud, toneless voice, "Nooo." I gave John a silent bravo. He continued to play with the truck, and we read our story. He stopped banging—to listen!

John's behavior in the first weeks stood in stark contrast to the other children's; it was a pale strand among brilliant ones and thus more discernible. John's mother did not participate as a teacher until the Friday of the third week, so I had not talked with her. During the third week before she first came, my notes on John looked like this:

1. Parents did not come to first night meeting.
2. John can talk.
3. He *seems* to have very poor muscle coordination—large or small.
4. He comes to and leaves school spotless and unruffled.
5. He has a *good* stubborn streak. That, to put it positively, may save him.
6. He ignores and is ignored by other children. My genuine, overt affection gets to him (I believe this, although I cannot know for sure).

7. He has never used the toilet or shown any discomfort at not using it.

8. He occasionally sits near me but usually stands—psychic fatigue—his fatigue must be great.

9. His general health is good—no runny nose, no absence from school.

10. I have seen him watching a child paint, but he refuses if a brush is offered to him.

11. The stiffness of stance, or refusal, evaporates if I take him in my arms—he is like a rag doll.

12. I cannot forget that he is a member of a lonely, striving family in an almost all-white community and graduate school. It is 1958: the Cooperative parents last year tried hard but reported to me, "We didn't do much for Ralph," John's brother. I count on my San Francisco years to help me here and look forward to becoming friends with John's mother at school.

These notes are almost verbatim with what I wrote during the first weeks with John. I have deleted only what I consider to be too speculative or intimate and not necessary to John's story.

When Mrs. Wilson finally came, I suggested that she devote her time to John, which she did. She got him to paint, to play in the sandbox, and generally to try much more than he had done before.

John's painting was like a two-year-old's except that it was neat and controlled—not surprising for John. He put on the paint, and then his mother would change the paper and he would continue on the clean sheet in an almost trancelike state. At least he was painting!

Mrs. Wilson made some magnificent origami birds. She did not expect the children to make any, knowing they were too complicated, but the children loved them, and we hung them on the "chandelier" we had made for the children's work. Hanging from a bare ceiling I-beam, the chandelier could be lowered or raised by a rope and pulley. Such I-beams have their uses and should be left uncovered! John stood near, with his mother the center of an admiring group. Mrs. Wilson was at ease and was obviously pleased with the children's response.

After school, another participating mother was critical of such difficult objects being made. She missed the higher priority, which was Mrs. Wilson's pleasure and, consequently, John's. I was misled that first morning, however, and saw John's and Mrs. Wilson's tie as stronger and more

reciprocal than it actually was. Much later she spoke to me of the gratifi-
cation of getting to know her child thanks to the school setting!

Back, now, to how it worked from morning to morning or even from
hour to hour. I left John alone often and measured his growth by his ability to join a group or at least move to the edge of it at his own initiative. I
still hugged him and, at the right moment, I hoped, I would push. One
must learn different approaches with each individual child; there can be
no formula or substitute for tentative trial and error, for analysis of the
different dynamics involved in the child, group, and adult settings. John,
in spite of himself, began to try. He would walk outside with the others if
the door was left open for his return. If he was offered a paintbrush at the
easel, he would sometimes paint, but I did not see this activity as something that caught him.

He used the toilet at least once, but I didn't see or help him, nor did
any other teacher. Margie had reported at home: "You know, John has a
voice like this"—she imitated the very low register, indeed like John's
voice—"and he is all brown, all over . . . even his behind." She had seen
him go to the toilet one morning, she reported.

With the cold weather coming in November, we began to use the
large room upstairs for the more noisy and boisterous play. A specially
designed tabletop was turned into a slide. There were small sawhorses
for riding and big boxes for making bridges. There were beanbags and
traffic signs to keep tricycles going around instead of into each other.
(Almost everyone learned to read Slow, Stop, Dangerous Curve, Children
Crossing, and so on.)

But for John, all this offered a different and self-invented pleasure. He
endlessly pushed around a small sawhorse, like a two-year-old. Unlike a
two-year-old he seldom bumped into anyone or anything, thus showing
his maturity in that regard. Was this his first use of both hands together? I
think so—it was the first I observed.

I now felt secure enough with John to insist that he come outside with
us, even interfering with his sawhorse pushing. I wanted him to taste the
boundaries of a school that, although easy about many boundaries, still
had some: no child, for example, left alone inside. He balked at first but
came along, and I felt he was becoming increasingly aware of the reality
of the nursery-school situation and, in so doing, was creating a new role
for himself. Shortly after my insistence on his going out, he selected and
looked at a book on his own. Bravo again, John!

In the early days he did not enjoy being with a story group, although
at his own initiative he came with us up the stairs and even climbed into

my lap occasionally. I did not believe he really listened at first, but I was happily proven wrong. So trucks, sawhorses, stories, and human interaction gave me confidence that we were on the right track. I was confident that he liked his school, but I didn't know for sure until this episode occurred.

Mrs. Wilson came to get John one morning after he had been absent twice, and I remarked that I was glad he was well again. "Oh," she assured me, "John is almost never sick. It is the only way we can punish him—to keep him out. He loves school so." I swallowed a gasp and asked what he had done that required such punishment. She responded readily: "He is so stubborn—won't eat his breakfast on time, won't get into his clothes fast enough. Spanking doesn't faze him, so his father just told him he couldn't go to school unless he changed his ways."

Now, Mrs. Wilson told me this with no awareness that it was a shock to me. I begged her to use some other punishment and told her how we missed John and how much he regressed after he had been out, that it took almost a morning for him to participate again. By this time Mrs. Wilson and I were building a friendship; I tried to make my response as off-hand as possible so she would not feel my genuine misery at such a tale. I think it worked; we *did* become friends, and John didn't miss as often.

There was still almost no conversation from John. He was silent except for an occasional "No!" in that deep voice. I surmised that he could talk, but I did not hear him do so until there came a breakthrough.

But another kind of breakthrough preceded any language communication, and perhaps with John this sequence is significant. How can one be certain in the realm of a disturbed four-year-old's self-pacing for development? John had stood next to me at a table of children who were cutting, stapling, pasting, and hanging. There had been that flurry of cutting spirals out of round, fairly stiff colored paper, attaching them by thread to a short stick, and then laughing at our spiral "kites." Some twirled the sticks above their heads or ran with the spirals twirling behind them.

John stood beside me, silent and watching. He had been such a faithful observer of the various paper activities that I took a chance and put the blunt scissors in his limp hand, held a paper within the open blades, then closed his fingers so the scissors cut. He dropped the scissors the moment the cut was complete. He looked at the cut, and I said, "It cut." That was the extent of the conversation during the next ten minutes. John picked up the scissors, closed them to cut, and dropped them. He did not move any other part of his body—just his hands: pick up, cut, drop; pick up, cut, drop. From then on, John added cutting to his growing repertoire of accomplishments, everyday for awhile, then tapering off. He did not make *things,* he was just cutting.

I remember well the second time Mrs. Wilson came to participate. After the first hour of work and play, I asked her if she played the piano. Her response was a broad smile and "I love to play; I was a music major at college." What an hour we all had! She played anything requested by the children or me, and we sang or danced or clapped or all three. I had only to hum a tune, and Mrs. Wilson was carrying us off to that world of music that she loved and could create for and with us. Was John pleased? I think so, but this was his mom's morning. The next time I saw her she volunteered, "I really enjoy participating this year." We hugged each other.

John was absent too many times before the holidays, with no reason given when he returned. The first day back to school after the holidays there was no John. No John, that is, until suddenly the door opened and a grinning little boy in a cowboy hat stood looking at us from the doorway with his mom behind him, both beaming. Still grinning, John took off his hat, threw it into our circle, and called out, "I comin' back to *my* school."

And so he did. He came, he saw, and he continued to conquer. My further notes on John show a steady joining into school activities, with ups and downs but mostly ups. One or two high points will close this saga of a gallant little boy at nursery school.

Mrs. Wilson and I became friends, and she shared with me many miseries as a result of racism and some joys. With too little progress having been made by the 1990s, we still must ask, with J. P. Comer and A. Poussaint: "How have black children fared since Emancipation? . . . They have consistently borne the devastating effects of white racism. Many have shouldered the double burden of growing up poor and black. Some have been damaged so severely early in life that their chances for a happy, productive adulthood have been small." [12]

One day at a story time we were on blankets on the floor, with John on the edge but listening. The story was *The Red Balloon,* which was becoming a special book for these four-year-olds. [13] I was still paraphrasing and shortening the rather long text.

There was a chorus of "read it again"; Gregg added, "and read it *all.*" Everyone settled in, so I was confident we had reached the time when I could indeed read every word of the text. I loved the attention and pleasure of the eight or so children. Another chorus: "What is a pupil?" And we laughed at that other word for *us!*

Such a session usually ends with the quiet of joint appreciation, and so it was on that morning. John broke the quiet with a little joke, knowing it was a joke: "I not a pupil, I a boy." We all laughed with him while he smiled as other children picked up his lead: "Me either, I'm not a pupil. Me either . . . a pupil. I'm a girl. I'm a boy." Watching John's face was to share his triumph.

We ended school with a picnic in the mountains and a day of hiking and exploring. Mrs. Wilson was one of the five volunteer mothers, and together we watched John climbing fences, racing across meadows, wading, digging, laughing—a pupil or boy—in his own school on a mountain.

The following year John's mother sent a kindergarten picture of John, smiling broadly. "John likes his kindergarten, although it is not as good as his nursery school." For me, the lasting character of John's progress was assurance that he had truly helped himself and his family. Would it be enough to enable him to continue and to thrive in this racist country— This is not a question a teacher can answer—except to say that he had already found his own great strength.

In the Hall of the Mountain Queen—And Southward to New Mexico

Was it Terry, our dancer, who tapped my own early dance memories? Or was it Greg—Greg with the red tutu hastily tied over his jeans, gliding or leaping, his delight in movement propelling him at any moment unself-consciously among us? We had two Gregs this year, Greg and Gregg: "My name ends with two 'g's,'" he always reminded us. Greg the younger one was less talkative. (Basil's whirlwind joy had lived again and again in my memories, he who had brought the Russian Ballet to Emerson kindergarten in the thirties. Nearer in time our daughter, Julie, at age sixteen, had been dancing for three years with an Austrian teacher. Her friend Gretchen and she had needed no reminder of their weekly lessons, where they were the oldest and the tallest.)

When old memories are braided together with newer ones, wisps become strands that can grow still stronger. With the dance, which expanded this year in the Co-op School, my four-year-old San Francisco self once again knocked at the door. I stand in the cold but enchanted basement of St. John's Presbyterian Church. My shivering comes less from the cold than from excitement—thin, black slippers and in my two hands a thin wooden rod. Once my feet move to music, that memory is gone. How did this brief interlude come? What stretch of early life does it represent? Any clue is lost or deeply buried, but I keep the fragment, it does not fade. That early and joyous awareness of commitment is something I value as a teacher of the young and as an avid lover of ballet.

It is not always clear what spark ignites a group of young children to invent and extrapolate, but with these children and the dance, there was no mystery. We had Terry. Quiet and shy at other times, Terry was transformed when she danced; she took most of us with her through dance into a world of make-believe.

Within days Terry had gathered around her a troupe of girls, an auspicious beginning. What circumstances encouraged the unfolding that brought this new life as the weeks went on? As is often true, I find a cluster of possibilities.

In the beginning Terry and her "school" danced to a piece or two from *Swan Lake,* especially "The Dying Swan." They danced, watched, and repeated before an appreciative audience of boys. In the early sessions, only the girls danced.

Hunting through the records one morning I found Grieg's *Peer Gynt Suite*—kings, mountains! I knew the girls would welcome it, and it might catch the boys who sat there on tables and sawhorses, watching contentedly. (These records had somehow just appeared. To parents, bravo!) Only a brief verbal sketch was necessary—storm, morning, kings with their court—and there before our eyes it all came alive. Although the boys did not join the dance at first, I had a sense they wanted to. "Will you, won't you, will you, *won't you join the dance?"*

"Props," I thought, "we need props." So I called a sewing bee of parents together; bought tulle and other materials, ribbons, and artificial flowers; and in one evening six of us made tutus in rainbow colors of tulle with clusters of artificial flowers on each. We made gold paper crowns, many wands for wielding—with silver stars on the ends—and cut soft black wings that fit onto arms. Another bravo for parents! Little did I realize at the time where those wings and a new dancer, young Steven—who at first had not even watched—would take us.

"The play's the thing wherein I'll catch . . . ." and so we did. For many mornings there were "performances": actually snatches from *Peer Gynt Suite* that might not have been dignified as performances except by the dancers themselves. We had four kings with wands, clusters of tutus, winged creatures hiding in under-the-table caves sleeping through Norwegian storms; morning waking, stretching, and calm. Program music was written for the child in us all, certainly for these children. Terry, who listened and interpreted and invented, was our guide and in every sense—for a beautiful time—our inspiration.

After a particularly long session one morning, the children collapsed beside me on the floor. I thought at first that it was only fatigue, but as I put an arm around Terry and the other around Alexia, I felt wonder—did the children also feel it? Terry certainly heard the music transformed within her and followed it with delight. To some degree she was sharing not only her dancing but also her beginning understanding of this ancient and primitive art. We were all enriched.

The music and the dance still echoed within some of us that morning, and I began to speculate about what it all meant, what it was telling us. Fear of the storm? Hiding to keep safe? How the stretching told of morning, as did the music and the calm? And then I reminded them that you don't always use words to tell or to communicate.

Humor took over! Covering my mouth with one hand, I waved with the other; of course, I was "saying" goodbye without talking. And then I frowned, and the boys especially yelled: "You're mad, Mrs. H.! She's mad!" So we giggled. Faces tell! Greg put on a wide grin—he's happy. And what about "surprise"? With that we all looked at each other and fell to giggling again.

After some exploration I stood up to signal that it was time for arriving parents. No one wanted to leave. Their need to continue was so clear that I sat down again, wondering how to end without spoiling the mood entirely.

It *was* time to leave, I reminded them, but I would tell one last short story about creatures who communicated without words. I had read recently about the circling and wagging dances of bees and the beautiful investigations of Karl von Frisch. [14] To these so-recent dancing philosophers, a telescoped version of how bees tell distance and direction made interesting copy. I promised to bring in the story from *Scientific American.* "You mean bees *tell* that way?" Alexia's voice carried wonder and amazement for the whole group. "Gee!"

There was quiet, and then Gregg, who until recently had been only a faithful observer of our dancers, got up and shuffled along the floor in his heavy oxfords, giving his realistic interpretation of a bee doing one of its dances. "He prolly goes like this." After a few inches he stopped and wagged himself in a most incongruous imitation of a bee. But it was not incongruous to even one child: all eyes were fixed on Gregg's next move. He preceded a right turn with two waggles. "If he's gonna turn this way, he's gonna do this." Others got up and experimented with new signs.

Finally, downstairs went the bees. But apparently they arrived as children; there seemed to be no trouble with child recognition by mothers. The speed of metamorphosis!

The next morning I brought the *Scientific American* that tells and shows bee communication in the story of the Rundtanz and Schwanzeltanz. As the children arrived I wondered who, if any, would remember. Gregg and Alexia came in together, saw me by the piano, and ran over. "Did ja bring it? Where is it?" "Did I bring what?" I teased. "Oh, you know," Alexia smiled, "the bee story."

I pointed to the magazine "for later." Off they went until after juice time. After gulping his juice I watched Gregg carefully retrieve the magazine and wait for me and the others. I noticed that newcomers to the dance of the bees were gathering too.

Those who had been part of the earlier discussion enlightened the newcomers, who hadn't heard the amazing tale. I was delighted to listen too. Alexia, Gregg, John, and others enacted and told it in rather great detail; they certainly *had* listened and remembered. Finally we began our magazine research.

Diagrams and pictures were pored over, the magazine was passed from hand to hand, and odd bits of new information emerged from the children's own experience. Alexia had eaten honey from a honeycomb and had noted the shape of the individual cells. With a stubby piece of chalk she drew a tiny hexagonal figure on the blackboard—technically a difficult feat. We counted the six sides and added "hexagon" to triangle and square and circle: new ideas, new words.

"My brother is already six, and my sister is even older," interjected Tim. Joel added his mundane but accurate observation: "But you know, that sticky stuff, yes, that wax, I don't like it—it sticks to your teeth." "Yeah, I like it better in a jar—no wax."

The dance finally urged us past these interesting byways, and back we went to dancing or signaling bees. We explored other, more human ways to signal. We explored hand clapping; fast could mean run, slow could mean go slow. On and on, good sense and nonsense intertwined in this four-year-old world of inventing: clapping hands, stamping feet, turning around. And, I added, no one else would know what they mean except us!

Embedded in these minds were still more possibilities and variations not scheduled, not planned. One morning when Anita was with the dancers, she introduced her first language—Spanish—seeing the relevance of another way of talking. With Anita's help we practiced how to count to ten and reviewed how to say yes and no. *Si* was easy, but Anita insisted on a clipped Spanish vowel sound for "no." I sang from my high-school Spanish memory: "A donde a donde ha ido mi perro, a donde a donde se fué?" "Oh where oh where has my little dog gone, oh where oh where can he be?" Our appreciation for Anita grew. She could speak and understand *two* languages! No one learned very much Spanish, but Anita's mother came to school one day, and we made flour tortillas and learned how to shape them *de mano,* by hand. Anglo parents asked for the recipe because their children demanded Mexican bread such as we had made with Anita's mother. From dancing to tortillas and back again went the good life in nursery school!

Frank Luther's "Trip to the Zoo" was revived and had a new reception. "And when I clap-clap-clap my hands, the monkey claps-claps-claps his hands, monkey see and monkey do, the monkey does the same as you. And when I shake-shake-shake my head, the monkey shakes-shakes-shakes his head, monkey see and monkey do, the monkey does the same as you."

Some mornings we had to divide the group in half, because with so many choosing dance there was not enough individual space and time. Both boys and girls now danced. The sawhorses were saddled and ridden to Wyoming, with records of Agnes DeMille and Aaron Copland. I added favorites of mine from home, such as a Mozart horn concerto, and watched the wild dancing to that beautiful music—Terry, Greg, Tim, Alexia, Anita, John, Gregg, and even the cowboy Steve!

Another happy accident occurred that altered directions and broadened horizons. Steve stopped me one morning. He had taken no part in the weaving, but he had obviously overheard our talk of Indian weaving because he said: "My Dad has *real* Indian records." We were all impressed. What did that mean, what were *real* Indian records?

Steve brought to school next session a field recording, and the children heard for the first time the high Pueblo chant and watched Steve begin the characteristic deliberate footwork: toe-heel, toe-heel . . . another form of the dance! Steve and I had independently watched such dancers not far south of Boulder, but Steve and his dad had brought the haunting chant to life by dancing at home themselves. Some of the children joined Steve while others sat, listened to the recording, and watched with awe— an awe, I somehow sensed, that bordered on fear. Nothing quite like this had been experienced by these four- and five-year-olds. Recorded in the field with a natural setting for a background—no walls—the monotone chant is sung to a repetitive beat by the drum accompanied by rhythmic steps pounded on the hard ground. There *was* fear in some faces and a pushing even closer together while we listened.

My familiarity with and admiration for the Pueblo Indians along the Rio Grande allowed me to become an interpreter but only partly to allay fear. I felt a need to do this, but I was not certain how to proceed. Then young Jim showed me the crucial first need: to recognize and talk about the fear. Jim climbed into my lap, something he had never done before. But when he felt threatened, as he did by this record, he knew from his home how and where to seek comfort—with an adult. I held him close, talking to another child. But then Jim, with a gentle touch, took my chin and turned my face toward his, saying with trepidation: "They won't come out of the record, Mrs. H., will they?" Reality for the four-year-old, we know, is a sometime thing, even for Jim, already a good reader. Holding him closer I reassured him that they would not come out, but, I said, "The record is such a good one that it *sounds* as if they are close and could come out."

Jim's courage in speaking about his fear that the Indians might come out was received by the others with respect and some empathy. I decided that others' fears might need some defusing and began to tell of my family's last visit to see and hear Indian dances. It had been at Santo Domingo Pueblo where many Indian children had danced in the plaza, along with the adults. As soon as the Indian children came into the story, into the dance, attention and listening began increasingly to replace anxiety. I could see it and feel it.

"After we watched the big dance," I continued, "very much like the one on the record Steve brought, David, Julie, and I took a walk among the adobe houses where all those children dancers lived. And there, outside their houses now, practicing without any drum, were the children, still dancing, their bare feet pounding on the ground—toe-heel, toe-heel, toe-heel, just like Steve's record! Some were very young, only three, but they were trying to dance just like their daddies and mothers and grandmothers and grandfathers. They still wore their costumes of small embroidered blankets and held fir branches in their fists. And then, one grandfather came out with his big drum and played. Big children and little children gathered, because they all loved their dancing and their grandfather who beat the drum."

More than once I had to repeat parts of this memory, elaborating on details as I felt the healing effect and the excitement of the *children's identification with the Indian children dancers.* Even at a distance, around three hundred miles, a far older culture spoke through its children to these children. Without pictures but with sound and a storyteller, this new bridge was being built. It was not until later with the children dancing to this insistent beat—toe-heel, toe-heel—the record of accompaniment—that I saw the strangeness of this different culture first fade and then be embraced.

In my teaching that year, this small history was a special joy. One always carries a strand of sadness for these native people. The culture of Pueblo Indians along the Rio Grande, still intact in the face of terrible odds, was and remains a talisman of courage.

Some of our props, the wands, became essential for the Indian dancing. With a wand in each hand to give the deer four legs, I showed the Indian way of being a deer. Pictures of the Eagle Dancers called forth the black wings. So it was that Batman was finally eclipsed, along with Grieg. On the first such morning, eagles flew with the deer as our own two drums replaced the phonograph. I can clearly see the eagles soaring as they made their way among the slower deer.

I hope a sense of history was begun. Early roots may not be remembered, but they must exist when later learning thrives, as it does in some. On any morning now we could take off southward to New Mexico, back in time, dancing our way or looking at pictures and following stories from my own and Steve's experiences. For me, this represented the role of grandmother. What grandparent does not know the joy of responding to the demand, "Tell about the time when you were naughty" or "when you hid from your brothers in the laundry box." [15]

This chapter has led a life of its own in the telling. It started with Terry and her ability to communicate through dance rather than through words. When the Rundtanz and Schandtanz bees took over I thought that would be the end of the theme. But when the living is good, live children have a way of extending or of asking for help, and live teachers are needed! Steve had brought his recording of another kind of dance—one that existed close to us in miles but that traced back through great stretches of time. No wonder these early Americans dominated our dance for awhile. We were in touch, however briefly, with the flow of history—an awesome experience for any age.

Notes

[1]Throughout this book I refer to Frederick Allen's emphasis on the significance of "asking for help."

[2]Anna Freud lectured at Radcliffe College in 1952–1953. See note 3.

[3]See Anna Freud, *The Writings of Anna Freud*, vol. 4, 1945–1956 (New York: International Universities Press, 1968), pp. 75–94, where she answers teachers' questions. For the psychoanalytic view of children in early schooling, see pp. 560–564.

[4].Jean de Brunhoff, *Babar and His Children* (New York: Random House, 1938).

[5]From Hans Otto Storm, "Eolithism and Design," *Outlook* 4 (winter 1971), pp. 37–43; quoted p. 40. Reprinted from the *Colorado Quarterly* 1, no. 4 (winter 1953).

[6]Elsa Beskow, *Pelle's New Suit: 1874–1953*, trans. Marion Letcher Woodburn (New York: Harper & Row, 1928).

[7]Emily Dickinson, Poem 1,263, in *The Complete Poems of Emily Dickinson*, ed. Thomas H. Johnson, (Boston: Little Brown, 1960), p. 553 .

[8]Francis Darwin, *The Life and Letters of Charles Darwin*. 2 vols. (New York: Appleton, 1887), vol. 1, pp. 3–89.

[9]For related episodes see Chapter 4, "Only Ben," and Chapter 9, "Turn Here."

[10]Robert Louis Stevenson, "My Treasure."

[11]Francis Darwin, *The Life and Letters of Charles Darwin*. 2 vols. (New York: Appleton, 1887), vol. 1, pp. 3–89.

[12]J. P. Comer and A. Poussaint, *Black Child Care* (New York: Simon and Schuster, 1975).

[13]A. Lamorisse, *The Red Balloon* (New York: Doubleday, 1956).

[14]August Krogh, "The Language of the Bees," *Scientific American* 179, no. 2 (August 1948).

[15]For such travels into the recent and past, see Ann Nolan Clark, *In My Mother's House* (New York: Viking, 1941).

7: South End Kindergarten

Turn to the East

In 1962 David and I were invited to a summer workshop aimed at generating fresh ideas and inventing styles for teaching elementary-school science. The workshop was under the aegis of Educational Services, Inc., whose patron savant was Jerrold Zacharias, a physicist at MIT. Under his able leadership a group had recently developed a radically new physics course for high schools.

More important for young children, this group had also been making plans for an elementary-school science program. In summer 1961 they met with educators from African countries recently liberated from British and French colonial rule. Babs Fafunwa from Nigeria had helped to define this group's goals. Perhaps in Africa a fresh start could be made, freed from the baggage of moribund colonial schooling. With our own entrenched elementary-school habits, which almost totally neglected children's science, we could profit from this innovative freedom; they, in turn, could benefit from our work and resources. A joint venture would be helpful and indeed became so.

Our own involvement in the project diverged often because of our different backgrounds. David was to begin by harvesting ideas and planning for good, simple laboratory equipment and imaginative guides for teachers. For me there were, I believed, more fundamental concerns: a focus on the atmosphere and provisioning of classrooms for early learning, not memorizing.

We had intended to return to Boulder at the end of the summer, but the sudden tragic illness and death of Francis Friedman, the very able head of the elementary-science project, left it without a director. David was prevailed upon to take over, obtaining a last-minute leave from the University of Colorado. We were thus to stay and work in the Boston area for what became two years.

I was a sometime-consultant for the Elementary Science Study (ESS). But I took time to explore and enjoy a big city with its museums, to renew old friendships from the war years, and to spend many glorious hours in the Widner Library at Harvard. The fall rushed by, but after the holidays

I became restless. I think it was that very disquiet that again opened my eyes and my mind to the human undercurrent flowing all around us.

As a consultant to ESS I had been invited by some of our summer-conference participants to give workshops for teachers in what was called the "target area" of poverty in Washington, D.C. A marvelous group of young teachers and supervisors, mostly black, had been eager attendants. This was in the early Kennedy times when hopes were high—even mine. During those trips to Washington I discovered a superb school run by Meg Borden Kline, now of the University of Massachusetts in Amherst. We became lasting friends.

The South End

A further shift in my focus came by chance on a cold January afternoon in 1963. Waiting at Harvard Square for my bus to Back Bay, where we were living, I took the Dudley Station bus. What made me focus on four pale and silent children—the oldest no more than twelve—waiting beside me? It was not just the boy with one very short leg and a crutch who alerted me, nor even the telltale pale faces or their faded clean clothes that didn't fit. It was primarily the wariness one recognizes in children in public who "know they don't belong." They are the silent ones, the silent minority. I lost these Cambridge white children in the crowded bus, but watched them get off at Central Square. From the time of that brief encounter, my blinders were off and my vision was widened. Reality met my early memories of teaching in the Depression years in San Francisco and of a visit to a migratory workers' camp in the central valley of California in spring 1938. Boston 1962 felt like Depression 1930.

The bus for Harvard Square early in the morning was filled with middle-aged black women. In the late afternoon similar tired women boarded the bus, and the sign above the driver had been changed to Dudley Station. Where and what was Dudley Station?

I stayed on one afternoon and found Dudley Station in the midst of a region called the South End. This was near where my tired traveling companions lived. They were evidently daytime servants to an elite group in the ambiance of Harvard Square. Many of our friends lived around Harvard Square. But although that bus was linked to Dudley Station, as poverty to affluence, only the poor used it. No friends I knew had ever been to South End.

Exploring further much later, I was unprepared for the amount of misery and squalor, the number of liquor and slightly less-visible drug outlets, that existed in South End. In the North poverty was not found in alleys but in ghettos that could be passed by—but not, I was to discover, by all. A group called the Northern Student Movement did not just pass by. I became its oldest adjunct member. Most of its members were college and high-school age; I was almost fifty. The year was 1962, when gentrification of the South End was far in the future.

Plotting for a Kindergarten

I sought out the Northern Student Movement (NSM) meeting with the local NSM leader, Lucia Clapps, a student at Simmons College. All doors were immediately opened to me. I went to meetings with Lucia and met students from Simmons, Harvard, Boston University, and other colleges in the region.

In the atmosphere created by the commitments and hopes, by the benign preconceptions of those students, the project of the South End Kindergarten was born. Of course, there was more to it than my appreciation of the conscientious desire of these fine young people to help the children of inner-city Boston. There was more than my wish to offer NSM apprentices some experience beyond the limited offering of courses in "remedial tutoring," which, I guessed, was a conventional expression of a genuine desire to help. My dear friend, Jane Casstellanos, had summarized the weakness of this approach for me: "What is needed is not remedial work but a first chance." There was, I recognized, a strong pull on me from my San Francisco past, where I had learned and left so much of my young self with Depression and migratory families. Their gallantry and affection had never left me. But living in a small college town had narrowed my vision.

In our fifteen years in Boulder, the children I had known and taught were from middle-class and sometimes affluent families. They had given me new professional understanding. With age and experience here and now in the 1960s, I wanted and needed to close the circle I had begun in the 1930s. This was a chance to touch and enter the lives of our most forgotten; to observe and help them show and develop their strengths. I had no doubt that they would. But I was appalled by the poverty of South End, which was worse than I had known in the Depression years in California, although not worse than that of the migratory workers. Then and now, such conditions remain in the richest country in the world.

Having sought and found a group such as the Northern Student Movement (NSM), I was emboldened and empowered to move into plans far more ambitious than I otherwise could have undertaken. I was not alone. I went to meetings with Lucia and listened. I listened on at least two levels: first, to see whether and then how I could be useful; next, to apprehend what these students were all about, how they viewed their own usefulness. Although so far they had worked only at a remedial level, they were already on their way.

What had never come up, I soon realized, was prevention. It was at that beginning juncture, I thought, that we together—children and teachers—might create a paradigm of young inner-city children's learning. None of us could bring about economic and social reforms, those sorts of prevention we all knew were primary and desperately needed. But, I argued with myself, a small group of neighborhood children could exemplify, might even dramatize, the possibilities that could be realized within a classroom that nurtured and helped to realize children's native commitment to learning. I dreamed, gathered resources, and began to plan and plot. When Martin Luther King moved on Washington in that summer of 1963, our daughter, Julie, and friends were there. Our voices sang out together with Washington from Boston.

Through Lucia I met Mel King, one of the local sponsors of the NSM. He was already wielding educational and political influence in and around Boston's black community, influence that would grow in later years.

A House of Our Own

On the first morning when Mel King, Lucia, and I met, talked, and walked upstairs in South End Community House, I was awed—awed that such light, simple, but attractive and appropriate rooms, too long vacant, were being offered to us for a kindergarten. Thus, suddenly, Mel King gave us the GO! In that old settlement house kindergarten, across decades of neglect, the spirit of Jane Addams welcomed us.

Later, as we assessed and organized, rejoicing in the almost empty rooms, I opened the door of a large closet. Glorious relics from the past, long unused, were waiting. For me it was a coming home to a place I had never been before except through books. From the spiritual grandparents of us all who choose such work—Jane Addams, Julia Lathrop, Lucy Sprague Mitchell, those marvelous women (see Bibliography)—this old neighborhood house, so long forgotten, came to us intact. Many decades before in Chicago, Jane Addams had seen the strengths in the new, bewildered immigrant families, and her settlement houses supported them.[1] This empty kindergarten, old but well preserved, was a lineal descendant, but for decades no one had cared or dared to see the strengths of these later bewildered families migrating north from the background of southern slavery—until now, in the year of Martin Luther King's march on Washington.

Out of these same closets came large, hollow wooden blocks, paint easels, a spacious empty dolls' house, and more.

So here in that wonderful old building, in the midst of a forgotten and decaying inner city, surrounded by ignorant, sad, and punitive schools, we were preparing to demonstrate the possible with local children. The physical arrangements reflected previous incarnations of the kindergarten traditions as I had known, adopted, and adapted them. I was curious to see these transformations in this new time and setting, to note how they succeeded and how they needed to be altered to meet the conditions of life in the radically altered world of 1962. We had fallen heir to a fabulous beginning of long ago.

My rage, long smoldering at the abuse and neglect of "a third of our nation," as Franklin Roosevelt had declared, was rekindled. Hope took over—for a summer.

Family Lives and Recruiting

What struck me at the time and has remained was the diversity and the strengths of so many of these inner-city families—from the poorest to the most comfortable, black and white. The neighborhood of South End House contained a few families that were not deprived, although they were not rich monetarily. They were primarily black families whose personal lives were often enriched by their concern with more than the lives of their individual members. Rhonda and Michael King were children from such fine homes. Tommy, Charles, and Freddy came from homes that were loving, although meager.

At first Mel King felt his five-year-old son, Michael, should not be permitted to come to the kindergarten. "It wouldn't be fair, he doesn't need to," he argued. I believed strongly that we needed some such fortunate children, and the right words came to me—that we were not running a "segregated school." Mel grinned, and although Michael was never

The South End staff in front of the doll house. *Left to right:* Maureen, Jeannette, Lucia, Sally.

encouraged by his family, he chose to be there at every session; the other children and the program prevailed. Rhonda's mother heard about our school, telephoned the South End office, and begged us to take her child.

To our knowledge Rhonda and Michael, both black, were the only children who showed awareness of the stirrings and hopes for change, for black civil rights, that were gaining wide attention across the land. We opened the school long before Martin Luther King's momentous march on Washington. Rhonda and Michael gave, and everyone gained. Without the horizons such children could already see and share, our other children would have been further deprived. I knew, from my entire professional life's experience, that a good school can, if the numbers are reasonable, provide for each and for all.

From an Italian family we had Freddy. His mother brought him on the first day and was friendly and delighted to have him in the school. I never saw her again, there was no need. One could see reflected in Freddy a great deal of affection and care. Our sad little Allan, so neglected and abused, was welcome to play on Freddy's porch. Freddy was a pleasure to all and made school a further part of his good life. His wildness was the result of delight in his world. Tommy, another white child, also enriched us all (see Jeannette's notes and watch Tommy as the summer unfolds).

A few children wandered in and out of our mornings: friends, relatives, and chance attenders. In this area it was not uncommon to play with a stranger or a visitor. Christina, "a twisty little girl," as Maureen, our secretary, called her, came to school just once.

We came to know a few families. One day Lucia and I left South End House, cutting through an alley to the office of the Northern Student Movement. A taxi that was coming toward us, going too fast in that unpaved, rubbled dump-heap, slowed because of a small girl in the middle of the alley. The child, whom we would come to know as Denise, had on a suggestion of an old, adult-size pajama top, pushed a broken doll in a falling-apart canvas cart, and stared at us as we eased her out of the center of the alley. From a near basement door her mother thanked us in friendly fashion. We stopped to talk.

The contrast hit us immediately between the alley's neglect and filth and the ease and well-spoken manner of the child's mother. With interest, she listened to what we told her about the proposed kindergarten and took seriously, we hoped, the invitation to send her child. The mother smiled and said, "She is real spoiled, she needs school. You want to go to school, Denise?" Remember, at our feet was this quiet mite, dirty, half-dressed, with the muscles of one eye not properly working, letting the eyes sometimes cross. A faint smile on her face would come and go.

As we were about to walk away a man, sleepy or doped, looked at us over the shoulder of Denise's mother: "How much does it cost? What does she have to wear?" Our answer was: costs nothing, wear anything. Denise's mother closed the interview with dignity and said, "Denise, say thank you to the teachers; do you want to go to school?" The wisp of a child grinned and nodded a yes, so sure her assessment after her mother's obvious friendliness toward us. Lucia and I walked on feeling our first child had been enrolled, holding sad thoughts about so much of the scene we had just encountered.

One noontime after all of the children had left school, Denise's mother arrived out of breath, asking, "Where is Denise?" She had been to the store. She was frightened that I had let Denise go home with "Robert." "Who was he?" Once we realized that in the street Robert was known as "Pete," Mrs. Stuart relaxed and agreed that Pete was completely reliable. Nevertheless I walked with her, and there on her doorstep was Robert Pete—carefully waiting with Denise beside him.

In the fall and early winter of that year, we would meet some of the children on Saturdays for a trip or a workshop. Denise and her sister, Lorraine, would attend if we called for them and brought them home.

One late December afternoon our daughter, Julie, home from college, and I took the girls back to their basement rooms. Their mother and father answered the door and invited us in. "It is cold, come in and get warm." This was rare in South End, but after the kindergarten experience I was remembered and trusted. Denise and Lorraine dropped our hands, walked together across the bare room, and sat—as if habitually—in a basement window seat and stared out on the dark alley. In the center of the room sat a silent, staring young man, present merely in body. I knew that he was drugged. Ignored by all—including us when the first shock was over—these silent young men almost ceased to exist, even in body. Other lives, so sparse and meager, moved quietly around the drugged individual.

Julie and I stood in that neat, bare, ugly basement room that contained no sign of the season or even of food. There were a very few cracked dishes on an open shelf and two straight chairs near a bare table. We stood, talked, and were made welcome. Then, with nothing as inappropriate as a "Merry Christmas!", we said goodbye.

For blocks we walked with tears in our eyes, trying to interpret what we had just seen, awed at the courage that came through the situation. Julie finally said to me, "I have felt that you exaggerated, Mommy, that you overreacted. But you have undertold it."

The substance of this chapter—recruitment—becomes too complex for my own voice to tell it. This text is based on the original report I compiled from the notes of all five of the staff: Lucia, Jeannette, Sally, Maureen, and myself. The report was written for our patron organization, Educational Services, Inc. It was to be a "background" document for a legislative battle, but that battle has never been fought. What *did* come of it was Head Start—in which I later became involved.

Unlike the other stories from my life as a teacher, this tells of a drama, set on the different stages within South End House and the surrounding neighborhood, which we could not all observe or interpret equally. Relying on that report, I have quoted here, sometimes extensively. To give credit where credit is due and to convey the richness of our lives—children and teachers—in those six summer weeks, I cannot do otherwise.

It is time for other voices. Jeannette, one of the half-time teachers, tells of her recruiting efforts and introduces us to Allan and Tommy.

JEANNETTE: Allan's flat was visited first in the afternoon. A grand-mother did most of the talking and sounded very earnest about send-ing him. At the time, sitting in the bedroom/living room, were her two daughters. One, very young-looking, was sitting in a corner holding a 3-week-old baby. When I asked about the baby, her face was still, and without emotion she gave his age. The other woman was possibly Allan's mother? She took no interest in the kindergarten project and said nothing during the time I was there. From what I could see from the hallway very quickly, there was one other room, containing two double beds, and a bathroom. I pray there was more to the house than I saw—for a grandmother, two daughters and pos-sibly husbands, and six children.

Allan did not come to school the first day. So during that session I went to see if he could come. Everything was quiet in the house when I went up the stairs, about 10:15 A.M. After a few knocks a woman did come to the door, holding her blouse shut, and said no, the child could not come. I hesitated and then asked again, could he not come with me. "No, he is asleep," was the answer. And then, from behind the door I heard a little voice say "hey!" and again "hey!" She turned, looked into the room, and again said no and shut the door.

F.H.: The continuing story of Allan, never quite resolved, will reappear. Jeannette continues her search:

JEANNETTE: Around the corner from South End House, off of an alley, there was a tiny grouping of two-story wooden dwellings. Leaning a little this way and that, they had a precarious appearance. Several entrances opened onto a tiny courtyard that had room for two giant-size dogs, a dog house, children's toys, and, I believe, a sandbox. After a greeting from a smaller dog, Tommy's mother came to the door. My first impression was that she took little care of herself and her home, that she was not a pretty woman. The spirit of her house made me quickly change my mind. She was very friendly in the course of the conversation and said she would love to get rid of Tommy for the morning. Although he didn't seem quite so delighted when she turned around and asked him if he would like to come, she agreed to send him.

Tommy did not come that first morning, and the next morning I went around. He was shy and reluctant, but his mother was strong about his going. Later she said, "I couldn't keep him home!" He came steadily. That second morning the father was there, washing his face in the sink, a handsome and kind-looking man. When the conversation centered around the pets, they both spoke with lightness and joy. They asked me earnestly whether I wanted a dog. They were fond of the little one but felt they could not keep him. So deeply did they feel about the death of the kittens they had given away to some ruthless people, that with this dog they were emphatic about being more careful. Their sensitivity and gentleness was an unusual and beautiful thing to see. And indeed I felt sure that this family relationship must be something quite special.

F.H.: It certainly was. Watch Tommy all summer. Lucia adds to the account of recruiting, with new names to the cast of characters.

LUCIA: Jeannette and I went out two days with leaflets containing information about the summer kindergarten and the afternoon drama-music workshop. We worked mainly on Rutland Street and Rutland Square. In most cases we saw children on the street, asked if their mother was home; if she was we went into the house with the child. Jerome, Jackie, Barbara, and Lewis were signed up this way. While walking through an alley, we found the four of them playing in a backyard. Robert was also there, but he had already been asked. Jerome and Lewis came away from their play to show me their house. The mother was very willing to sign them up. The whole clan was very regular in coming to the afternoon program but were seldom up in time for regular kindergarten attendance.

The mother made no special attempt to get Jackie—her 6-year-old "niece from New York"—up and ready. Jackie came in the beginning. Then for some reason she would avoid the kindergarten, although she would come around at noon after time was up. In her distrustful, half-fearful manner, she was sticking around almost, it seemed, to test her anticipation of our reprimanding her. For what? We could never be sure, though we had some idea she might have taken something from the kindergarten. We knew she had been kept home for a day as a punishment for having taken something from the corner store. Everyone on staff was concerned for Jackie, and it seemed our continued openness to her did most certainly affect her. We welcomed her whenever she came, without question about her previous absences. Evidence of this became clear in the last two weeks. Her willingness to sing and dance in the afternoon program was very noticeable, and by then she came regularly to the morning kindergarten.

Very clear in my memory is little Robert, listening while I told of the program. He listened without saying a word, like a little old man. I read into his silence a suspicion not confirmed by his later involvement. At the time he seemed to say, don't bother me with all your tricks; I know these games all too well. Seeing the expressionless face of his mother, the ever-present invitation in the eyes of his father, and the uncurtained, broken windows of their second-floor rooms may have affected my expectations of this child. I certainly questioned my own prerogative in offering him a summer kindergarten when he seemed already to have experienced more of the sad realities of life at the age of 6 than I probably will in a lifetime.

When Robert's mother did not show up at registration Jeannette and I went to the house and registered him. We registered his sister, Shirley, for the afternoon music program. Their mother's minimal response when giving her consent might have foreshadowed Robert's failure to show up the first day. When I went to get him I found mother and son sitting at the window, watching the drizzling day. I asked if I could take him over to kindergarten. She said she would send him. I went on to Rutland Square for others, not knowing whether she had meant it. But on arriving back at South End, I found him just arriving with his mother. She left and I walked with Robert up the stairs. I watched with much anticipation as he entered the room where a group of about five children were around a table blowing bubbles. To my surprise he approached the table without hesitation and entered into things completely, as he subsequently did the whole summer—never missing a day.

Will give in to a temptation to indulge in a story about these two children, Shirley and Robert; it seems to say much about our attempt to understand what things and how things affect kids brought up in our inner cities. Although we had seen their father in the house, I did not recognize him till two weeks after we had begun work with the children, as one of these guys always on the street corner. He stepped out as I passed with Shirley, to identify himself as their father and ask whether he could come to school and have us be his teachers too. In the many similar incidents that followed, Shirley showed herself to be much more conscious of and disturbed by what was going on than Robert was. She once stepped back—after we had passed her father, who was sitting in a car and had called out one of his remarks—and said to him, "Why don't you shut up!" We know how much she had taken in by her performance, recorded in Maureen's notes, of a

drunken woman so soberingly realistic. Shirley often went into this
act in the afternoon drama workshop when playing "statues," where
"one comes alive" from the stilled position one has landed in after
being twirled. The other kids would watch intently, aware somehow
that this was a little too serious, a little too realistic to be just play.

Robert, on the other hand, doesn't show the weight of what he sees
around him. Found him one day standing on the corner with another
kindergartner (Denise) and her mother witnessing a very drunk, half-
clothed white woman being dragged by police from the sidewalk to a
paddy wagon. His very normal "hi, Lucia!" greeted me without looking for my response to the scene—indeed, as if it were not there.
Franny has pointed out the importance of such significant differences
in the attitudes of the kids.

F.H.: Lucia and I had spoken of these differences. Some children, like
Robert, draw a curtain around themselves and allow only those
things of true interest or value to enter. One sees it, one reads of it in
literature.[2] I continue these observations with those of a young beginning teacher who is already on her way:

LUCIA: Both children have performed exceptionally well in most things.
The creativity of Shirley's dialogues in the afternoon drama workshop, in different role-play—the witch in *Snow White*, the sister in
Hansel and Gretel—and in the dance and fill-in spots in songs; and that
of Robert, most notably in his work with wood, making creations
resembling no particular object but with sticking-out movable parts
with a great sense of balance. Such things have offered evidence of
well-fed imaginations.

I've already given one instance of the kind of relationship the kids
know with their mother—recalling Robert watching the wet day with
her from the window. I remember also a conversation with the two
children one morning. They were always the first ones to arrive in the
morning, sometimes when we ourselves arrived, at 8:00. I asked this
day whether they didn't have a magic alarm clock inside that got
them up so early. Shirley said no, they got up at 6:30 with their
mother when she got ready for work. I said, "Oh, does she wake you
for breakfast?" "No, we just get up." "Do you hear her moving
around?" "No, we just kind of know when she wakes up."

Without construing this as some kind of mystical communion, I'd
like to say that these children do have in their mother someone who
cares very much—someone on whom they can rely—and though

they spend most of their time with each other (she works all day), they must know a real closeness with her. This security, in spite of an unemployed, wandering father, coupled with very wide exposure may account for the quality of their work. They have been to the zoo, swimming on the commons, riding the swan boat—lived in New York originally—and have had such of the "little things" as putting baby teeth under pillow for surprises.

To expand on this alluded-to strength these children find in each other: it is one of the most beautiful friendships ever, especially considering their closeness in age (7 and 8) and difference in sex. Have *never* seen them argue; often protect each other. Never forgot the look on Robert's face when we suggested that we walk ahead on our way to the car when going on a trip. Almost crying, he pointed upstairs, saying, "But she (Shirley) doesn't know the way"—fearing we'd leave her, even in his real anxiousness to bound ahead. Shirley had that precise response once at the playground when Robert was in line for a drink of fountain water and started for another part of the play area. Seen once again when the boys were deciding whether to let any of the girls (then in dance class) be in a play they were working on. Shirley's name was suggested. All (Robert vocally included) decided only Shirley would be included.

F.H.: Lucia's report now mentions two new arrivals, Gail and Anthony, of whom more will be told. She adds a new paragraph to our concern for Allan.

LUCIA: We went to check on the single boy next door (Allan). Heard three little boys through the blind, called in "hi!" and heard a "shh." Then a quiet "shh" after one of the boys had made a sound. Was it their mother? We don't know. Earlier she had seemed anxious to have them come. We came back here for the three once more. The children said their mother was shopping.

Jeannette's first visit to Allan's household deserves a sequel. A six-week interval is long enough to see some children at least begin to thrive, and those our story will follow. In the main they are from gross poverty but have, nevertheless, some essential human support in their backgrounds. For the Allans of this world, however, even a year, or ten, is profoundly problematic. For this child we gave perhaps a few drops of nectar in the sieve. In the sequel he can be lost among the other children.

MAUREEN: As I approached the front entrance to the main room of the kindergarten class, I felt it was going to be an unforgettable day for me, but the thought of Allan flooded my mind. Who is Allan? Well, Allan is one of those children who doesn't have any particular responsible person to care for him. He is a child in an atmosphere that takes only children like him. He is a loving little fellow, sweet as can be, but something needs to be changed.

JEANNETTE: Allan is well known to other little children on Rutland Street. The first day Shirley saw him coming to class she said, "He can't come!" I heard another whisper, "He comes into our house and steals food." The little dazed look, the voice that uttered over and over, "Can I have a nickel, can I have an ice cream, can I have a sandwich?" Says he's hungry, and you wonder if there was ever a time when he knew the feeling of being full, stuffed, happy, and contented.

One night at dinnertime he waited for me outside the South End building. Naively I said, "You go home and eat your dinner, and I will go inside and eat mine." "Nobody home, no food at home," the little face replied, tilting his head and looking up at me with a puzzled expression.

MAUREEN: Sally and I had climbed twenty-one steps to bring Allan to class with us this last week of school. We got to the top of the stairs, and Sally knocked on the door a few times but received no answer. I told her to please try again; she did, and a female voice asked "Who is it?" It was a voice which told me we were being a disturbance. Sally asked if Allan was ready for class; the voice said he was still sleeping. We then wanted to know if he was coming at all. We heard Allan's voice, a very soft "yes."

Without Lucia and her associates, who were already working in the South End area, a great emptiness would have existed in my professional life. This diary of South End, which they made possible, is dedicated with loving appreciation to those children of that summer 1963 kindergarten; to their parents, who sent or allowed their children to come; to Mel King, who gave us a place to live and work; and to the young women who made it possible: Lucia, Jeannette, Maureen, and Sally.

Occasionally we needed equipment and a bit of cash, and the Elementary Science Study came to our aid. They paid Maureen, who needed a summer job; the rest of us volunteered. Sally was employed every afternoon for her needed salary.

Day One: No Children

In his everyday life, play is the child's natural form of expression, a language that brings him into a communicating relationship with others and with the world in which he lives. Through play he learns the meaning of things and the relation between objects and himself; and in play he provides himself with a medium of motor activity and emotional expression. [3]

It was a day, our first! In which:
We have no children;
We have children.
We send three children home.
We send out s.o.s. for staff volunteers.

F.H.: Not unprepared were we, in any usual or known sense, but who— WHO—could be prepared for the realities of what I could only believe were those of a new and unique world?

We started kindergarten after two weeks of getting ready. We had set aside the last Friday and Saturday for registration. Imagine our naïveté in thinking that in the South End one could post signs, talk, and give churches notice of a free kindergarten and expect more than four to turn up. Well, we did just that, and four did turn up.

Jeannette and Lucia returned an hour later full of excitement and success; we were immediately busy with supplies for all, including new arrivals. We tried to keep paint jars full, needles threaded, the playhouse from being flooded, fingers from being hammered. A first day feast!

And first impressions? Children, except for two or three, were very independent. By their actions they asked to be left alone to play and work in their own spacious "school." By 10 A.M. we had about ten children.

Very little talking, much communication. No one would allow a story or book to be used. No one could stop to gather for juice or talk or—Individual problems recede in this kind of a group—are masked?

My initial pleasure in these rooms was multiplied by the children's immediate recognition that this was *their* place. It overflowed with appropriate materials, with nooks and corners away from any traffic, low windows, a colorful welcoming atmosphere. The children would, in fact, expand their work and play here throughout the summer,

Jeannette with Robert, Louis, Shirley, Anthony; me with Jackie in my lap; and Rhonda's head.

refusing trips or even, for some time, much garden play. We watched them on Monday, Wednesday, Friday for six weeks. As we came to know the hovels many of the children lived in, we appreciated their delight in these sparse but welcoming rooms.

Having valued the tradition of Jane Addams and rejoiced in this Boston scion of it, we were now blessed by the return of the very life it had been built to save and to serve. And here, if only to underline these reflections, I tell of the "wild boys" that first morning, of their capture and expulsion—installment one.

Into a buzzing, self-directed group of children there came from the "public" playground that first morning three small white whirl-winds. Their choice for a first serious maneuver was to storm a tall hollow-block tower that was taking form in the main big room. This animate tornado, in the form of the three 4- and 5-year-olds, raced into an adjoining room and returned, with grins at the destruction they were spreading. The block builders stood statuelike, black and white faces fearful; the three young white hoodlums defied Lucia's

A time in the garden.

and Jeannette's attempts to protest or interfere. I judged that *this* moment required my presence.

I grabbed the ringleader, carried him to the open front-entrance door, and stood him down. As hoped, all eyes were on me and my captive (Perry, as we were to learn), including those of the other two miscreants, Johnny and Stevie. In the attentive silence it was an easy matter for Lucia and Jeannette to bring the other two close. We literally held the three by the door while I stooped down and found myself saying something like this: "This is not a school for babies who cannot yet take care of themselves or others. Lucia and Jeannette will take you back to the playground, and when you have grown up enough and can take care of yourselves, then please come back to play and build."

Feeling like an ogress, I took solace from the restoration of peace and play. I hoped the message I had given the young rascals, and intended for all to hear, was well received by the other white children. Three girls from the playground stayed happily with us. Here there would be no bullying, intimidation, or ugly racism. (We later

Left to right: Michael, Shirley, and friend.

learned that only white children were welcome at the public playground. It was obvious that Perry, Johnny, and Stevie had been
allowed to taunt and harass their black neighbors.)

With this episode I became a head teacher! I realized that although
I had played this part before (see Chapter 6), I had never before actually sent children away from school. At our brief after-school meeting, Jeannette, Lucia, and I discussed what had happened. From
Lucia's notes I quote the saga of taking the three back to their playground, which was public but segregated.

LUCIA: Johnny and Stevie offered some resistance to holding my hand,
but Perry bolted altogether—running ahead, peeking around corners
at us, etc. Arrived at playground; supervisor looked very upset. She
said well, yes, she knew they were devils but felt Perry especially
needed a more disciplined situation than the playground offered
since he'd be going to school in the fall and just couldn't be controlled. Asked me to speak to Perry's mother, since she was anticipat-
ing his going to our kindergarten.

Mother was outside—came to see what's up, since she could see from her window to the playground. We all went inside her flat, Perry in the lead. She had yelled to him to come inside. He scooted into a back room, periodically poking his head out for comment. We explained [what had happened]. She said to Perry, as if to say you little devil, "Oh Perry, you've been a bad boy." He returned a "yep" in a very matter-of-fact tone. Can't recall our conversation in between—about four minutes. Perry finally called, "Time for them to go, Mom," speaking to her as a fellow conspirator. Mother shrugs a what-am-I-to-do-with-him look. We left. Perry had won.

F.H.: Watch the "uncontrollable" Perry's return after a week and his behavior throughout the summer! Once Perry had decided to take control of himself, he did.

Day Two: Exploration

Exploration:
of equipment: paint, blocks, clay, water, prism, magnets, wood, and
    tools;
of yard;
of unseen boundaries;
of wild animals: ants, flies, grasshoppers, caterpillars;
of tame ones: each other.

F.H.: Even on this second day one could see the children, shy or bold, showing us their ways of relating to adults, to each other, and to materials. What initial trust! What expectations! What unexpected truths to be understood! The challenge of beginnings and of having such young allies as the by-now four associates: Lucia, Jeannette, Sally, and Maureen! (As I had requested from Lucia and Jeannette, we now had two young adults to match the color of most of our children.)

Sally and Maureen, our two new volunteer high-school assistants from the Northern Student Movement, came for their first morning. From now on each of us, child or adult, would try to fit individual strengths together and to influence plans and direction for the days ahead. The dedication and value of these four were clear to me from the beginning.

We never got to the yard on the first day. We did today and drank juice sitting in a wobbly circle on the lawn. Jackie, beside me, tall and bony, pointed out a fly near us, and I covered it with cupped hand. Michael dashed in to get a jar (his suggestion). Paper-topped jar with imprisoned fly passed around for all to see. First general interest shared. Little shy Denise noticed spots on fly and remarked on them to teacher Sally. A great hunt among bushes, grass, and trees followed.

Children, I thought, were involved because this was a new slant on their own "here-and-now" environment. They were momentarily fascinated by "hunting," and at a suggestion at end of morning, we freed every "catch" to fly or walk away. As one should expect, the children's reaction to their giving of freedom was positive and connected, perhaps with the satisfying and new glimpse of what one could see and discover—as if the letting go itself were part of that fresh view? We talked about it in our staff meeting.

JEANNETTE: Shirley, our big 8-year-old, climbed into the top bedroom of the dollhouse, legs and everything, all crunched up inside. And then came a muffled, happy voice, "See, look, I fit."

F.H.: When we furnished the dollhouse, the children would move all the furniture into one room. It was an "apartment" house to them. They knew no other.

Gail loved school and reflected a loving mother—she was less inhibited than her brother, Anthony, and seemed to be able to seek and take from us what she needed. Anthony had been in school for two years; he, I judged, was traumatized. I was much too optimistic about Gail's sturdiness—not concerning the summer itself, since what we offered was grist for her little mill, but as to her inner strength for coping with the hostile world of Boston public kindergarten. Who could?

What a child is Robert. It was difficult not to watch him constantly in the hope of understanding how a child gets this kind of independence and self-direction.

Anthony—so silent and watchful and such a loyal follower of Robert. I underestimated the strength of this quiet one, I believe. Both Robert and Anthony could read; they would be second graders in the fall.

Tommy, though shy, was a great little human—well on his way. He was from that kind of helter-skelter home that was rich in important things—one could surmise this from his activity. Enjoyed playing ball. With Anthony, interested in making a garden.

Michael, Mel King's son, was what one would hope to find in a child from such a fine home. Hope he keeps coming. We need his strengths and his wider background. He shared it with us.

After a couple of weeks Lucia came to me, saying, "Franny, things are going so well here, I think I should go help at_____; they need it." I remember responding honestly, as well as selfishly for our children and for myself—that she was one of the main reasons things were going so well, and I needed all of the staff to be on deck. That was true, but I did not know the worth of her alternative choice. I hope I ended by saying that of course it was hers to decide. She stayed, to my delight.

Day Three: Too Much Praise

Return of Steve and John—not Perry.
Pulley, paint, drills, and saws.
Michael makes a discovery about magnets.
"Children of restriction."
Who is young enough to come?
Too much praise becomes a villain.

F.H.: Partly in response to the behavior of our wild trio from the playground, I had made changes: moved woodwork into a big room of its own and turned the sturdy wood jungle gym upside down, making the lower platform a ceiling with a rail around it at adult eye level. We secured an arm for a pulley wheel, complete with rope and plastic bucket. This was introduced with ground rules: two at a time to use it, no more; never lift or lower heavy things. Reasons were discussed. The pulley instructed and delighted the children, two at a time, all summer. The ground rules were never violated. Immediate and good feedback, that!

Two of the wild trio, Stevie and Johnny, returned with every peace offering known to 4-year-olds. Tentative smiles and expressions of "I want to come" and "I mean to try." Still absent was the ringleader, Perry. Of course, we welcomed the two and expected no more serious trouble. Getting them on the upside-down jungle gym, with the new pulley and bucket, helped that first day. From the playground five boys and girls are now coming—of course, all white. Watch them. Their behavior is revealing; and remember, none of them is much over five: Stevie and Johnny, who returned today, and now Susan, Elizabeth, and occasionally Donna.

MAUREEN: Donna and Mary B. seemed to me to be children of restrictions. They always seem to await the opportunity when an adult isn't around. They seem to want to do things, but there is something holding them back. Timmie, a younger brother, came today and walked right into the program.

Now that the program has been fully established, children of all ages are coming. At our teachers meeting, Mrs. Hawkins says we need to set up a program of less adult interference.

F.H.: Although newly arrived herself, Maureen was prescient about the B. children.

We stayed easy, but not too encouraging, about the older newcomers. If they came and did not demand too much from us or push at the little ones, then they felt welcome.

Maureen refers to an important discussion. Praise from adults was becoming too much the form of reaction to woodwork, paintings, and so on. For the children and teachers, I hoped to keep the activity itself satisfying and motivating. What these children brought as strengths (their self-direction and self-motivation) I hoped to encourage rather than to decouple from their activities. When children—all children— are inventing and learning, it is not adult praise they need but recognition: a resonance, a shared and thus steadying enjoyment of their valid work.

Day Four: Focus on Jackie

Sawdust is for smelling, feeling, gaining attention.
Jeannette looks at the Bs.
Anthony and Michael at work.
Once upon a time.
Two young Turks.
Focus on Jackie.
Tears and fights in the yard for Tommy and Freddy.
Diane examines a drill.
Sawdust is drill dust is sawdust—for Robert.

What is floating?
Louis comes to school with "an older trio."
And we hear of "suckling cups."
The Bs. go home dirty.

F.H.: By the end of this day, our fourth, these children were coming into focus for each of us in different ways. We were recognizing similarities and differences. Among our girls, Jackie was a mystery. Competent Robert was becoming more and more inventive. Older Louis came today and brought his abiding curiosity. The three Bs. (Timmie, Donna, and Mary), quiet but active, moved into the playhouse as "permanent" residents.

What struck my older, professional eye at this time about the three Bs. was that they still came, played, learned, and were as whole as they were, as open with their troubles, as structuring for their needs and joys. I missed the troubles brewing with Timmie; in his sisters' shadows I thought he was OK. A humbling mistake.

I turn attention to Jackie. She came in the beginning and gave glimpses of her brilliant mind, both in kindergarten and in the afternoon program. But something was happening to keep her away from kindergarten. She might show up at noon during the teachers meeting, but until the last of the summer she was wary of school. At our teachers meetings we speculated. Had she taken something? Was she teased by other children? Why did she so love going to the library with Mrs. Hawkins and a few others one afternoon? Her complete involvement when she returned in the last two weeks surprised us. Now we fear her basement "home" held her in the mornings—in some way literally held her.

Knowing what I now know, many years later, I am fairly certain Jackie was being abused and that this occurred over time. Watch this 6-year-old. She may help us with others.

MAUREEN: Donna, Mary, and Timmie B. got very interested in certain things and started to crawl out of their shells. During the sawdust period, they played with it but kept running back and forth to wash their hands. (Outdoors later they made mud pies, and the same procedure of hand washing as with the sawdust was observed.) Timmie cried for no apparent reason.

F.H.: On Timmie: As we were soon to realize, and as will be seen on this and succeeding mornings, Timmie's tears were tripped by his getting slightly wet or dirty. Although I believed his total misery was also a threat, which freedom of a new kind posed (these troubles are not unrelated); I see in retrospect that I should have been more adept in helping to design his school environment. The fact that he was damaged emotionally and was abused at home, which we later confirmed, is no excuse for me. I failed Timmie by default. I thought he was like his sisters; I had much more to learn about child abuse and its so often selective aspects.

The very materials that fostered Donna's and Mary's growth—at their particular stages and with their psyches—seem to have been responsible for Timmie's trouble. He was drawn to paint, to water play, and to do similar activities in the way his sisters were; but too late did I realize that he, the youngest, would be unable to cope and would be brutally punished for "getting wet" or "getting dirty." Our old-shirt aprons were especially scorned by the boys as demeaning, and we did not insist that they use them. Could we have made Timmie wear one? Would it have been a small protection in the entire situation? I cannot say.

JEANNETTE: Donna and Mary B. stood apart from the group and the materials in their first times at kindergarten, before they moved to the playhouse. They would string beads in patterns but in an indifferent manner. They wore an expression of interest yet uncertainty about whether they should join in with the other children. It was not shyness but, I think, a feeling of superiority. It is difficult to say.

These particular children have a component from their home of feeling better-than. Is it protective? It is coupled with a hidden longing in them? A longing for what is not understood but at the same time is desired. As Donna and Mary, through this summer, allow themselves to sample and participate and change . . . one begins to have some insight into their previous or initial starting place as observed by all. The two girls are only superficially similar, but their individuality is masked until they break through and are released from self-consciousness into participation with their environment—material and human. Then their self-selected way of navigating is impressive.

It was interesting that the behavior of these youngest three mirrored that of their older siblings, whom we had in the afternoon groups—Gwendolyn, 7, John, 8. There are twelve children in the family, who live in a row house, immaculately clean and in good appearance from the outside. Brick. The house is a part of a small cluster, bordered on one side by a school, the other side by the street. Thus, they are largely set apart from other neighborhood children. They play only with the children living right next door, some of whom are their cousins. The B.'s father is a minister. Their color is very light; they are immaculately clean and well dressed.

The clothes problem in kindergarten with the B.'s also was seen with the older ones in the afternoon. Gwendolyn could not sit on the floor and, unfortunately, refrained from taking off her shoes in dance class. How my heart ached because she seemed to long to move like the others, but with the handicap of her slippery shoes, could really do no more than scrape them along the floor, laughing at the mistakes of the others.

In the school garden the B. children made the discovery about mud pies—mud and water—on a pie plate; Donna stirred it, beat it, pressed it, it oozed between her fingers, and she was radiant. Much too busy to even speak as she made the pie, washed her hands, and repeated the cycle over and over. The intensity of both of them was grand—Donna leading, but even Mary getting her fingers in it with delight. They tended to feel freer when adults were not around, confident in their ability and freed from some of their restraint.

F.H.: Coming to know the neighborhood hazards, one may understand this family's parents' fierce restrictions without condoning them. See Maureen's comment at the end of this day's notes, and follow these children throughout the summer.

I had brought a big box of sawdust, which I thought the children might mix with wallpaper paste and water, thus making a sawdust maché. (My Farm School children had found this good for modeling and liked its gooey-sticky quality—but not these children!) Before we got started making the maché, however, I realized that the sawdust itself was new to the children and would be fun to investigate. So, I kept the box partly closed and invited the children to come up, close their eyes, and feel what was inside. High interest and patience for turns after a few "me firsts" were ignored. No one guessed—even when the children smelled the sawdust. Attention stayed, and finally we looked in the box, handled the sawdust further, and talked about it. No one had ever knowingly seen any before.

With turns for stirring and pouring water and adding dry paste, the mess was a good consistency, and most children refused to touch it. A few did. Some of the stuff made its way mysteriously to the playhouse as a cherished but gruesome food, and I left it there for the day. Some cleanup that was for the staff. Never again!

From Jeannette's record I return to the mystery of our Jackie.

JEANNETTE: Jackie arrived late today as usual. She was observant enough to remember that one of the trees in the playground was the same as one she had at home. Didn't want to leave school. Her interest was caught first by hammering two pieces of wood together like a + sign, and then she carefully painted each side a different color. She also painted at the easel, primarily stripes of different colors. One misses in her face the flicker of a laugh, a dance in her eyes. She is fearful, I think, afraid. Her face does not move.

Jackie will often come back after all other children have gone, seriously and shyly come in while we are gathered around for our teachers meeting. We have noticed that her fears seem even more pronounced when she comes to kindergarten than when she is on the street. In the early weeks I saw her smile only once, and that was when she was teasing me by not coming off the fire escape and I was being stern (afternoon session). Her concentration in painting or wood is adequate. She is silent most of the time, and thus it is difficult to know how much she discovers or understands. She works primarily by herself, with little communication with her peers, and she rarely works with them on a project. (Perhaps the equipment poses a constant temptation?)

F.H.: We postulated at our teachers meeting that Jackie may have taken some equipment from kindergarten and been severely punished and forbidden to attend kindergarten.

LUCIA: Diane held the hand drill upside down to examine it. She twisted the small drill bit and watched it make the gears and handle turn.

F.H.: Robert came beside me holding a piece of wood with many holes drilled in it. I started to comment on the difference in the size of the holes (he had used different bits), but he just stood and held the board until I tumbled—he meant me to see something different, the drill dust made by drilling. When I reacted, he was satisfied and walked away. No language, but lots of communication. What appreciation for the box of sawdust—drill dust!

LUCIA: They played with the boats—in ponds—made of large split truck tires—in the water, but they filled the boat with the water. They thought this was the way to use them?

Children *shoved* the boats along. Impatient with the slow floating motion—not familiar with the way things move in water, or just natural impatience with slowness?

F.H.: As our understanding of how and where these children lived fell into place, we realized that the chance even to use water, to play with water, was rare. One kitchen, one bath—not always in working order—was normal in a house for three, four, or five families to share.

In the garden, Maureen records the continuing investigation of insect life.

MAUREEN: Barbara, Sharon, and Louis—an older visiting trio 9–10 years—showed a great interest in the caterpillars Louis and Mrs. H. had caught. Louis said, "I like to explore the bottom of their feet, you see, they have like suckling cups." To demonstrate what he meant, he took the clear plastic, which acts as a door to the cage, and placed the caterpillar on it (then from underneath one could observe the feet!). Mrs. Hawkins and Louis were talking and talking: "How did you get interested?" Mrs. H. asked him. This was a very easy question for him. He answered, "Through a friend." He said that he had had over one-hundred and fifty caterpillars. He waited to see them make their cocoons, but they never did while he was there watching. Mrs. H. asked him if any of his caterpillars became butterflies. "No, they just became white, mothy, and beautiful, but they looked like butterflies." Moths!

F.H.: Louis had been so interested in caterpillars, moths, and butterflies that he and I had enjoyed a collecting afternoon; he showed me where he had found many caterpillars. I asked our ESS friend, George Small, to give us the knocked-down parts of a butterfly cage, and Louis and I put it together. Louis was incredibly clumsy and inept with tools—the 5- and 6-year-olds are better. Louis is "staying" with Jerome's family. Mother? "Father in hospital," he told me.

Maureen's comments for the day end on a premonitory note. We were to realize it only too late, even after today's recognition and discussion of the B. family's special condition and of Timmie's troubles.

MAUREEN: The Bs. were dirty when they returned home today. This could be a problem.

Day Five: Oh Say, Can You See

The Bs. stay home, and Lucia makes a call.
Bubbles, numbers, and "a flick of the wrist."
Elizabeth and Susan in focus.
"You remember me, my name is Perry."
Diane thaws.
Where is Jackie's world?
The new city out of blocks.
"An' when the saints go marching in."
"Oh say, can you SEE" with Louis leading.
Lucia and Gail share a bubble-walking.

F.H.: Today Jackie stays in focus, from different angles. Michael King's salutary influence is a bonus. His family "lets" him come because "he wouldn't stay away."

Maureen reports on the continuing concern for the B. children.

MAUREEN: Lucia Clapps went to see the Bs. today. She got to the door, and the oldest boy went downstairs and came back up. "My mother said she is busy and what do you want?" Lucia said, "We missed the children at school today and hope none of them are sick. I want to know if we'll see them on Friday." He immediately says "yes." "We'll be looking for them."

F.H.: Lucia's quiet time with Gail delights my teacher's perception of a student teacher—as does Jeannette's observation of Shirley giving brother Robert all her bubbles! Sally and Maureen complete the caring quartet this teacher is blessed with.

JEANNETTE: At the bubble table a great game of "who has the most bubbles" was started: Shirley, Michael K., Robert, and three others. They were going great guns. Shirley, after awhile, gently pushed all her bubbles over to Robert's pile and exclaimed, "Robert won!" This is but one of the many examples this summer of how close a relationship this brother and sister have built up. One afternoon when we started on a trip, Robert discovered that Shirley was not there. He was horrified that we would possibly go without her and propelled himself home to get her. We really wouldn't have left her.

LUCIA: Haven't recorded dates on these incidents, but [they occurred] about this time: Recall becoming conscious of Gail one day. Just thinking about her—not deciding she needed more or less attention or any particular work—just wondering about her responses to things, which so often must be interpreted because of her silence. Very struck by an incident indicating clearly that she was somehow conscious of my thinking of her. Sitting at a table where about five children were blowing bubbles. Was talking to someone on my left when Gail on my immediate right called me to look at her bubble, which was moving along the table as if walking. She did not watch my reaction—was not interested in recognition—wanted only to share this excitement. We may not always have such clear reminders of the kind of transfer which takes place between people. Again underscoring the importance of teacher attitude and expectation of the children.

MAUREEN: When Perry (the last of the three playground children to return) arrived in the morning, acted very uninterested, but after he was led by Mrs. Hawkins to the workshop, he said, "You know, you got good hammers here. I'm gonna come every day."

F.H.: Perry had face to save. He was not uninterested, just brave to return at all—and understandably defensive. When he took my hand and we went to the wood room, he was grateful. Then the tools spoke to Perry, as I had hoped they would to all these wild ones.

JEANNETTE: I was working with the wood in the workshop when I turned to a little boy working intensely beside me and said, "What is your name?" He replied, "You know my name!" I said, "Have you ever been to kindergarten before?" He said, "You remember me, my name is Perry." It hit. This was the little boy [who] had been sent home the first day because of his wild behavior. How well I remember the dash home—Perry dodging in and out of alleys, my trying to act calm and poised as minute by minute he put blocks between himself and me. He was so under control this morning, so diligently knocking in the nails, that I had not recognized him.

MAUREEN: Jackie—[the] only child who didn't respond to anything. This was noticed by Lucia, who said that she didn't believe it was willfully done.

JEANNETTE: I do not quite understand what Maureen meant in her statement about Jackie that she "didn't respond to anything." I did notice in the course of the summer that in certain situations Jackie,

her body stiff, would clasp her head in her hands and not move for
long periods. Bent over and still, she could not verbalize what was
wrong. I doubt if she knew. She worked herself out of it each time
and would soon join the group again.

F.H.: Jackie, still our most enigmatic and injured. Her face is stiff from
long use as a mask. Her eyes seek, search, and judge. One afternoon
about this time I took Jackie and Jerome and three others to the main
Boston library. She was as at home in that large, strange central
library as she is here—which is to deny that she feels "at home" anywhere. I read in her eyes a constant indictment, "You won't really
rescue me either, will you?"

Maureen's observations conclude the record of this eventful day;
our kindergarten is indeed under full sail, and the wind is steady.

MAUREEN: Michael—very busy and self-reliant. Talked about making a
gas station to Mrs. Hawkins. Mrs. H. said, "You might need some
money?" He wasn't slow to answer her, he said, "Yeah, we could
make it." He paused for a moment and said, "You know, you're having a real class here, it's just like the New Boston."

Michael had a round magnet which had nails hanging on it. He
knew there was some connection between the nails and the magnet.
When he gathered the nails on it, he saw them hanging onto each
other, and he said, "Hey, the nails are magnets too!"

Instead of having story time we had song time. Michael sang,
"When the Saints Go Marching In," and he knew each word to it:
"And when the rev, and when the rev. . . . Dear Lord, I want to be in
that number when the Revolution comes."

Louis—our "older inspiration," said that he had a song to sing but
we'd all have to stand for it, it was "The Star Spangled Banner." It
was sung with inspiration, and his posture was great. I've never seen
a boy his age with such pride and hope in what he was doing. It was
shown on his face.

Day Six: No Timmie

The Bs. return—Donna and Mary, no Timmie.
"Is THAT supposed to be a seesaw?"
Anthony speaks, and Gail too!
Colors from colors.
"Getting to Know You."

F.H.: Another quiet day. But Donna M., from the playground, emerges in just such an atmosphere—on a livelier day she could be invisible. She reminds me of some of the quiet ones who ask too little—and receive too little.

MAUREEN: One piece of equipment was a "balance board," designed for investigation, with wooden blocks for weights.

LUCIA: Robert's examination of the "seesaw"—a board 8 ' × 6' on a low fulcrum. The wording of his question—is THAT supposed to be a seesaw?—made it clear that he suspected there was something special about it.

MAUREEN: The group mixed its own colors (for the paint easel). The colors I saw were purple, brown, orange, and green. We had not before taken a group aside to do such a thing.

F.H.: Here developed one of those pleasant tangents—unplanned but rich in side considerations. It was over color mixing. A small group was excited, of course, about the first changes in color, such as red plus yellow giving orange, blue and yellow giving green, etc. But another kind of excitement accompanies such a digression—and that, I suspect, has to do with the element of fun and encouragement a teacher adds to a hitherto unsuspected or forbidden or barely permitted activity. A kind of conspiratorial delight can pervade and is not inappropriate—considering the taboos and cautions and limitations we surround our children with in too-neat classrooms.

MAUREEN: Mary and Donna B. came a little late, but as soon as they arrived they started in immediately to the program. They were rather silent, but about sixty seconds after arrival they started to play and do other things. I am not talented for the art of singing, but I started to sing "Getting to Know You," and they made me a star. Mary wanted me to sing it for her, and Donna followed with the same request.

Day Seven: Butterflies

Butterflies in South End.
And animal stories.
A quiet, consolidating sort of day in which no momentous events are reported.

Day Eight: African Rocks

Shirley reflects a part of her world and we all react.
Elizabeth helps Timmie.
Timmie's world comes to school, and we admit defeat.
Sally is caught by a real and symbolic drama between Anthony and
    Freddy.
Japanese flowers and African rocks with American children to "gaze
    in disbelief."

F.H.: This overflowing day needs little comment. Maureen's notes are
    becoming more and more useful for steering our course; all of our
    young staff are a pleasure to the children and to me.
        Sally's quiet ways allow her to observe an auspicious highlight
    with Freddy and Anthony. What a day! What a crew!
        First, a confession from Maureen.

MAUREEN: Robert—a heap of projects from the scrap-wood pile. As
    soon as he was finished, he gathered them all in his hands to take
    them to dry. Because his hands were full he said to me, "Open the
    door." I hesitated and asked him what was the proper way to ask for
    anything. He couldn't care what I thought about what he did, so he
    piled [everything] in one arm and opened the door for himself.

F.H.: Robert escapes Maureen's scrutiny from here on, but she records a
    drama none of us can forget.

MAUREEN: Shirley put on a show "of all time" for us. It was a show
    which I shall never forget, even when I'm old, at least I hope that
    much. It was all in play, yet it seemed so real and natural to me.
        Shirley was dressed in heels, lady's dress, and pearls (from the
    dress-up box). For more than an hour she played the part of a drunk-
    ard. She kept saying, "I'm drunk." . . . She fell on the floor, kicked her
    feet in the air, yelled she was drunk, and believe me, she looked like
    it, too! Her eyes were like those of one possessed by alcohol. I believe
    her part deserved an Emmy, it was that good in my opinion. Shirley
    left the workshop and went somewhere else. I asked her where she
    had been. "I in' know," she replied. Then she went to the bubble
    table and started to blow bubbles, still insisting she was drunk. She
    messed up the table, so to speak, then she left the children at the
    table still watching her and went over to the make-believe train with

a mouthful of the liquid that makes the bubbles. She approached Diane with the mouthful, blowing bubbles in Diane's face; Diane raised her hand at her. Shirley saw that I was there and immediately left Diane alone.

F.H.: My own reconstruction of this instance began with alarmed whispers in my ear. It was either Sally or Maureen whispering that Shirley was acting drunk in the workshop. What should they do? One has a first reaction to such news—which is at least to dispel the alarm with the way one replies. I tried to do this and suggested they observe but leave Shirley alone, not discouraging, not encouraging her. I promised I would be along soon—not wanting to add to their alarm by rushing.

To appreciate the significance of this instance for the young staff, one should remember that this was the first on-the-spot appeal to me about any of the children's behavior. It took little insight on my part to recognize the quality of deep and anxious emotion accompanying the communication. Our Shirley had brought to school a great big slice of the kind of life most of us know about but that all of these inner-city children knew intimately—the assistants and the children themselves. The way we reacted to Shirley's performance was important to Maureen and Sally. I was the receiver of their alarm, and I sensed fear in the entire atmosphere. Suddenly I represented that other, superior, white world—of school, established middle-class morality?—known mainly through past schooling (see A Boston High School at the end of this chapter for the story of Maureen and Sally's high school).

It would be hard to overestimate what was happening on this kind of morning, and it would be equally shortsighted to interpret second-grader Shirley's drunken woman suddenly in our midst as anything less than a symbol of forbidden fruits brought to a now trusted table. On the faces of the watchers, adult and child, one could read "What will happen? What do you think? What will Teacher say? Is it all right? Is it all wrong? Should we watch, laugh, look away?"

So, we reasoned later, at our noon meeting and after. Shirley dared to bring to school some of life as she knew and lived it on Rutland Street. Bravo to her and for our school—that we had communicated the permission.

I went into the workshop without watching Shirley except covertly and joined children who were busy with wood. As I went by Shirley I patted her gently and gave her an offhand smile by which I meant to deemphasize rather than to encourage or interrupt. As I went about other involvements, I continued to observe. What struck me in the first few minutes was the receding of apprehension and tension in the young volunteers. Once the nonjudgmental, professional reaction had become clear to them, they could somehow turn away from me and my response and let their own professional response develop. I hope they felt released. At least that's how I interpreted their behavior. We were becoming a team, and since I was not at all threatened or shocked by the children's behavior, they need not be.

So much for my initial action. What of Shirley and her peers—actors right in the middle of the stage? What did one wish to convey to them? Permission, yes. But certainly more than that. Permission coupled with less emphasis, acceptance with a minimum of interest? Some such subtle combination. One could argue here about what should have been conveyed once permission was accepted. Merely to discourage would be wrong, I believed. What I hoped to do was to compete—in the way a good life can compete—by providing wide choices. Follow this morning to see how it went. I see Robert later with Lucia and me on the street when a white woman is being dragged into a paddy wagon.

Not the least concern in such an episode as Shirley's drama is for the self-image of a child, as it is tied inevitably to the image that child has of a parent. How to accept? Not judge?

MAUREEN: Donna B. was very self-reliant today. Painted quite a lot by herself and didn't cling to Mary as much but rather associated frequently with others.

Elizabeth from playground was very kind to Timmie B. when he wanted to help her wash the dishes.

Timmie played house today, he was trying to put up the ironing board but had difficulty; he then left it and went to help Elizabeth wash. He soon left that and started to pump up a tire tube.

It was time to go to the yard, and so once again Donna B. made mud pies and puddles. I then saw her bringing Timmie over. He was crying. Donna later told the reason why he cried. I was not there to hear what she had said because I had left the scene. I was soon told by Mrs. Hawkins and Sally. . . . He was playing in some water and spilled it on his shirt. Sister Donna said he was crying because he was going to get another beating from his father for having his shirt wet.

F.H.: I was trying to reassure and comfort Timmie who was sobbing quietly but convulsively when his sister Donna walked near and pulled
up Timmie's shirt to show me his badly lacerated and still bloody-
raw back. "He cry 'cause he father goin' give him 'nother beatin' for
gettin' wet." She left Timmie with me in the same condition of misery. I felt sick and was totally unable to think of one thing to do for
Timmie, except to hold him gently close, not further injuring his back.
He leaned toward me.

So, we had inadvertently been responsible for that particular
bloody beating. I felt then that Timmie would not return to school.
How or why the two older sisters were permitted to come, as they
did all summer (after Lucia went to ask for them once again) we cannot know. Was Timmie the sacrifice? Often only one child is. Or were
only boys so lacerated in that large sad family? I contrasted Charles's
wet shirt and his gentle father coming to get him, only the session
before.

But now, to cheer us all, we must turn to Sally.

SALLY: After working with his project, Freddy notices an empty box. He
opened the cardboard box and jumped inside. Since the room was
not particularly busy, I watched him with interest. Here was a little
boy amazed by such a simple thing as a cardboard box.

He pulled the flaps over his head, looking so cute that I wished I
had had a camera, but the best was still to come. Anthony (who is colored, Freddy white) had the same look of amazement on his face. It
seemed as if he read in Freddy's face, "Come play with me. My parents don't mind because your skin is darker than mine. Please come
and play with me."

Soon, Anthony was in the box too. Here were two children playing
together—not one black child and one white child but TWO CHIL-
DREN. This was one of the main experiences that made me decide
that this is where I belong (working with underprivileged children),
learning as they learn, because no other field I am sure can be as
rewarding to me as helping children to learn and play side by side,
unaffected by prejudice or fear.

F.H.: To my personal and to future children's delight, Sally announced
that she wanted to go to college, then into teaching. A week later
Maureen announced her own resolve to go on to college—in social
work. Both girls did follow those careers (see A Boston High School
at the end of this chapter).

MAUREEN: Rhonda—As I entered the workshop where she was working, she got up and held my hand, leading me to her work. "Let me
show you what I did," she said. "I made purple." She had mixed blue
and red paints on the board. She then added that she had a PURPLE
THUMB.

Anthony worked with wood but hung around Freddy, his pal
from the episode of the box. Laughed a lot over Shirley's act.

Mrs. H. worked with small groups of children. She brought some
objects (Japanese water flowers) which, when placed in water,
opened to flowers and had many beautiful colors. The children recognized the changed form, and we had some interesting comments.
Robert said, "Ooh, it's getting big." Shirley was astonished. Gail said,
"Them are worms?" And so the comments kept rolling our way.

The whole class was called together, and Mrs. H. said she had a
surprise in her basket. She shook the basket so that the group would
hear sounds made by what was inside. She asked them what they
thought it was. Once more she received several answers and questions such as the following: Was it alive? Checkers? A belt? A toy? A
drum? Bread? Something to eat? But when the basket was opened,
there were large rocks [from Africa] of many beautiful colors. . . . The
children were amazed at the colors. . . . [They were] magnificent—
amethyst, pink quartz, green jade, and others.

F.H.: As Maureen records, I used rocks for a mystery game of "What's in
my basket today?" With the sound these large rocks made in the
deep, covered basket when I shook it, the children were fascinated. I
got Lucia to ask the first questions—"Can you eat it?" etc., and soon
the beginnings showed of children understanding something of the
logic of the game Twenty Questions. Maureen reported that "the children were simply excited over the rocks, it was something just to
gaze at their little faces as they looked in disbelief." Interest lasted a
long time, and all were delighted to see and hold the pink quartz, the
amethyst, etc. Shirley, bless her, asked, "Are they from Africa?" They
were! Such were beginnings for category games.

Robert's gaiety was a joy to see. Was he reacting to sister Shirley's
acceptance of us, her now daily attendance, our warm welcome to
her?

Shirley's drama echoed around us after the children had left and
we were having our daily, if brief, noon meeting. Shirley's overt
reflection of adult life posed itself as a stark opposite to Timmie's battered back—and what hidden horrors it revealed.

The strict, religious, devoted, but fiercely punitive regime at the B.'s home conformed rather closely to one pattern the slum dweller has for escaping its bondage: "Spare the rod and spoil the child. . . . Parents are responsible for their children's delinquency!" The stern declarations of law and order—advising on how to protect your children from the degradation of these slums—were all on the side of the Bs. As Jeannette had said, the children came immaculate and starched; they were not allowed to play with anyone of doubtful reputation; they took music lessons, had glasses when needed. They never wandered in the street . . .

In such matters, how can one dare pass judgments? For me, it is better to ask another question first. What evidence of damage to the human soul can be seen? For me, in this case, the answer lies in children's behavior and activities. The behavior and participation of these children in morning and afternoon programs, compared with Robert's and Shirley's, for example, was by now so striking it implied that a drunken reaction to life in that street, like that of Robert and Shirley's father, was the less destructive one. Can one really know this, and how can one even say it? At that meeting of our young staff, it was not my right to do so. I tried to express my belief that both patterns were pathological but understandable in the cruel, disordered society in which these children were forced to live. The variables were legion, but we could learn much if we would study these children with a historical compassion and thoughtfulness. Timmie we had lost, and in our sorrow we felt frightened even to wish him back. The feel of that thin 4-year-old shoulder, the bloody back, still remind me of failure. I was never to see him again. Dylan Thomas was wrong, of course—after the first death there is another and another. . . . But certainly he was right: they are all one.

Day Nine: No One Wants to Leave

Colors and prisms, mobiles, games, and puzzles.
Formal language.
Air and pumps, balance, and a story.
Stars, a quiet moment, and NO BOOKS, please.
Structures tall and small; attribute blocks.
Twenty Questions and a top.
The old beloved tools and "a voice of pride."

Digging for roots.
And no one wants to leave.

F.H.: In the intensity of this day I stored no memory of five adult visitors.
One wonders what they made of our ways.

In the rhythm of our days, we of the staff continued, in time available, to discuss all this life we were a part of. This ninth morning was the halfway point; but since the closing date had not yet been set, we knew this only in retrospect.

The previous session we had all seen, with misery, the world of Timmie. It lay beyond our direct powers of amelioration, but it was heavy on us. Did the growth of his sisters, Donna and Mary, soften his misery—or did it intensify it? Such questions remain. The previous session had also provided a stage for Shirley; we discussed what we had been able to learn by watching through children's eyes—their reactions to a slice of their out-of-school life. It had been role-playing at a high level of sophistication.

And so came Friday with its own character—unpredictable except in its excitement, vividness, and uniqueness. I had borrowed some puzzles, games, a kaleidoscope (with empty cartridges so one could insert any small pieces to become the mulltimirrored image), and a large, handsome singing top. Until now, I had not felt the need for this type of more "programmed" equipment. Programmed, that is, by adult designers who think that when the toys are played or worked with, they will transmit to the children the intelligence that designed them. They sometimes can, but only if children's curiosity and intelligence have already grown to meet the challenge. This morning's reactions give clues that some children were ready.

If we had provided, in the early days of South End, an abundance of adult-structured, sequenced games and puzzles, I believe the pattern of learning would have been adversely affected. I submit this statement as a hypothesis but one strongly supported by my past mistakes in having done just that—in having failed to analyze what was communicated to those beginning schoolchildren when I overloaded the environment with "puzzles" and the making of pleasant-enough artifacts, teacher-directed. I believe that when this is done, the children receive an implicit message: "Figure out what the right answer is—what the adults have embedded, what you must learn." In our too-brief staff meetings here we tried to carry on discussions of these deep but vital matters.

The material itself is not often seen as possibly carrying its own message embedded, available, sometimes with a little help. Watch Michael with a magnet, Robert with a drill, or Gail with bubbles. We remember young Diane with the workings of the drill, Rhonda discovering that red and blue paint make her thumb purple. Since our days were filled with such inventions and discoveries, we could directly observe the powers to teach that lie in some materials.

And now, but only on this ninth day, I did introduce new materials—attribute blocks. These had been originally designed for "logic" teaching, classification involving attributes of shape, size, and color. They are also extraordinarily adaptable to the many uses children may put them to, uses often "logically" far more complex than mere classifications. I thought to find out about our children's use of them.

Maureen recorded how I started.

MAUREEN: Mrs. Hawkins, sitting on the floor, started to play with the attribute blocks. She had the children close their eyes, then she'd take away one of the shapes to see if they noticed any changes when they opened their eyes. Freddy said, "I saw that missing" and pointed to the empty space where a triangle had been.

F.H.: The informality of this introduction of games with these blocks was planned to fit into the total offering, and it seemed to work. Children began building with them and making up games.

MAUREEN: Rhonda was walking around with no specific thing to indulge in, but she noticed Mrs. H. and the game going on with the attribute blocks. She quickly became a part of it. Freddy didn't always catch on to the way the blocks were being taken, but he knew the colors. Soon it was Rhonda's turn to close her eyes and have one of her blocks taken. When she opened her eyes she said, "He took the red triangle." She was correct. Robert joined the group, then Elizabeth. All soon understood what was going on.

F.H.: Transformations: A board is a board is a train is a balance! Michael used the balance board the most, on its low fulcrum on the floor; he stood on it and walked back and forth, watching and feeling it go up and down. Freddy took the long board and ran it straight across the floor, calling it a train from rapt attention.

With satisfaction one observes two children (Michael, a mature 5, and Freddy, a young 4) work essentially side by side and build for their own needs and levels. Does this small episode throw any light on the rather murky arguments over heterogeneous and homogeneous groupings? If narrow provisioning and one-answer materials are prevalent, older children will get "the" answer first and thus dominate the scene. But if not, then not!

I highlight in my memory Freddy at the dollhouse, too charming to miss. He would curl up in one of the top-floor rooms, where he fit if he assumed a fetal position. With eyes closed, he would take a "brief nap," climb down, stretch, and go off refreshed.

In the midst of such a morning, a teacher's radar screen is overflowing. The new materials—the attribute blocks—are being used along with the old, and there was a hum of self-direction and involvement that one assesses with satisfaction and renewed curiosity.

The variety of responses to a set of small shapes—stories told, analogies discovered, patterns and structures designed—reflects a new phase in which these children are listening with their own well-tuned ears and investing new materials to become part of their own experiences. I focus my observations for more specific clues, and the design for the last weeks begins to take form.

MAUREEN: I sat and sat watching for a time these enigmatic children at work. But they soon left me alone with Freddy. He slapped me on the shoulder from behind, not in violence but to ask my approval of what he had done. But then I heard running feet; I gazed behind to see a head, a head that was peeking from behind a board. It was Gail's; she was getting dressed in Shirley's favorite dress. Lucia called me to see Tommy's creation, and I said so long to this drama.

F.H.: What Tommy was doing must be carefully told. He had built a tower on a base of three regular blocks on end, with a round, flat piece of Masonite on top. Then on top of this were three more blocks and Masonite, supporting in turn a third story. Each story was defined by round, flat pieces of Masonite in the structure. The tower was already taller than Tommy, and he had a piece of triangular Masonite in hand and was gently testing the tower's steadiness against his taps. Small taps and the tower would lean, settle, and become still. Again and again he varied the strength and place of the taps; watched, waited, tapped again, and finally—on purpose—did hit hard enough to topple the structure. Then the entire process of building the tower and testing it was repeated. No wonder he found it hard to leave! Balance!

I nominate Tommy for the next earthquake commission.

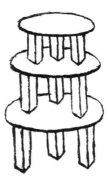

MAUREEN: The children were by now gathered around in a circle, listening to the description of a new surprise. Finally a big spinning and
singing top, which was beautiful in color, was shown to them. They
were fascinated by the way the individual colors disappeared as the
top went around. They remembered in the discussion that they had
seen the colors before. They were then asked to form a bigger circle,
and Susan refused to hold Charles's hand, protesting that it was
dirty. It wasn't that bad.

F.H.: All the children's positive response to some types of group gathering strengthened my reliance on continuing it. The gathering Maureen speaks of here was to introduce the top—which was concealed
at first; I hid it in its box. Was it that it had the element of mystery,
of what was in the box? Or the fun of question-response, with by -
products of humor introduced among more sober questions by Lucia
and Sally over "Is it as big as an elephant? Small as an ant?" All of
this silliness provided us with one of the few types of group experience the children were finally ready for. More "logic." It was propitious as a beginning but would have evolved as the children's growth
dictated wider needs over a longer period.

Trouble? Yes. One top, many children, fatigue after too much sitting at the end of the morning! But read Maureen's final report.

MAUREEN: In the woodworking room we have five children at work.
The sounds of saws, hammers, and drills surround me, the voice with
pride from a child having succeeded in driving a nail through a piece
of wood. The room was suddenly silent, but once again the sound of

the apparatus began. Rhonda came to me, showing me a "flashlight" that she had made. The workshop was now occupied by Gail, Robert, Tommy, and Rhonda, also Anthony. The children all seemed surprised at the time. They didn't want to go home.

Day Ten: "A Moth Could Be Sleeping"

Hot weather! 102°F.
"A moth could be sleeping."
Foolish answers to untimely questions.
When is a group too large?
A moth's first flight to watch and follow.
Freddy's song.
Tempers, age, heat, and Perry dives into the pool.
$1 + 1 = 1$.
Dali?
And no one wants to leave.

F.H.: Elizabeth, one of the playground children, "clings" to the butterfly cage in Maureen's notes. I missed that. I could have built on it or gone alone with her to hunt butterflies. Another chance passed over.

By now we might well have divided the children into smaller groups more often. But time was short, and instead I thought about a final week with small groups as an alternative. We could, in fact, have used five days each week for these final times. For that matter, and for the children's sake, we could have used five days a week from the beginning. The staff simply could not have given the time.

MAUREEN: Mrs. H. brought the butterfly cage with a caterpillar, which had changed to a moth. Robert was sitting on his haunches looking at what was inside the cage. Lucia called me over, telling me that Robert had something to show me. I guess he figured I should have known what it was. He was silent. Mrs. H. later told me that when she brought the cage to Robert, she thought that the moth was dead, saying to Robert, "Robert, you know, the moth could be dead." He responded, "Well, it could be sleeping." He gently shook the glass for awhile, and presto, it was alive.

Robert was given a prism, he said that he saw rainbows—"pink," blue, and yellow. Freddy placed the prism to his right eye and remarked that he could see Lucia from the prism though she was sitting beside him.

F.H.: Children fascinated with prism—of course, and they exploit it rather fully on their level, so much so that the prism was one of the few things to disappear. Meritorious theft? Another such was a screwdriver! I bought two more.

MAUREEN: In the garden Mrs. H. took the cage to show the children, with the moth and a caterpillar. The children made their circle so all could see. Perry said, "I can't see." "Move back and the circle will get bigger," said Mrs. H. Michael remarked that the legs of the moth looked like black-and-white stripes. Perry insisted that he wanted to go back upstairs.

Robert wandered away from the others and went to sit on the steps by himself. He saw a butterfly and ran after it. Perry was getting quite irritable, and once more he said, "I want to go back up." Lucia took him and a few more upstairs. I followed them in order to get the outdoor apparatus for those who were staying out.

F.H.: It was seldom possible by now to keep the older children in a body in the yard. Their own work-play going on in the room was too engrossing—especially to the older ones. Young Diane and some others often asked to go to the yard.

MAUREEN: As I joined the children, the moth from [the] cage made his first flight. Michael, Freddy, Charles, and Lorraine were watching the moth. Michael said, "We should have brought the magnifying glass" and went upstairs to get it. We started to look for the cage, realizing it was missing. I went upstairs, only to find Elizabeth clinging to the cage, refusing to let me have it.

F.H.: Should have had more than one cage! When we released our moth it flew off; we waved and called "good-bye!" "Thank you," the moth seemed to say by its flying. The moth settled near, and we ran to watch it settle on a branch. Then it flew to a tree and settled again. Children following were delighted and stayed near—no one trying to touch or catch. We had freed it, it was learning to fly.

MAUREEN: Inside, a make-believe swimming pool was invented today, and it was delightful to see the children take their shoes off and "plunge in," as if in a real pool. It was continually being enlarged by pushing blocks back and adding more. Freddy said, "Somebody is

knocking down this, I don't want nobody to knock this down."
Tommy and his cousin (who was visiting) were the only ones at work
in the workshop.

F.H.: It was such a hot day that my subconscious must have suggested
the swimming pool. The children who dived in stayed, and somehow
we all felt cooler! What nonsense! Perry actually looked puffy from
the heat. 102° that day in South End.

MAUREEN: I was asked to return from the workshop to the scene of the
swimming pool. Some of the children wrestled a little in the pool.
Lucia tried to explain to Perry that he shouldn't go on the so-called
diving board because he was liable to be hurt. Perry wouldn't listen
to anything, he just said, "Move, move outa' my way, and leave it
alone." He rolled the tire tube into the middle of the pool, screaming
as he went along. Michael said, "Perry, get out of here." Freddy
called for help because he had fallen on some blocks; he wasn't hurt.
Stevie was pumping air into another tire tube. Shirley started to
scream, and everyone joined her. All interest in the pool vanished.

   Perry started to have a dispute with Freddy; he told him, "You
can't get in my house." Freddy left him. I was aroused by Robert
singing to himself, "See you later alligator, after awhile crocodile." By
now Freddy was running up and down. I returned to the workshop
to find seven busy boys. Mrs. Hawkins was supervising, and she had
to give them another lesson on how to be careful with the tools.
Freddy entered and had to be seated. These children were soon copying each other in the making of helicopters.

F.H.: And getting wild in the process. That Maureen sees what the children were making as helicopters is interesting. In fact, the children
were using strips of Peg-Board Masonite as moving parts in a free
manner, unstructured and inventively. Once the word "helicopter"
was mentioned, the jig was up, and most began to make helicopters.
Sometimes—as here with tools and 102° temperatures, "copying each
other"—children get wilder and wilder, possibly leading to injuries.
It was easier for me to spend a half hour in the workshop with the
children than to ask a novice to cope with a difficult, degenerating situation. Another side of this troubleshooting had to do with the copying. This may be related to the kind of notice or praise given—to one
child, for example, which others may then seek to emulate. It is not at
all a simple matter for beginning teachers to understand. I remember!

MAUREEN: The workshop was occupied by Michael, Perry, Johnny, Stevie, Freddy, and Tommy. Freddy was now the only one hammering, while Michael, and Johnny were painting structures they had made. Mike F., Tommy's cousin, then took the red paint and painted his fingernails. Michael K. said to me, "Hey, yellow and blue makes green!" I was very impressed by his discovery,

I went to the playhouse room, which was dripping wet with clothes washing, and stayed for awhile. Then I rejoined the group to hear Mrs. Hawkins say, "I'm going to take Freddy across the street." Time to go. Robert was taking money from his shoes, Perry stood by the piano, Stevie was playing with the balance board. And so it was near the end of another busy, irritating, hot day for us in the kindergarten at the South End House. Yet the children were reluctant to leave.

P.S.: I was told by Mrs. Hawkins that earlier in the morning Robert [had] brought a pan to her which had contained water some days before but was now empty. How come? He wanted to know where all the water had gone to and so she asked him, "Robert, do you know where the water might have gone?" He quickly answered, "I don't know."

Robert said to me when he was leaving, "You, you're a nutty, nutty, nutty girl." He also told one of his friends the same.

LUCIA: Notes here refer to Robert's question, which had spread among the children. A number of kids were asked about the disappearing water. No one had ever heard of evaporation. Liz said it went into the wooden flowers (Japanese)—having a notion of it being soaked up. Robert said it leaked out. Someone else said it spilled.

Day Eleven: The Mailman Cometh

Temperature 103°.
The big ones come to school.
Maureen and Lorraine read a story.
The mailman cometh.
Temper, temper everywhere.
Married girls and flower girls.
Fire engine—trash can.
Freddy shines, and Charles learns to measure.

F.H.: The heat this whole week! On an earlier hot day before school began, when young men who were members of the Northern Student Movement were helping us move in, someone turned on the garden hose, and they all stripped to their jeans and had a cool sprinkle. Mel King spoke to me about it; a neighbor had complained. Prudery, prudery!

The variety of sustained work-play activities degenerated while a few children and I were gone to buy more hammers. But the dominant and continuing mode now is that of a purposeful getting busy—on one's own.

At the hardware store the children had unanimously chosen full-size hammers over small ones: "The heavy ones! The heavy ones!" was their joint cry.

Maureen continues with a familiar topic.

MAUREEN: It started out to be a day of confusion because the visiting older children numbered eight or nine. They were just walking in and out. But let's get back to the B. brothers. When the two of them walked in the door, sister Donna said, "I'm going to tell on you!" Perhaps this was because they were here? I looked around, and Freddy was busy talking to himself, saying, "New York is a big city. It's a *big* city."

I went to the almost empty playhouse. Johnny entered, followed by Lorraine. I asked if anyone wanted me to read a story; after all, I was seated right at the table with the storybooks. Brenda said, "Nope." Johnny said, "Not me." Lorraine (Denise's sister), who is 7, said, "I would, yes." I read her a story, and she showed great interest in it. Elizabeth was playing nearby while I read. She got interested in the story and drew closer.

F.H.: During this heat wave, every day above 100 degrees, tempers were short all around. Our weaknesses showed: my age, the girls' youth and inexperience, the children's narrow and harassed lives at home. I missed "mailman" Rhonda; was glad Maureen took the step of reading to Lorraine and Elizabeth.

Had the mores been less strict in the South End, I would have taken all the children to the yard and sprinkler—wearing panties. I knew this would cause trouble at the Settlement House; these days reflect such frustrations also.

The older visiting Bs. had asked to mend the dollhouse. We had furnished it with plastic furniture; we finally understood why we always found all the furniture in one room! The children *lived in one, sometimes two rooms* of what had once been spacious family homes.

Maureen takes note of conversations overheard.

MAUREEN: The big children were hammering, and blocks were being tossed around. Suddenly Donna asked me, "Can girls GET married to girls?" I was amazed at the conversation, . . . but I didn't have any choice but to listen. I answered, "Of course not." Elizabeth said to me, "Donna and me are gonna MARRY him." Stevie was the object of their conversation. All of a sudden Stevie told me, "I ain't making you nothing." Donna told Stevie, "You can have two girlfriends but not to marry." Elizabeth chimed in with "Donna is going to be the married girl, and I'm going to be the flower girl."

F.H.: Perry put his foot into his clean cup four times before he got juice on this hot day. I took him aside, where he waited—chastened—until last, when he was ready to come back and have a clean cup.

MAUREEN: Freddy did a very admirable thing today. He spilled some juice on the floor, and Johnny saw it, but he didn't know who had done it. He said to me, "Look, someone spill, who spilled it?" Freddy quickly said, "I did." They left for the yard, all except Shirley. She wanted to build a house.

F.H.: The quixotic Freddy may have his troubles, but they do not have to do with deceit or guile. His dad took him home, remember, happily, with no shirt.

Maureen finishes the day for us.

MAUREEN: Many children were in the workshop. They were very playful, and it didn't seem as if they wanted to go home. When it was time to go, someone was starting to paint.

The day was a very busy and tiresome one because of the heat and the big children who came in. At [our] teachers meeting, which wasn't very long, we tried to decide who from the older group should and shouldn't come. Lorraine (Denise's older sister), we decided, wasn't any trouble and should be encouraged to come.

I've never told of the pouring of Charles's bubble liquid. He was in the habit of pouring an overflow into cans from the coffee pot, but today he measured the mixture about an inch deep in the cans—with care and accuracy. This was wonderful, in Lucia's opinion.

Day Twelve: Fishing

Brief haven.
Robert's extraordinary project.
Mother Diane with cradle, doll and hammer.
Plenty of fish.
Kaleidoscope for Rhonda.
Tommy finds one will give two.

F.H.: Tommy and Robert had never read an essay by the engineer-novel-
ist Hans Otto Storm. But they and others were prototypes for Storm's
description of children at serious play. He observed them well:

Children, when they construct things in play, normally play after
the eolithic fashion; a pointed board suggests the making of a
boat, and if the toy, in process of construction, begins to look less
and less like a boat, it can conveniently be turned into an airplane. . . . Select the child who appears most ingenious in the
making of this class of toys, . . . *give him a simple plan which must,
however, be adhered to until completion, and usually his ingenuity
gives way to a disheartening dullness"* [italics mine].[4]

Maureen caught something of the essence of such serious play, the
style of it that Storm called eolithic.

MAUREEN: Robert came out running to Shirley's make-believe house to
show Lucia his project. It was extraordinary and beautiful, in my
opinion. Shirley quickly told him, "You better don't get them clothes
dirty." The way she said it, it was worth hearing.

Mary started to get a store organized in the vicinity of the clay
table. Somehow, instead of Robert being the father, he was now the
son, and his sister was the mother. He went to the store to get the groceries, but he returned only to find his mother still mopping. Freddy
came running through the room and was gone. Robert followed him.

Johnny, Mary, Brenda, Diane, and Tommy were in the workshop
acting very busy. Diane had a doll and cradle in her arms, and she
tried desperately hard to hold onto them and hammer too, but I
believe she sensed her trouble, and the hammer won out over the cradle. She got a piece of wood, and with her hammer she went to work,
but being the baby she is, it was very difficult for her.

Robert and Brenda pretended they were fishing. Of course, we who are working with them know perfectly that there wasn't a pond around, but on the other hand, they knew it too. It was just clean fun they were having, and I thought it was amusing the way they kept running back and forth to show us what they had caught.

F.H.: The "catch" was prodigious! Fishing poles, line, with magnets for hooks, and almost anything—with a bit of the right kind of paper clips attached—did for a fish. Then Lucia and children began drawing fish and putting a staple in each. As can be read, Maureen was caught too! Compare her observation here with her early notes. All self-directed.

MAUREEN: At 11:05 the children in the workshop were working in complete silence, no conversations whatsoever. Rhonda came in with the kaleidoscope and started to play with it. Mrs. H. told her that she could put anything small enough into the cartridge. Rhonda wanted to know if a nail could go in, and with the answer she received—"try it!"—she placed it in herself. The first thing that had been inserted was a bolt, Mrs. H. had done it; but Rhonda wasn't the type who wanted to be shown a second time. The shop was now very quiet. Stevie and Tommy started to hammer.

Tommy said he was making a bridge, but he needed help, and Mrs. H. came to give it to him. He took a piece of wood—wanted two—and she asked him what he could do to make two from his one. He said, "I don't know," but she didn't take that for an answer. She asked him to look and think, and this time he thought awhile and said, "You *saw* it!" *He placed the wood in such a position that he did saw it into two equal pieces.*

Tommy wanted to make a door, but we didn't have any hinges. Mrs. H. took him to a real door to show him what hinges were. She then asked him how many hinges the big real door had. He looked and said two. She asked him if they were in one place. He said no, one was on the bottom and one was on the top.

F.H.: We began a door with tape hinges, and the next session, with Lucia's help, Tommy finished. With Tommy this kind of help is legitimate—he will not be a copier, ever—and he had begun the door. Maureen's saga continues.

MAUREEN: Donna B. got her dress soiled with paint. I had to help her get the dress clean again. When I had the paint out, she showed me some more spots. . . . I had to fight them too. I wanted to.

Tomato juice was served, but the children didn't care for it. "I don't like it," "I don't want it." We had more don't like its than don't want its. I hope you understand what I mean! The B.'s liked it, and Stevie did too.

Day Thirteen: "How Do You Spell Love?"

Mail bags!
And letters!
How do you spell "love"?
Paul Klee.
And clay to mold.

F.H.: What a morning! I had promised my young associates that the harvest would come, even if only when we were no longer around to see it. But here it was. One may not set a date for such a breakthrough or forecast any particular episode, but after enough experience one sees the good grain forming and knows that with protection it will grow well. We had seen and shared small indications, but much had been taken on faith. This week we have reaped, with joy. For me the children's breakthrough regarding writing and reading was exciting, if predicted; but the excitement of the staff was a lovely bonus.

Today began before school when I remembered the pleasure and fun other groups had experienced with large brown paper bags and junk "letters" to deliver. Brenda had brought me a "letter" the Friday before, but I had been too preoccupied to carry her implied suggestion further. She had delivered such mail before. Remembering clues from the children, on this morning I realized they were ready for new input from the staff.

So, I tied string through punched holes in a couple of large paper bags with the edges folded over several times. In them I dropped a few old IBM punch cards for letters.[5] When Robert came I offered him one of the "mailbags" with a bare suggestion—the bag does the trick. With more children, more bags were needed; and the lovely quality of fantasy entered at once—allowing many mailmen, more IBM letters, and invented letters or drawings to be sent, received, and deciphered.

At first I would "read" a letter out loud that had just been delivered to me: "Dear Mrs. H., I hope we will have cookies with juice today, Love, Shirley." When the message is changed quickly and is obviously made-up, humor and silliness dominate, and anyone can "write," "read," and deliver.

Then the few who could indeed write (or copy) caught a bug. "How do you spell Lucia?" "How do you spell Sally, Maureen, Mrs. Hawkins?" "How do you spell love?" For those who hadn't yet learned to write letters, crayons were needed for pictures and make-believe writing. Even baby Freddy had a fine time making the few letters he knew, running in all directions, so that his green sheet with a different color for each letter resembled the work of a young Paul Klee. Thus the work was easily adjusted for all levels; many real letters were dictated to me or copied by our older ones. Delivering and receiving went on and on, with the magic and logic of reading and writing the central theme to be savored and built around—avidly.

Lucia, having been on the receiving end of many love letters in the far wood shop, came to the door with eyes shining. "What is happening? I need paper and crayons!" Letters were now flowing in two directions. "Is this what you meant last spring, Franny?" she asked, "when you were pleading that we observe and trust these children in this setting?" Oh yes, Lucia, It certainly was!

With the exception of a sign or two ("Store," "Open," "Closed"), this was the first turning toward the printed word, less startling for our youngest. But it should be remembered that stories told and books read had been shunned by most. Robert, Shirley, and Anthony could read. Joy in stories (perhaps their own, written first?) would come—summer is too short.

Maureen takes us farther into the morning.

MAUREEN: I arrived finding Mrs. Hawkins playing in clay with Robert and Shirley. Well, she wasn't playing in it, she was just rolling it around in her hands with a direct motion.

F.H.: I *was* playing. Clay available on a table was being ignored, I decided to try a more direct method—getting in myself. It worked; some wonderfully weird and free things were produced. I seldom finished anything I started but kept making fresh starts and talking about them. "This is just a thing, I guess, but I want it tall and big—Maybe now I'll try a turtle—Gail's is certainly growing."

MAUREEN: Donna and Mary B. entered the front door and went directly toward the playhouse. Shirley, who was still with Mrs. Hawkins at the clay table, said, "I know where they're going, they're going to get the buggy." She said it almost disgustedly because they always love to play with the carriage. Mrs. Hawkins called out to Donna and Mary. She wanted to know if Mary wasn't going to give her a hug. I felt this strange because the children weren't accustomed to this type of arrangement from her. The Bs. just made it a habit of rushing to the playhouse whenever they came in. Today Mrs. Hawkins said, "I'd give you both a hug, but my hands are dirty, and since yours aren't you could give me one instead!" Mary came over and leaned against Mrs. H. Both children grinned and hurried off to the playhouse.

F.H.: I felt suddenly confident this morning that these two strange, silent little girls were ready for and needed to add some human warmth to their lives from us. The slowing of their steps, their coming toward me signaled willingness, and the leaning against me must have relieved some stiffness (see Mary hugging Maureen later in the day).

A first-aid station was started by Rhonda, who efficiently acted as the nurse in charge. Mary B. was her first patient, with a sick finger. Rhonda fixed the finger with cotton and soapy water, and Mary was quickly sent on her way. Incidentally, Mary's finger was "bleeding" red paint.

Teacher Sally, seeing what Rhonda was doing, asked her to fix her finger. Rhonda started by soaking the cotton in water and placing it on one of the wooden circles from the workshop being used for medicine to see if it was dry enough. Sally got a little impatient and asked the nurse when her finger was going to be taken care of. Rhonda told her, "When I get ready." She then got one of the sticks we used for mixing paste to put in Sally's mouth. She wasn't about to fix a finger, but she wanted to pull a tooth. She took the stick and wanted to look in Sally's mouth to find out which tooth needed pulling.

MAUREEN: I withheld my interest from Dr. Rhonda for awhile, not willingly though.

Tommy came and went directly to the workshop. I returned my interest to Rhonda once more, just in time to see her mopping the floor. She had spilled water.

F.H.: This morning we felt some of the half-willing-to-come children would come if we went out again to bring them. We decided a week ago to let Sally and Lucia go to certain children's homes, but later we decided to take advantage of having fewer children and to work with them on an individual basis. We all felt it had been worth working with fewer children, as we had done, and being alert to opportunities when possible. No lesson plans for us.

MAUREEN: Today some children's homes were visited by Lucia and Sally. They went to Mrs. P.'s home first to find out why Gail and Anthony, who have come so faithfully, had been absent for a week. Their mother told them the reason they hadn't come was because she had had a baby, and there wasn't anyone to bring them. She said she had left them with a friend while she was in the hospital, and she didn't want to impose by asking her to bring them.

Lucia told me that our Anthony, Gail, a crawling baby, and Lorraine (8 years old) live in an "apartment" on the fourth floor. The stairs were very dangerous, without rails from the second to the fourth floor, very shaky. The living room was very big; it had a bed in it and nothing else except a crib with the new baby.

Lucia suggested that she could take them to school, but Mrs. P. said they were about to have some oatmeal, and she'd have her husband bring them or someone walking across Tremont Street.

Lucia and Sally returned with Jackie, Denise, Lorraine, and Allan. Yes, Allan. That's the only name I know him by. Allan seemed very competent with tools, and the others received him well.

LUCIA: Freddy is the only one who plays with Allan outside of kindergarten. They live across the street from each other. The others have been warned to stay away from Allan because he "steals." Confusion about who is home to take care of and feed these children—always hungry, always eating candy. Some difference in attitude developed by his brief attending of summer kindergarten. Others aware of his competence with tools. He also insisted on writing his own name on paintings and a coat hook, where most of the others watched as we wrote theirs. Some children watched as he printed his name, Allan. Don't know what previous reinforcement makes him enjoy writing his name. Has been kept back in the first grade.

MAUREEN: The children worked in groups, and it was a day for playing mailman. They were interested in dictating notes by a teacher for a teacher. It was remarkable to see their interest.

LUCIA: Brenda seemed to enjoy the mailman play so much. Never saw her more involved with anything. Never can tell who will take [to] what [and] when. Pointing up again the importance of offering a number of different things for the kids to get into.

F.H.: As she often did, Maureen observed significant details.

MAUREEN: At juice time, Freddy still chummed with Allan. Allan had a scar over his left eye, and Freddy asked him, "How come you got that?" Allan said, "I fell down," and Freddy immediately took an empty cracker box and knocked him on the head with it. I guess it made Allan angry, and he folded his little fist, but he didn't hit.

Mary B. surprised me today. I was sitting in a chair, and she came on me from the back, with a hug for history. She had never done this before, but she wanted to cling to me. I was happy over the whole situation. I can never tell my real feelings. Denise, seeing what Mary was doing, started the same thing. I was sitting on the floor with the children, and Denise came from the back with a hug and a kiss from this world. Take it from me, when some of these children hug you and try to kiss you at the same time from behind, you've got to be able to stand your ground.

F.H.: Love is contagious. Denise asked for affection often but this is different. Mary hugging Maureen was an important first step.

Day Fourteen: Instruments, Important Notes

Instruments made, hugged, and taken home.
Two mailmen.
Jell-O making—smoke or steam?
Hose reigns, and joy.
Jackie can stay.
Sleepy hands.

F.H.: At a noon meeting we spoke of many of our children's lag in language usage, of the contrast between their abilities and their language—in spite of observed gains. Two or three were well on their way, but others were not yet. Lucia had spent a day with friends and their loquacious 3-year-old. She was shaken by the contrast. Such a family-centered pleasure as exchanging thoughts, sharing experiences, and recounting adventures—all that can come at so young an age. Misery shows and prevents development.

Some of our families here—if they can be called families—are too heavily laden with despair, fear, and hunger to be able to do more than use language sparsely and only when necessary. Lucia's visit with the 3-year-old reminded us. The language precocity of Michael King and Rhonda we had taken for granted. They were 5, they lived in comfortable homes, they belonged to families.

MAUREEN: In spite of my haste to make it on time this morning, Sally and I went to Allan's home on the way to school. We went because we wanted him to come to class and because he wants to come, and the only way to insure his coming is to go for him.

I was quite sad about the surroundings of the place as it was the first time I had ever seen the so-called home of any of these children. We knocked on the door but had some difficulty in getting anyone to answer at first. We were greeted by this young woman who didn't seem to know if she had an Allan living there. Well, Sally told her why we were there, and she said that he would be coming later.

On my way from Allan's house, I had to ask myself a few questions concerning this problem which we are all faced with. In this world of sadness and uncertainty, I often have to ask myself what gives me the authority to freely state my opinions on these children, what on earth ever gave me the blessed idea that I might be a better person than some of these [people] in this area. Well, I come up with answers which only were meant for me to try to believe myself. And I still wonder—how, when, and where?

F.H.: Maureen was born and raised in Jamaica, and she received her early education there, not in the United States.

Robert and Anthony and two or three others had come today before I arrived. One of them found a large box of wide and thin rubber bands behind the piano. I had brought it days before to use for sounds and had lost it! So now together we took time to construct very simple musical instruments. The children were fascinated. Shoe boxes, large and small ones, were strung with different widths of rubber bands. The boys hugged their boxes when they were not strumming them. "Can we take 'em home?" The sounds from large boxes and rubber bands were rich and deep—changes came from box size, band size; we experimented. Another door opened!

Now to Maureen's early morning report:

MAUREEN: The children were very busy when I arrived. I tried to see what was a possibility in the main room, and I immediately sat down to find out. I suddenly felt a weight which I knew I hadn't brought with me. I glanced around to see the beaming face of Mary B. It was simply thrilling to have the feeling I had then. This was something I had wondered about.

Brenda was the first one to start off the mailman trip. Anthony soon copied the idea. Now we had two mailmen.

I was still sitting when I saw teacher Jeannette bringing Allan. The first thing he did was paint, at least he started to. He saw a ball on a nearby table. Believe me, it was something to see, the way he ran at the ball, hugged it, and said, "Ball, ball." I wanted to shed tears for him and myself. Why? It was a feeling which surrounded me.

Freddy and Shirley were painting. I looked through the bathroom and saw Denise and Donna exchanging slaps between themselves. It appears that Donna had [kept] the carriage for quite some time, as was usual, and Denise wanted to use it, but Donna wouldn't permit her. It was settled by Mrs. Hawkins, who has a marvelous way of handling situations like that.

F.H.: What I do in such an impasse situation is not marvelous, although it may seem so to beginners, but it IS logical. It does indeed have a magic quality, that of trusting the two who are at war and providing them with new alternatives for their still-small repertoires of conduct. It goes something like this: I speak to the out-one, here it is Denise: "You watch, Denise, Donna will share with you after she has a longer turn herself. *You* don't grab." This puts Donna on her mettle. They both have new roles to play—one to be patient, one to be generous. And I leave the scene. The two are then center stage together, with trust from me rather than commands. It often works.

Maureen introduces a new occupation, once more revealing something of South End life.

MAUREEN: The children were taken to an empty room to make Jell-O. It was another instance for anyone who has a feeling for children to have seen. Mrs. H. cautioned the children not to come near the hot water. She asked, "Now, when hot water spills on you, what happens?" They answered, "You get burn." When she brought the hot water in she asked if they knew what was coming out of the spout. A few of them said it was smoke. Lorraine said it was steam.

JEANNETTE: Our great circle, sitting on the floor with the giant mixing bowl in the center, gave everyone an excellent view of the Jell-O-making process. They noticed the colors of the different Jell-Os put in [and] the smell. And when the hot water was poured in, each one understood and did not move from his spot. The first label given to the steam was smoke. Lorraine suggested steam. Jackie led off with squirts from a plastic lemon, then each had a stir, and we resigned ourselves to the long wait before we ate it—next session.

MAUREEN: They all had a chance to stir the mixture. Jeannette asked them how many had eaten Jell-O before. The reply didn't have me gullible because I couldn't believe that only four out of more than a dozen children could be that fortunate. I couldn't place it in my mind as an actual fact.

In the playground later, Mrs. Hawkins got the splendid idea of bringing out the hose and giving the children wet feet. They were enchanted with the idea. Denise, Jackie, Robert, Perry, Gail, Shirley, Brenda, and Allan all had their shoes off. Diane said she wanted to, but somehow I didn't think it might be okay. Mary, Anthony, Freddy, and Tommy didn't participate with the others in the water. They were otherwise involved.

JEANNETTE: My lack of coordination with the hose finally got Jackie's dress very wet at the bottom. She was concerned, although she was so eager to wiggle her toes in the mud and cried for more. She gave us the familiar refrain, looking at her wet clothes, "I will get a beating." I tried to convince her that it would dry. Very shortly after, Jerome came and said Jackie had to come home. The family was going out somewhere. She was then quite worried but proceeded to leave like a trooper. I told her I would go with her and explain that it was my fault. She was still hesitant but I know sad to leave all the laughter and fun. When we got out on the sidewalk, . . . I asked if Jackie could stay, and the man answered yes. She quickly pulled on my hand in the direction of the kindergarten, and we ran back. . . . When she arrived back at the steps leading into the garden she blurted out happily, "I can stay!" Of the two of us, I do not know who was more delighted.

F.H.: Although I felt wicked about daring to turn the hose on, I did it anyway! The summer was ending, and then Jackie's dress got wet! In the South End one doesn't . . . We tried very hard to keep the hose on feet, but there is something about a hose . . .

Teacher Sally reports on this day's end.

SALLY: As Perry finished his project he said, "All finished. Boy, are my hands sleepy!" He then painted it red. He was the first one that I've

seen who made a platform since the children had been using the
tools. He said, "I'll let it dry and take it home to my mommy." Robert
was the second one to make a platform. Really, I don't know if he had
copied Perry or vice versa. Soon all the children began to make them.
Robert called his a door, Perry called his a hut.

Rhonda hit her finger while hammering and started to cry very
hard. Even after her finger was bandaged, she still cried and wanted
her mommy.

Johnny came into the workshop; he soon started to copy Robert's
door. Mrs. H. gathered the children around the piano. She asked
them: "What did you hear coming down last night?" Donna Murphy
said, "It was all over my parlor floor, mother left windows open last
night." Before Donna said this, the children had answered "rain" to
the question. Charles said, "I didn't [hear rain]." . . . Mrs. Hawkins
asked if the flowers liked the rain. Someone said no. Rhonda said her
corn grew in rain. From then on the conversations became very mingled, and it was hard to keep up with them.

F.H.: It seemed "mingled" throughout, as though just to contribute was
enough, but now at last we do have conversations in small groups.
Hooray!

Day Fifteen: A One-Eared Rabbit

Clay becomes a one-eared rabbit.
Robert looks and thinks.
Allan "kills them all."

F.H.: Allan begins to dominate my thoughts. I have returned more than
once to his history as we know it from the recruiting days and
through the summer, but the overall misery shrouds my understanding. As a beginning we have Jeannette's description of his living
place, with its two teenagers sitting silently, one with a baby. That
was haunting to us all. I think of Allan's rather constant bewildered
attendance; almost as if each time he is brought he is surprised and
pleased we are still here—Freddy, many other children, and welcoming adults. Is he sedated or just constantly hungry?

But now I turn to Robert and Shirley and their mother to cheer me.
These two never miss a day. I met their mother just once when she

was in front of their rooms holding a bag of groceries. I thanked her for sending her wonderful children. She smiled wanly and took a plum from her bag for me. I felt rewarded and in awe of this silent, gallant young woman. Lucia has expressed her appreciation throughout. The father of this small family is often on the street, drunk. With compassion I tell this; with wonder I see the magnificent care the mother bestows, the security the children know through her.

Work with clay has always, in the good tradition, been one of the basics in the kindergarten. Watch Robert, as Maureen reports—matter into form!

MAUREEN: There were five children, plus Mrs. Hawkins, working at the clay table. The clay was very inviting, it gave them a desire to make objects from it.

Robert was working with the clay, trying to make a clown. The neck and head kept falling over. He took it apart and made the neck even longer; it fell again. Mrs. H. told him, "Now look at it, Robert, and think." He quickly said, "I see," broke its head off, and made the neck shorter. When he was finished with his clown, he took a piece of clay and flattened it out in his hand. He called it a watermelon at first but changed his mind and called it a sandwich. Well, as we know, changes take place, and the sandwich became a pocketbook.

F.H.: Maureen has caught the essence of a great moment, to be in on a work of Robert's. It started as a rabbit-clown, smooth and clear of cracks, with one central rabbit ear on a head and long neck. He brought it to me, carefully holding the too-long neck with its heavy head: "Won't stay up," his typical thrifty use of words. We both looked, and I asked him, "What can you do to help?" He turned to the figure and questioned doubtfully, "Make it bigger?" "Go ahead and try," I encouraged. Robert pulled the neck taller and thinner, and of course that made matters even worse. I said to him, "Look again, you can figure it out yourself." Confident that he could, I heard his next words. "I SEE!" And with dispatch, as Maureen reports, he broke off the creature's too-long neck and made it short enough to hold upright both the head and that one long ear!

And now Maureen captures an event that tells its own dark story.

MAUREEN: Anthony and Freddy were fishing with magnets on string and poles, and they were waiting for quite some time before the fish started to bite. John was working at table number two. At this table we had paste, crayons, scissors, safety pins, paper, and sets of the attribute blocks. Johnny took the blocks and mounted them one on top of another. Big square, big circle, big diamond; small triangle, small square, small circle, but then big triangle. Seeing a mistake to his own plan, he quickly removed the triangles and stacked them in reverse order. He seemed to be building from size and color. Jeannette and I couldn't help but watch him. When he saw us staring at his moves, he got up and walked away. But he returned to put the blocks away in the box.

Allan came in and went directly to the clay table. He seemed to want to be everywhere, touching everything at the same time, but then he played with the magnet for a long time. Mrs. H. told me . . . that he was playing with the magnet and some nails. When Allen saw that the nails were hanging onto the magnet and then to each other, he dipped again, held it up to eye level, and yelled: "All them people fighting, all them people fighting." Roughly, he pulled the nails off and yelled, "Kill 'em all, kill 'em all!" He pictured the nails as people fighting, I suppose, and he didn't like the situation, so he just wanted to destroy these people?

At first, when he went over to the make-believe fish pond, friend Freddy said, "Hi there." Allan said, "Oh shut up, Freddy."

Freddy left Anthony fishing and went away for awhile. Gail joined her brother, Anthony, to fish. When Freddy returned he didn't like it and pushed Gail onto the floor.

Just recently, rereading, cutting and editing those days of South End, I think I have understood this small but very instructive scene embedded in Maureen's and my notes, waiting for some twenty-five years to be pulled together and understood—or rather, to be understood so that it could come together and inform us. Because I believe the sequence is so significant, let me repeat Maureen's works "Anthony and Freddie were fishing with magnets on strings and poles, and were waiting quite some time before the fish started to bite. . . ."

"Allan came in, then, and went directly to the clay table. He seemed to want to be everywhere touching everything at the same time." Maureen then includes in her notes my story of Allan with the magnet and nails: "When Allen saw all the nails hanging on to the magnet, de dipped it again, held it up to eye level and yelled, 'All them people fighting! . . .

All them people fighting!' Roughly, he pulled off all the nails, saying as
he did, 'Kill 'em all! Kill 'em all!'"

To appreciate Allan's reaction to the nails and magnet it is useful, if
poignant, to recall Michael King's delight and awe with the same phenomenon, and to remember that these two boys, both Black, lived within
a block of each other. But there sadly the similarity ends. We never
learned who was Allan's mother, or who was responsible for him.

What Michael did and said—in Maureen's words—"Michael knew
there was some connection between the nails and the magnet. When he
gathered the nails from the magnet he saw them hanging to each other,
nails from magnet and a beard of other nails from magnetized nails. He
said, 'Hay, the nails are magnets too'"

Now return to Allan's next move, leaving "all the people fighting."
He walked directly to the two fishermen, who were his special friends.
Freddie even turns to Allan and says, "Hi there!" Allan, still with his previous experience, I think—"Kill 'em all!," then replies, "Oh, shut up,
Freddie!" Freddie left Allan for a while and sister Gail joined Anthony to
fish (there were plenty of poles with magnets). "When Freddie returned
Allan didn't like it and pushed Gail to the floor." What Freddie didn't like
was friend Allan's rejection—which he took out, then, on Gail? This chain
of violence, and its seemingly aimless aspect, suggests a frightening paradigm—especially for later years.

Days Sixteen, Seventeen, Eighteen: The Last Week

F.H.: Part of me, as I review and remember this last week, felt set apart
from the excitement of life in the broader world of summer 1963—
with the interracial milestones being reached and mounting concerns.
Our daughter and some friends were joining Martin Luther King in
his march on Washington. Julie had been in South America leading a
student group and had come to Boston before going to graduate
school at Johns Hopkins. Our Gloucester Street flat overflowed with
the comings and goings, sleepings and eatings of Julie and friends
getting ready for the march.

At the kindergarten, with our free and flexible ways, especially
now that we knew each other, I had been longing to explore the children's learning patterns in a more formal way: with small groups. A

luxury, this—for any teacher who has ever wondered about the effects of changed settings and the magic of smaller groups or one to one; who with too many children has not dreamed of how he or she would react if I . . . ? What would happen if I paired those two? What if . . . ? I was remembering the refusal of the children, at the beginning, to give their attention to any formal or directed pursuit. Would they have altered this behavior?[6]

I was also fully aware that this refusal would cast the darkest of shadows over their narrow school experience, dragging them on toward lives of failure.

In the attribute blocks, as I had hoped, we found materials that aroused children's curiosity, that led them to accept a trusted teacher's guidance. We had only a week remaining, but this week, with the previous five supporting it, could at least point toward what our MIT physicist boss, Jerrold Zacharias, supporting all our summer's activities, would call an existence theorem, a demonstration of possibility. We could open the door, at least a crack, on a world in which learning could flourish among children who came from conditions of radical exclusion, segregation, and poverty.

For all of this fascinating summer, my husband David quoted Aristotle as saying that one swallow, or one fine day, does not make a summer. I can add that one fine summer does not make a good life— though it may help. Were such a six-week school as ours extended for a year, perhaps a decade, the experiment could be complete. In the meantime, there is some published evidence that supports our optimism, though far too little of it.

One of these studies that I mentioned elsewhere is of an intervention with two approximately equal groups of young orphans (all classed as mentally retarded). One group, by practical necessity, had been left to lead dreary and sterile orphanage lives. The other had been placed under quasi-maternal adoptive care in another institution, in humane and stimulating conditions. Three years later, careful observation and tests, including the I.Q., showed large and obviously significant gains, including those of test scores, in the "experimental" group. What is most remarkable, however, is that one of the original investigators, Harold M. Skeels, did a follow-up study of the same individuals in adulthood, when the qualitative differences between the two groups were stabilized, and obvious beyond any doubt. [7]

In all the vast literature on I.Q. and the like, there have been few studies of the direct effects on the lives and learning of young children, of radically improved environments. There is no other longitudinal study, I believe, confirming the major and irreversible effects, from childhood to adulthood, of early life experience.

The story of our last week is surely no evidence of grand educational achievement, but a careful reader may find, in the story of it, that indeed we were on our way toward a higher level of trust, rigor, and learning than would have been at all possible when we began.

Feeling encouraged in my plans by the wish of the young teaching staff members to try their wings without me, I turned the main group of children over to Sally, Jeannette, and Lucia, taking Maureen with me. In this way I would have the privilege of taking one or two or a few throughout the mornings. What happiness!

In an empty adjoining room I had set up a simple, almost stark arrangement: a low round table, a few small chairs, and several sets of the colored attribute blocks. I added construction paper in the same four colors as the blocks, and on each piece of colored paper I had outlined the shapes of individual blocks.

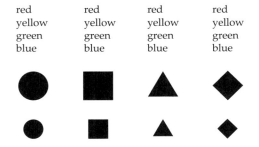

So this small set of thirty-two wooden blocks became the projective material around which we proceeded. Earlier I had been struck and delighted by the children's first informal use of the blocks on their own. The blocks had given the children separate suggestions for ways to use them. Some had matched colors with no attention to shape; others had stacked shapes, forgetting colors; and a few had made structures in a kind of marching-along order. The youngest had built with care and affection structures that might be seen as having been built without thought but that in fact had required small muscle and good mind because of small size, matching angles, and similar constraints.

By chance, young Freddy came to school first this morning, and I lured him to the block room. We sat comfortably side by side, and as I began to fill the green paper with the green shapes. Freddy took a yellow paper and found the blocks he decided to use. No words, but judging from his unusual concentration he was having fun. Maureen came in and noted Freddy's first words: "I'm goin' to do that one too—what is that called?"—pointing to a big red circle. His focus was on shape rather than color.

As happens with some young, closure is sudden, and so with Freddy.

MAUREEN: He looked away for a time; all interest seemed to have gone elsewhere. He looked tired or bored. He left.

F.H.: I suspect that—looking around—Freddy missed friends so important to him, as was the hubbub of his own kindergarten next door. He had been a happy representative of some of his cohorts.

In came Robert, Anthony, and Shirley. Robert's eyes took in the entire scene; still standing, he immediately filled each colored sheet with its matching blocks—color, size, shape—with speed and in an offhand manner, as if to say, baby stuff! Then he sat down and began to build across from me with a fresh set of blocks. Now the other two sat down with us, Anthony with Robert, Shirley with me.

Responding appropriately to the relative quiet and formality, I observed that Anthony and Shirley each took a set of the attribute blocks, gently dumped them, and—without a word—two different structures took shape. Before Anthony had finished his house with a wall, Robert announced that he had a game "for all of us to play— you too, Mrs. Hawkins." I joined with my own set of blocks, and we were off. Robert placed a small red triangle in front of himself, and so did we all, following our leader. "Now your turn to be first, Anthony," Robert pronounced, and silent Anthony put a large yellow square next to his red triangle. We took turns, building a pattern of colors and shapes. But soon Shirley had trouble. She seemed unsure about following, and Robert tried to help her. Watching, I realized that because she was sitting across from the two boys, she was confused by their moves because of right and left. I suggested she move next to them, and her troubles receded.

Although there were no "me first" arguments, three pairs of eagle eyes monitored all moves. First came Robert's "Ya only supposed to take one."

When given my last turn I added a new move, trying to encourage the children's additions: "I'm going to fool all of you. I'm going to try to fool you." "Not me, you can't fool me!" Only a smile from our Anthony. Now all those eagle eyes watched my hands, and I pushed my last piece over to Shirley's structure. Shirley promptly moved her corresponding piece to Anthony's. Then it was Anthony's to Robert's and Robert's to mine. Nice bit of symmetry, that last. "Ya didn't fool me!"

Another round was requested, and when we finished Shirley reminded me again, "Ya din' fool me." As usual, language was sparse, but attention was riveted, with grins of pleasure abounding among these 7-year-olds. (Shirley was 8.)

The boys left, and Shirley stayed on and on, the two of us alone! We had a very warm time—playing, inventing, and laughing at ourselves in a nice, conspiratorial way. After another "Robert game," as Shirley called it, I began by making a row of pieces, mixed shapes, all blue, and under it a row of red, again of mixed shapes, Shirley said, "I can do that." She did, and then said "ah done it!" I looked at what she had done and said, "You found all the shapes; what about the colors?" (She had put in a blue triangle instead of a red one.) With mock horror at herself she identified and corrected the color. Putting her hands over her ears she moaned "Shh" and then beamed—amused at herself. How Robert and Shirley reflect their loving mom!

Shirley took a turn as leader. She tried to fool me: "This gonna be funny." She alternated colors in every second and fourth row, keeping the first and third in one color. Before I could finish understanding her invention, Shirley left with Allan and an older sister who had come for the first time. But Shirley returned quickly to check my pattern and was delighted to see that I had successfully copied her invention.

Observing the two of us, Maureen makes a very perceptive observation.

MAUREEN: Shirley was suddenly very polite. Everything was, "May I borrow— Thank you." This was brought about by the way Mrs. H. had been asking for things, saying, "May I borrow," etc. I suppose Shirley liked it.

F.H.: Shirley was responding to the fun and intimacy of our association, just the two of us. She listened and copied my language, so that I was cued to take advantage of her rapport with me. It is a simple evaluation when this happens. It is a kind of relationship in which learning abounds. When the climate of a room lacks harmony and fun, all sorts of learning recedes. Inappropriate behavior takes over.

Shirley and I continued our fun with each other and the blocks; what was reassuring was that though she appreciated and took cues from me, she kept her attention on the change-cue itself, introducing her own new variations. Here is another Shirley challenge: I had to match each shape in a left-hand column with a different color and size—except triangles, which were to be of [the] same color. Not bad; it looked so random at first. Then it was my turn. When she had matched one of my setups with colors and shapes, she looked puzzled and realized, with insight and pleasure, that her big ones were the color of my small ones and the reverse. "Hey, what's this?" she observed, and together we laughed at how this must be, since any one set of the blocks had just one of each kind. My husband, David, remarked that night, "You're both going beyond the intentions of the attribute blocks designer. You're both on your way to becoming mathematicians." Good materials allow this.

As Shirley walked away, Jerome came in and looked at the now-scattered blocks. I urged him to stay—should have known better. At school he was always unobtrusive. Yet at the library that very afternoon, he was to be one of the smiling, happy explorers. In a school worth its salt, real experiences and choices abound.

Let me return to the enigmatic Jackie. She came in quietly to our makeshift annex, spoke to no one, sat down, and started to explore with a set of the blocks. She had put herself next to me, and since we were briefly alone I could watch her fascination with the blocks. For a long time she was busy making lovely flat designs and then some complicated standing structures—all in silence, as usual. But she was staying especially close to me, touching, and it was obvious that she chose this intimacy. *First Shirley, now Jackie in this setting!* So different these children, so concentrated in their attention!

This rare one-to-one time is especially revealing with a mysterious child like Jackie, especially when she has chosen it. Such times are crucial for getting to know any child but particularly the deeply troubled Jackies. Knowing a child only as part of a group or on the street or in a shop, one can see as many different profiles of that child as there are settings. Sometimes—as with Jackie—one can't easily fit them together in the round to make a whole child. But a time comes, by chance or by plan, of being close to each other, away from others, and then some convergence emerges. (A walk with one child around a block can result in new insights.)

Soon after she first came to us, it may be remembered, Jackie disappeared, although she came occasionally after kindergarten. Now in this last week she had returned. How could I compare this silent returning one with the Jackie who raced around Boston's central library that afternoon when I took her with Jerome and a couple of others? She had the map of the enormous public building so well in mind that she led me with excitement from space to space—"All newspapers here . . . children's books here"—as though she were a local docent rather than a South End waif living temporarily with many other children in the basement of her "aunt."

With her rather bony skeletal structure, skeletally mature for one of only 6 or 7, came flashes of brilliance yet also that wariness one comes to expect in abused children. What was her past, with her masklike face and rare smiles? Yet we saw the joy she had with Jeannette; her awareness and holding her head.

Other children came to my lair. Still using only sets of attribute blocks, we would line up four different shapes, get all but the child who was "it" to close their eyes, then have them open them and guess which one piece was now clutched in a hand behind the back of the child who was "it." "You took the big red square!" If there is any doubt about the empowerment of a young child who is sure he or she knows which one has been taken, try this under similar circumstances. See the shining eyes, the smiles on the faces of Gail and Anthony, even of Jackie and others who had not yet been fully able— as far as we knew—to equal the Roberts and the Tommys in their readiness to grasp and structure their own enjoyment of learning. The responses of these previously "withdrawn" ones provide a litmus test to be studied.

Following many eager rounds of play, I varied the repertoire by bringing out a paper bag in which we could dump all the pieces of one set—large, small; triangles, circles, diamonds, and squares; red, yellow, green, blue. The child who was "it" would reach into the bag, not looking, and would find by touch what another asked for—"a big circle." Then we made a discovery. If one reached into the bag and didn't look, one could feel and find the shape and the size but not the color. Our eyes had to be used for that! When Jackie asked me to "find a round, green, small circle," we all laughed because I finally had to look to give her the color she asked for.

The bag passed from child to child. Sometimes, instead of describing a piece in words, a younger child would hold out a triangle or square and say to another, "Find me one of these." When I asked Jackie for a triangle, she responded, "Do you want a big one or a little one?"

Robert joined us, and to my surprise the usually silent Jackie volunteered to explain the game to him. Jackie gave him an easy one, "Find a big diamond." But, says Maureen in her notes, "He had difficulty at first in reasoning with the hidden shapes." Jackie had used thrifty language to explain the game and showed with her eyes that she was delighted to challenge Robert and instruct him.

After Robert met Jackie's challenge, he introduced his own game— a variation on the one he had invented before. The others had to copy this, and with precision. He would make a three-dimensional structure, and the others had to copy it precisely. So we continued to build and play together.

When Maureen returned, she remarked on one of our new games.

MAUREEN: A bag with blocks was given to Mrs. H., who encouraged the children to ask her for anything they wanted. And once again the adjectives started to roll!

F.H.: On the third morning, however, the children with me seemed tired, and we all rejoined the others for the rest of the day. It had been a bright display of ideas hatching and language leapfrogging. Appropriate to the young when school goes well! We were at ease with each other, and were building on our summer together. There was a new level of precision and communication. These children were ready.

Joining the others in the big room, we found Michael singing "When I first came to this land . . . I was not a wealthy man." It seemed a timely benediction, and the few who knew the song joined in. Verse followed verse before a rapt audience. The city hospital had been packed away, there was no evidence of the swimming-fishing pool or of fish so carefully made and caught.

On the last day, the children were given paper, crayons, and felt pens to take home. Almost everyone walked rather sedately out of the recently bustling playroom. The workshop was already neat and almost empty.

Although it was the last day of the South End Kindergarten, it was the first day that almost every child seemed ready to leave and knew we were ending our school. Two stayed, waiting, I thought, for a goodbye hug. But not so. Anthony, with a beaming face, spoke in his usual gentle, almost inaudible voice: "Teacher, our mother says for you to come home with us to see our new baby."

When Anthony and Gail gave me this invitation, I hugged them and was happy to prolong the parting sorrow of our last school day. Holding hands, the three of us left South End House. I couldn't quite believe that Mrs. P. had been so thoughtful, so generous as to invite me. The little I knew about her from these two children, with their excruciatingly gentle ways, their faithful and appreciative attendance, was enough. Through her children we trusted each other. I felt already welcomed. Little did I realize how I would need the children's protection.

Walking in the bleak, troubled neighborhood was, as usual, a hazard, but between the two, with their shy but happy invitation to bolster the three of us, we flew along the block. I understood by now that they lived in only a couple of rooms, and when we entered the dilapidated building in which they lived I released their hands and suggested that they lead the way to their mom and baby sister.

Anthony, with a smile, went ahead on the stairs to the second floor, turning back to encourage me—and well he might. The railing disappeared before we reached the first stairway landing. I stopped and looked down at the dark basement, now two floors below. "How many children? . . ." flashed through my mind. Then I looked up: the entire next flight sloped into the stairwell. No rail remained to the third floor. Anthony, seeing my hesitation—perhaps my fear—encouraged me: "Go like this, teacher, our mother says to go like this." And there they went with their little thin bottoms pressed against the "safe" inner stairway wall. I joined them, and laughing now, we slid our ways to the third-floor attic. We were greeted by a less-than year-old baby who had already been carefully taught to hug the inside wall of the long railless landing as she crawled along.

Mrs. P. met us with a smile and welcoming words. "Come on up, come right up." Amenities exchanged, she led us into the large front room so that Anthony might show his teacher the new baby. In her gentle way Mrs. P. encouraged Anthony to tell me "what you have named your baby sister." A beaming Anthony and I went over to the crib, and he whispered, "Carol, I named her Carol."

The crib was near the center of the room. A seemingly catatonic man (doped, perhaps?) sat in a chair in the middle of the room. I guessed this was the father. I ignored him, as did his family. (Since he was the third such man I had encountered that summer, I too could pretend he was not there.) The crib, the chair, and a neatly made double bed piled with clean laundry furnished the large room.

We moved back to the hall, chatting about Anthony and Gail, about how much we at school had enjoyed the two of them, of how well 7-year-old Anthony read. Then Mrs. Parker, looking at me with a clear and affectionate manner, took my hand and said, "Mrs. Hawkins, I want to thank you especially for teaching Gail to play." She continued: "We don't send our children to school until we have to, it is too horrible, but now I want to send Gail to kindergarten." Never in all my years of teaching had a parent I had seen only twice—when she had first brought the children and now in her attic rooms—been so in tune with the deep needs of a particular child, been so clear about what a school had tried and hoped to do. We hugged each other—for a long time.

I tried to untangle my emotions as I slid my way down and out into the filthy street. I felt loved and appreciated, but I was so sad that I could barely keep back the tears. Knowing the hideous truth of Mrs. P.'s words about those 1963 Boston schools, I wanted to run back and say, "Don't send her until you have to. You are right, don't send her!" But with five children (there was an older sister in school), the sad, miserable husband, that stark and dangerous place to live, and the not-well-hidden physical hunger, she would do what she must. I remain in awe of such gallantry and intelligence as I met that day with Anthony and Gail and their slender, beautiful mother and baby Carol.

A Search for Anthony and Gail

After our school was over in fall 1963, Lucia and Jeannette and I tried to keep in touch with as many of the children as we could. We met a few times at South End House. It wasn't hard to find some of the children. When it was warm enough they lived on the streets, and we just turned up on a Saturday and held little reunions. We would go with a child to his or her living place and check in. We were remembered. Yes, we would be told by the mother of Denise and Lorraine, the children could go with us. "Anywhere away from here, with you and Lucia!"

One of our memorable expeditions was to the Franklin Park Zoo. We met at South End House and left in a taxi: Robert, Shirley, Anthony, Gail, and their 8-year-old sister, Sonia; 9-year-old Pat from the afternoon class was with us too.

The afternoon was a sheer delight for all of us. There was the usual, and some unusual, excitement about the animals. "Hey Teacher, look at the big rats!" Those "rats" were small wallabies. There was cotton candy, but everything else was topped by the children's ecstasy over the spacious green meadow and the wild, tree-covered hills adjacent to the zoo. We found small green apples, climbed trees, rolled on grass.

We came back by bus, with spirits wilting as we approached South End. Robert left us at the corner and walked to his house alone. The joy was past. Before we crossed Tremont Street to Anthony and Gail's house she asked me, "We go backa school now?" What appreciation for the summer weeks!

I did not see Gail's mother during the fall months. Finally, one day I rode my bike to South End and went to their old flat. It had been gutted by fire, but the outside was still intact. Next door was a youngish man who covertly observed me and remarked, "No one around there!" I told him I was looking for Gail and Anthony's parents. Looking off in another direction he said, "Ain't no one around here; it burn." I tried again, did he know what had happened to the family? "No," he responded, "they gone." I finally realized he wasn't going to tell a stranger anything. But I decided to take a last chance—that he might have heard of the summer kindergarten. I introduced myself as Mrs. Hawkins, the teacher who had run the kindergarten in Mel King's South End House and who had taught Gail and Anthony.

To my delight he *had* heard—these proved to be magic words to him. He stood up, took the clean cardboard from under himself, put it next to him, and said, "Sit down, Mrs. Hawkins, sit down." I steadied my bike and sat beside him. We talked—not for just a few minutes but for a half-hour at least. From this new friend I learned honest, furious reactions to life off Tremont Street in Boston's South End in 1963.

As if to illustrate his indictments, we were often interrupted. My new friend stood in front of me protectingly while a violent man, drunk or drugged, broke bottles on the curb and yelled at us. My friend said, "This what our children have to grow up with." He was giving me a glimpse of the life of nearby children. He volunteered the information that Anthony's parents had moved to Columbia Point (a new high-rise, low-cost housing project on Boston Harbor). [8] "Get away from rats there, at least; they sure had 'em here." My next question made him laugh. "I hope," I said, "that no one was hurt in the fire."

"Ya don't think someone set the fire with people in it?" he replied, looking at me with incredulity.

"Of course not," I amended the question hastily and continued. Did he know where Charles had lived, in that now burned-out brownstone building, or where he and his family now lived? This brought another homily.

"Nah, ya don't go near anyone's room les' you invited. They'd say ya take something." He didn't know where Charles had moved to. He had never been in "their" room.

If it had not been for my faith in Anthony's mother, in her courage already seen against terrible odds, I would have had little faith left, after a visit to Columbia Point School (as another sequel to our summer's work). Sometime after my return to South End and the burned-out house, I made my way to Columbia Point and was allowed to enter the silent but full school building. The principal gave me permission to see Gail and Anthony, and I went to Anthony's second-grade class. Anthony came with me into the hall, and we spoke briefly. I didn't see a single smile in that silent sterile room, nor from Anthony. His teacher volunteered, however, "Anthony can read, you know, he is bright." How anyone could be "bright" in that atmosphere I do not know. I gave his teacher a blessing, although a minimal one.

Going next to the kindergarten I saw fifty children, all black, each at a desk, with one white teacher. She was sitting at her neat desk—with a scowl on her face. When I asked to speak with Gail this teacher checked a seating chart and called to Gail, who walked zombielike to the desk. No equipment was visible.

I took Gail's hand, and we walked into the hall. There was no sign of recognition, no words, little life evident in that thin five-year-old frame. Stooping down, I hugged her and then led her back to the mockery of a kindergarten, where a dark hole of silence and total inactivity waited to swallow her.

Had Dylan Thomas known there would be this kind of death, what might he have written about rage at this early dying of the light? In more recent times, Johnathan Kozol has continued his saga of the "death at an early age"—in school and out—that remains endemic among so many of these, our children.[9]

A Boston High School

When the Boston public schools opened that fall of 1963, I had a telephone call from Maureen. Their Burke High School had refused to allow Maureen and Sally to transfer from the "commercial" program to "college prep." Further, the school had demeaned itself in no uncertain terms. "You are not college material, so why don't you go south to a Negro college . . . only there do you have a chance."

These were fighting words to me and to David. I promised Maureen and Sally action and turned up at the high school almost immediately. I was armed with two well-deserved letters, on proper stationery, commending the girls for their summer work with the South End Kindergarten and the Elementary Science Study, signed by ESS Director David Hawkins and myself, Frances Hawkins.

After formally presenting the letters to the principal and, with roguish diplomacy, thanking her high school for having produced two such fine and well-educated students, I joined a meeting of the Parent-Teacher Organization in the auditorium. Fortunately, few parents were there to listen to the principal's "welcome": an immediate and vitriolic tirade against these parents and their children. "How can we teach your girls to speak correct English if you don't speak correctly at home and if you don't make your girls come to school every day?" I wanted to hide my white face in shame as I sat next to Maureen and listened to that shameful "welcome."

Maureen and I consoled each other on our way to see her very nice and appreciative English teacher from the previous year. He was white, well educated, and Maureen had enjoyed a good year with him. Then we visited her present English teacher, who had just failed her on an English test after two weeks in school. Her first spelling test had been marked "0" because all the words, correctly spelled, had been capitalized!

We listened to each parent and daughter who preceded us being put down and scolded. All of the teachers I had known, who in their ignorance and frustration had failed children, came crowding into that room. I silently rehearsed all the ruses I had practiced as a child defender before another shabby court. These were sad memories, but I needed them, hoping that somehow I could get this teacher on Maureen's side rather than further alienating her.

Miss Arnold, as I shall call her, smiled at us and, looking me in the eye, said, "Maureen's mother, I presume?" Overlooking the implied scorn in her voice I answered that no, I was not her mother but her good friend and her employer from the summer. Miss Arnold looked at Maureen with the manner of sympathy normally reserved for the helpless and said, "Maureen finds it difficult, don't you, dear?" With that, I knew my next move. Assuming correctly that Miss Arnold had not a clue that English was spoken in Barbados, I looked her in the eye and said, "You know, Maureen and her family have recently come from Barbados." The teacher turned to Maureen and said, "Why Maureen, I didn't know. You must come to me for help with your English!"

Later Maureen whispered to me, "You see why I can't think in that room. I just can't think." But over the year Maureen managed to do so; she and Sally graduated, although not with honors—except with the few of us who knew their courage, their stories.

There is a sequel. Their high-school grade averages were still not too high, and we conspired with a respected friend who was the superintendent of the Newton Schools, Dr. Gibson. David wrote to him, urging that the girls be admitted to Newton Junior College. I remember he said that although the girls needed this special chance, he thought the college needed them as well. They were admitted, and their subsequent academic and professional records tell a story that Burke Girls High School would never have foreseen or allowed.

In the story of this high school I remind readers of the distinction I made in an earlier story, the one of my first year of teaching—the distinction between the extreme case and the merely exceptional. This school may have suffered from extreme disabilities, but it was, as we well know, not exceptional. The fact that the ending turned out as it did only emphasizes a deep institutional pathology.

Both girls wrote to us later. Maureen's letter, written after a year of college, is long and witty, part of it in good Spanish. The young lady who had been "failing" English had an admirable college Spanish teacher. She loved Newton Junior College. She and Sally were the only girls among seven blacks in a student body of 479. She found the teachers great and the student body lovable.

I also had a letter from Sally in fall 1963, which, with her permission, I quote:

Dear Mrs. Hawkins,
   This has been the most rewarding summer of my life. I have worked with children before but never experienced such joy from such simple folk.

As I try to prepare myself for college, with such nuisances as college boards and achievement tests, I feel discouraged and wonder if I'll ever make it, but then I look back over this past summer and know I must go on, I have to. If I don't, what will become of all the Jackies, the Tommys, the Roberts, the Shirleys, and, dear God, the Allans in the world. Somebody has to help these kids. They have helped me—they have shown me that nothing is impossible, just fight, fight with everything you have, and you will get there someday, somehow. I am sure that every person with a goal could reach it if they had such wonderful PEOPLE as the kids of Rutland Street, Rutland Square, and so on, and yes, even the playground group to give them confidence.

Thank you, Mrs. Hawkins. I feel indebted to you, for if I had not volunteered—who knows what my life would have been like, probably at some desk typing meaningless letters when deep inside I would have known there was something better to be done. You helped me find my goal with your loving and unselfish ways. Thank you ever so much.

— Sally

Maureen has a Ph.D. in social work from Boston University and is a lecturer at the University of Barbados. Sally has an M.A. in child development from the University of Illinois. She has had a long successful career in early childhood education, working in Boston and New York. In a study conducted some years ago in Boston, her classroom was chosen for inclusion; the report observes that the teachers, as well as the children, were having fun!

Notes

[1]Jane Addams, *Twenty Years at Hull House, With Autobiographical Notes,* introduction and notes by James Hurt (Urbana: University of Illinois Press, 1990).

[2]I mentioned in the Introduction an example of such a child-mother relationship in Sean O'Casey, *I Knock at the Door* (New York: Macmillan, 1950), "His Father's Funeral," pp. 57–75.

[3]Frederick H. Allen, *Psychotherapy With Children* (New York: W. W. Norton, 1942), p. 125.

[4]Hans Otto Storm, "Eolithism and Design," *Colorado Quarterly* 1, no. 3 (Winter 1953); or *Outlook* 4 (Winter 1972), pp. 37–43.

[5]Leftover valuable junk in our culture, these from our godson, Philip Dow, at Harvard.

[6]For all of this invaluable study, seldom if ever a model for others, see Bibliography under Child Development, Harold M. Skeels. The investigations took advantage of a major

intervention in the lives of young orphanage children, already classified as mentally retarded, with very low I.Q. and other developmental scores. A conspicuously stimulating institutional environment, found for these children, produced developmental improvement in the short term, approximating normality. A twenty-year longitudinal study found that their three-year gains were quite uniformly sustained into adult life. These lives stood, moreover, in complete contrast with those of the equal group that had unavoidably been left behind in the orphanage. Almost all, left in the orphanage after those two decades, were still "institutional cases."

If only for reasons of humanity it should be a scandal, in our affluent world, that such radical interventions are almost vanishingly rare. If only for reasons of science, says my husband David, more such studies of radical intervention could provide quite direct evidence for understanding the relations of our biological nature and our human nurture. That sort of understanding, he continues, is now largely buried under masses of inconclusive I.Q. population-statistics. That sort of study cannot easily distinguish between cause and coincidence. From my own working life the story of Ronald (Chapter 2) is such an extreme case; and the intervention was radical!

[7]See my reference in the bibliography to the work of Dale R. Meers and to the work of Harold M. Skeels and associates.

[8]A "low-cost" high-rise housing project soon overtaken, in its turn, by its isolation, the sterility of its architecture and provisioning, and the misery of its inmates.

[9]Johnathan Kozol, *Death at an Early Age: The Destruction of the Hearts and Minds of Negro Children in the Boston Public Schools* (New York: Houghton-Mifflin, 1967).

8:   England and Africa

In the early 1960s, when David and I made that initial move east, we did not stay put in Boston. Our work during those two years led to an association with schools in England and later in Nigeria, Kenya, and Uganda. We continued to visit these areas throughout the 1960s after we had returned to our university base in Boulder.

We were drawn to England first by stories of remarkably good primary schools and of those who were working to support their development. Our first associations, which have continued to the present, were in Leicestershire. There indeed we found Infant and Junior schools (ages five to seven and above, and seven and above to eleven and above, respectively) that delighted us and rekindled our hopes for children. Under the benign encouragement of Stewart Mason, the Director of Education ("Superintendent") for Leicestershire Authority, there flourished a small advisory group whose work had already fostered incredible skills and enthusiasm for improved education of those county children in their county schools.

My first visit to one of the Infant schools, with about thirty children ages five to seven, reduced me to tears. I remember the teacher's surprise at my pleasure in being among children who were moving about and so deeply engaged. At one table some were weighing and recording: "Six conkers [chestnuts] weigh nine ounces." Three were setting up from a cooking cart, getting ready to bake in a small portable electric oven. Two children were weighing each other under a sign that read HAVE YOU WEIGHED YOURSELF TODAY ? In the game corner two children were concentrating on a game of chess. A boy and girl were hard at work in another corner, continuing a collage of the Pied Piper. The teacher told me quietly, "They've been at work on that for three mornings."

Before I left, the teacher said, "But why have you been so surprised, Mrs. Hawkins? We got it all from you in America, from John Dewey." I responded with sorrow: "But too few there ever knew of him or were allowed to make use of him in the United States except in fee-paying private schools."

On that first visit we were taken to the schools by our longtime friend Bill Browse. He was then assistant to Leonard Seeley, the Advisor to the

Junior schools, whose place he later took. We met Vivian Gibbon, adviser to the Infant schools. The imprint of her longtime commitment was visible in the many good classes we saw for younger children. We had tea with Stewart Mason and came to understand that his quiet, steady support of the Leicestershire Advisory Centre, which his vision had created, lay behind many of the achievements and good beginnings we were coming to know.

Headmistresses particularly captured this teacher's heart after the San Francisco variety of principals I had known. These women all had backgrounds of good teaching and were still frequently found working with a child or a group. First-grade teacher Mary Brown, who was a teacher when we first met her, made me long to teach next to her—with her. She soon became a headmistress; one morning she said, "Take a moment, Frances, and go down the hall to see our first-year kindergarten teacher. Things are a bit untidy there, but oh, she is going to be a grand teacher." I saw and agreed.

On another early visit we met John Paull, then called the Environmental Advisor. His forte was in helping teachers link their classroom worlds with the richness that lay outside, in town or countryside or along the banks of a canal. John has often worked with us since—in England, in Vermont, and in our own center in Boulder, where he and his first wife, Dorothy, spent a year. They wrote a charming book that our Mountain View Center published: *Yesterday I Found.*[1]

During those Boston-based years a reciprocal working relationship evolved with the primary schools in England and Wales. We were invited to Leicestershire, Oxfordshire, and London, where David and I were in awe of what had been accomplished, by 1962, in these state-supported schools. David became involved with the Nuffield Foundation's Junior Science and Junior Mathematics programs, and we both took part in week-long teachers' courses over the next several years. English colleagues came to visit or work with the Elementary Science Study (ESS) in return. This working association continued into the 1970s, after we had worked in the African Primary Science Project—a cousin to both ESS and Nuffield—with English and African friends. This strong association continued in the 1980s with Canadian colleagues Skip Hills and Brian McAndrews, from similar backgrounds in Kingston, Ontario.

Ronald and Joyce Colton from Northumberland spent a year at our Mountain View Center for Teachers at the University of Colorado in 1966. We in turn spent a wonderful fall in 1968 at Ron's college in Ponteland, a suburb of Newcastle-upon-Tyne. Still later, the Coltons joined our Mountain View Center staff in the early 1970s and stayed until they left, to our sorrow, permanently for Australia in 1988. Their contributions to the center were many and deeply significant.

Nine kilometers from Newcastle-upon-Tyne in fall of 1968 we were given a charming apartment at Ron's College in Ponteland. The eastern end of Hadrian's Wall, which had once divided Scotland from England, is anchored near Newcastle at Wallsend, and parts of the wall were a short drive from the college. We promptly came down with what our associates called "wall fever." We frequently explored the ruins and walked that Roman wall from mile-castle to mile-castle.

Early in that English autumn of 1968 I was introduced to Shirley Pybus, whose extraordinary nursery class in the slums of Newcastle, 7 miles from Ponteland, drew me like a magnet. I volunteered there in the mornings, and David made a film, a composite day, of Shirley Pybus's nursery class.[2]

When I first saw the school and met Shirley Pybus and her thirty children, I could hardly believe its initial good impression on me, but that impression lasted and grew. The three lovely big rooms in the old, worn, churchlike, gray-stone city school were filled with life and color and spontaneity. The many paintings displayed on the walls, made by children under age five, were and remain the most magnificent I have ever seen.

That first morning I watched a four-year-old paint: sitting on the floor, scooting around the big piece of smooth paper, and dipping one brush after another into thick, brilliant color. The brushes were soft -bristled beauties, which came to a fine point when used lightly and spread a wide swatch of color when pressed.

Other children gathered beside me, squatting down, watching too, and then Shirley Pybus came and stood near me. I asked, "Where did you get such brushes and such thick, brilliant paints?" She smiled and answered, "Well, you've part of the secret, haven't you?" We were to share many secrets in the months ahead and in the years since. Much later Shirley confessed to us that she had been pleasantly surprised because "these Americans didn't concentrate on the children's poverty; they were not like others who had visited." Had such Americans never been to one of our own inner-city schools?

Wor Gloria

San Francisco, New Mexico, Boston, Washington, D.C.—none of my U.S. residences had prepared my ear for the music and variety of speech in the north country of England. Other parts of England and Scotland had taught me to listen with great attention so I could understand the language of the three- and four-year-olds; these Geordie children could not understand my American-accented English. Denise, in Shirley's class, who was almost five, looked out the window early on and announced in a lilting voice, "Missus 'awkins talks A-mer-i-caine!" We all giggled at that summation, and, with surprisingly little effort and much desire, I began to change. Interesting that these Newcastle children understood the elegant, flawless English of their teacher.

I must have picked up some of the local rhythm fairly well, because the young ceased to giggle and simply accepted my language and my presence as that of another teacher, no more. But then, children are experts at language, so the adjustment may have been totally theirs—at home David objected: "I wonder, Franny, if you can keep that singsong at school?"

What was more exciting for me about the language in this class was the reflection of the local culture in the sometimes rather different use of familiar words. The possessive pronoun *our*, pronounced *wor*, appeared often in the children's conversation: "wor mum, wor da, wor Mary." A criticism was softened by the way the possessive was used. Wor Tom was kept within the circle when he offended rather than being left outside. If guilt was somehow shared by this device, so too was accomplishment. So it is that wor Gloria's name, in my memory, is a double one.

By any name she was mercurial, enchanting, and maddening—wreaking havoc across a landscape of people and things when she was feeling out and becoming deeply absorbed if water or sand or painting or a book invited her attention. She told me proudly one day, with her special lilt, "They won't have me in that other nursery school." This was reported with a modest dignity that made me look with altered respect at this scruffy three-year-old who took pride in besting "that other nursery school," adults and children. Shirley had overheard Gloria's announcement and whispered to me, "She speaks the truth, you know, they wouldn't have her."

No ordinarily abused child, this one: neglected, a ragged, penultimate member of her family of nine children. It was a rough-and-tumble life, Shirley assured me, with few good things but—one surmised—not small or mean, just frightfully poor.

Gloria and I originally met over the issue of a locked door, one locked to keep her and others out, for a time, of the tiny teachers' room. There, children would come to explore new materials with me, and we found that the door had to be locked if a child within was to have more than just a brief turn—to English children "a try"—with batteries and bulbs, colored drops of water, balances. But girls like Gloria could storm a castle's keep—as no doubt her ancestors had done in that border land with Scotland hundreds of years before. As I came to know later, it was not just the locked door. For our Gloria, "tries" were a call to battle; if hers was not the first try, she would surrender as readily as she would the last headland to her castle.

On our first encounter over the locked door, I, who was bigger, won. Gloria showed her disdain for such a test of mere strength by not coming near the little upstairs room for a long time. She ignored me, really, as did many of the other three-year-olds, who found the nursery rooms themselves to be a paradise that sustained their days. It was the four-year-olds primarily, or a troubled three-year-old, who used the small room and its materials—but that part of the Northumbrian story remains to be told elsewhere or seen in our film.

Most mornings were lively and filled with laughter, and they yielded abundant evidence of just how well and how at ease these children were with using the paints and clay, the blocks and water and sand. They also listened to stories raptly and with participation and joined the singing games and dancing.

There were surprisingly few tussles among so many children—thirty—with only one teacher and two aides. This was a reflection not only of the incredibly well-supplied three big rooms but also of the ambience within—and also, specifically, of Shirley's ways of reacting to arguments and fights. Usually and deliberately, troubles were simply overlooked. Minimal teacher interference and minimal taking sides has this effect among a group of children. It was a special delight for me to see it exemplified in this day-care situation where my role was to observe and assist, not to design.

Gloria was the only child I ever saw punished; not only did she deserve it, but the punishment fit the crime. She had run past four children who were washing for lunch and had scratched each face with her well-aimed fingers. Finding four screaming children and a beaming Gloria, Shirley lifted Gloria to the top of the high lockers—where she couldn't jump down—and left her there while life went on beneath her. It was the only time I saw Gloria cry—wholeheartedly and loudly, ignored by all. After about five minutes Shirley, in passing and matter-of-factly, asked, "Can you remember to keep your hands from hurting other people?" Yes, Gloria nodded. "Then wash for lunch," Shirley reminded her as she was taken down, slightly but definitely chastened. This school would have Gloria because she would have this school.

After some weeks of many happy mornings, I decided to come occasionally in the afternoons. This followed my realization that I was becoming stereotyped in the children's eyes. Each day I was greeted with requests: "I go upstairs today? My try now?" Fair enough, I was usually upstairs. Some of this thought was my own rationalization. The important reality was simpler: I was just plain curious. What went on in the afternoons? I wanted to see the children's behavior in the afternoon setting. I knew it would be different from the mornings, but I didn't know how.

Curiosity is its own reward, at least for teachers. On my first afternoon at school, when the children began slowly to wake up from naps, I was watching them. By chance I noticed Gloria and a couple of others putting on their shoes and stockings. I joined them to help and to talk. One child asked for a story. "Read a story, Mrs. 'awkins."

But I wanted to change their usual afternoon routine. "No," I responded, "I want to sing you a song." They cuddled close, and I sang them the "Riddle Song"—"I gave my love a cherry." [3] There they sat, Gloria next to me, intent and listening and ever so quiet. "Again, sing it again." We had just enough time for "What are little boys made of?" before mums and older sisters and brothers began to arrive to take away my rapt audience. It was some time before the last child could be coaxed off the largest rocking horse or from saying goodbye to the guinea pigs, gerbils, and mice. In schools where living is good, parting is often such sweet sorrow.

Many new images lingered in my mind, especially that of the transformed Gloria. It was clear, of course, that a morning of the kind these children experienced, followed by a good and quiet lunch and a two-hour sleep, could achieve transformation. Contrary to what I have often seen in the United States—with its casual or hectic lunches for children—these children ate well from a variety of foods, were seated comfortably and carefully served by Shirley and the two aides, and enjoyed some protective etiquette and formality, such as flowers on each table.

A day or two later at an afternoon session, Gloria woke rather early and was walking past me when she stopped, looked up at me, and asked softly, "Sing me the apple song?" Would I! We found a far, quiet corner and were joined by Denise and Steven, who were almost five and who played games or "read" books quietly during nap time. No one joined in the singing, but there would be time for that in this school, where Shirley knew what was important and tried to build on it.

Later I began to put Gloria's socks on her, and she complained, "My toe hurts, see?" I did indeed see a red toe, stubbed or picked at perhaps, and then I thought—soaking, a bath! Gloria's perpetually damp panties had seemed too trivial a justification for bathing a child, but a sore toe required some such treatment. I laughed at myself as we four gathered ourselves together. Ever since I had first watched the delight these children took in their rare baths at school, I had been wanting to share in it.

Gloria's response to my bath offer made it clear that she too was ready and willing. My own bath memories returned—not from my childhood home, where, with four children, baths were swift with no dawdling, but from my grandmother's, where the pace allowed time for a proper bath with scented soap. No luxurious shower has ever felt as delightful as my grandmother's enormous sponge squeezed by her again and again over my shoulders—and later the nightly bath with our own small daughter, when talk and bubbles and water were such a pleasant way of winding down the day.

Shirley's school was a fine place to "bath" a child. There was a big sink—high enough for the comfort of the adult, deep enough for the child within, and in this case low enough for Denise and Steven to see and assist. (It occurred to me later that these two older ones had never been bathed at school; there were three or four who were always immaculate, always well dressed, from middle-class families who valued such a good school.) Assistance was indeed needed: there was soap to be found, a rubber frog, and another rubber animal or two or three. In the center of our concern sat the beaming and glistening child, transformed, gracious, and sharing her bath toys with Denise and Steven. When her tangled hair was washed and close to her head, Gloria resembled the most adored baby ever caught on canvas. We all admired the transformation and felt part of it. Gone with the faded, damp, too-big hand-me-downs and the runny nose were Gloria's prickles and defensive ways. For these few minutes she could bask in affection and admiration, as if she had tried on another possible self and found that it fit.

It was finally time, and so I wrapped our baby in a big soft towel. I carried Gloria, with her attendants near, to a low bench to be dried. I wanted to stay and finish this so-satisfying episode, but my professional sense won out, and I gave Gloria over to Denise and Steven. I saw how gently and possessively they were helping to dry and care for her and observed Gloria's loving response, It was proper for me to withdraw. From the hall I watched, unseen. With slow competence Denise and Steven dressed "their" child, savoring every moment. And Gloria? Through all this she showed not the slightest impatience or disdain. It took Steven a long time to buckle her sandals, but Gloria held still and cooperated. The three remain in my memory, caught in one of those tableaux of daily living when only a little help from adults is needed to ensure some of life's goodness.

I take an episode from E. M. Forster to end Gloria's story. Miss Abbott has just returned to Italy to "rescue" the storybook baby from his "poor" father, Gino. At first she refuses to touch the baby, but then she wavers:

> "May I help you to wash him?" she asked humbly.
>
> He gave her his son without speaking, and they knelt side by side, tucking up their sleeves. The child had stopped crying, and his arms and legs were agitated by some overpowering joy. Miss Abbott had a woman's pleasure in cleaning anything—more especially when the thing was human. She understood little babies from long experiences in a district, and Gino soon ceased to give her directions, and only gave her thanks.
>
> "It is very kind of you," he murmured, "especially in your beautiful dress. He is nearly clean already. Why, I take the whole morning! There is so much more of a baby than one expects. And Perfetta washes him just as she washes clothes. Then he screams for hours. My wife is to have a light hand. Ah, how he kicks! Has he splashed you? I am very sorry."
>
> "I am ready for a soft towel now," said Miss Abbott, who was strangely exalted by the service.
>
> "Certainly, certainly?" He strode in a knowing way to a cupboard. But he had no idea where the soft towel was. Generally he dabbed the baby on the first dry thing he found. . . .
>
> She sacrificed her own clean handkerchief. He put a chair for her on the loggia, which faced westward, and was still pleasant and cool. There she sat, with twenty miles of view behind her, and he placed the dripping baby on her knee. It shone now with health and beauty: it seemed to reflect light, like a copper vessel. Just such a baby Bellini sets languid on his mother's lap. . . . For a time Gino contemplated them standing. Then, to get a better

view, he knelt by the side of the chair, with his hands   clasped before him.[4]

An African Alliance

I have mentioned some of the good times that have interrupted the writing of this book. One is recorded in *The Logic of Action.*[5] Some episodes not included in the present book have been documented in *Outlook* and elsewhere.[6] Others, such as "Commerce City, USA," are found only here. There is another, to me major, story, not published previously, that I shall speak of here. It tells of another world I joined, and it speaks to an alliance I still puzzle over—between poetry and fiction, with their differences and similarities, and the kinds of narration I strive for in my own stories.

The stage was tropical Africa: Kano, Enugu, Awo Amana, and Lagos in Nigeria in the spring of 1965, followed by the summer in Karen and Nairobi, Kenya, and Entebbe, Uganda. This was before the devastating Biafran civil war and the horror of Idi Amin in Uganda.

That 1965 spring-summer with African teachers and children has somehow remained unwritten—a hallowed time, perhaps, too set apart in my mind? The legacy of the months remains; it stays and pervades when I take time to recall. It is also a personal legacy of the mystery of friendship, the oneness of the human family on a continent of color—of mountains and lakes, of thorn trees and flame trees; overflowing with misery, promise, dance, and celebration of life itself.

Isak Dinesen (Karen Blixen) captures this life with precision. When I first read her *Out of Africa,* I wondered if I would ever get to Africa. [7] Perhaps then by its presence it would unlock some of the mysteries of the friendships Karen Weishopf made with Kikuyu, the Massai, and Somali and of those our daughter made during a semester in Chile before the Pinochet disaster. Those I met later in Africa did just that for me, but a special magic enhances the continent itself—from my Yoruba and Muslim friends in Nigeria to those in Kenya and Uganda.

Nothing had prepared me for my first landing in northern Nigeria in early 1965. When that plane landed in Kano—with its camels well back from the runway, undaunted by the noise of our landing, waiting to be useful; where we were met by tall Hausa attendants, slender and handsome in their knee-length, smart uniforms of starched cotton, speaking elegant English—I was totally disoriented and delighted that anything could be so new to my fifty-one-year-old eyes and mind.

The ancient city of Kano enchanted me, and the delight remains. Early in our conference, "court" was in session. We sat on the earth among hundreds of Kano citizens, watching the judge during his monthly visit on a distant, stagelike platform with plaintiffs and defendants filing slowly by. I couldn't see his robes well, but the colors, even at a distance, were brilliant.

Among the riotous color and life of the marketplace we found incredible riches—such as scissors that worked, fashioned from pieces of automobile fenders. Through one of the fourteen gates of Kano was the village of dyers. There we found deep vats dug into the earth, filled with dye of indigo blue, steaming endlessly, heated by hot rocks on ropes that were lowered and retrieved, we were told. Philip Morrison and I stood in awe, walked around. Phil was sure, he said, that this system came down, unchanged, from biblical times.

On another morning we visited an open-air school under a great spreading tree, where the Koran was being memorized. The children and their Koranic teacher were happy to have us. Suddenly this was just like home, where bored school children rejoice at any interruption.

After delicious evening food, young men gathered, anxious to talk, to get some idea of what we were up to with the teachers—joining, we surmised, in a search for good science. We couldn't resist putting on little sideshows, so eager were these curious youths. I remember hanging pendulums, with sand-filled gourds for weights, from the low eaves of the hotel roof. When our young friends first began swinging a pendulum widely into orbit, all was joyous pandemonium: "Sputnik! Sputnik! Sputnik!" It was 1965, what else?

One evening our visitors brought three or four types of drums and gave us a concert. My favorite was a "talking drum," its tone modulated by squeezing it under an arm to change the tension and tone of the drumhead. I bought one and experimented with the range of its "talk." General amusement accompanied those efforts, and one brave fellow called out: "Oh madam, what you have said!"

Later that summer I joined colleagues in East Africa for a conference. There we worked with teachers and children of Entebbe—the former British capital of Uganda. That conference was to mark the beginning of the African Primary Science Program, a commitment among African countries that continued for many years.

Before returning to the United States I joined our good friends Mike and Wendy Savage, who were living in eastern Nigeria—later Biafra. After a fascinating week with them in the village of Awo Amana, I flew to

Lagos and then to the United States, returning later to Uganda. But before I arrived in Uganda I stopped in Kenya, where I visited the village of Karen, named for that marvelous Danish authoress Karen Blixen (Isak Dinesen), where I spent a day in a school for forestry workers' children.

A School in Karen

Before Uganda there was a school in Karen. The morning flight—Nairobi to Entebbe—took off without me. I had asked to visit a Kikuyu school in the village of Karen, some miles from Nairobi. I'm not sure whether I was drawn by the school or the chance to see Karen Blixen's old house or both. Joan Honey, a capable school adviser from Nairobi, took me to Karen. There in the forest we found the long, low building, and Joan Honey introduced me to Mrs. Kibathi with her forty children of differing ages, promising to be back two hours later.

Mrs. Kibathi and her forty children engaged me for those two too-short hours. The English lesson was just beginning when I walked in, and I sat quietly to listen. "We shall begin again for Madam Frances." Each of those forty children, ages perhaps seven to eleven, beamed with anticipation and sheer pleasure. Ragged uniforms and runny noses receded. Eager children sat on the edges of worn benches at worn desks, and Mrs. Kibathi began.

"Once there was an old woman . . . who lived in a large black pot. Now, who knows what a pot is?" Half the class raised their hands, and one child explained in good English just what a pot is and what it is used for. The story continued, with other welcomed pauses for participation. If a child was slightly incorrect or not explicit enough, Mrs. Kibathi would listen, pause, and gently ask, "Who can aid him [or her]?" No one was put down, no one was bored, and the whitewashed adobe school overflowed with good spirits and avid participation. The children displayed an amazing facility with the English language. I note in passing that this was but a few years after Kenyan independence; English was becoming a common language among several tribes, along with Swahili.

Geography came next, and Mrs. Kibathi invited me to take charge and show where I lived, had traveled from, and so on. With chalk and blackboard and willing help, we drew a map that included the United States, England, and Africa. Some thatched houses and an airplane completed the cooperative drawing.

Too soon it was time for lunch, and the children left. Mrs. Kibathi took me to her small thatched-roof house for tea. She asked, "Madam Frances, do you understand how a teacher can follow a lesson plan?" I answered, "No, Mrs. Kibathi, I do not understand how a teacher can follow a lesson plan, unless she [or he] pays no attention to the children; but I have come halfway around the world to be asked such a good question!" (In Berkeley-Oakland in 1935, Principal Anne Bradley had set us on course: "One does not need to follow a lesson plan, but in retrospect ask yourself: What did we do instead?")

We chatted over good hot tea from a thermos and delicious buttered bread. Before going off with Joan Honey, I promised to return with my husband at the end of the summer. When we did return Mr. Kibathi, the teacher's husband, was also there to meet us. Mr. Kibathi and David got into a discussion of algebra that required writing a formula. Mr. Kibathi scratched it on his bare black arm and remarked, "One of the advantages of having black skin!" All summer my letters, with pictures and adventures, had been sent to the children in that Karen school, and the children had written back to me.

I returned to Nairobi—and missed my flight to Entebbe! The next day I found passage there in a small plane. A very obliging pilot welcomed me and flew low as we skirted the northern shore of Lake Victoria and once around the great falls that mark the beginning of the White Nile. The American "tourist" has never forgotten!

Zenna

A farewell to Africa and to our summer associates was celebrated formally at an end-of-summer banquet. It capped off a tearful day of parting with students in the five local primary schools where we had worked. Babs Fafunwa, the recent minister of education in Nigeria, and I had worked with three teachers on the physics of sound. I learned more physics than I taught.

Early on our last day, as if to underline the sweet sorrow of parting, one of our Sudanese refugee children walked the three miles from her living place to hug us and wave a last goodbye. In perfect English, just one of her five languages, Zenna gave us her last-minute thoughts and hopes. She was shivering in the cool tropical morning in her worn, sleeveless pink uniform. David took off his sweater and helped her pull it over her head. She smiled her thank you, the car pulled away, and we watched

Zenna.

Zenna recede—with the sweater reaching almost to the hem of her pink uniform, baggy on the elegant slim child—waving until we could see her no more.

Zenna exemplifies for me something of the spirit of this book, although she appears only here. Always, on any morning and around any corner, there is the possibility, the likelihood of surprise, delight, communication—of some vision of the Goddess of Anticipation. In such an atmosphere miseries can recede, lives can be enhanced and strengthened to bear what cannot be changed and—sometimes, perhaps—to change that which should not be borne.

Notes

[1]John Paull and Dorothy Paull, *Yesterday I Found* (Boulder, Colo.: Montain View Center, University of Colorado, 1972).

[2]*Northumberland Children* is available on videotape from David Hawkins, 511 Mountain View Road, Boulder, CO 80302.

[3]Karpeles and Sharp, *English Folk Songs From the Southern Appalachians,* vol. 2 (London: Oxford University Press, 1932), p. 393. It was fun and fitting to be bringing back to England a legacy of folk songs that had come to the United States over two hundred years before.

[4]E. M. Forster, *Where Angels Fear to Tread* (New York: Vintage Books, 1920).

[5]*The Logic of Action: Young Children at Work* (Niwot, Colo.: University Press of Colorado, 1985).

[6]*Outlook*, Journal of the Mountain View Center, University of Colorado; published quarterly 1970–1986. Now in the University of Colorado Library, Boulder, Colorado.

[7]Isak Dinesen, *Out of Africa* (New York: Modern Library, 1952).

9: Mountain View Center

Beginnings

In 1968 we left Boulder for two and a half years: first for Cornell University, then for our year in England (see Chapter 8), and last for an academic year in Princeton at the Institute for Advanced Study. When we returned to Boulder in 1970, we were ready to expand our efforts in the Boulder schools. With good seed money from the Ford Foundation, we launched the Mountain View Center for Environmental Education (MVC). The label *environmental education* was still new, and it could mean what we wanted it to mean: education through the environment, through children's and teachers' living engagement with the world around them, and not just lessons about it—not until the engagement itself was firm. Despite negligent university support in the decade that followed, it became a center for teachers who were seeking help in their professional development.

In 1970 we held an initial summer conference, with advisers and teachers from England, New Zealand, and some of our U.S. associates. Before long we were giving small weekly workshop-courses for teachers and receiving invitations to work as visitors in classrooms.

For that first year we had two fine teacher-advisers from England, John and Dorothy Paull,[1] and for the first and second years we had Elwyn Richardson from New Zealand.[2] For them, as for us, the work with the Oglala Sioux we soon became engaged in was an introduction to the Native American. It was a far different sampling, happily unpremeditated, from the mix of Boulder teachers—a mix drawn from our nation's melting pot, still so half congealed. I shall hold up the mirror for a child's-eye view of our evolving style of work at the MVC.

At our new center we quickly accumulated a staff of ten and were joined by a part-time ten-year-old volunteer, Ken, who haunted the center in the after-school hours. He became our curator of salamander and fish. Through him, various inhabitants of University Pond found their way to John Paull's indoor ponds. Transplanted duckweed thrived under Ken's hand and eye. Once he took me to University Pond to see a large snapping turtle, knowing just where to find him.

One afternoon we went collecting. For a boat we took a large plastic wading pool. Ken and a friend paddled expertly around the shallows an d collected nine minnows with their small nets. It was a lovely afternoon of "messing about in boats" that my husband, David, came over to see, and Kenneth Grahame was with us in spirit.[3] Ken came faithfully and usefully for some years, until high school claimed his full attention, but he belongs to the Mountain View story.

The style of our work with Boulder teachers and others from nearby districts is suggested by the following pictures, all by our staff member Tony Kallet, musician and editor of our Journal OUTLOOK.

In this work I specialized somewhat, with Jane Richtmeyer and Joyce Colton, introducing teachers to Native American weaving, with field trips for collecting native dyes for the yarn.

It was our eventual mastery of a Hopi-style braiding that created the dancing-belt we proudly gave to our friends in the pueblo of San Ildefonso, New Mexico. They had traditionally known this braiding art but, like much of their ancestral technology, had lost it.

My own next undertaking was with native Americans in South Dakota, in the Pine Ridge Reservation of the Oglala Sioux, the once-great tribe of the Black Hills. Visits there led to a year-long engagement that involved and educated all our staff.

My next major work was with the Head-Start program, newly commissioned in Boulder. To tell that story I first go back to an earlier enegagement with Head Start, both before and during its beginnings. Our work with the Boulder program is a story worth telling. Some of those teachers are still by friends.

Jane, Joyce, and I learned this braid from the Hopi tradition (*previous page: top*) and made the dancing belt for Gilbert of the San Ildefonso Pueblo?here with his mother, Isabel (*previous page: bottom*), and with the three sashmakers after presenting the scarf to Gilbert and his mother (*above*).

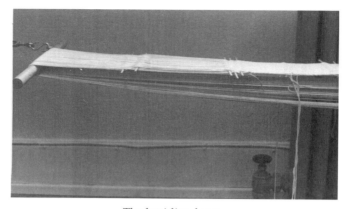

The braiding loom.

When Gilbert first took the belt in his hands he said, "You did it, you did it right." He was testing the stretch of the braided material—woven does not stretch.

A child's view of the plant room at Mountain View Center; his favorite.

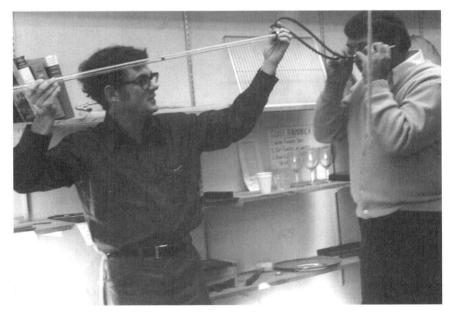

Tony Kallet and Carols Mena—two staff members.

In the plant room, Ron Colton and visitors from fifth-grade class.

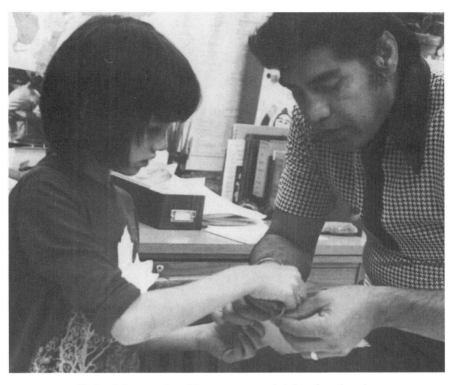

Carlos Mena and a visitor; some work takes four hands.

"Will more batteries make it brighter?" "Yes!"

"We made the whole thing balance!"

From polygons to polyhedra.

For sorting marbles by size.

Some string geometry.

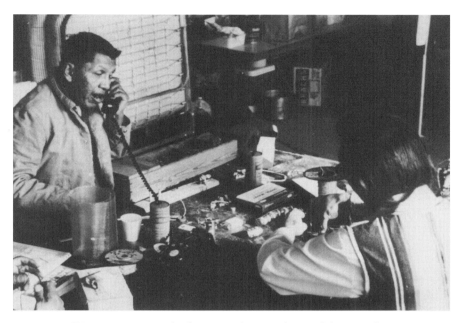

Wiring up some telephones in the Manderson lab: it works!

Project Oglala

For most of 1970–1971 we spent every other weekend on the Pine Ridge (Oglala Sioux) Reservation in South Dakota getting to know the Oglala and giving a prerequisite science course—Natural Science 101—for adults seeking a degree and certification to become teachers. Thus Native Americans might finally become teachers of their own children. All of this began not long after we had opened our doors to local teachers in Boulder and were planning and starting programs for them. How did this diversion come about?

When the opportunity for our involvement suddenly appeared, we surmised, somewhat wildly, that it might become a special kind of opportunity for the new center, a way into some close encounters with what we knew to be the sad condition of most schools run by the Bureau of Indian Affairs (BIA). Indian children in these schools were not expected to learn much because they were, after all, Indian.

The Volunteers in Service to America (VISTA) Program during those years was described as a kind of domestic Peace Corps. The program that

This tower will survive many scissor cuts!

Making a wind machine.

created our opportunity was designed to advise and support young volunteers in helping with the economic and educational development of the Pine Ridge Indian Reservation. There were already around fifteen young volunteers in that southwest corner of South Dakota, eager but untrained for one of the jobs they were asked to do: tutoring. [4] Working in local school situations on the reservation, they were to provide help for a wide range of children, beginners through young teenagers. The older Indian students were being paid 75 cents an hour to "help" with the young ones.

A colleague of David's, John Carnes, called me one day about his niece, a VISTA volunteer on the Pine Ridge Reservation. She had called him for help with the summer schools they were staffing as tutors. Leonard Pinto of the Sociology Department at the University of Colorado was one of the sponsors of this program and also sought our assistance. Our staff was dubious at first about what might become a major diversion of our resources. But we all ultimately agreed, with excitement, that any such diversion would teach us as much as it would those who were to become our Oglala student friends. In short: Would I fly to Rapid City at once and give some of my time?

Conduit pipe sold for household wiring, a Lakota xylophone!

I seized the first chance to do so, taking along a toothbrush and a collection of good "junk" from the center. Dowell and Jean Smith met me. He was a graduate student in sociology at the University of Colorado, and she was a primary teacher of young Sioux children. We drove to Porcupine, about seventy miles into the reservation, and talked antischool-establishment talk.

The next day Jean left for work in Pine Ridge, and Dowell and I set off for school A. Dowell was an ingenious driver over these unpaved roads, and his conversation sparkled; I listened and began to learn.

School A

The day was already hot when we reached a small old school building that had been set aside for VISTA use. Nearby was a modern one that, except for its water tower, could have been lifted unaltered from any U.S. town, east or west. In the old building we entered a room that was almost empty. On a table there was a decent but decrepit typewriter. We met a handful of children, around eight years of age. There were a few peripheral teenagers, acting and looking bored. A young VISTA volunteer was directing a "treasure hunt for candy" reading game. One child was typing instructions: "Look under the table." Interest seemed minimal. The VISTA volunteers did need help.

A child hovered near me, from friendliness I sensed. I asked her to read what I began to type, guessing she could read but prepared to prompt. She—Fern—read each word as I typed: DO YOU WANT TO BLOW BUBBLES? She needed help with the last word and then typed: YES. Her friend Jackie caught the scent of fun in the air and came over. Fern typed my original question, and Jackie typed an affirmative answer. We three, plus comers and goers, were soon on our way down the road to Fern's house to borrow soap.

Fern's grandmother and I discussed our little project, and one of the plastic glasses I had brought was filled generously with detergent. Grandfather shook hands. Older girls put their dishwashing aside and joined us. All were laughing, chatting, and helpful. I still see the smiling grandma, holding in her apron wrapped bars of soap for our project. "Why don't we do it here?" one of the group asked me. The life and warmth of that household and its cool, shaded yard were tempting. Had I not been a new school visitor, we would have stayed.

Tiny flowers were abundant as we neared school again, and we all picked a few. I joked happily and called the flowers "teeny-weenies," to the amusement of the girls. We came back to the school and watched the older children on a trampoline. Tom Casey was a great instructor for a few older boys, who obviously admired and respected his expertise.

"What are you picking?" one teenager asked me. With amusement Fern answered, "The teeny-weenies." So much for picking up language along with fun.

Water was fetched by car from a mile away. Bubbles and delight followed. The trampoliners joined, and we used all the straws from my kit. Bubbles were carried far downwind. On wet surfaces half-bubbles formed, and others were blown inside of them. Rainbows took form and were discussed with wonder.

After about an hour of experimenting, a fitting climax of bubbles came about that was completely new to me. Three or four of us, with our plastic glasses touching, began blowing into them slowly but simultaneously. The mass of bubbles climbed up between and upon us. Soon six of us were in a tight circle, delighted with the great magic column of bubbles rising between us. Finis; except that Jackie said, "Let's do the bubbles together once more!"

The plastic magnifiers came into use. Teenagers almost spoiled the fun with their disdain for these low-power lenses, which were ×3. But the magnification held the younger ones, as I have found is generally true. Fern, holding her bubbles at a distance, said, "Hey look, they [some reflected children] are upside down!"

In an article by Dowell Smith that we published in the Mountain View Center magazine seven years later, he reports on this episode of my first visit to Pine Ridge.[5] He refers first to the widespread belief among the Euro-American teachers and principals of the BIA schools that Indian students are "silent and withdrawn." He also describes the narrow ethnographic studies of the "culture of poverty" that once, incredibly, purported to explain this "language deprivation." He speaks also of more recent studies that suggested reforms in the education of Indian children, obvious and needed. I quote from Dowell's article:

> What these and other studies do not address, and what I want to illustrate when I return in a moment to that dusty schoolyard, is the *process* of cross-cultural education. I especially want to stress *the value of focusing on materials and the natural environment as subject matter which can reduce cultural conflict while leading naturally to inquiry about varying cultural patterns of organizing this basic knowledge.* . . . . I propose . . . to continue describing the first encounter

Frances Hawkins had with country-full-blood-traditional Ogla-
las—an encounter which led to seven years of continuing
involvement with Oglala education by the staff of the Mountain
View Center. [emphasis added]

From his recollections as an observer more detached than I, he tells
his story of that visit, some of which I omitted from mine. For example, in
a section on plateau surfaces he discusses the elegant, patterned bubble
that could be blown inside a wire cube I had fabricated from pipe clean-
ers. Was that a real bubble? I go on to quote Dowell's observations as a
young ethnographer, one already skilled in reading the ways of Oglala
life:

At no point did cultural content become an issue during this
encounter. Yet a number of significant cross-cultural events took
place. I want to focus on three of these: the children's pattern of
work; Franny's visit to the grandma's home; and the teacher's
role in focusing on intellectual development rather than cultural
conformity.
    As we left the school, Franny commented that these children
spontaneously cooperated to blow bubbles together. In her several years of working with children and bubbles, no young group
had ever come together quite like this. Thinking back, I realized
that, throughout, the children had been free to follow their own
cultural roles about peer interaction and child-adult relations.
They were not given orders, they were not disciplined, they were
not judged either on behavior or on their thinking. Yet they had
been exceptionally "good" in both respects. What went right?
    Encouraged by example and by their natural curiosity to pur-
sue the bubbles wherever they led, there was no occasion where
defiance was possible or necessary. Where there was withdrawal
or hesitation, a relevant example and special encouragement
came easily. If these failed, the moment was allowed to pass as
easily as the bursting bubbles—not unnoticed, interesting, but
not judged good or bad. Neither student nor teacher had failed.
Genuine suggestions like "Look at the rainbow moving around
the side of this bubble!" were impossible for the children to meet
with indifference. However, these same children had been "discipline problems" for the young VISTA, just as I once heard a kindergarten teacher on the reservation complaining that her

students were "unmotivated and undisciplined." Marching was her favorite activity.

Today's children implemented their own pattern of self-discipline and group interaction. They helped each other, encouraged, explored, innovated, revised, explained, and expressed puzzlement in their own ways, not in ways imposed on them. There were conflicts, distractions, doubts, but these were resolved—or left to a future time—without recourse to authority or threat. Each of the children became engrossed in some phase of the projects and thus transformed the teacher into a co-seeker working with them, not someone they were working for.

Here Dowell returns to his description of the dominant pattern of relations between the Oglala and those who come from the outside as teachers in the BIA schools. "Home visits" are required of the teachers, although most avoid them and those who don't find them awkward. The "silent Indian" again!

Dowell refers to the fact that I was soon invited into the home of Fern's grandmother. He suggests

that it was her focus on nature and its wonders, her emphasis on example and encouragement, her concern for the puzzled and perplexed among the children, and her non-judgmental demeanor [that precipitated the invitation]. These are all fine qualities of grandmas everywhere—the teachers of young children for aeons past. But not only grandmas. The young adults among the VISTA who exhibited some of the same characteristics also found it a matter of course to be in and out of Indian homes.

I quote Dowell's final summary here because of the way he contrasts the response to what a "grandmotherly" teacher—although one undoubtedly from a Euro-American background—can offer with the standard educational offerings the Oglala, since our conquest of them, have usually been expected to accept. I use his words as part of my commitment, expressed in other parts of this book, to "tell it like it is."

But I also quote him because of the clarity with which he gets to the essence of a way of teaching children, a way that happens to be my own and that of others as well—although of far too few in our society. If praise is due, we can accept it from a Dowell Smith because his attention is not on us—as though he is a kind of inscrutable magician—but is instead on a kind of praiseworthy practice that can be understood and adopted more widely.

All this leads to my final point about the teacher as co-seeking enthusiast, engrossed with nature, a prepared seeker of knowledge, a person genuinely concerned with learning about the things around us, coming with us to see things in new ways through engagement and imaginative manipulation, serious reflection, and organization.

All too often in my work with adult Indians I found that the focus of their formal learning had been on conduct and demeanor. Teachers were genuinely concerned to help them assimilate European culture. Thus, their strengths and skills were disregarded both as resources they possessed and as places to begin. For example, people who could carry out complex mathematical operations in their daily lives would recoil at the simplest textbook example of multiplying fractions. When shown that they could already do such operations in their heads, they were in turn amazed and angry—amazed that math was interesting and easy, angry that they had been humiliated and convinced they were dumb in school. Yet, because they had dropped out of school and because they lived in a strong culture, they maintained a faith in themselves and an interest, like Franny's, in the natural world around them.

Franny's successes in the visits we made that summer day and in situations I've watched since then are intimately connected with her intense interest in the concrete world around her. Perhaps I should emphasize that this interest has never seemed feigned. Indeed, it is infectious. She had often had me out well before breakfast digging yucca roots for soap, other roots for dyes, collecting rocks, finding sticks to make God's eyes, making bubble frames, examining plants.

With regret one leaves such children. Chance being as it is, we might not meet again. What a commentary on their school, that these children do not thrive there!

School B

We entered a similar stark, bare room later that same day, furnished only with two or three tables and chairs. There were five or six little ones and eight to ten teenagers. Some of the latter were playing cards, some were cooking "hamburgers" (hard, black, thin meat) in the tiny kitchen, with pleasant boy-girl banter.

Just before arriving here we had stopped where some children were swimming in a shallow, pleasant lake. Two ponies waited nearby. I waded in, and the two or three older children were friendly—although just barely. I asked whether they were teaching the younger ones to swim. "No, the teacher does that."

Amid the barrenness of this second room, some rocks on a table were a welcome sight. They were being used for a game, perhaps? But again there was little reflection inside that building of the world outside or any evidence of sustained activity or interest. There was horsing around, in which the teens teased the younger children. Morale in general was a mixture of pleasant boredom and chips on shoulders.

With one lively seven-year-old boy, Todd Yellow Cloud, I began picking up sticks outside and then making *ojos de dios* with yarn I had brought.[6] Instant attention. Todd was a master designer and craftsman, with immediate understanding and pleasure as his guides. A small, slightly spastic girl became industriously involved, although her limited dexterity interfered. A third girl was adept and excited, but her bus came, so she took beginnings home to finish.

The little slow girl worked and worked with no prompting, but her eyes were wandering, and one felt that little satisfaction accompanied her efforts. She missed the beauty because she lacked the skill to place a new round of yarn just touching the previous one. Whereas Todd's grew in brilliance and elegance, hers resembled the efforts of an intoxicated spider. I should have had more free-form branches for her to use in a less narrow way. In a class one would be challenged to find some releaser for such a child's slumbering joy in the world of creating.

Todd, whose ojo grew, listened to my suggestions and produced a two-level pattern. He looked at the result, thought, and then said, "No, I don't like it." So he undid that part and produced a stylized but elegant ojo. Here is an example of that marvel of both design and "eolithism."[7] A child who is following some private star is able to try out another path and discard it because of some inner-directed sequence. Is some of the possible variation filed away, to be useful later— I suspect so.

Dowell suggested we take Todd and a friend home in our truck. I watched Todd Yellow Cloud very carefully protect his ojo by placing it tenderly between the pages of a comic book. I wondered about the reception at home, hoped and believed this child was secure in planning to unveil what he had made before appreciative eyes.

I was not disappointed. We drove the boys up a hill to a cluster of two or three houses. There was a rather large pine branch under which sat adults and children, a hand-turned washing machine, and so on. Driving away very slowly, Dowell and I watched unobtrusively. Todd went directly to one adult and put his comic book in her lap. Then all drew near and seemed to share in a great pleasure. Our road turning obscured what happened next in this familial opening and sharing—a seven-year-old's contribution to a gathering of his appreciative family.

Picnics and a Workshop

Bunches of dried "wild turnips" with their tails braided together were for sale at a church fair we visited. [8] I asked Dowell about these edible roots in situ. The Smiths in turn asked their friends, John and Cordelia Attack Him, to come by some evening and take us turnip hunting. They came with their daughter, who was curious and friendly and lively. She spied the yarn; with two sticks and a word or two, she was making ojos.

In the cool of early evening we drove on dirt roads, through gates, and into a soft, hilly grassland with a few small pines in the draws. John Attack Him led us. We drove down, up, and around until John suggested we stop at the next mound.

Setting sun on smooth, lovely hills, companionship, and a search for wild turnips—all of these ingredients combined to involve us through a magical two hours. John spotted turnips where we could not see them, and we kept digging until dark. The tail of that small root is often nearly two feet long, and the earth was so grass-rooted that the turnips were difficult to dig. We came to understand John's insistence that forked crowbars were the best implements. We had only shovels.

Later that week David came from Boulder to join me, and he met Len Pinto, the Dowell Smiths, and some of the VISTA volunteers. We picnicked again and dug turnips at the same spot. For a workshop we were to give I wanted yucca root instead of soap to bubble, so Dowell and others unearthed a large root nearby. [9]

This time all three Attack Him children (ages nine, seven, and six) came, as did Cordelia's two brothers. Insects were spontaneously collected—beetles, grasshoppers, and others I was unfamiliar with. Plastic jars I had brought kept the short-term captives. Good food from Jean Smith, songs in Lakota, trading of jokes, a brother's stories translated by Cordelia. I quote from a report David wrote:

> No one of the Vistas I had talked to had seen the bluebirds below the Smith's house or had noticed anything about the local rock, a

very fine-grained siltstone. When I mentioned what I thought was their need to learn, Cordelia told a brother—he spoke no English—and he promised to show me "sand crystals"—selenite, I think, with embedded sand. That brother, a very quiet man, was a medicine man. . . .

After the digging and much shared and general pleasure we watched the sunset in the big sky and heard Lakota songs—Cordelia and her brother—including the warrior's death song.

In a lull I asked at large, "Suppose you woke up in the night and didn't have a watch. How would you know the time?" I was thinking still of some of the Vistas and their own education. Cordelia snapped: "I'd turn on the radio!" And then, knowing the point of my question, she joked: "I'm a fine Indian; I must have been 'made in Japan!'" But Cordelia translated my question to her brother, who then spoke quietly in Lakota and at length. Her translation was briefer; but what he said was that through the night there were constantly changing sounds, the night sounds of birds and animals; there were changes in the sky with the seasons, but through the night as well . . . Cordelia told me, sadly, she could not translate it all, she didn't know the English words for much that he spoke of. Two worlds, not just two languages. Our loss.

But here is the possibility of something we are after, for Indian children and white. These are well-educated people, in spite of the schools; for their world, better than we.

At the workshop the yucca root made fine soap bubbles. It had once been prized as a shampoo, Cordelia told us. It was "supposed" to make hair grow longer, she laughed.

The potato cellar, where we were holding the workshop, was a great place. Steve Langley, one of the most committed and competent of the VISTAs, had a fine-art workshop there, and he invited us to move in. Other VISTAs came, some with their aides.

David got some electrical materials going—batteries, wire, bulbs, and the like, as well as small mirrors for playing with light. We brought along the insect zoo and a screened box with a few local butterflies. More ojos were made, and the visual delights of food-color droplets in still or stirred water were observed and played with.

Reactions were rather typical for newcomers. We had a time to warm up and some genuine use of materials, but it was mainly a diagnostic session—on both sides.

During that year we were given a large old one-room schoolhouse. Sometimes we had as many as twenty adult students attending our course every other weekend. Half of our Boulder staff would prepare gallons of stew, chicken, or beef with vegetables. The other half would drive the two hundred miles from Boulder with materials for the course and sleeping bags. It was a beginning to be cherished.

Head Start: Retrospect

The few of us whose professional lives had revolved around the beginning years of children shared a renewed—if tempered—hope in the early 1960s. Once again the needs of our youngest were coming into focus. Some of us had experienced the WPA nursery schools of the Roosevelt years, the Lanham Act nursery schools—federally supported—and good cooperative schools. All over the United States, there had been fine nursery schools to free women for war work during World War II. As always, the good beginnings soon faded. This has been our history: much learned, so much lost so quickly.

That history made it hard for me in 1963 to shake off a rather pessimistic sense of deja vu. Could it be different, this program that was to become Head Start? Could it survive, perhaps even flourish?

It was early fall 1963. David and I were still working in Cambridge when a conference was called by our parent organization, Educational Services, Inc., at MIT's Endicott House. The educational zeal and fine hand of Jerrold Zacharias were again involved—to formulate strategies and plans for a new, federally supported educational program that would prepare young children for school a year or two ahead of time; to give them, indeed, a "head start." Many knew the public schools had largely failed the poor children of rural areas and inner cities. Professionals who had been involved in early-childhood education were called together from around the country to confront the issues and propose remedies.

The report of that conference was to become a position paper in later congressional debates, culminating in legislation sponsored by Congressman Adam Clayton Powell. It was shepherded through Congress by Powell and his immensely capable legislative assistant, Deborah

Wolf. This law became a key part of the Johnson administration's poverty program.

My contribution to that conference was to present the initial 1963
report of the South End Kindergarten (see Chapter 7), "A Demonstration
of Possibility."

A small minority of us who had backgrounds in early-childhood education argued for the need to look closely at the quality of beginning programs, to start small enough to support the best that was already
available, then to expand in successive steps—each guided by cumulative
experience and staffed by some of those who had previously been
apprenticed. Without such experience and apprenticeship, what has been
learned is lost.

For that very reason, Jerrold Zacharias had asked me for names of
experienced old-timers in the field, and all but one had been invited. That
one, argued a young man from Washington, was too old! So we lost the
invaluable guidance of Dr. Lovisa Wagoner, of Mills College in California. She had been the main and forceful figure in the setting up of excellent preschool care in the wartime shipyards of California.

But all of this concern with the substance or quality of early- childhood
education was put aside in the push to "start big." We had allies, but not
enough. Among the allies was our physicist friend Philip Morrison, who
supported our minority report. He coined a maxim: Slow can be fast! A
similar piece of wisdom, from ancient Rome, was included in our high-
school Latin book: *Festina lente,* make haste slowly!

The members of that early and continuing minority remained always
hopeful and involved, however. We supported director James Hymes
from the University of Maryland, for example, in his well-informed
attempts to build in quality from the beginning—fighting, among other
things, to keep classes small and to enrich their narrow provisioning.

In the second summer of the national Head Start, 1966, I was invited
to Mississippi to give a series of workshops for teachers from Gulf Port to
Jackson. I was both encouraged by and fearful of what I saw. Some local
teachers and all of the children were great. I was warmly welcomed in
each Head Start I visited. Teachers were delighted to choose directions
from among my offerings: water with siphons, simple weaving with colored yarns, string telephones, homemade drums, drops of food color in
still or swirling water, and large, clear plastic jars.

Most northern advisers, however, failed to see or to communicate
what was essential: *how to build on the strengths and the uniqueness of these
Mississippi children and teachers.* What were the signs? Let me give one or

two small examples. In a school in Jackson, hidden on a back shelf, I happened upon a guitar made from a cigar box, which I strummed with delight. A teacher came over and said with embarrassment, "Oh, one of the parents made that old thing. . . . It's just homemade, and we aren't supposed to use old things like that." Then she hid it. My appreciation did not impress this teacher, although in other, similar instances teachers were surprised and appreciative to find a white northern adviser who warmed to local talent and to the children's ways: to allow and enjoy, for example, a four-year-old's solo descant after a song was finished. On that occasion all faces turned to see my reaction to this soloist before they allowed themselves to join their pleasure to mine.

When I shared this teachers' respect for an older woman "with no training" who had a group of three-year-olds happily engaged in dramatic play, we agreed that she could teach us all—she who confessed to me that she had loved and raised eight children! "Some advisers," I was told, "don't understand our having her here." I especially admired an occasional grandmother sitting in the hall, mending or sewing, with one or two children always beside her, talking, rocking, pleased with each other in an atmosphere of mutual learning.

One northern adviser who understood, harvested, and spread delight was Lucia from South End Kindergarten, now herself a Head Start adviser. She was with me during my stay in Gulf Port and Jackson and had been in Mississippi for several months.

In Jackson I was introduced to Head Start "charts." This occurred in a pleasant church setting with lively teachers who greeted me warmly. The open space between the pews and chancels made a spacious area where some children were happily building with blocks. I joined in, sitting with them on the carpet. We were all builders together, and I was pleased that the teachers beamed with amusement, although they were not sure they should approve—of a teacher on the floor.

"Mrs. Hawkins, would you take the sound table this morning?" For a moment I didn't understand. The gravity of tone made me think I was being invited to lead the children in prayer. Recovering my wits, I looked around and saw the "sound table." As the children gathered chairs to sit before it, I read: "TH" IS THE SOUND FOR THE WEEK . My eyes registered nine objects, painted with great care and detail on the large cardboard above the table. I was appalled at the chart, and I wasn't even certain what some of the objects were. The thimble was bigger than the throne, and the thumb strongly resembled a larger bit of male anatomy.

Pointing to the elaborate throne, I asked the children, "What is this?" With delight they called right back, "It's the king's chair. That's the king's chair!" So much for the sound for the week, *TH*! The children and I had fun talking and proposing. Would the king also have a table? And what would he eat? The sound for the week, *TH*, went out the window. I made no apology to the teachers for my misbehavior. I knew the whole idea of a sound for the week had come from some northern place on high. The teachers seemed relieved and even pleased at my irreverence.

My impressions of what was going on in these Head Starts began to crystallize in Jackson. I found these urban children to be inventive and even more ready for all sorts of pre-science activities than most other children, but such subject matter was little understood or valued in the "northern curriculum." I had with me a few easy-to-carry bits of material, and in one school a chance came to use flashlights and small stainless-steel mirrors. Several children at a time used the flashlights to "climb" the branches of the spreading oak trees outside, to jump off the end and return to the trunk, then to follow another long, twisty branch.

Next I introduced the steel mirrors. No one seemed able to catch the sun and send its beam to climb the trees until Sam had a turn. He was an expert, and we all watched him with oohs and ahs. Sam had two club feet, which made walking all but impossible. His expertise with hands, eyes, and mirrors delighted and instructed us all. Concentration and happiness took turns in Sam's face! And appreciation and new admiration for Sam were formed among the rest of us, children and teachers!

But there were troubles. The teacher-child ratios we had fought for had obviously not been explained and were not understood; as a result, the staff was poorly used. Instead of having each member work some of the time with a small group, one staff member would rote-"teach" seventeen children at a time while the others made charts or decorations or engaged in would-be housekeeping. (Those good cooks, bless them, often took two or three at a time as "helpers" in the kitchen.)

My observations, which were made long ago, were reinforced in a recent Head Start study by Lorene Quay and Olga Jarrett. [10]

> We observed informally that Head Start teachers spent a great deal of time preparing beautiful bulletin boards and engaging in other creative projects while the children were present, without directly involving the children. . . . Teachers . . . need to be encouraged to spend less time in such activities as interacting with other adults in the school, . . . to encourage children to initiate more contact with them, and . . . to initiate more contact with the children.

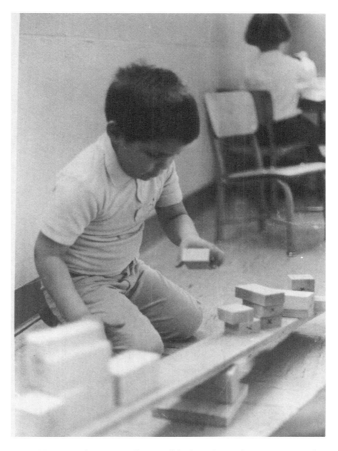

There were ten blocks of pine and ten of balsa. Scott begins to explore with the blocks.

The play continues. Because I knew the dense blocks were smaller, I chose them and won.

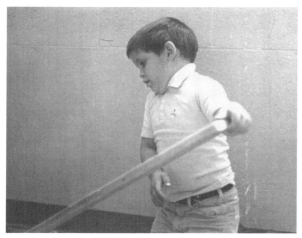

Without a word Scott stood up; and gently slid all blocks off of the balance board. He then chose all large balsa blocks for me, and the dense smaller blocks for himself, and said; as he turned the fulcrum upside down, "Now, we'll play it my way."

Scott's pleasure in realizing he had discovered some secrets of balance show in his anxious anticipation for his turn.

My experiences in Mississippi strengthened my beliefs about the potential of Head Start and underlined my fears that this potential would be overlooked or denigrated. I did not anticipate at the time how deeply I would later be involved.

Boulder got its own Headstart program in 1967, and I was invited to be involved in its beginnings. I already knew some of its staff, and others soon became friends and colleagues.

For the children, and their teachers, I found or produced a variety of materials, including some for play with the phenomena of balance. We had evolved many such materials during our work in the Elementary Science Study. These included rounded fulcrums on which boards would balance, and different sizes of wooden blocks for balancing. These included blocks of the same size but different densities, for example pine and balsa. And thereby hangs a tale.

It was during a visit from Boston our friend and colleague Allen Leitman, who came with his always-ready camera. I invited almost four-year-old Scott, as I shall call him, to "play a game with me." I did so partly because he was watching me so intently as I unpacked all the balance equipment.

Still later: the young Archimedes and a friend.

Once I put the balance-board on the fulcrum Scott picked up a block and put it on the high side, and this brought it down. This delighted him, and now it was my turn; the game was on. Because I used the denser blocks, I won.

Then Scott stood up and slid all the blocks gently off, stating, "Now we'll play it my way." He systematically passed all the light-weight balsa blocks to me first, turned the fulcrum upside down, and gathered the denser pine-weights for himself.

Allen caught the whole sequence with his camera. It is one I cherish; it reveals, through action, something of the knowledge and analytical powers of one almost four-year-old mind—of a kind that many adults, and some developmental psychologists, might regard as impossible.

Head Start: Sequel

This early association with the Boulder Head Start had been brief; we soon left again, first to Cornell University, then for a year in England and a final year at the Institute for Advanced Study.

In 1972, when our MVC was well launched, the Head Start teachers came to us again and asked us to be their in-service advisory group for the year. Jane Richtmyer, our center's artist in residence, our craftswoman par excellence, joined me from the beginning of our involvement. Soon, with the efforts of the Head Start teachers, our work took off. Betty Kellogg documented our work with her superb photographs.

Our commitment as a Head Start advisory group was to help the teachers grow in skill and understanding. I shall speak later of our work with specific children, which teachers and others could observe. Our work with the teachers, we decided, would not occur in their classrooms unless we were invited. Such a procedure would have required too - radical changes, taking from the teachers their collegial status. We chose another and less invasive way to do our work. We set up our own Mountain View Annex classroom in one of the Head Start buildings. Here children could come from the four other classrooms, and teachers could observe how we worked with their children: with fewer children at a time, different materials, in a different atmosphere. I return to this part of the story later.

We had no intention of running any sort of "model" Head Start room, something to be copied. What evolved instead, with the staff's understanding and support, was a room where a small group, or even just one child, could come away from classmates and teacher for an hour or two. The room could be viewed through a one-way mirror so teachers or visitors could observe if they wished. Occasionally a child would become the observer.

Our teachers were also given half a day a week of workshop and seminar time at the Mountain View Center, on the campus of the University of Colorado. Some of this time was devoted, of course, to discussion of the work and the children. But a major part was given to the teachers' own engagement in whatever subject matter they chose.

For this workshop time we gave the teachers a variety of choices. After discussion, their initial choice was Plants: Growth and Reproduction. The excitement of choosing their own investigations is usually the most neglected part of "teacher training," a neglect that robs them of their knowledge of where to start.

This plant work was guided by Ron Colton, our associate director and an incurable botanist, horticulturist, and teacher. Spores came first, in their elegantly small brown cases—taken from the underside of the leaves of the maidenhair fern. They were developed in damp, sterile-covered petri dishes and not only rewarded us with their initial brilliant emerald display but on sterile peat moss also took us into the world of very large numbers. In the second stage, when a miniature fern appeared, celebration reigned.

Other sorts of plant reproduction were also explored: propagation from leaf, stem, a piece of a leaf, and seeds. At the teachers' request we made large bottle gardens to be assembled and wondered about: how to invent "gentle" tools for planting through the small neck of the big bottles, lying on their sides or upright; how the plants could grow in a sealed bottle; where they would thrive in relation to the light. The involvement was deep and concentrated, and we were all impressed.

One afternoon I noticed teacher Angelita standing back from her bottle garden and silently weeping. When I asked if she was unwell she answered, "Oh no—it's just that this is the first beautiful thing I have ever made."

There was more than one unforeseen spin-off from that work on the growth and reproduction of plants—although it had less to do with the growth of plants than with that of the teachers.

We were planning a trip to a local greenhouse to buy seedling plants. I suddenly felt the enthusiasm was being suspended, withdrawn. My first probings were unsuccessful, but finally one brave soul spoke out. Looking at her teacher friends, hesitating, she broke the silence with the subject they had all been discussing privately: "It's just that we, Franny, don't go into places like that nursery and flower store." There, suddenly, loomed the wall—the wall between the middle class and poor minorities, in this case poor black and Hispanic minorities; a wall still felt or seen by the people it was once designed to exclude—mostly invisible nowadays to those who "belong." A one-way wall!

Earlier, in the days of the Boston South End Kindergarten, I had invited Maureen and Sally to lunch in Harvard Square. "But we don't go to Harvard Square," they protested. When we were in fact eating lunch there, we giggled because now they could not say, "We don't go to Harvard Square." How long, how long!

One day the parents asked the Head Start teachers an interesting question: What was the use of, what was the reason for, blowing bubbles in class? We took this as an indication to all of us that it was time to have

Barry, a salamander, and a frightened child who just a week before would not take off his coat.

Spray it all? Again?

Making rain for the salamander: Thor and Billy.

"Hey look, I can make my own moving pictures": Billy.

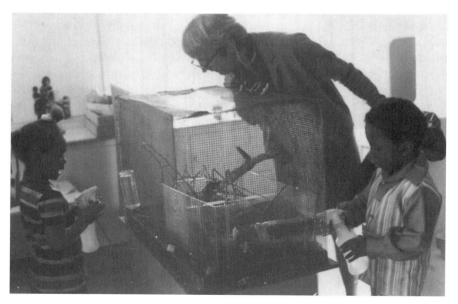

Robert and Judy inspecting our house for mice.

In our dry climate, spraying our mice cage became a favorite task. A mixture of peat moss and soil was just right for mouse tunnels if lightly sprayed often.

Dickie came daily. He might return with his group to his class, but return with the next group bringing his gentle charming manner. He chose our ways and room—never a trouble—always busy.

Siphons, syringes, and a stream table for young geologists.

an open house for parents and teachers. Plans were hatched; what developed was a glorious Mexican cooperative dinner and an evening for exploring materials in what we called environmental education—education through the environment.

Good food knows no one country. About fifty parents, teachers, and staff wandered and ate and explored. We were learning with pleasure the diversity of the Americans of Spanish descent in Colorado. Some were fifth generation or even more, their ancestors having settled in Colorado when it was still New Spain or New Mexico and was not yet a part of the U.S. West. A member of our own staff was, by comparison, a newcomer: Carlos Mena was born in Los Angeles; his parents had come from Mexico.

The "bubble frames" (wire frames to dip in soap solution to make what mathematicians call plateau surfaces) and other soap-film materials were there on nearby tables to give their own answers to the question, "Why bubbles?" And there were books as well. [11] But rivaling all else was the weaving room, with its samples of work in progress, patterns of Indian and Spanish origins.

It was an axiom of the center that good teaching depends on a teacher's own love, understanding, and continued pursuit of subject matter, whatever that may be. When teachers' lives have been deprived of any wholehearted enjoyment of the things of the world that can engage young children, then a first priority in helping them, as we sought to do, must be to let them discover that enjoyment as adults. We did not attempt any little lessons on "how to teach." The examples we provided, in our own special classroom, gave more to their teaching, I believe, than any homilies on the art of teaching we might have provided.

Jane and I, with faithful volunteers, worked at Head Start four mornings a week. Betty Kellogg soon joined us with her magnificent photographic art. Her work is informed by her skill as a teacher.

We also had a darkroom! It was a pass-through hallway joining two classrooms. With all doors closed it gave us a superb space where we could huddle with flashlights and colored theatrical gels. What lovely times! One of the Head Start supervisors from Greeley, Mr. Martinez, squeezed himself into our darkroom with four children and me one day. Beams of green (*verde*), red (*roja*), yellow (*amarillo*), and blue (*azul*) played on walls and ceilings. We would take turns, and a child might say, "Guess what color I'll use!" On and on it went for half an hour or so of play, of beams of light and color. Mr. Martinez walked near me as we returned to our room, and I realized he had tears in his eyes as he continued, "And not once did you say 'blue, that's blue' or ask 'what color is

that?' They all learned the color names from playing—and in two languages!" So much for the traditional mindless routine of teaching four-
year-olds "their colors"—as if their world did not naturally abound in
them with their names attached! Or if not, as an easy spinoff of good play.

We cannot know in advance the ways a small child in trouble will
choose to help himself or herself, but we do know how to prepare settings
supplied with good materials (which I call *universals*) from which a child
can choose and then give us guidance in maintaining an atmosphere for
learning. For this Head Start room we selected phenomena from the
world around us: water, sand, color, light and dark, shadows, balance,
magnetism, small animals, plant life.

Nothing was prepackaged or predesigned. What was properly expert
and predesigned were the variety and also the expertise of the staff in
observing, diagnosing, providing, and extending what children chose
from that variety.

Elaine Hill was a daily volunteer, already a fine preschool teacher
who wanted to learn in this new kind of situation. Barry Kluger-Bell was
a graduate student in physics and a part-time staff member at the Mountain View Center; he came occasionally. Jane Richtmyer I have mentioned
already; she was an artist and editor whose intellectual curiosity about
early learning never lagged. And as also mentioned earlier, Betty Kellogg
was a superb photographer whose early experience as a teacher can be
seen in her selections of subject and sequence in the illustrations.

I anticipated that we would find talents and strengths that would
help us to uncover further strengths. For that sort of therapy my background, from San Francisco to Boulder to Boston, promised me the fulfillment of a dream of possibility. I was sure that the course and speed of
therapy in these small groups would be such that the children themselves
would be learning to help themselves. [12]

Jane and I had played originally with the idea that art for the young
should be conceived not solely as painting, clay modeling, and similar
activities—so often just watered-down adult activities. Here there would
be expression and invention in all of the children's engagements. And so
there was to be.

Teachers soon began to send us children, a few at a time; children in
some sort of trouble, developmental or more profound. The troubles varied widely. Watch Judy, who tried, very successfully, to run her home
classroom. Her teacher was frantic, although amused, and could not quite
cope with such a takeover. When she came to us, Judy usually brought
her friend Robert, who was painfully shy and seldom spoke. They were

good for each other's particular constellation of habits. After some weeks Judy stopped being her unmanageable, too-adult self and seldom returned, busying herself in a more childlike way in her own classroom. Success, we believed. Robert, in turn, became less withdrawn.

Darin came because his last-year's adjustment to Head Start, as a three-year-old, had been to sit in an aide's lap and be read to. A good enough first adjustment, but he seemed stuck there until he came to us and learned that he could live well on his own.

Then there was Billy, as I shall call him. He came on cold days with no protection from the weather—in shorts, no socks, a cotton jacket—and spent his time eating, looking for food, and disrupting everyone with his persistent separateness. He was an abused child, we soon learned. Over the weeks with us he expanded and could use the equipment with delight and forget about food until snack time or lunch. Later he had to be removed from his "home" by action of the court. He came to us during this change.

The speed and assurance with which even such children settled in were a constant encouragement to us and our ways. The small groups; the abundance of phenomena from the real world that allowed significant choices for engagement; a staff that was competent and eager to learn, both with and from each other—it was little wonder that we all thrived and healing raced. Yet the specter of what could not be changed—poverty—permeated almost all our lives, those of teachers as well as children.

From one classroom came Bruce, diagnosed as brain damaged. His behavior was unfocused or only briefly focused. His delight in batteries and bulbs and a train to use such lights on seemed therapeutic; we encouraged his attendance with us. He was in less trouble with us, although his level seemed unchanged.

A local child psychiatrist, Dr. Schultz I shall call him, had been consulted about a few of the children. He came to our annex one morning to observe Thor, who often engaged in rather frantic and destructive behavior at home and in his own classroom. Thor was now spending his mornings with us, and Dr. Schultz came to observe him. The assessment he made of Thor, of our staff, and of our equipment and classroom climate was startling. Let me summarize.

The doctor, appropriately, was sitting at the back of our big classroom while four children, including Thor, were busy with the usual paraphernalia and with each other. By now they enjoyed working alone or in small groups, where each could use different equipment rather than always "sharing"; that was a part of our design. Sharing was a dominant theme of the home classrooms. Structuring for individuals, on our part, was both understandable and understood by us all.

But back to Thor. Two children left that morning after the first hour, and Thor and another boy stayed on. Dr. Schultz talked to me for a few moments. The gist of what he said was this: He couldn't pick out Thor by his behavior; which child was he? I indicated Thor by his continuing activity at the deep-water tub. Dr. Schultz watched for a minute and said, wonderingly, "I have never seen a classroom like this—with such skilled teachers and such great equipment." I tried to indicate to him how the small size of the class freed us all and how materials from the real world were indeed a blessing for children of four, especially for those who were in trouble. He said he would stay for a few minutes more to watch from behind the glass, which he did.

As was common, there had been other visitors to our annex that morning, and one of the supervisors, a friend of mine, had met Dr. Schultz leaving the observation booth. He made some comment about what he had seen and concluded by asking a remarkable question: "But aren't we rewarding bad behavior by sending such a child to such a classroom?" A child like Thor, privy to a violent home situation, whose mother had recently been expelled from her apartment along with Thor and a new baby because her boyfriend had shot himself in the leg while attempting to shoot her? Tell me, O puritan Dr. Schultz, would you send Thor to a prison for four-year olds? Where? An orphanage perhaps?

"Tell it like it was." Lest I seem merely angry, I refer back to my story of an event from long ago in which I emphasized the distinction between evils that are genuinely exceptional and those that are only the extreme of a continuum.

"Tell it like it was." It is against this background of events that Thor can now show us something of how children in trouble can acquire courage in a classroom with good materials, time, and small numbers—therapy?

My mind's eye sees Thor quietly at work, with a small siphon he had happily and speedily learned to start with a plastic syringe, bringing water to his sand, rock, and mountain world at the wet-sand table. Darin was at work at the deep-water tub; others were with the salamanders and the mice, blocks, and woodwork.

Good! Thor could work alone! (The crisis at home was still raging.) He was so deeply engaged that I withdrew my long-distance attention from him. But not for long. A small pitiful wail found me: "Franny! Look! The water is all gone!" Tears were gathering.

Fortunately I felt something, I believe, of the significance of the big, empty plastic jar on a shelf above the sand table. It was as if he had said "look, Franny, even at school it happens!" I canceled my immediate reaction, to go to him and take him in my arms, as unprofessional. Instead I called to him across the room, smiling to reassure, and said, "I see; but you can fill it yourself at the deep water—and Darin can help!"

He looked toward Darin and made his way, with his empty bottle, to the deep water. Darin, I knew, had also heard. Thor stayed there filling, playing, and talking to Darin and finally came near me lugging his half-filled plastic jar. "I did it, Franny! I did it!"

If psychotherapy does not make possible a series of such small self-help episodes in the life of a four-year-old in trouble, then what else can it possibly be good for?

So we thrived, with teachers' cooperation almost paralleling that of the children. The reasons for sending a child or allowing a child to come varied. Some sturdy ones we allowed to come because they provided ballast and took complete care of themselves. After a time, when things went well, they usually chose to stay in their own home rooms.

Some sturdy ones came uninvited, like Dickie. He would walk past his own room, take off his jacket, and say to me, "Hi, Franny. Guess I'll feed the mice. OK?" He not only made his own way among the riches but often took some less inner-directed friend along with him. Occasionally, because we needed room for a newcomer with priorities, I would send Dickie to his own classroom; an hour later he might be back, unobtrusively making a dam in the stream-table.

What more? The telephone company at our request had supplied the center with real telephones. Hooked up properly, they could be used to talk to a friend across the room; such conversations were reflections snatched whole from these children's lives—conversations with abusive neighbors, with police, with friends.

Batteries and bulbs and wire were favorites, especially when Barry Kluger-Bell was with us. As our playful graduate student in physics and a part-time member of the center's staff, he had a coterie of followers in the Head Start Annex. [13]

From classes next door a teacher might come to observe a child sent to our setting. At weekly seminars we could then discuss what they had seen. An occasional parent came. One was Thor's mother: "At home he is climbing the walls!" More discussion was needed for Thor. But her frantic misery was lessened, we hoped, by seeing him so deeply engaged.

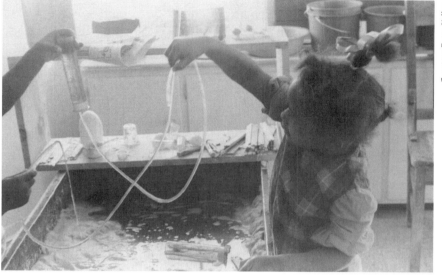

Judy: "Look, Robert, I can stop my siphon!"

"Look! The bubbles get smaller when you beat them with the egg-beater."

Robert's peanut butter factory (*above*).

Peanut Butter Delivery Truck.

Courtesy Betty Kellog.

Andrew and F.H. listening to their "rain makers." Africa introduced me to these tubes. Using hollow stems and nails to interrupt the fall of sand grains—one heard gentle, musical sounds. (Repeats by turning the tube upside down.)

Elmira with carpenters. Elmira loved her work as a parent aid—as did the children..

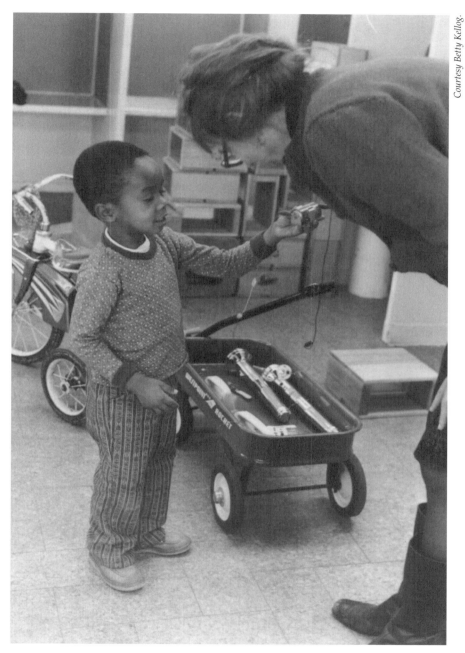

Courtesy Betty Kellog.

Andrew delivers flashlights and batteries to Jane from our faithful and versatile delivery truck.

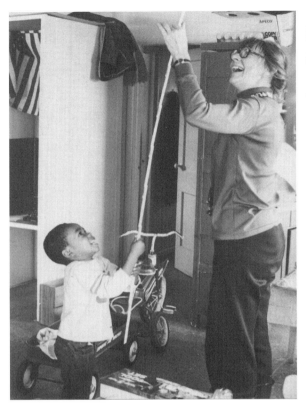

Courtesy Betty Kellog.

"Look, I can touch the ceiling!"

Courtesy Betty Kellog.

Judy and Elaine. Two hands are needed, sometimes four.

Courtesy Betty Kellog.

Reggie, our supervisor.

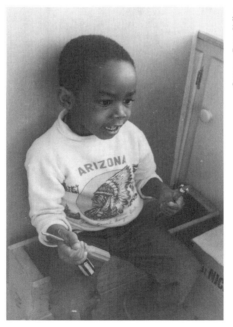

Courtesy Betty Kellog.

A corner on the tools!

Courtesy Betty Kellog.

Judy tries the typewriter.

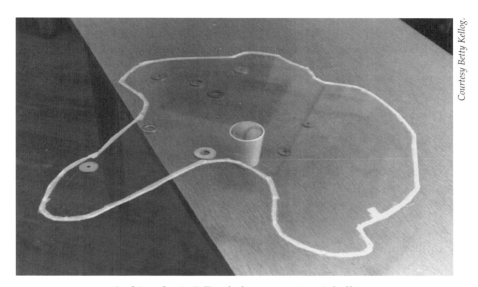

Courtesy Betty Kellog.

Archimedes in 2-D: a balance on a tennis ball.

Courtesy Betty Kellog.

Friendship begins over magnets, with many fine discoveries—not the least a growing friendship.

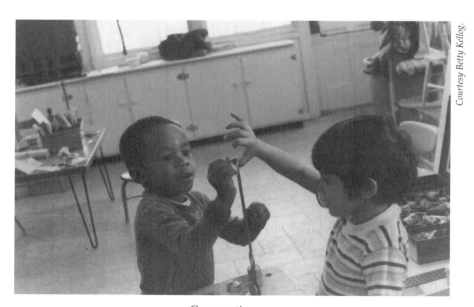

Cooperation . . .

. . . learning, . . .

. . . and sharing.

Courtesy Betty Kellog.

Our almost-silent Robert would talk over our "electric telephone"!

Andrew stands out vividly in my memory, for reasons worth considering in some detail; his problems were less serious and obvious than some other's. Two weeks passed before I realized that <u>Andrew</u> was always with us. His teacher, Gwen, had neither brought nor sent him; he just found us and moved in. When I put all of this into focus I realized why he simply fit in and why we, busy with the demanding ones, had overlooked him. Andrew always seemed busy in one place or another, if unto himself. He was especially occupied when his group was being escorted back to its own classroom, I noted. The pattern was similar to Dickie's, except that Dickie might accompany his group back to its classroom, then return five minutes later with another group. Andrew was more direct.

We began to count Dickie and Andrew as good ballast for our more demanding visitors. But one morning Gwen came by and found Andrew beside me looking at a book. She and I walked away to have a few words and returned to Andrew. "We wish you would come back to your own class, Andrew; we miss you." Without looking at Gwen he responded: "You're not my teacher. This is my class. You don't even like me."

Gwen and I agreed later to "leave him for awhile." She did not have to assure me that she *did* like him; I knew she did. I wondered if what he wanted to say was rather, "You don't even know me." *Exact* language may be a barrier for some of the four-year-olds, a fact that leaves their thoughts beyond recovery.

What did Andrew's behavior reveal over the next weeks? Contrary to my expectations, his initial moving from one activity to another, always "busy," was a fixed pattern rather than a reaction to his new classroom. He seldom stayed long at a choice or finished making or doing a self-selected project. He loved to take the small red wagon, fill it with an odd assortment of items, and pull it around the room, calling out to all, "See ya later, I'm on my way!" He appreciated my Woody Guthrie, "I'm on my way, an' I won't be back!"

After some weeks I was still mystified by Andrew. Too agreeable, charming, self-effacing, somehow in a safe groove? He seemed to be giving me clues, but I couldn't interpret them. So it can be with those who don't make waves—they can be puzzling. I finally began to sense that Andrew, like a few others I had known, lived carefully behind some sort of facade that had served him in the past but that he needed to break through. These are the fascinating, tough puzzles that challenge us until fresh insight can grow. As his pattern began to challenge me more and more, I sensed I must be alert to some chance to spend time alone with Andrew. How?

As happens when we are ready and cunning, we see and seize a propitious moment. It came when Andrew arrived early one sunny morning and I was outside looking toward a field where last night's light snow defined every shadow of rock and hummock and bush. Andrew saw me and called, "Hi Franny, come on, let's go in!" There it was, that school pattern that had to be followed. I had to break it. "No," I called, "come on out here! I want to show you something." He argued, but I was firm, and reluctantly he joined me. I pointed out a far cottonwood tree, saying that it was where we were going. He tried to lure me back to school but finally came with me and stood, uninterested, as I tried to find a bug under a rock. No ruse worked. He dragged himself along and then played his trump card: "Let's go back, Franny, I have to pee!"

I knew how often Andrew had to pee and was about to give up, but I was inspired instead to offer the cottonwood as a place to go behind. That proved irresistible. He reached the tree at a run, went around to its far side, and had a good pee. I offered to race him back to school, feeling that my plans had gone astray. But no. Andrew saved us. He stooped down to "find a bug under a big rock." By the time we approached school our arms were filled with treasures—including every rock or piece of wood I had suggested to him as worth collecting for whatever purpose. He moved slowly as we neared the school. We were both aware that we felt good about the trip we had made together.

Gradually over the next days, Andrew grew less dependent on his previous routine and became more spontaneous. I began to understand. In my insistence that he come with me that morning against his will, I was exerting, as I rarely do, one of my adult-teacher prerogatives. The sheer assertion of my being in charge had allowed Andrew to let go, had joined his hidden wish and need to be a child. The walk itself was a culmination of inner growth. Had his correct choice of a classroom started it? His realization that I was different and was not afraid of him? I use a question mark because we cannot absolutely know how a four-year-old like Andrew files and assesses the multiplicity of segments involved in his home or classroom life. Had this new situation not felt right for his needs, he would not have chosen it or stayed. In some such sense he was asking for help in taking the next step. That kind of asking is what Frederick Allen referred to in stating the "fundamental thesis" of his *Psychotherapy With Children*. When a child or an adult asks for help, he or she is halfway toward the cure. [14]

Only much later did I learn some details of Andrew's life. There was no abuse in this family, no neglect or poverty. His parents were divorced, his mother and he were living with her parents. Mother worked full time, and his father lived and worked thirty-five miles away. They all "loved him and took care of him." No wonder Andrew was always packing his little red wagon and getting on his way. It was his solution to the way many people live today.

In his chapter "The Function of the Family in the Child's Growth," Allen refers to the fiction of Thomas Mann and quotes Malinowski speaking of "the impossibility of envisaging any form of social organization without the family structure."[15] As the reasonable child he was, Andrew felt the need to forego spontaneity, a drastic choice for anyone but especially for a four-year-old. He was subtly on guard, to somehow fit into his distressed but loving family, wanting to be genuinely occupied as a child.

This story of a special classroom is a summary, rather late in my teaching life, of much I have learned about children—first from the Emerson years, then from the South End Kindergarten. Among the diversity of their troubles—superficial or deep—lies an equal diversity of potentially redeeming talents, often buried. Teachers, when they become curious and committed detectives, can help uncover these talents and provide some of the ways of strengthening them.

Notes

[1]John Paull and Dorothy Paull, *Yesterday I Found* (Boulder, Colo.: Mountain View Center, University of Colorado, 1972). Together they wrote a story of the children in her Leicestershire classroom. See Chapter 8.

[2]Whose *In the Early World* I have discussed in the bibliography.

[3]One of David's better-known essays, "Messing About in Science," was inspired by Kenneth Grahame's classic, *The Wind in the Willows.*

[4]Interesting! This well-meaning but utterly inept notion of "tutoring" had been given, seventeen years earlier, to volunteers of the Northern Student Movement, for their work with children in the South End of Boston.

[5]Dowell Smith, "Bubbles and Children: A Small Ethnography of Cross-Culture Learning," *Outlook* 26 (Winter 1977), pp. 20–27.

[6]The *ojos de dios* are traditional decorations of the Huichol natives of Mexico, colored yarns wound contiguously over crossed sticks or, in our more free-form appropriation of the idea, over three or four smaller branchlets from the fallen branch of a tree.

[7]Hans Otto Storm, "Eolithism and Design," *Colorado Quarterly* 1, no. 3 (Winter 1953); reprinted in *Outlook,* no. 4 (Winter 1971), pp. 37–43.

[8]This is not a relative of our garden turnip; according to our fellow staff member Ron Colton, it is a member of the *lupin* family.

[9]Nonnabah G. Bryar and Stella Young, *Navajo Native Dyes* (Washington, D.C.: U.S. Department of the Interior, Bureau of Indian Affairs, 1967).

[10]Reviewed in *Phi Delta Kappan* 22 (May 1987), pp. 703–704.

[11]For example, V. C. Boys, *Soap Bubbles and the Forces Which Form Them* (New York: Anchor, 1959).

[12]Here, as so often in such matters, I refer to Frederick Allen, *Psychotherapy With Children* (New York: W. W. Norton, 1942).

[13]At this writing (1993) Barry is a staff member at the Exploratorium, a science museum in San Francisco.

[14]Allen, *Psychotherapy With Children* .

[15]Brontislaw Malinowski, "Kinship," *Encyclopedia Britannica* (14th ed.), vol. 13, p. 403.

10: Consulting

Turn Here

In recent years I have been invited to be an observer-critic in schools for the young and in colleges for their teachers. This has been a challenge, a chance to learn, and great fun. The episode I consider here was taken from notes I made during a week at a college with a laboratory school—a week memorable for the kindness I received, for friends made, and for what I learned.

For some of us—perhaps it is age—memory becomes excruciatingly selective. Whether in a museum, at a concert, on a trip, or in a school, I seem unintentionally to carry a sieve. I sometimes think of it as a winnowing basket for selecting out and keeping the grain. The grain I want to discuss here came in the form of two small boys, not yet five, who defined for me and with me something of the strength and weakness of our better schools, their own included. With my winnowing memory and my notes, I will try to tell their story; it is ours too, of course, we who seek to understand and thus to provide well for the young.

Records of episodes such as this provide only the tip of the iceberg of their significance. What I hope for and seek in rethinking such a morning with children is further insight into how action was triggered and informed, not overlooking the less obvious dynamics inherent in the situation.

The outdoor space and provisioning of the laboratory school, with its large sprawl of sun and shade, was ideal for children and reflected its designers' understanding of the kind of place where play-cum-learning could, should, take off. What puzzled me as an observer was the rarity of that element of taking off—of deep, sustained involvement of imagination, of unique group or individual transformation of the well-designed equipment and the available raw materials. Yes, I had seen it and felt it, but too fleetingly. In this ideal setting I saw the boredom of both children and adults outweigh the excitement.

On my final morning I walked toward a far corner where I saw a boy in a tree. Near him in another tree was another boy. The boys weren't climbing, they were just *there* in the small trees—content, I judged,

315

away from the groups of children using tires, jungle gyms, sandboxes, and tricycles.

As I came closer, slowly entering their sphere and looking at them, my judgment of their mood changed. They too were bored, and I thus felt emboldened to join them. Under the first tree I slowed and stayed and saw at eye level two immaculately new tennis shoes. With admiration I commented on the deeply grooved, handsome pattern of the soles. The response dispelled my shyness. The boy lifted one foot at a time and out-lined with a finger the grooves and edges, with an appreciation the young often have for new shoes. Then, unexpectedly, he said, "My name is Kenneth." With a long, searching look he stared at me, and I realized he was silently asking my name. After giving it, I felt that having intruded, it was up to me to strengthen our initial bridge to friendship, those tennis shoes. I had noticed a wide, damp place under a nearby faucet and asked Kenneth (as I have called him) if he thought his shoes might make good prints in the damp, sandy earth.

By the speed of his descent from the tree, I judged Kenneth's enthusiasm for such a venture, and we found ourselves standing and speculating about precisely where to test the pristine soles. For a moment, forgetting what I had rather recently come to understand about pounds per square inch, I feared he would prove too light to impress clear prints, but to our joint pleasure the laws of nature acted on the just-right mix of soil, sand, and water and two clean, clear sole prints appeared. Kenneth's care in stepping in and out seemed well calculated; it was not chance. He was coming into focus for me.

We stood in admiration, and the forgotten little boy (I'll call him Lester) came around to see. Of course, he wanted to make his prints. The three of us examined his plain-soled oxfords and wondered whether they too would make prints. Kenneth and I were doubtful. Lester, who must have been a young four, was less dubious as he stepped carefully into the damp soil. I grabbed a twig to outline his shoes, just in case, and while Lester stood importantly still, Kenneth took the twig and outlined Lester's shoes. We now had two sets of prints to admire. Unable to resist, I stepped into the dampness, but not too close to the small prints, and waited while Lester outlined my plain-soled oxfords.

The boys continued to stand respectfully before the prints while I, in some quandary, stood behind them. What next? It was not the time to bow out, and although the boys were involved, I felt they were unable to contribute enough to make the play their own and carry on. It was my

move, and the sequel was uncertain. Neither of the boys seemed to be a talker, so clues remained largely nonverbal. Thinking to increase their preoccupation with footprints, I picked up the discarded twig and etched a "circle road" around Kenneth's left footprint and Lester's right one, saying, "I shall make a road here."

This was simply a holding operation on my part, but Kenneth came to my rescue. He took a twig and drew another circle road. "I don't want the road to go between my prints." So pronouncing, he drew a circle to enclose his own two footprints.

By thus taking his first initiative to alter or change my input, Kenneth clearly signaled a developing partnership I could count on. By his use of my word "road," rather speculatively introduced by me, he indicated a desire to continue in some such endeavor and to use one part of my input, altering it for his own purpose. It is easy to miss some clues

because of their telegraphic speed and their subtlety, but personal relationships are built or abandoned around their presence or absence and
the comprehension of them. Adults must re-apprentice themselves,
retune their ears and minds; most children send and receive easily with
peers.

With confidence now in Kenneth's readiness, I again began to make a
road in the earth. Both boys, Kenneth and Lester, provided themselves
with sticks, and a city map—or was it the city itself?—began to take form.
Kenneth soon emerged as the pacesetter, with Lester and me as rapt assistants. Behind us now was the prelude, with its slow tempo, in which my
part had seemed of necessity too powerful, too directing. Once such a
juncture is passed, exact sequence defies even careful notes. Let me try,
however, to take the rapid and intertwined action and, by means of its
substance, to reconstruct something of how two children, each in his own
way, made the play his own on one of those mornings to be remembered.

Near their free-standing kindergarten room was a large box of
assorted scraps of wood and other nice junk. This became the supply
depot for our budding enterprise. As the old roads were abandoned, new
roads defined a growing community. Both boys were indefatigable in
trips for supplies. Kenneth, as a city planner, remained the boss. Lester, I
realized, was very much his own man and didn't seem to mind. Concerned with developing small areas within the overall plan, he began
work on the airport at a far side of the "city."

From my new and appropriate place on the sidelines, I could watch
grandiose plans taking form at my feet: there was the sea, a beach—a
"swimming beach"! Ideas tumbled out of two well-stocked brains, and I
could contribute from my less active role as sidewalk observer without
fear of interfering.

Amid all this hubbub of activity instigated by the two boys, I decided
to remain. My concern had initially prevailed and then kept me there; I
sensed a hunger for an adult presence—an involved but not dominating
one.

I am convinced that we too often make a virtue out of a necessity:
with too many children to be attended to and more pressing matters at
hand, we withhold our involvement and careful observation, although
conditions invite it and time allows it. It is as if we come to believe that
not to ever give sustained attention to anyone is better than to give it only
to a few when circumstances and conditions do allow. It is sometimes
argued that adults should enter the work-play only to get children
started, to increase the visible learning, to widen repertoire.

But although many such factors may weigh heavily, in special situations, I have come to know that deeper considerations may be at stake and must be understood to form a facet of the adult's participation. By always bowing out of children's affairs just when the children take over—which may be necessary in a crowded classroom or a big family—we may communicate a shallowness of concern. Some children couldn't care less; they are the lucky ones. But once we accept the great challenge of engaging the bored and the narrowly involved, of helping them reclaim their birthright, the quality and honesty and duration of our engagement are crucial.

An involved child may certainly influence a withdrawn friend, but as adults it is our business to *know* about involvement and to examine ways of affecting the ambience around us. Children come to respect one's sometimes deep involvement with just one of their number when—and if—their own affairs are part of the propitious climate.

Fortunately for those of us who teach the young, feedback is not slow in coming. Receding boredom always releases strengths. We observe this release in renewed, less clumsy efforts; in the transformation of materials; in the "hatching of wonderful ideas" (to use Dr. Eleanor Duckworth's phrase); and from a multitude of other specific manifestations. None of this is new, and it is too fundamental to be spoken of so briefly here. But what I miss in the field of early education is the intellectual curiosity that grows from pushing further these subtle, sustaining, or fostering matters. Is it because they are subtle that we dare not examine or discuss them? Especially in large classrooms, where atmosphere and climate have to substitute for adequate staff, pursuing and understanding such matters should have high priority. It can enhance the atmosphere of learning; it is a major protector against burnout.

I return to the children's action, as raw materials were being stockpiled and transformed by young minds in transit. What was taken from the box as an interesting rectangle of styrofoam arrived at the construction site as a dock. Once in place at the oceanfront, the dock required boats. So the classroom was raided for properly scaled boats. Judging from the quantity of cars, trucks, and boats that returned, that classroom was very well stocked, and the children were at home with its surplus. After more trips by Lester for airplanes, the two workers again settled in to build their city. Lester had carried back an oversized giraffe on one of his trips, and it stayed as the first and only wild animal in Lester's instant zoo. Kenneth was initially uneasy about the animal's size, having a clear sense of scale, but he did not rule out the giant giraffe. When things go well, tolerance is a by-product. Lester settled in at his airport/zoo and left Kenneth and me to our concerns.

How the need for signs arose I cannot remember. Whether Kenneth went to search for signs or whether the small formica samples he encountered on a trip suggested signs to him is not clear. When Kenneth returned from the penultimate trip he brought back two good handfuls of small colored rectangles, saying importantly and directly to me, "I have to put up signs." The pieces were so signlike in size and finish that I wanted to commend him on his foraging skills but, knowing that would be superfluous, I offered instead to be his sign painter. Kenneth dumped the blanks in my lap and dashed off for something to write with. He returned with a "mission accomplished" look, carrying a felt pen. "I got deep pink; it's a good color to use." And so it proved to be. To Kenneth's specification, I printed the first sign:

I asked if he wanted an arrow pointing in the correct direction. In his circumspect way, Kenneth thought about this and then looked at his road system: "Yes, and make the arrow go this way." His arm gave me the direction, and I wondered whether he really did have the directional idea clearly in mind. I need not have wondered. The city-planner-turned-traffic-planner planted the sign securely at an intersection so the arrow directed the traveler to the Lester Airport.

With mutual effort and satisfaction we continued the set of signs, and Kenneth stayed steady of purpose and in command. He re-created a lost time for me in his distillation of a city while creating a satisfactory microcosm for himself. As a reader of confusing urban highway signs, my nostalgia grew:

And then a kind of disembodied fancy informed Kenneth's last order, which I followed exactly. The sign "Turn Here" was set at the intersection of two roads. Where did the indicated road go? What unexpected delight waited at its end? No one asked, no one told, but I was happy to be with this young man who brought a bit of faith and fancy into his city's invisible inhabitants' lives.

I backtrack to speak of the genesis of a river. It provides a nice paradigm of a way in which a child who is using his or her own mind well can pick and choose and discard from a willing and cooperative adult's mind. When the "River" sign was in his hand but the river itself was still only in his mind, Kenneth stood and studied his landscape. I believed he was wondering what to use to make a river, and I suggested that a blue ribbon might be found to make it. With quick scorn he rejected such a representational idea. "I will make a river out of blocks." My initial reaction was personal—I felt slightly miffed. My professional reaction—tardy—was to feel deep confidence and satisfaction as I watched blocks expertly used to define a rushing stream, with waves, on its way to the ocean Kenneth imagined his city to be near.

Meanwhile, at the Lester Zoo the giraffe stared in silent, solo occupancy from a block cage as Lester managed his busy airport. In classic parallel play, this younger four-year-old had been content and busy. The fact that he stayed suggests his contentment with us. But I wanted to include him before I said goodbye, and so I offered to make a sign for his zoo. Yes, he would like that: "Say GIRAFFE. And with an arrow." When I was ready for the arrow's direction, he used his arm as Kenneth had, but when he put the sign in place I was amused that for him the arrow was just dressing—he pointed it away from the zoo. The Lesters will work fast enough on their own timetables—if, that is, they are not forced into other people's.

Finally, I reluctantly got ready to leave the small city and its builders. Kenneth, "to see the city from up here," climbed to his early notch in the tree. From there he delivered a benediction. He passed his right arm slowly over the miniature community below him, raised one foot, pointed to its sole, and said, "And it all started with this!"

Jack's Secret World

The nursery school I visited one day was for children ages three to six, described as emotionally disturbed or with "learning problems." The children were referred by physicians, by other nursery schools, or, as in Jack's case, by public kindergartens. Hence, they were "at risk." I call this school a negative paradigm. In my sampling of the current universe of nursery schools and kindergartens, it was more typical than its high medical school credentials and its evidently large budget had suggested.

Before any children arrived I was shown the well-stocked classroom long enough to approve of its basic provisioning, and I was briefed about the staff and the good teacher-child ratio. By format and intent, this was an "open classroom." By any purely formal criteria, the staff was adequately educated and qualified. What seemed a possible luxury to me was that in addition to an adequate teaching staff, each child was assigned a part-time therapist-teacher (TT). (Such special assignments had been made in Anna Freud's nursery home for six German concentration camp orphans.[1])

I was invited to observe the classroom activities from an excellent observation booth, where the one-way glass and the acoustics worked well and where I did not feel too cut off from the action. I settled to the pleasure of not being responsible to anyone—except to myself for my own learning.

My colleague-host pointed to a tall child who came bouncing into the classroom. I cannot remember her exact words, but the tone of her voice still chills me: "Oh, that one has to be subdued in the yard. . . . Kindergarten can't handle him . . . impossible." So young Jack, as I have called him, came bouncing into my focus already damned. We shall observe how incorrigible he was.

Alone and no longer being briefed, I could watch Jack. His TT had left him near the door. He may have been subdued outside, but now there was devilment on his face, liveliness in his muscles, and, I mused, a "how to amuse them today" attitude reflected in his stance and manner. I promptly forgot the rest of the classroom. Jack's TT was for the moment occupied elsewhere. I watched Jack go forth looking for fun or trouble, both he and I wondering where he would find it. He stopped by a low vase with golden leaves and took out one brown cattail already fraying at the top. I thought he would shake it and scatter the "million" winged seeds over the heads of all—not dull havoc to wreak with that elegantly packed marsh plant. Then I saw Jack's attention focus on the denuded stem at the top. With care, he broke off the spare top stem. After a moment his interest seemed to shift again, not away from the brown cattail but more intently on the velvet-textured object he held protectively in his small brown hand. From that moment I was his silent partner and admirer.

Jack continued to probe the looser seeds at the top very gently with the testing finger, his eyes on the finger's probing. What bit lay under his private microscope? The vast numbers of seeds? The way each seed was attached to the stem, the way the seeds were attached to each other, or how each looked when partially released? I couldn't know what he was thinking, perhaps all this and more.

Only after a long, delicate examination did Jack make his selection: one helicopter seed. By such care he showed me much about his concentration and dexterity and something of what was important to this—I now surmised—remarkable child. He held up the one seed and blew softly, matching his blowing to the delicacy of his miniature glider. The seed traveled, while Jack and I (from behind the glass) watched until it was lost somewhere in the large classroom. Content in face and posture, he gently put the still-intact marsh plant back into its vase and moved on.

The door to my observation booth opened. Startled, I turned to see my hostess coming in. Hoping to protect the delight in the scene I had just witnessed and to forestall another unprofessional attack on Jack, I asked his age.

"Five." "He is tall," I began, "and . . . " Before I could recount his investigation, she was off: "Look at him there wandering about . . . can't settle down to anything . . . does nothing . . . trouble to all."

Filled with shame at such remarks, I did not respond but turned away to the protection of observation and was again left mercifully alone. The intrusion had caused me to miss some of the action with Jack. When I observed again, the TT was restraining him, holding his arms against his sides, saying seriously (but not angrily), "No, you can't do that." Jack wriggled expertly out of the TT's grasp. I shall never know what "terrible" thing he had done.

Jack stalked away to some low shelves where a large plastic hourglass caught his eye—and a hard blow from his clenched fist. So much for you, TT. The timer was well constructed and was filled with tiny colored beads instead of sand. Colorful and intriguing, it was an object boys like Jack cannot resist. He must have noticed the beads jump at his bang, because this "hyperactive" child's next move was, as I was coming to expect, logical and patient. He examined the timer with his hands and eyes, finally trying to get it open.

He was as respectful of this object's construction as he had been of the cattail's packing. He tried to unscrew any part that could conceivably be unscrewed, but with no success. The upright wooden posts were examined and again gently tested to see if they could be pulled apart. All efforts failing, Jack carefully put the timer back on the shelf and gave it a friendly, gentle, good-bye pat. The pat was enough to cause another jump of the beads. Jack stopped. I soon realized it was not the jump itself but the sound of the beads as they moved that caught his attention.

With delight and evidently with some recollection of similar sounds, Jack grabbed the timer and immediately transformed it, as children will in their "eolithic" way,[2] into a magnificent soft-toned maraca. He accompanied its rhythm with a playful joyous dance. From side to side the timer-maraca made its muted rhythm, and Jack made his soft, following steps. The dance was for himself. The fact that I could share it with him was grace.

The dance did not last. The TT had seen him and called from across the room, "Put that thing down, Jack, and get busy putting blocks away." The dance held briefly, but the TT was bigger, and in the manner of a top sergeant he insisted that Jack get started stacking blocks left scattered by another child.

Halfheartedly, Jack began to stack the blocks, initially kept at it by the watchful eye and straw-boss manner of the TT, who yelled encouragement of a kind from across the room: "Come on . . . keep going . . . pile them neatly!" In quiet despair but by now with no surprise, I watched the scene. Who was handicapped? Jack was not, at least not yet; but how long could this young victim of conventional misdiagnosis or others like him survive a conventional treatment that was inappropriate even for the genuinely handicapped?

Although discouraged, I continued to watch. I heard soft sounds—musical, gentle, and strangely muted. Looking at Jack's mouth I realized that some of the sounds were his. I couldn't identify the other sounds until I concentrated on Jack, still on his knees. He would lift a block that was already in place and drop it on another block. He was matching the marimba-like sound of good dense wood against good dense wood with his voice and matching it well.

In this quiet classroom, conversation with children had been scarce all morning—except for constant idle talk among the staff, which is seriously unprofessional in a setting where children are living and where learning demands involvement and repays alertness to that observed life. There had been no encouragement or reason for Jack to talk, so I was reassured that he did hear and had responded so acutely to rhythm and tone. Jack was communicating; a responsive adult could have reciprocated through music, through other instruments, or perhaps, at first, by selecting some of these hardwood blocks for tone and supporting them—like xylophone blocks—for an even better sound. In that way one could participate in Jack's discovery and help him extend it. Under these circumstances, however, I could only enjoy his discovery vicariously, appreciating the key he had found for releasing musical tones from wood.

The sounds had been a lovely by-product of the routine of stacking. But the TT, with his eagle eye for deviance, had seen Jack's slowdown and interfered: "Stop that fooling around, Jack, and GET going." The behavior of this well-meaning and consistently inept young man showed him to have missed all of Jack's perceptive actions and to have zeroed in only on the behavior to be corrected or—to use the word he had probably been trained to use—"modified."

I wondered where and how the professionally needed kind of therapy and teaching, communication between patient and therapist, had been lost, somehow regressing from a time at least sixty years ago when it was widely shared.[3] Was professional curiosity, with its skill and ability to alter its focus, also mislaid? Was some preconceived formula continually being trusted? It was as if Jack had been prejudged to be incapable of innovative response. I quote from Frederick Allen:

> This book emphasizes the values of what people have and how they can be helped to use their present capacities to effect their own changes. We begin with the fundamental thesis that no one can effect change in another person without the participation of the person in whom change is desired. This is as true of children as it is of adults. The focus lies in what people can be helped to achieve and not in what is done to, or for, them to bring about

change. Taft has this clearly in mind when she states: "The word *therapy* is used instead of treatment because in its derivation there is not so much implication of manipulation of one person by another." Therapy is concerned with a process and must give full recognition to the essential participation of the patient in this process. As Taft says: "Therapy cannot do anything to anybody—hence can better represent a process going on, observed perhaps, understood perhaps, assisted perhaps, but not applied." [4]

I tell Jack's story to teach, not to condemn. When the last blocks were in place and I had heard that impersonal and inevitable "Good boy, Jack!" I turned to the room, which was as neat and seemingly untouched by children's hands as a certain sort of teacher could desire. I thought of the untidy midmorning array of work-in-progress, which some colleagues and I had come to expect and cherish and to interpret when snack time came to punctuate the day, giving us a fresh moment for overall evaluation. I wondered if other children's buds had been nipped on this morning. There were no signs reading: CHILDREN AT WORK—BE BACK SOON. A teacher or therapist or observer misses many clues, but here and in similar classrooms I feel the ground rules intentionally or unwittingly hinder any deep involvement. In numbers, this staff was luxurious, to the point of overstaffing. Laissez-faire policy could not be blamed, as it often can. The culprit seemed rather clear: no curious adults were in communication with curious children.

A teacher announced snack time in a loud voice, and the ten children walked sedately to the low tables. Jack, two other children, and Jack's TT sat directly under my one-way glass window, and I hoped to hear a bit of conversation among the four people in this intimate setting. At the table there seemed to be an easier atmosphere of selection and self-direction among the children, who were sitting on big pillows instead of in chairs. I relaxed. Children poured their own juice and took generous handfuls of an attractive nut-raisin mix. Jack was the last to take the juice pitcher and once more displayed his precocious concerns.

He stopped pouring juice just short of overflow, and I thought he had been careless for the first time in judging amounts or that he was preoccupied. I did not appreciate the purpose of the near overflow until I saw Jack lower his head to observe at eye level the lovely, convex curve of the liquid surface, the meniscus. After a brief confirmation of this phenomenon, he carefully added a few more drops—one, two, three—as one still can when overflow seems certain. Not breaking the delicate protective film of the liquid, he again lowered his head to check in silence and with satisfaction. From observing this brief but expert maneuver, I was certain that Jack had long since filed away the existence of this particular phenomenon and thus was able to retrieve it for enjoyment and curiosity. (It is a phenomenon many of us adults, being uninformed, have never really noticed. With luck, we may have been shown the phenomenon in a science class much later in life than kindergarten.) I cannot say if the TT saw or wondered at Jack's small demonstration.

As some children will, Jack approached his nut mix with care and selectivity. All raisins, one by one, were eaten, then the slivered almonds. The children ate and drank, silence reigned, and then Jack pulled his bright, comfortable pillow around himself and began to rock gently from side to side. The other two children picked up the rocking rhythm and smiled at each other in the first genuine communication I had seen: that of shared fun. I looked at the TT, still hopeful—optimist that I am—that he might smile or even accompany this new rhythm with a song, extending a beginning offered by the children, but the TT had been differently programmed. He stopped the entire endeavor by swiftly removing Jack's pillow and saying smugly, "You can sit more quietly without your pillow." Is this to be called "positive reinforcement"?

I have come to see the basic handicap that pervades our schools and clouds our understanding of child development as a poverty of intellectual curiosity. The *American Heritage Dictionary* lists the first meaning of *curiosity* as "a desire to know or learn, especially about something new or strange." *Webster's Third International Unabridged Dictionary* lists several archaic entries that have a negative connotation: "a blamable tendency to desire to inquire into or seek knowledge . . . or to inquire too minutely into any subject," "undue nicety, subtlety, or fastidiousness," and "nosiness."

Whether it is intended or not, one can read in this long definition a certain developmental view of the attribute *curiosity.* By the time of old age, curiosity may have been corrupted to be the equivalent of prying. For us to encourage children to give up life-enhancing curiosity too early is to interfere with one of the very means by which we all learn. I submit young Jack as a typical case of the positive definition given by dictionaries. He and many others—labeled hyperactive, learning disabled, or disruptive—bring to school their weak and their strong ways, their "odd" ways, of unpacking the world. These children are too often met by adults who, fatigued and poorly educated, cannot recognize this intact curiosity and build upon it because their own curiosity has been so severely damp-ened and damaged.

For key members of a society—the teachers of the young—to lack curiosity is a profound handicap. It is very rare for an infant to be born so damaged congenitally that he or she completely lacks that capacity. I select the word and concept *curiosity* because even with seriously retarded children—retarded genetically, congenitally, or functionally—enough of a spark of curiosity exists to ensure their humanity and to allow for some learning, if . . . It is the *ifs* that the state of the art should address. Thus far it has done so inadequately.

Commerce City, USA

Most of the teachers I came to know at the Mountain View Center I met through the courses, seminars, or workshops we gave weekly after school or in the evenings. I would be invited to work in classrooms, or groups of children would come with teachers for a half day at the center. Music, art, math, embryology (when Max Braverman was in residence), weaving, and such offbeat titles as "Don't Have Animals in the Class-room—Unless . . . " became favorites. But Sarah Padilla, as I shall call her, came to us by none of these routes.

She telephoned and made an appointment with me for the following week. She was in her first assignment as a second-grade teacher in a bilin-gual classroom and needed help, "especially with some of the children; boys who are truant too often and uncontrollable." Remembering my own first teaching position, I looked forward to helping Sarah.

Sarah volunteered information, but she did so in a curiously colorless manner. She had done her practice teaching at the University of Colorado with a fine teacher. I could appreciate her request for help with some of her children. I thought it indicated that other aspects of her teaching were on course, but I came to know that Sarah was asking for a more personal kind of help. I think in retrospect that had I realized this early on, I would not have agreed to go to Commerce City. I regret that my intuition did not alert me to another human being's personal need, but I have no regrets about getting to know and to work with the children in Sarah's second grade. I drove our van full of "junk" on the afternoon before I was due to spend the first morning in her class.

As I drove to Commerce City, I wondered where anyone lived among the smokestacks and trucks and sprawl that constituted this suburban area of Denver. I was never to know for certain, but I was told that "most of these children live in trailers."

I arrived at the school with the aid of a good map Sarah had kindly drawn for me. As I arrived she and most of her twenty children were just leaving. I asked for help from the two boys who were the causes of Sarah's concern. They joined me with eight-year-old pleasure, and a few trips sufficed to carry in branches, mountain driftwood, pinecones, a map globe of the earth, yarn, clay, and boxes to be opened. By the time the van was empty and well explored, we were friends: Pedro, the leader (the "constant truant"); Timmy, his cousin; and a couple of their buddies.

The classroom was so bare, neat, and untouched that I should have known at once that it was the young teacher who was in the most trouble, not the children. But for foul weather or fair, my course was set. I wanted to know these children and the scene where they lived. This was a new opportunity to be embraced. Sarah and I spent a pleasant hour together stowing the things I had brought and planning for the next morning, talking and becoming friends.

As I walked into the schoolroom the next morning, the door opposite me—from the playground—was opening and closing as the children came in. How I would have loved such a room—with outdoor access, a low sink and drain boards, low eastern windows, tables, low shelves, and *space*. I joined the group of children on the floor around Sarah and her guitar. It was a friendly way to start the day. But in spite of Sarah's expertise, there was no liveliness, no enthusiasm. I was mystified. Time would unpack some of the dynamics of these twenty children with one young adult.

After a couple of songs, with children still arriving, Sarah suddenly rose and stared at an entering group. I saw Pedro poised in the doorway with an entourage of several other children. He was standing there quietly, beaming.

Somehow Sarah signaled me that she felt faint. I rose and started toward Pedro. Suddenly I saw what Sarah had seen: around his neck, punched for stringing like mittens, were the two bloody ears of a deer. I had seconds to recover and speak. Grasping the psychiatrist's technique of reaching for the obvious, I asked, "Someone in your family, Pedro, has been deer hunting?"

"Yup," he said, "my dad."

Trying not to look too closely, I removed the strung ears, saying I would hang them where they would be safe, high above an out-of-the-way blackboard. With Sarah pale and off to the side and Pedro center stage, I sat on the floor with the children and invited Pedro to give us some details. With relish he did so, although briefly. The other children and I listened in rapt silence.

I had recently learned one small fact about Alaskan Indian caribou hunting, so I felt I could ask Pedro if his mother did the butchering, the cutting up for roasts and steaks. "Yup," he answered, and we were launched on a discussion of the meat and its distribution. It would go to friends and family, primarily to the latter. Cousin Timmy showed us with his hands how big a roast would come to his family. (This was in response to a mistake I had made in assuming cousin Timmy's family might get a half. "No," corrected Pedro, "only a roast.")

Timmy, who was pale and wary in contrast to his ebullient cousin Pedro, was so self-effacing that I was unprepared for his short but personal statement in recognition of me. It was the first and last such statement from any of the group. I was simply accepted. Looking directly at me Timmy said, "You look like a grandmother." I felt well introduced as many eyes focused on me, even Pedro's. "You are right, Timmy, I am a grandmother, and one of my grandsons is in second grade in another city." I stopped because I felt I was getting out of touch with what Timmy had intended to introduce with his statement. My instinct was right.

With attentive silence encouraging him, Timmy continued; "We lost *our* grandmother." Silence again held. With little confidence about what to say, I tried, "Grandmothers get old, and we miss them when they die." But once again, in the unexpected quiet of the room, Timmy kept to his course, still kneeling while we all attended. "No, my grandma didn't die, my mom said we couldn't keep her anymore because she was drunk all the time. She came back, but we couldn't keep her." Compassion erases the immediate sequence.

From this first visit I was understandably and continually stunned by further evidence of need, by the openness most of these children showed in signaling, in guiding me to supply something of what they lacked—those in trouble and those few already on their way. They informed me and themselves. We were on our way as a group.

At first I felt, although still without understanding, that this sad classroom, if not the lives of its children, could be altered. As it developed, these children filled a niche in the range of my experience that had been mostly empty. I had known the children of the middle class, children of migratory farmworkers, and those from the slums of cities large and small. Now I was with another overlooked pocket of children—those of underpaid blue-collar workers, coming to school from the trailer houses of a new, sprawling, unkempt suburb. Some were Spanish speaking, perhaps still in touch with a countryside that several generations ago had been taken as part of the Spanish Empire, overrun in turn by my own ancestors.

They were ready to learn, these children, but in a sterile curriculum how long would that be the case? Perhaps by picking out some of their actions, voices, and visions—as I have done throughout—I can communicate something of Commerce City's uniqueness, of my brief role, of the still trusting behavior and talents of these children. I cannot identify what had gone well for some children, but I was certain something had.

I had brought enough stuff to keep everyone wondering and exploring. With hand lenses they were taking a first or a fresh look at seed pods, branches, rocks, and mountain driftwood. Some used paper and pencil and drew, with only a suggestion. Joshua soon showed me seeds, closely observed and carefully drawn—winged ones, smooth ones, and furry ones. I was impressed with his skills of observation and drawing. Later Joshua brought another drawing of something I could not recognize. He pointed to the large, elegantly forked bare branch. Because I recognized his obvious skill and pleasure and judged that he had hurried this one, I felt justified in urging him to look more carefully and try again. After awhile he returned, beaming, with a stunning drawing that reflected his close observation of branching and the swelling of the wood at branch points.

A few children tried the fresh clay I had watered and allowed to get to the proper consistency. That was to be expected. But what I found unusual, what was to become a passionate preoccupation—also begun that morning—was weaving. I had made small cardboard looms, warped ahead of time, with much brilliant yarn provided for weft. I had warped a variety of shapes, some radially—circles—so the weaving would spiral around. Squares and rectangles were also included. José and his brother, David, began to weave at once (José was nine years old, David seven). From the wide array of colors they both chose black. David's was on a round loom and progressed with an occasional copper-colored strand. José's become a banner—red and black for *La Huelga* of the lettuce-picker's strike that had been going on for so long at that time. I felt we were touching reality and were in communication on a widening front.

On the next visit the weaving had taken over so engrossingly that I, as a teacher, needed to understand why. There is beautiful weaving in our Southwestern traditions, both Indian and Spanish, and this I had anticipated. But not all the children in this class were bilingual, and the Anglo children were equally involved.

I kept alert for clues and was given an important one by seven-year-old Dorothy. She came to me for help, as she had before, but this time she was in tears, holding her now-finished small round weaving. Sorrow poured out: "Look," she said, tears falling, pointing to the pink and blue and yellow weaving, "it's so bad where I began. I didn't know how. Can I take it out and do it right like the last part?"

In spite of early mistakes, the weaving was quite lovely. These circular looms absorb mistakes. I put my arm around Dorothy, and we looked together at the circles of color. What raced through my mind was Dorothy's constant and sometimes annoying need for reassurance. She had asked for much help and especially for much praise in the beginning. I had an idea: "Look, Dorothy, this is the history, your own history, of learning to weave. You can look at this and say, 'Why, I can see how I began, here I didn't know how very well, I went over two instead of one; but I learned, and then—it is perfect all the way to the end!' Now turn it over and do another." Dorothy thought about this. The tears stopped, and slowly she walked back to her group of weavers, still properly intent on her first weaving. The next visit she brought me an elegant and flawless circle in different shades of pink, with novelty yarns—some nubby, some plain—all done without consulting me!

I valued the returning independence of this child. She had seemed so hesitant and untrusting of her own abilities, so dependent on adults. I would like to believe she felt new power from learning a desired skill and reflecting on the history of that learning; that it freed this unsure child to call on her earlier abilities once again. I say "again" because, with rare exceptions, young children's abilities as infants and toddlers *are* alive, to be quenched or rekindled with our help. In the beginning it may have to be a joint enterprise—ours to supply an atmosphere, a bit of honest know-how; theirs to want to persevere until the sweet taste of success itself lures them on. So it seemed that Dorothy's thoughtful persistence, with some confidence in her on my part, kept her on course.

With this vignette I became aware that I was hatching a theory about the obsession to weave.[5] But let me return to José and David, whose different but deep involvement adds to our understanding.

When José's small rectangular banner for *La Huelga* was almost finished, I joined him where he worked alone on the edge of things. He had come to me for no help, and yet there, almost finished, was an elegantly striped red-and-black banner on a rectangular cardboard loom. "José," I began, "you already know how to weave! Someone in your family must be a weaver." We looked at the straight selvage, and I commented that he already knew how to keep the edges straight, not curving them in like an hourglass. In his shy way he traced and appreciated those straight edges, and I feared he had no intention of speaking. I tried in Spanish. I waited. "My grandma weaves," he began, and I could respond appropriately. He seemed pleased to have me near, so I stayed, "Does your grandma live with you and your family?" "No," he answered, "she lives in Raton."

We were in familiar territory for me, and I invited José to go with me so we could find Raton, New Mexico, in the map book I had brought with the globe. There it was! And I was sure José could read it (I had been told he had been held back because he could not read), although I did not test him. I was to find that indeed he could read. We returned to his weaving, and although José was silent I judged he was reminiscing about his grandma, about Raton. I sat with him a moment longer, wishing, as I recall, to prolong our communication. I asked him where he was born. Still smiling and musing, he answered, "In Pueblo." Back we went to the atlas, this time to Colorado, and he found Pueblo with only slight help from me. José looked up at me, saying, "You mean the place where I was born is in that book?" Such delight, shared, is more than doubled. I left José to finish his flag, thinking, I imagined, of being in a book, perhaps of being a weaver.

How different he was from his brother, David, who seemed to have no shy or cautious moments. The brothers were friendly to each other, but then David was a friend to all. "Hyperactive" was the fashionable, unprofessional label. No one seemed to know José's history, beyond that he had been held back. Certainly he kept his own counsel, and David was too busy trying and experimenting with everything and everyone to provide me with a clue. As for many of the boys, wild Pedro was David's favorite *compañero*.

Because of his many loyal attendants, I was delighted when Pedro decided to "make" a weaving. Only one of his band, David, had tried to do so. Pedro's circular weaving was done with abandon and amazed me by staying together, because it quickly became a frisbee. It was hardly a weaving, but at least he had made one!

With so many small weavings we wanted to show them off. Could we make a mobile? A driftwood branch that had stood stark and beautiful since our first day together might do. To balance the mobile from the ceiling by a single strand of heavy yarn required a sense for balance, and no one was bored with the care and advice necessary to solve such inherent and self-selected problems. The place for each weaving to hang with its own bit of yarn (through a punched hole) required further testing, but finally all of the weavings were hung above our heads on the suspended branch, now transformed into an elegant mobile. Many children had woven on each face of their cardboard looms, and the changing colors as they slowly turned were enchanting.

To keep the mobile balanced through new additions had required continuing trial and error, with much laughter. It was a nice introduction to unequal and many-armed balancing, a topic we could easily have moved on to. But here among these weavers I felt a need to prolong this escapade, not to move on; so I carried spurs to my thinking home with me. What next? How further to enrich?

I knew little about the reading or writing abilities of most of these second graders. I decided to try a cooperative story with them: "How to Weave." The suggestion appealed to them, so we began. It went something like this:

HOW TO WEAVE

First you put the warp on.
Then you thread a big needle with yarn.
Then you go over and under and over and under.

I added a blue line going over and under, and the children cheered.

I asked myself, "What next?" No one wanted to remove a mobile to take it home, and so I asked the group if I could borrow all of the weavings to show to the Mountain View Center, which had contributed the materials. The children were pleased, and, with their help, I dismantled the mobile and carefully packed each loom for transporting.

I sent a letter from the center signed by each staff member. I made twenty-five copies, and their teacher, Sarah, gave a copy to each child. The letter was rather formal, expressing appreciation for the work and the colors and patterns. After two or three weeks that letter—from which I had received no feedback—popped up in the following way.

Quiet José stopped me with one of his always significant statements: "I'm glad I won first with my weaving." I was mystified. Was he imagining some event? I asked him to tell me more about being first. He called his brother David from across the room and told him to go and get THE letter from his jacket. This was done as if José was accustomed to being in some sort of command, a facet of both boys that was new to me. David went to the hall and returned with a grubby, folded piece of paper. José opened the letter from the Mountain View Center and read silently to the place he wished to show me: "You see," he announced, "here it says: 'We especially like the colors you used: black and red, black, rainbow colors, pink, etc.'" With satisfaction he looked at me, saying, "You see, mine comes first!" And so it did.

I tried to sort out what these two had made of the written word and then took a chance with David, who, although so ubiquitous, was with us for the moment. "David," I questioned, "would you like to read the whole letter to me?" A pause, and then José explained, "He can't read without his glasses." "Where are they?" I pursued. "They are in his jacket pocket," José responded before David could answer. At my request, David ran to get his glasses, came back, and read the entire letter—with a bit of help from his big brother. Bravo! my heart sang. These slow ones, these children who so lovingly reflected their homes, gave me parts of themselves I might never have seen: competence hidden away, for safety, in coat pockets. That need for safety reflects on us all and, until we appreciate it, is to our shame.

Alfredo did not come until the second week, but I had been visited at the end of my first day by a pleasant young therapist who had been testing Alfredo and trying to understand him. Sarah had reported that Alfredo was constantly truant and was unable to read. He was abused, she thought, neglected by his "prostitute" mother. The young therapist added that this child "didn't talk." He understood that since Alfredo was not doing well in school he would not like to talk about it, but "he doesn't even want to talk about after school or what he does at home." I was not impressed with this insight since the therapist spoke no Spanish, but I became interested in Alfredo. I decided he must be a sturdy character to have confused so many people.

The following week Alfredo was in class, but only briefly. He spent most of his day in a special class for "learning disabled children" down the hall. I had spoken briefly with their young teacher, Mrs. Martinez, and, wondering what sorts of things she did with the children, had invited myself into her room. She seemed pleased, and I was reassured to see that the room was not uncared for. There were few interesting materials, but few children and an obviously caring teacher drew Alfredo there. She and I spoke in Spanish—mine rusty, hers perfect; the Spanish-speaking world is tolerant of our attempts.

On my third visit Alfredo stayed in class with us. I had brought colored paper, scissors, and staplers, which attracted him. I joined him, and we talked as we worked. Alfredo was completely bilingual, and I asked him if he would help me with my Spanish. "Sure, Franny"—from the first moment there was no embarrassment or refusal to talk. Indeed, he didn't stop talking in either English or Spanish. Suddenly he was telling me about his grandfather in the San Luis Valley. "He goes hunting up in the mountains, and he gets a deer, and he skins it, and the skin looks like this." On a piece of paper, Alfredo drew a rough outline of a flattened (drying) deerskin. What did I know about skins? A picture from my recent edition of *Ishi* came to my mind, and I asked Alfredo to cut out his paper "deerskin" so I could show him something. [6] As I told him of Ishi and his deer and rabbit hunting long ago, I started to cut the drawing of Alfredo's deerskin in the Indian manner: into one long, thin, continuous strip. Alfredo was so intent that he asked if he could finish it. He had understood my cutting and went on, and finally we had a very long, thin strip of "rawhide" made from one small, chunky "deerskin."

I promised to bring the Ishi book the next week so everyone could see the pictures of Ishi, who had lived at the foot of Mount Lassen in California. Alfredo and I went on talking, and I asked him, "Alfredo, does your grandfather speak Spanish?" He chuckled and answered in Spanish, "Oh Franny, you know ALL grandfathers speak Spanish." This was a silent boy?

The next week I brought the book, and I brought my husband, David, too. Both were appreciated. Alfredo and Big David—as the children immediately named him—got a large sheet of paper, cut it in a thin rectangular spiral—round and round and round—and disappeared outside to measure how far that one piece of paper would go along the side of the long building. A small band followed. It became an exploring mathematical morning that was much fun, with Alfredo and Big David especially in the know.

There was an always-empty "science room" across the corridor from Alfredo's special-help teacher. It had been properly designated the "Science Room." Within it were shelves lined with *untouched kits of good science equipment,* unused kits of Elementary Science Study units (David had been involved in their development about fifteen years before). During my last weeks at Commerce City, half the class and I would go to the science room. Balancing was by far the top choice of the group. Pedro was in his element. He understood some fundamental principles, such as whether to use an equal or an unequal arm balance. He observed the phenomenon instead of trying to guess what to add or subtract to achieve balance. He was excited, as were his cronies, to find such apparatus at the school. The children were pleased to use it and to invent other forms, such as balance boards with blocks for weights.

Had no one else ever found this room? Who had ordered all of these good kits? Someone from "middle management" who was tied to an office chair, remote from the school, responding to some call from above? I never found out because no one I talked to had any knowledge of or interest in the room. It was a mystifying phenomenon but one that is common in our schools and critically symptomatic, I suspect, of their ills—for science teaching, surely, but for much else besides. All the teachers I met invited me to come work in their classrooms. Like their children, they were bored.

Before my last day at Commerce City, I received a letter from the class. It had been written in very readable wobbly print by Wesley, one of the seven-year-olds who had no obvious troubles. The letter was signed with four names. I have paraphrased it here for continuity: "Dear Franny, How are you? We are fine. We want to tell you about where the water goes. We put a cover on one of the jars, put it on the radiator, and no cover on another. The covered jar didn't lose its water. The open one evaporated. Water doesn't go into the rocks. We didn't put in any rocks."

Wesley and I had become friends over a forlorn empty fish tank. It *did* contain big rocks and enough water to cover them. He had recounted to me that they had to put water in the tank almost every week, and I had asked him where he thought that water went. Wesley had answered, "Into the rocks."

I tried to keep the question open in the following weeks by bringing in containers and covers. But long before that letter arrived, I had moved away from the topic; it had seemed to me, wrongly, to be a dead end with these children. Wesley's concerns, as exemplified in his cogent letter, remind me of another facet of learning: the passage of time. When a child has learned to file information that matters and can then retrieve it, even much later, that child is on the way. I hoped the information Wesley sent to me reflected his teacher, Sarah's, similar growing abilities to file and retrieve. I keep alive the same hope for myself. It is a life-enhancing talisman.

With regret, one leaves a band of children or a teacher such as Mrs. Martinez. I am often asked whether I know what happened to a particular group or a certain child. No, with exceptions I do not know, in the sense that is meant. What I *do* know is that the children often changed themselves and developed well in the altered atmosphere we achieved together. As we know when we take time to assess, strengths are increased when they are sought and challenged. Mrs. Martinez knew this too. We talked about Alfredo before I left. She wanted me to know that he was doing much better, and she gave me credit for it. I was not surprised, but I was delighted to hear it and to have her warm to the subject of what children need to let them expand and use their own resources.

Before we parted, Mrs. Martinez asked me a question: "Where do you come from, Mrs. Hawkins?" In our few remaining minutes I gave her a sketch of my teaching and learning. I encouraged her to continue to trust herself and her children and not those "experts" who had coached her unless their advice was to help her to seek and learn, to believe that helping a child find her or his strengths was the magic key. Together we laughed that I didn't really come *from* there—because I was still there, trying.

Notes

[1]Anna Freud and Sophie Dann, "An Experiment in Group Upbringing," *Psychoanalytic Study of the Child* 6 (1951).

[2]Storm, "Eolithism and Design." Storm used *eolithism* to mean the kind of human behavior in which "ends" are suggested and, even for the first time, invented only when interesting new materials have come to one's attention.

[3]See Jessie Taft, *Dynamics of Therapy* (New York: Macmillan, 1933), on the nature of this communication.

[4]See Allen, *Psychotherapy With Children,* p. 46.

[5]For many in this group, school was not a challenge. It was not cruel, as some are, but it failed to use their strengths or to invite the confidence that comes with those strengths, with their ability to learn. There were no anticipations of their talents, and no good materials were provided to invite those abilities.

[6]Theodora Kroeber, *Ishi In Two Worlds: A Biography of the Last Wild Indian in North America.* Deluxe illustrated edition (Berkeley: University of California Press, 1976 [1961]). Earlier editions lack many of the splendid illustrations included in this deluxe version.

Bibliography of Sources and Resources

The field of early childhood development and education has been, for the most part, narrowly conceived, meagerly addressed, and widely denigrated, but not by all. There is a good body of literature written by a few pediatricians, therapists, and developmental psychologists that can help define important generalities of childhood character and growth. But in teaching, unique encounters occur with individual children and groups that give even the best theory a depth and sparkle it cannot by itself provide. Great writers—of novels, autobiographies, and biographies—can add to this shining array, as can stories told by informed and enlightened teachers.

Here are writings I especially value, with comments on a few. Favorite lists will vary from teacher to teacher, but they will all cluster around the universals of childhood.

Teachers' Art

Armstrong, Michael. *Closely Observed Children: The Diary of a Primary Classroom, Writers and Readers.* London: Chameleon, 9-19 Ruper Street, 1980.

Biggs, Edith R., and James R. Mclean. *Freedom to Learn: An Active Learning Approach to Mathematics.* Ontario: Addison-Wesley Ltd., 1968.

Featherstone, Joseph. *What Schools Can Do.* New York: Liveright, 1976.

Kohl, Herbert. *Thirty-Six Children.*
A story by a young teacher who discovers one of the great secrets of the art.

Paull, John, and Dorothy Paull. *Yesterday I Found.* Boulder, Colo.: Mountain View Center of Environmental Education, University of Colorado, 1972.

Richardson, Elwyn S. *In the Early World.* Willington: New Zealand Council for Educational Research, 1964.
If I had to choose just one book by a teacher about the children who are taught, it would be this treasure by Elwyn Richardson. He chose the title from Irene's poem, a thirteen-year-old who was one of the older children in Richardson's New Zealand class.

The blue heron stands in the early world
Looking like a freezing cloud in the morning.

Throughout the book Richardson includes his developing insight as a new young teacher, along with that of the children. "Since some children could absorb information well, I thought it reasonable to value this the most. It was easy [at first] to place more importance on rote learning than on conscious understanding by the child."

The classroom included both Maori children and those of English ancestry—the first from New Zealand's involuntary minority population, the second the children of English farmers. One can detect these background differences primarily through the wonderful photographs throughout the book. The differences in background recede when individual differences thrive, as they do here in the community of such a school, in this atmosphere of cooperation, invention, and learning.

Tolstoy, Leo. *Tolstoy on Education: Tolstoy's Educational Writings, 1861–1862.* Selected and edited by Alan Pinch and Michael Armstrong; translated by Alan Pinch. London: Athlone Press, 1982.

Deep truths he saw over a hundred years ago in teaching his peasant children.

Child Development

Erikson, Joan M., with David and Joan Loveless. *Activity, Recovery, Growth: The Communal Role of Planned Activities.* Postscript by Erik Erikson. New York: W. W. Norton, 1976.

Escalona, Sibylle K. *The Roots of Individuality: Normal Patterns of Development in Infancy.* Chicago: Aldine Publishing Company, 1968.

This is an overlooked classic, a twenty-year study of early roots. I quote Escalona:

We have known for a long time that children born to poverty, neglect, and family disintegration tend to be less able intellectually and to run greater risk of psychological impairment than children from stable and nurturing backgrounds. For many years this discrepancy was ascribed to genetic inferiority on the part of some ethnic and socioeconomic groups, as well as poor nutrition, harassing life conditions, and poor medical care.

Infants respond differentially to external stimuli of identical physical nature, receiving greater or lesser doses of stimulation as a function of a biologically rooted characteristic of the perceiving organism.

We are of the opinion that much of the research in child development has suffered from the fact that psychologists strove to adopt strategies and concepts analogous to physics rather than to biology. In point of fact, we consider that the psychological and behavioral study of human development falls within the scope of general biology.

Lewin, Kurt. *A Dynamic Theory of Personality.* Translated by Donald K. Adams and Karl E. Zener. New York: McGraw-Hill, 1935.

It was fortunate in summer 1939 that my practical experience could become tuned by seeking good theory. I had three and a half years of teaching experience. That summer, at the University of California at Berkeley, I studied briefly under Kurt Lewin and George Stoddard. There I found good theory.

Shinn, Milicent Washburn. *The Biography of a Baby.* New York: Addison Wesley, 1985.

Skeels, Harold M. *Adult Status of Children With Contrasting Early Life Experience: A Follow-Up Study.* Monographs of the Society for Research in Child Development, vol. 31, no. 3, 1966. See also *Outlook,* no. 5 (Spring 1972), 26–38. The Mountain View Center for Environmental Education, University of Colorado, Boulder, Colorado.

This is a report of a little-known and all-too-rare longitudinal follow-up study of intervention research on childhood development. A group of very young orphans were removed from an Ohio State orphanage. Traditionally, they would have been doomed to the "low-IQ status" that would lead to continued institutional care. They had been placed for temporary adoption in a highly unusual but stimulating environment: a home for "feeble-minded" young women. Each child had an adoptive "mother" and more than one doting "aunt." They had then been returned to the orphanage. A two-year follow-up study had shown impressive gains in health and well-being.

The longitudinal study that is the substance of Skeels's report, which was done about twenty years later, showed that the group had maintained those gains, markedly different from the "contrast" group that had been left in the orphanage and been doomed to "feeble-minded" status.

Wagoner, Lovisa. *The Development of Learning in Young Children.* New York: McGraw Hill, 1933.

Therapy

Allen, Frederick H. *Psychotherapy With Children.* New York: W. W. Norton, 1942. Republished in *Bison Books in Clinical Psychology* . Lincoln: University of Nebraska Press, 1979.
Since I first became aware of *Psychotherapy With Children,* I have never been alone in my teaching. Allen never tells me what to do but, rather, describes how to assess a situation through more observation so that fresh ideas are uncovered, new paths cleared.

A parent [or teacher or therapist]can guide and define the conditions in which a child can become responsible, but he can never MAKE a child feel responsible. . . . Adolph Meyer had this in mind when he said: "By the person's spontaneity I mean that which the person may be expected to rise and to rise with on his own, su sponte, with his sponse and response, and finally responsibility." . . . Children with personality and behavior difficulties can be helped to help themselves. (Foreword, p. 7; quoting from Adolf Meyer, "Spontaneity," Proceedings, Illinois Conference on Public Welfare, Mental Hygiene Division, 1933, p. 25.)

In his last chapter, "Implications of a Therapeutic Philosophy," Allen speaks of the creativeness of human differences and turns to the fiction of Thomas Mann (*Joseph in Egypt* [New York: Alfred A. Knopf, 1938], v. 1, p. 4):

But lo, the world hath many centres, one for each created being, and about each one lieth its own circle. Thou standeth but half an ell from me, yet about thee lieth a universe whose centre I am not but thou art. . . . For our universes are not so far from each other that they do not touch; rather hath God pushed them and interwoven them deep into each other, so that you Ishmaelites do indeed journey quite independently and according to your own ends, whither you will, but beside that you are the means and tool in our interwovenness, that I arrive at my goal!

Meers, Dale R. "Psychoanalytic Research and Intellectual Functioniong of Ghetto-Reared, Black Children." *The Psychoanlytic Study of the Child,* vol. 28. New Haven: Yale University Press, 1973.
My own experience—as a teacher of just such children as Dr. Meers refers to here—surely confirms his view of the effects of ghetto life. Their below-average distribution of I.Q. scores is usually attributed to some otherwise unidentified "racial factor." Meers has shown that this ghetto culture is not only one of deprivation, but that it can quite positively shape a whole system of attitudes inimical to school life and learning, especially—I may add—to schools quite unprepared to deviate from their standard-

ized "tracks" unprepared to help children find their special talents and strengths. Meers's patients typically have consolidated views of themselves as less than beautiful, less than adequate, as marginal children of marginal families in an ambivalent "racial" community. To these quite correct generalizations, an imaginative teacher, standing in a quite different and far more participative relation to these children of the ghetto, can add that they also can have learned much we value, and acquired hidden strengths for learning. Along the standardized tracks our schools mostly lead them on, these strengths go unrecognized.

Meers's survey provides an excellent brief discussion of the investigations of Skeels and others that I refer to next. His bibliography refers also to his own fine work, well worth studying by teachers of the young, and a review and critique of the international day care as it existed in that time (1970), and mostly still does.

Skeels, Harold M., Ruth Updegraff, Ruth Williams, and Harold Williams. *Study of Environment Stimulation: An Orphanage Preschool Project.* University of Iowa Studies: Studies in Child Welfare, New Series no. 363, December 1, 1838.

Skeels, Harold M. *Adult Status of Children With Contrasting Early Life Experience: A Follow-Up Study.* Mongographs of The Society for Research in Child Development. Serial Number 105, 1966, vol. 31, no. 3. Reprinted by the Univiersity of Chicago Press, 1966. See also *Outlook,*' no. 5, (Spring 1972), pp. 26–38. Boulder, Colo.: The Mountain View Center, University of Colorado.

The two Skeels citations listed here report a little-known study and an all-too-rare longitudinal follow-up of intervention research on childhood development. A group of very young orphans had been removed from an Ohio State orphanage, a life that traditionally would doom them to the "low I.Q. status" of continued institutional care. They had been placed, as a practical matter, for temporary adoption in a highly unusual but stimulating environment: that of a home for "feeble-minded" young women, each child with an adoptive "mother" and more than one doting "aunt." After that they had been returned for adoption to the orphanage. A two-year follow-up had shown impressive gains in health and well-being, including the customary tests of I.Q. and the like. The longitudinal study that is the substance of Skeels's repport, some twenty years later, shows that the group has indeed maintained those gains, in sharp contrast with the fate of a "contrast" group that had unavoidably been left in the orphanage and doomed to "feeble-minded" status. It was that two-year study, reported by Stoddard and Lewin, that had so outraged Professor Terman: that adults of low I.Q. could help, dramatically, to raise the I.Q. of young children otherwise doomed, like themselves, to institutional life. See Lewin.

Literature

Darwin, Charles. *Life and Letters of Charles Darwin, Including an Autobiographical Chapter.* In two volumes. Edited by his son, Francis Darwin. New York: D. Appleton, 1887.

Dickinson, Emily. *The Complete Poems of Emily Dickinson.* Edited by Thomas H. Johnson. Boston: Little, Brown, 1960.

Edel, Leon. *The Life of Henry James.* In four volumes. Philadelphia: J. B. Lippincott, 1953 et seq.

Forster, E. M. *A Passage to India.* New York: Harcourt Brace, 1950.

Gorky, Maxim. *My Childhood.* Translated from Russian by Margaret Wittlin. Moscow: Foreign Languages Printing House.

James, Henry. *What Mazie Knew.* New York: Scribner, 1897. Reprinted by Penguin Classics, 1985.

James, Henry. *The Art of Fiction and Other Essays.* New York: Oxford University Press, 1948.

Murasaki, Lady Shikibu. *The Tale of Genji: A Novel in Six Parts.* 2 vols. Translated from Japanese by Arthur Waley. Boston: Houghton-Mifflin, 1935.

> In his introduction Arthur Waley tells us that Shikibu Murasaki was born about A.D. 928. The observations such young ladies were so adept at making are no less profound because the success of their lives at court depended on the development of just such awareness and understanding.
>
> Lady Murasaki consistently displays her insights about life as she lived and saw it. In speaking of the young Empress Akiko, whose service she had just entered, Murasaki comments: "Thus she had gathered round her a number of very worthy young ladies. They have the merit of sharing all her opinions, but seem in some curious way like children who have never grown up."

Nijo, Lady. *The Confessions of Lady Nijo.* Translated from the Japanese by Karen Brazell. Stanford, Calif.: Stanford University Press, 1973, p. 156.

> Among the upper classes, babies were not reared by their mothers. The baby Lady Nijo speaks of in this quotation is the first of the many she has borne that she keeps by her side for several weeks.

> It was a safe delivery, and the child was a boy; but curiously enough I had no feeling for him. . . .
> I was told there was not even a wet nurse available. While one was being sought in vain, my poor baby fell asleep at my side. It was not long before he was soaking wet; underneath. That would never do, I thought, and I quickly changed him. As he lay again sleeping beside me, I began, for the first time, to understand the depths of a mother's love. For more than forty days I took care of him myself, begrudging every moment he was out of my hands.

> We have new names for and long discussions of "bonding," of what happens to a baby and its mother when life is rather normal. But it is reassuring to learn that Lady Nijo, whose court life had precluded any such normal engagement, nevertheless discovered and tells us about this phenomenon across six centuries.

O'Casey, Sean. *I Knock at the Door: Swift Glances Back at the Things That Made Me.* New York: Macmillan, 1960.

Tolstoy, L. N. *Childhood, Boyhood, Youth.* New York: Penguin Books, 1964.

Woolf, Virginia, *A Room of One's Own.* New York: Harcourt Brace Jovanovich, 1989.

Anthropology-Phenomenology

Geertz, Clifford. *Works and Lives: The Anthropologist as Author.* Stanford, Calif.: Stanford University Press, 1988.

> I first heard the name Clifford Geertz when David and I were teaching at the University of Michigan in 1980. We were invited to join a weekly lunch club of people who taught there, and one of the authors who was discussed was Clifford Geertz.
>
> Once again another discipline spoke to this teacher of the young. With this author I returned full circle back to my senior year at Stanford, when I had found Malinowski making sense to my ways of working and thinking about children. In a flash of remembrance I returned to my first contact with Malinowski.
>
> Chapter 4 of *Works and Lives* is titled "I-Witnessing: Malinowski's Children." Since I count myself as one of Malinowski's children, this chapter stirred my memory and imagination—I was immersed once again in working with children; seeing what is child initiated, teacher-observer initiated, child-with-child originated, child-with-

teacher hatched, child-with-child audience invented. Or, finally, just don't know! To be such an "I-Witness," to report and make it possible, as Malinowski hoped, is to escape from the dilemma of diary-versus-monograph.

Malinowski, Brontislav. *The Sexual Life of Savages in Northeastern Melanesia: An Ethnographic Account of Courtship, Marriage and Family Life Among the Natives of the Trobriand Islands, British New Guinea.* New York and London: Halcyon House, 1929.

Malinowski, Brontislav. "Kinship." *Encyclopedia Britannica,* 14th edition, vol. 13, p. 403.

Philosophy

Hawkins, David. "Nature Closely Observed." *Daedalus: Proceedings of the American Academy of Arts and Sciences,* vol. 12, no. 2 (Spring 1983), pp. 65–89.

When I read David the short passage Frederick Allen quotes from Adolph Meyer on the subject of human spontaneity (see Allen, *Psychotherapy With Children*), he brought me this essay, published forty-one years after Allen's book. With David's permission I quote:

> There is a marvelous continuity between the worlds of children's experience and the adult worlds. . . . The continuity is one of cumulative learning. Learning, in this educationally important sense of the word, is always in principle spontaneous. Man, said old Korzybski, is a time-binding animal. We store experience, well or badly, as the squirrel stores nuts. Not for a coming winter, though in a winter time the store may save us. But learning is always also, in some degree, induced. When it goes well there are teachers around, good teachers whose work is induction. In this essay I wish to use both these words, in a sense as technical terms. For spontaneous, I go back to the Latin *sponte,* of one's own accord, and still earlier to an Indoeuropean root *spon,* which is one of that vast collection of words derived from the weavers' art, to spin. In the hand of the spinner, the spindle is given an initial twist but continues for a time spontaneously, of its own accord or, as we may prefer to say, its own angular momentum. Children only learn well of their own accord. In this case, we need not wind them up to start the process. Nature does that. But in another sense, the learning they engage in can be induced; they can be led into association with matter that matches their readiness to assimilate and to make much of that which counts and that they might otherwise never gain access to. Induced learning is still, for children, spontaneous, if they are led, not dragged.

Hawkins, David. *The Science and Ethics of Equality.* New York: Basic Books, 1977.

"As is true of other deep issues, that of human equality waxes and wanes, appears and disappears like a comet, to return again in some later epoch. Like a comet it is altered, or should be, by every perihelion passage. . . . Marcus Aurelius the emperor and Epictetus the slave saw themselves, saw all human beings, as equally sparks of the divine Zeus, and as equally condemned to the inequality of their stations and duties."

Living with a philosopher of science whose Ph.D. dissertation was on statistical theory has given me license to ignore, in the literature of my profession, much statistical irrelevancy, much averaging out of human diversity, and much occlusion of that vital diversity among children the teaching art must constantly attend to and can delight in. This association, above all, has supported me in trusting my own intellectual curiosity, my persistence in seeking right environments for the diversity of young children.

In Chapter 4, "Abilities and Talents," David includes the sketch he calls "An Imaginary Profile of Concrete Abilities," a profile in polar coordinates. It suggests the differing strengths and weaknesses of any of us, adult or child, and the kinds of individuality that, it may be argued, are presupposed by the very idea and ideal of human equality—as by the teaching art.

Jones, Donald, and Stewart Mason. *The Art of Education.* London: Lawrence and Wishart, 1975.

Matthews, Gareth B. *Philosophy and the Young Child.* Cambridge: Harvard University Press, 1980.

It is reassuring to have a philosopher I do not know personally join the company of my Happy Few: novelists, physicists, and philosopher-in-residence. Gareth Matthews appreciates and elicits the early flashes of insight and reason in the minds of young wonderers that some of us learn to encourage, to trust, and be guided by. His text is woven around his careful observations and reports of child-level reflection and analysis. In this rich context, Matthews gives a telling critique of two important men in the field: Jean Piaget and Bruno Bettelheim.

There is a side to children's intellect, Matthews understands, an honest naïveté that adult life too typically discounts or suppresses but that philosophers especially have always struggled to protect and carry farther. It is a bond to which this insightful book elegantly testifies. It opens a new door on the subject of children's thinking.

History and Biography

Addams, Jane. *Twenty Years at Hull House, With Autobiographical Notes.* Urbana: University of Illinois Press, 1990.

Anther, Joyce. *Lucy Sprague Mitchell: The Making of a Modern Woman.* New Haven: Yale University Press, 1987.

The 1930s were the time of John Dewey's greatest influence. Lucy Sprague Mitchell knew him well, and the influence was mutual. She had studied with William James, Josiah Royce, and George Santayana. But her permanent direction and devotion were to the art of educating the young and that of their teachers.

Throughout my own life as a teacher I have known that time and place gave me great advantages. To speak of Lucy Sprague Mitchell's influence underlines a debt I acknowledge with pleasure. And to have the life of such a pioneer studied and illuminated by a fine new biographer, Joyce Anther, is an unexpected addition to my pleasure.

Bell, Quentin. *Virginia Woolf: A Biography.* New York: Harcourt Brace Jovanovich, 1972.

Bingham, Milicent Todd. *Emily Dickinson's Home: Letters of Edward Dickinson and His Family With Documentation and Comment.* New York: Harper Brothers, 1955.

Brooks, Van Wyck. *Helen Keller: Sketch for a Portrait.* New York: E. P. Dutton, 1956.

Fediaevsky, Vera, and Patty Smith Hill. *Nursery School and Parent Education in Soviet Russia.* New York: E. P. Dutton, 1936.
     Groce's book is a report of an unplanned spontaneous experiment on the human condition and clearly describes its outcomes. The book is a historical study of congenital deafness within a small inbred island community and of the evolution of a shared language.

Honan, Park. *Jane Austen: Her Life.* New York: Fawcett Columbine, 1988.

Kingston, Maxine Hong. *The Woman Warrior: Memoirs of a Girlhood Among Ghosts.* New York: Vintage Books, Random House, 1977.

Lane, Harlan. *What the Mind Hears: A History of the Deaf.* Edited and with an introduction by Harlan Lane. New York: Random House, 1984, Chapter 12.

Lash, Joseph P. *Helen and Teacher: The Story of Helen Keller and Anne Sullivan Macy.* New York: Delacorte Press/Seymour Lawrence, 1974.

Mandela, Nelson. *Long Walk to Freedom: The Autobiography of Nelson Mandela.* New York: Little, Brown, 1994.

Additional Research

Glass, Gene V., Leonard S. Cahan, Mary Lee Smith, and Nikola N. Filby. *School Class Size: Research and Policy.* Beverly Hills, Calif: Sage Publications, 1982.

Groce, Nora Ellen. *Everyone Here Spoke Sign Language: Hereditary Deafness in Martha's Vineyard.* Cambridge: Harvard University Press, 1985.

Critics of Our Schools

Coles, Gerald. *The Learning Mystique: A Critical Look at "Learning Disabilities."* New York: Pantheon Books, 1987.

Coles, Robert. *Children of Crisis: A Study of Courage and Fear.* Boston: Little, Brown, 1964.

Kozol, Jonathan. *Death at an Early Age: The Destruction of the Hearts and Minds of Negro Children in the Boston Public Schools.* New York: Houghton-Mifflin, 1967.
     Robert Coles's preface to this book begins: "I hope some of those congressmen who are now looking into the causes of riots will find time to read this honest and terrifying book by Jonathan Kozol, a young teacher fired from his job by the Boston school system for using a poem by Langston Hughes that was not on the prescribed list of 'reading materials.' He may even be called to Washington, and asked to tell our congressmen what he experienced in an awful, hellish struggle waged—of all places—in a city that fancies itself 'the cradle of liberty' and dotes on its illustrious past."

Macleod, Jay. *Ain't No Makin' It.* Boulder, Colo.: Westview Press, 1987.

Rose, Mike. *Lives on the Boundary.* New York: Penguin Books, 1990.
     A penetrating and moving account of the struggles and achievements of America's educational underclass.

Suransky, Valerie Polakow. *The Erosion of Childhood.* Chicago: University of Chicago Press, 1982.
    Describes what we provide by way of day care for our youngest; includes a few samples deeply and devastatingly observed. A must.

SCIENCE: For Teachers of the Young

Boys, C. V. Soap Bubbles: Their Colors and Forces Which Mold Them. New York: Dover Publications, 1959.
    This is the classic text. In his last Preface (1911) Boys boasts happily that because of his book "about two tons of bubbles are floating about in the world." How many since? Many beautiful phenomena on this mysterious edge of everyday life, an unfailing way into good science.

Thompson, D'Arcy Wentworth. On Growth and Form. 2 vols. Cambridge: University Press, 1959.
    There are many sources of ideas and materials for young children's science, but here I list only this one, because it is little known except to a small circle of scholars and scientists, and because many of the quite beautiful phenomena it deals with can be reproduced for classroom use, starting with young children's play with such as soap films and siphons, or drops of food color in water. This work was written for an audience perhaps mainly interested in its science, equally for those first interested in the style and beauty of many natural phenomena.

Afterword

A thoughtful reader of this book's manuscript suggested that it might well have an after-word, some final statement that says, with all possible brevity, what I would least like to be lost among the pages of a long story.

In accepting that suggestion I have decided to add nothing of my own; the story is told. I add, instead, a few lines from the philosopher who has long followed the writing of it, my husband David Hawkins. He says that for him the book brings one central idea, of practice and theory, to a sharp focus. To express it here, he has slightly revised an earlier statement. [1]

A proper and serious study of childhood would raise questions, I think, about one tendency widespread among us. In a novel of fantasy by Christopher Morley, [2] a group of children decide to send one of their number, magically grown up, as a spy, or emissary, to the world of adults. I have suggested, in the same spirit, that we adults need to send emissaries to the estate of childhood. But that may meet only half the need; we too easily learn only what we are prepared to accept. Being repelled, on our mission, by the typical formality and sterility of our institutional treatment of children, many of us react by seeking and advocating patterns of association which are arranged for easy two-way communication, warm and loving. If that is half the story, it is a half which needs redefinition when the other half is told.

Long before Bettelheim, Imanuel Kant had given profound support to the preposition that, in human affairs generally, love is not enough. The more magic gift is not love, but respect, for others as ends in themselves, as actual and potential artisans of their own learnings and doings, of their own lives; and thus uniquely contributing, in turn, to their learnings and doings.

---

1. David Hawkins, "I, Thou, and It," from The Informed Vision, Essays on Learning and Human Nature; Agathon Press, New York, 1973; pp. 48–62.
2. Christopher Morley, Where the Blue Begins, Doubleday Press, Garden City, New York, 1922.

Respect for the young is not a passive, hands-off attitude. It invites our own offering of resources, it moves us toward the furtherance of their lives and thus, even, at times, toward remonstrance or intervention. Respect resembles love in its implicit aim of furtherance, but love without respect can blind and bind. Love is private and unbidden, whereas respect is implicit in all moral relations with others.

To have respect for children is more than recognizing their potentialities in the abstract, it is also to seek out and value their accomplishments—however small these may appear by the normal standards of adults. But if we follow this track of thinking, one thing stands out. We must provide for children those kinds of environments which elicit their interests and talents and which deepen their engagement in practice and thought. An environment of "loving" adults who are themselves alienated from the world around them is an educational vacuum. Adults involved in the world of man and nature must bring that world with them to children, bounded and made safe to be sure, but not thereby losing its richness and promise of novelty.

It is this emphasis that makes me insist upon the third pronoun in the title of the talk, the impersonal "It" alongside the "I" and "Thou." Adults and children, like adults with each other, can associate well only in worthy interests and pursuits, only through a community of subject matter and engagement that extends beyond the circle of their intimacy.

Such reflections as these have grown from long association with Frances Hawkins—her teaching, her conversation, and now her own full story, bound up in this book.